Sundance Choice

For Writing Across the Curriculum

General Editor Mark Connelly

CENGAGE
Learning™

Australia • Brazil • Japan • Korea • Mexico • Singapore • Spain • United Kingdom • United States

CENGAGE
Learning™

**Sundance Choice
For Writing Across the
Curriculum**

General Editor Mark Connelly

Executive Editors:
Michele Baird

Maureen Staudt

Michael Stranz

Project Development Manager:
Linda deStefano

Senior Marketing Coordinators:
Sara Mercurio

Lindsay Shapiro

Senior Production /
Manufacturing Manager:
Donna M. Brown

PreMedia Services Supervisor:
Rebecca A. Walker

Rights & Permissions Specialist:
Kalina Hintz

Cover Image:
Getty Images*

For product information and
technology assistance, contact us at **Cengage Learning
Customer & Sales Support, 1-800-354-9706**

For permission to use material from this text or product,
submit all requests online at **cengage.com/permissions**
Further permissions questions can be emailed to
permissionrequest@cengage.com

ISBN-13:   978-1-4130-9945-4

ISBN-10:   1-4130-9945-9

Cengage Learning
5191 Natorp Boulevard
Mason, Ohio 45040
USA

Cengage Learning is a leading provider of customized learning solutions with office locations around the globe, including Singapore, the United Kingdom, Australia, Mexico, Brazil, and Japan. Locate your local office at: **international.cengage.com/region**

Cengage Learning products are represented in Canada by Nelson Education, Ltd.

For your lifelong learning solutions, visit **custom.cengage.com**

Visit our corporate website at **cengage.com**

Printed in the United States of America

The Sundance Choice Database

flexible and valuable!

You select the readings ... we provide your customized collection! Without a doubt, **The Sundance Choice Database** is the best way to provide your students with the reading selections that you want to teach—complete with rhetoric and writing instruction—at an ultimate value.

Featuring hundreds of classic and contemporary essay selections—chosen by English instructors from across the country—our unique database gives you the freedom to select only the essays or topics that fit your course. Each essay is surrounded by pedagogy that gets writing students engaged with the reading, and inspires them to do some original writing of their own.

A customized selection of readings made just for you!
The new *TextChoice* online system (**www.textchoice.com**) is the easiest and most flexible way to build your custom reader. Build your customized reader online, and receive a free evaluation copy!

It's never been easier to give your students an affordable, made-to-order collection of essays that you've designed . . . this PREVIEW and sample chapter will show you how.

An outstanding collection of resources—including our Comp21 CD-ROM—can accompany your adoption. See 6–8 for details.

Turn the page! Your brief tour starts now...

WADSWORTH
CENGAGE Learning™

Preview

utstanding pedagogical tools and visual aids
at draw students into each selection

very reading in The **Sundance Choice Database** engages and inspires hrough pedagogical tools and features—soon, your students are sure to begin original writing of their own!

Unlike any other custom database, **The Sundance Choice Database** offers full coverage of rhetoric, presenting topics that will benefit beginning writers as well as topics more appropriate for experienced writers. Additionally, a **model student paper** is included in each theme or mode, to give your students an idea of comparable writing.

Evaluating Strategy

1. What tone is established in the first sentence? What does the use of the word *victim* indicate?
2. Rendón includes a quote from one of his articles. Is this an effective device?
3. *BLENDING THE MODES.* How does Rendón use narration, description, and comparison in developing "Kiss of Death"?

Appreciating Language

1. What does the term "kiss of death" mean to you? Do you associate it with the Bible or with Hollywood images of the Mafia?
2. Rendón uses several Spanish words without providing definitions in English. What does this suggest about his idea of the United States becoming "acculturized" to Mexican-American culture?
3. Rendón uses both "Mexican-American" and "Chicano." What definitions of these terms are you familiar with? Do "Latino" and "Hispanic" have different meanings and connotations?
   by "cautious Chicanos"?

ng Suggestions

 of death" you have escaped in your own
 omised your future by taking

STUDENT PAPER

No Deterrence

Does the death penalty deter anyone? One of the main arguments people use to support capital punishment is deterrence the idea that seeing someone executed will make others think before committing a similar crime. In theory it might have that effect. If a gang member murdered a police officer or shot up a liquor store and killed six people, maybe executing him within a year of conviction might influence other gang members and younger people who admired him.

But today people spend years, sometimes decades, on death row before being executed. Stays and appeals delay executions to the point that any deterrent factor is lost. When a 38-year-old man is executed for a crime he committed when he was 19, who will be deterred? No doubt his gang no longer exists. The current generation of young criminals can't relate to him and don't see his fate connected to theirs. In addition, whatever shock and horror people felt by an outrageous crime has long worn off. Executing someone years after the crime becomes only an afterthought, a minor news item. Any deterrent power is long gone.

Sojourner Truth, *Ain't I a Woman?* ▪ Bruno Bettleheim, *The Holocaust* ▪ Nancy Gibbs, *When Is It Rape?* ▪ Michael Dorris, *Fetal Alcohol Syndrome* ▪ George Orwell, *A Hanging* ▪ Edward Koch, *Death and Justice: How Capital Punishment Affirms Life* ▪ Daniel Lashof, *Earth's Last Gasp?* ▪ Joycelyn Tomkin, *Hot Air* ▪ Anna Quindlen, *Horrors: Girls With Gavels! What A Difference a Day Makes. And If the Boys Stay Home—Well, There's a Lesson There, Too* ▪ Judith Viorst, *Bones Break, But Boys Endure* ▪ Ellen Goodman, *Girls Will Be Girls, Unfortunately*

Within each theme or mode, two **images** are available for selection. Each visual within the image bank is accompanied by questions, writing assignments, and collaborative activities.

Responding to Images

Responding to Images

Unparalleled pedagogy and visuals

Reflected in the Database's themes

Fourteen thematic categories are included in **The Sundance Choice Database** to help students identify with the readings. The latest issues are examined within the following themes:

- American Identity: Melting Pot or Mosaic?
- The War on Terrorism
- Medical Malpractice
- Reparations for Slavery
- Fatherhood
- Abortion: Roe vs. Wade at Thirty
- Islam and the West

- Capital Punishment
- Immigration
- Global Warming
- Public Schools
- America's Role in the Twenty-First Century
- Gender Identity: Raising Boys and Girls
- Welfare to Work

Medical Malpractice

The health and life of my patients will be my first consideration.
–The Hippocratic Oath

The problem with medical malpractice is that it occurs far too often. It is the eighth leading cause of death in America, killing more people than AIDS, breast cancer, or automobile crashes.
–Leo Boyle

The villain, I believe, is our legal system, which has become a free-for-all, lacking the reliability and consistency that are essential to everyone, especially doctors and patients. Most victims of error get nothing, while others win lottery-like jury awards even when the doctor did nothing wrong.
–Philip K. Howard

I am sure I could have become a millionaire by suing my father's doctors and the hospital. . . . But I didn't. . . . [T]o sue someone for failing to be the god we wanted strikes me as wrong.
–Alden Blodget

...OMFORT ALWAYS"

...icians in the United States had only a fragmen-...
...icine. Few medical schools were affiliated with ...
...not even accredited. Some medical schools did ...
...ve a high school diploma. In a few states it was ...
...al license in six months. Apprenticed to older ...
...earned primarily by observation. There were ...
...es, and little connection was made between ...
...pped with dubious medicines and crude surgical ...
...equently able to provide little more than emo-...
...eat many conditions, physicians attempted only ...

The War on Terrorism

How can you defeat an enemy who thinks he's on a mission from God? How? A hundred days and one war later, we know the answer: B-52's, for starters.
–Charles Krauthammer

The instinct to retaliate with bombing is an anachronism. Fewer than twenty men had brought us to our national knees. . . . The government's answer was that we were good and love freedom and these people are bad and hate it. That vapid answer came from a national culture that has lost its talent for healthy guilt.
–Daniel C. Maguire

[W]e hit Saddam for one simple reason: because we could, and because he deserved it and because he was right in the heart of that world. And don't believe the nonsense that this has had no effect. Every neighboring government—and 98 percent of terrorism is about what governments let happen—got the message. If you talk to U.S. soldiers in Iraq they will tell you this is what the war was about.
–Thomas L. Friedman

Real wars are not metaphors. And real wars have a beginning and an end. . . . But the war that has been decreed by the Bush administration will never end. That is one sign that it is not a war; but, rather, a mandate for expanding the use of American power.
–Susan Sontag

On the morning of September 11, 2001, President Bush was visiting a school. Informed that two planes had just crashed into the World Trade Center, Andrew Card, the White House Chief of Staff, interrupted the ceremony and whispered to the President, "America is under attack."
But was America at war?

mplete with customized technology integration

other publisher offers a custom database of this quality with technology
grated into each customized reader. When you adopt **The Sundance Choice
atabase,** you have the option of choosing from a menu of interactive technology
ools–each of which will be carefully integrated into your customized reader.

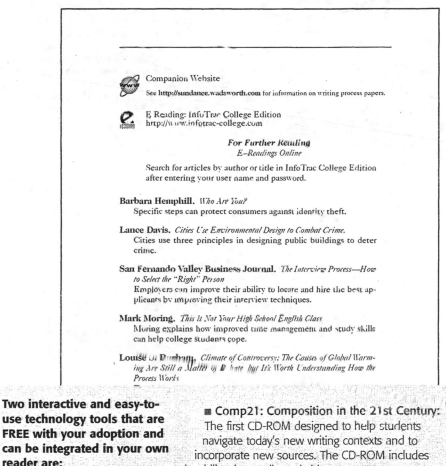

Companion Website
See http://sundance.wadsworth.com for information on writing process papers.

E Reading: InfoTrac College Edition
http://www.infotrac-college.com

For Further Reading
E–Readings Online

Search for articles by author or title in InfoTrac College Edition
after entering your user name and password.

Barbara Hemphill. *Who Are You?*
Specific steps can protect consumers against identity theft.

Lance Davis. *Cities Use Environmental Design to Combat Crime.*
Cities use three principles in designing public buildings to deter
crime.

San Fernando Valley Business Journal. *The Interview Process—How
to Select the "Right" Person*
Employers can improve their ability to locate and hire the best applicants by improving their interview techniques.

Mark Moring. *This Is Not Your High School English Class*
Moring explains how improved time management and study skills
can help college students cope.

Louise Di Dunham. *Climate of Controversy: The Causes of Global Warming Are Still a Matter of Debate but It's Worth Understanding How the
Process Works*

**Two interactive and easy-to-
use technology tools that are
FREE with your adoption and
can be integrated in your own
reader are:**

■ **Comp21: Composition in the 21st Century:**
The first CD-ROM designed to help students
navigate today's new writing contexts and to
incorporate new sources. The CD-ROM includes
visual libraries, audio and video
galleries, and collections of classic essays and
speeches to add texture and depth to student projects. The
CD-ROM is linked to each theme or mode in the **Database.**

■ **InfoTrac College Edition with InfoMarks™.** Each theme or
mode in the Database ends with a list of further readings on
InfoTrac College Edition with InfoMarks™, a fully searchable database offering more than
20 years worth of full-text articles. *See page 6 for a complete description of* **InfoTrac
College Edition.**

Reliable, cutting-edge web resources

That make research easy for students

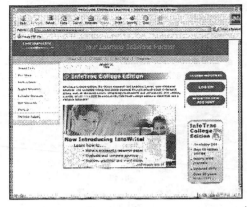

InfoTrac® College Edition with InfoMarks™

NOT SOLD SEPARATELY. This fully searchable ddatabase offers more than 20 years' worth of full-text articles (not abstracts) from almost 5,000 diverse sources, such as top academic journals, newsletters, and up-to-the-minute periodicals including *Time, Newsweek, Science, Forbes,* and *USA Today*. **NEW!** Your 4-month free subscription now includes instant access to virtual readers drawing from the vast **InfoTrac College Edition** library and hand-selected to work with your book. In addition, students have instant access to *InfoWrite*, which includes guides to writing research papers, grammar, "critical thinking" guidelines, and much more. Adopters and their students receive FREE unlimited access to **InfoTrac College Edition with InfoMarks** for four months. To take a quick tour of InfoTrac, visit **infotrac.cengagelearning.com** and select the "User Demo". (*Journals subject to change. Certain restrictions may apply. For additional information, please consult your local Cengage Learning representative.*)

Opposing Viewpoints Resource Center

0-534-12853-X

NOT SOLD SEPARATELY. This online center helps you expose your students to all sides of today's most compelling social and scientific issues, from genetic engineering to environmental policy, prejudice, abortion, health care reform, violence in the media, and much more. **The Opposing Viewpoints Resource Center** draws on Greenhaven Press's acclaimed social issues series, popular periodicals and newspapers, and core reference content from other Gale and Macmillan Reference USA sources. The result is a dynamic online library of current events topics—the facts as well as the arguments as articulated by the proponents and detractors of each position. Visit Visit **gale.cengage.com/OpposingViewpoints**. *For college and university adopters only.*

Online resources

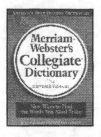
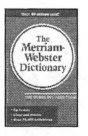

Table of Contents

1

Critical Thinking and Prewriting

*It is part of the business of the writer . . . to
examine attitudes, to go beneath
the surface, to tap the source.*
James Baldwin

Good writing is never "about" a topic—it has a purpose and makes a point. An essay about your summer vacation can be simply a list of places you visited and things you did, or it can focus on something deeper, something more significant, such as how visiting Mount Rushmore made you contemplate American values, how traveling together helped you appreciate your family, how spending a weekend in a cabin without electricity led you to discover how lost you feel without the Internet. A good paper shares more than facts and dates, first impressions, or immediate reactions. Good writing seeks to get beyond the obvious to explore ideas and events, to analyze people and ideas.

For example, if you decide to write an essay about your first apartment, your first thought might be to record every detail you can remember, trying to capture on paper what the apartment looked like:

On August 12, 2005, I moved into my first apartment. It was a flat on Newhall Street on the top floor of a hundred-year-old house. The living room was massive and had wood paneling and antique brass chandeliers. The dining room had a huge built-in buffet and china cabinets with glass doors I used as bookcases. The kitchen was L-shaped and narrow, but there was a pantry with lots of shelves. The battered refrigerator was old but spacious.

There were two big bedrooms. I planned to use the front bedroom for my study. The back bedroom was a bit smaller, but it had a great advantage. It was away from the street and shielded from the noise of traffic. In addition, there were awnings that blocked the morning sun so I could sleep late on weekends. The bedrooms did not have any closets. Instead there were large two-door wardrobes with built-in drawers. There was a spacious balcony off the front bedroom. It was covered by a redwood deck and had new patio furniture and an outdoor grill.

I had little money and had to get furniture from Goodwill and the Salvation Army. The floors were bare, but I covered them with old carpeting from my parents' house.

This approach will probably create an essay that lists physical details of minimal interest to anyone else. Before beginning to write, you might think about the topic and ask yourself some questions:

Why did I choose this topic?
Of all the possible subjects, why did you decide to write about your first apartment? What made you think of that rather than your first car, your last boss, a trip to New York, or a recent job interview? Clearly, something about that apartment made it significant. What did it represent to you? What events took place there that changed your life? Are your memories of this place happy or sad? Why?

What are the most significant details?
Instead of listing everything you can remember about your subject, select the most memorable details. Is the date you moved or the number of bedrooms really important?

How can I share my thoughts and feelings with readers?
Readers may not be interested in a room-by-room description of an apartment, but they may be able to identify with more universal experiences, thoughts, or emotions. How did you feel about moving? What change did it make in your life? What are the larger issues that other people can relate to?

What is the dominant impression I want to leave readers with?
Focusing on a single impression or message can help you select details. If you concentrate on describing your excitement about getting your first apartment, you can ignore irrelevant details such as dates, furnishings, and parking.

Considering these questions can help create an essay that has greater meaning for both you and your reader:

In August I moved into my first apartment, a great flat on Newhall Street. Although I could only afford to furnish it with battered items from Goodwill and the Salvation Army, I was excited. I was finally going to be on my own, free of my parents, my cramped room, my sisters' fighting, my brother's stereo. I spent two weeks cleaning, painting, and organizing the old flat into *my home.* I hung up posters of my favorite bands, stocked the kitchen with my favorite foods, and set the radio to my favorite stations. I was finally on my own, free at last.

But coming home from class, I was struck by the silence. Instead of hearing the drone of my brother's stereo, my sisters' laughing and fighting, I heard the hum of the refrigerator and the nervous tick-tick of an electric clock. I always hated that my mother watched soap operas but found myself turning the television on in the afternoon to hear the hated but familiar voices while I labored over algebra or ironed clothes.

On weekends I went home—not to raid the kitchen or borrow money. I had been adult, I had been responsible. I saved money over the summer and budgeted it carefully. I could easily afford my new apartment. I had hungered for a place of my own all through high school. But I never imagined what it would feel like to go to bed and to wake up in an empty house.

By thinking more deeply about a subject you can probe its depth, developing writing that does more than simply report facts and record observations.

Critical thinking involves moving beyond first impressions by carefully analyzing subjects, people, and ideas. Too often we rush to judgment, making instant assumptions based on what we think we know rather than what we can prove. We confuse opinions with facts, accept statistics without question, and let stereotypes color our evaluations. We allow what we "feel" to short-circuit how we think:

> Pete Wilson was a great quarterback— he'll make a great coach.
> Nancy's driving a BMW. Her new travel agency must be a success.
> Alabama improved reading scores 12% using this program; our schools should use it, too.
> Speedy Lube ruined my car. Two days after I went there for an oil change my transmission went out.

All these statements make a kind of sense at first glance. But further analysis will lead you to question their validity:

> Does a skilled quarterback necessarily know how to coach—how to inspire, manage, and teach other players, especially those on defense?

> Does Nancy even own the BMW she was seen driving? Did she get it as a gift, pay for it with existing savings, borrow it from a friend, or lease it at a low rate? Does the car really prove anything about the success or failure of her travel agency?

Alabama may have improved reading scores with a particular program, but does that really prove the program will work in Nevada or Minnesota? Could children in other states have low reading scores caused by other reasons than those in Alabama?

Did Speedy Lube ruin your transmission? They may have only changed the oil and never touched the transmission. Had you driven through a car wash the day before, could you just as easily blame them?

Errors like these are easy to make. Unless you develop critical thinking skills, you can be impressed by evidence that at first seems reliable and convincing.

AVOIDING ERRORS IN CRITICAL THINKING

Lapses in critical thinking are often called logical fallacies. In reading the works of others and developing your own ideas, try to avoid these common mistakes:

- **Hasty generalizations.** If your dorm room is robbed, a friend's car stolen from the Student Union parking lot, and a classmate's purse snatched on her way to class, you might assume that the campus is experiencing a crime wave. The evidence seems compelling because it is immediate and personal. But it does not prove there is an increase in campus crime. In fact, crime could be dropping and you and your friends could have the misfortune to fall into the declining group of victims. Only a comparative review of police and security reports would prove if crime is increasing. Resist jumping to conclusions.
- **Absolute statements.** Although it is important to convince readers by making strong assertions, avoid absolute claims that can be dismissed with a single exception. If you write "All professional athletes today are irresponsible," readers only need to think of a single exception to dismiss your argument. A qualified remark, however, is harder to disprove. The claim that "Many professional athletes today are irresponsible" acknowledges that exceptions exist.
- *Non sequitur* (it does not follow). Avoid making assertions based on irrelevant evidence: "Jill Klein won an Oscar for best actress last year— she'll be great on Broadway." Although an actor might succeed on film, she may lack the ability to perform on stage before a live audience. The skills and style suited for film acting do not always translate well to the theater.

- **Begging the question.** Do not assume what has to be proved: "These needless math classes should be dropped because no one uses algebra and geometry after they graduate." This statement makes an assertion, but it fails to prove that the courses are needless or that "no one" uses mathematics outside of academics.
- **False dilemma.** Do not offer or accept only two alternatives to a problem: "Either employees must take a wage cut, or the company will go bankrupt." This statement ignores other possible solutions such as raising prices, lowering production costs, or increasing sales.
- **False analogy.** Comparisons make very weak arguments: "Crack cocaine should be legalized since Prohibition did not work." Alcohol and crack cocaine are not similar substances. Alcohol has been consumed by humans for thousands of years. Crack cocaine has never been socially acceptable to most Americans.
- **Red herring.** Resist the temptation to dodge the real issue by drawing attention to something controversial: "How can you endorse the budget proposal of a member of Congress indicted for soliciting bribes?" Corruption charges alone do not invalidate a politician's policies.
- **Borrowed authority.** Avoid assuming that an expert in one field can be accepted as an authority in another: "Senator Goode claims Italy will win the World Cup." A respected senator may have no more insight into soccer than a cab driver or a hairdresser. Celebrity endorsements are common examples of borrowed authority.
- *Ad hominem* **(attacking the person).** Attack ideas, not the people who advocate them: "The only people who drive SUVs are spoiled, selfish baby boomers who don't care about the environment." The merits of the issue, not the personalities, have to be discussed to create a convincing argument.
- **Assuming past events will predict the future.** During the oil crisis of the 1970s, the price of oil soared from $10 to $40 a barrel. Alarmists predicted financial disaster, with Americans paying $50–$100 a barrel for oil to run cars and to fuel industry. But the dramatic price escalation was short lived. Price increases spurred exploration for new oil fields and launched conservation efforts. Soon the world was awash in surplus oil, and prices dropped to precrisis levels. *Past trends cannot be assumed to continue into the future.*
- **Ignoring alternative interpretations.** Even objective facts can be misleading. If research shows that reports of child abuse in your state have jumped 250 percent in the last ten years, does that mean that child abuse is on the rise? Or could those numbers reflect more rigorous reporting methods or an expanded definition of abuse so that previously unrecorded incidents are now counted?
- **"Filtering" data.** If you begin with a preconceived thesis, you may consciously or unconsciously select evidence that supports your view and omit

evidence that contradicts it. Good analysis is objective; it does not consist of simply collecting facts to support a previously held conviction.

- **Assuming that parts represent the whole.** Just because one or more patients respond favorably to a new drug does not mean that it will cure all people suffering from the same disease. In the extreme, because individual men and women die does not mean the human race will eventually become extinct.

- **Assuming the whole represents each part.** If 50 percent of students on campus receive financial aid, it does not mean you can assume that half the English majors receive aid. The student population in any given department may be greater or less than the college average.

- **Mistaking a time relationship for a cause (post hoc ergo propter hoc).** If your brakes fail after taking your car into the dealer for a tuneup, does that mean the mechanics are to blame? Can the president take credit for a drop in unemployment six months after signing a labor bill? Because events occur over time, it can be easy to assume an action that precedes another is a cause. The mechanics may have not touched your brakes, which were bound to wear out with or without a tuneup. A drop in unemployment could be caused by a decline in interest rates or an upsurge in exports and may have nothing to do with a labor bill. *Do not assume events were caused by preceding events.*

- **Mistaking an effect for a cause.** Early physicians saw fever as a cause of disease rather than as an effect or symptom. If you observe that children with poor reading skills watch a lot of television, you might easily assume that television interferes with their reading. In fact, excessive viewing could be a symptom. Because those children have trouble reading, they watch television instead.

STRATEGIES FOR ENHANCING CRITICAL THINKING

There is no quick method of enhancing critical thinking, but you can challenge yourself to move beyond first impressions and hasty generalizations by considering these questions:

1. **How much do you really know about this subject?** Do you fully understand the history, depth, and character of the topic? Should you learn more by conducting some research or interviewing people before making judgments?

Continued

2. **Have you looked at your topic closely?** First impressions can be striking but misleading. Examine your subject closely, asking questions, probing beneath the surface. Look for patterns; measure similarities and differences.

3. **Have you rushed to judgment?** Collect evidence but avoid drawing conclusions until you have analyzed your findings and observations.

4. **Do you separate facts from opinions?** Don't confuse facts, evidence, and data with opinions, claims, and assertions. Opinions are judgments or inferences, not facts. Facts are reliable pieces of information that can be verified by studying other sources:

   FACT: This semester a laptop, petty cash, and a VCR were taken from the tutoring lab while Sue Harper was on duty.
   OPINION: Sue Harper is a thief.

   The factual statement can be proven. Missing items can be documented. The assumption that Sue Harper is responsible remains to be proven.

5. **Are you aware of your assumptions?** Assumptions are ideas we accept or believe to be true. It is nearly impossible to divorce ourselves from what we have been taught, but you can sharpen your critical thinking skills if you acknowledge your assumptions. Avoid relying too heavily on a single assumption—IQ tests measure intelligence, poverty causes crime, television is a bad influence on children.

6. **Have you collected enough evidence?** A few statistics and quotations taken out of context may seem convincing, but they cannot be viewed as adequate proof. Make sure you collect enough evidence from a variety of sources before making judgments.

7. **Do you evaluate evidence carefully?** Do you apply common standards to evaluate the data you collect? Do you question the source of statistics or the validity of an eyewitness? The fact that you can find dozens of books written about alien abductions does not prove they occur.

CRITICAL THINKING EXERCISE

1. Review the list of topics and select one that you have strong opinions and feelings about.

the President	the war on	gun control	reality TV shows
underage	terrorism	high school	your boss
drinking	an NFL coach or	blind dates	daycare
worst teacher	player	sexual	raves
health insurance	gay rights	harassment	global warming
smokers	affirmative action	legalizing	the environment
SUVs	lotteries	marijuana	religion
your last job	cable news	cloning	rap music
suicide bombers	networks	proms	
	student loans	AIDS	
	welfare		

2. After selecting a topic write a statement summarizing your attitudes about it. Write a full paragraph or list ideas, or even words, you associate with this subject:
3. Examine your comments carefully and consider these questions:

- *What do I really know about this topic?*
- *Why do I feel this way?*
- *Would other people call my views unfairly biased?*
- *Are my views based on facts or assumptions?*
- *Can I provide sufficient evidence to support my opinion?*
- *Do I detect any logical fallacies in my response—hasty generalizations, red herrings, or mistaking a time relationship for a cause?*
- *Do I need to conduct research before I can honestly make a judgment?*
- *Are there alternative opinions? Do they have any merit?*
- *Could I organize a logical and convincing argument to persuade others to accept my point of view?*

Examining and challenging your values, ideas, and opinions improves your ability to express yourself to others and anticipate their questions and objections.

PREWRITING: PUTTING CRITICAL THINKING INTO ACTION

Writing is not only used to create a document, it also can be used to think on paper, to explore ideas, discover topics, develop details, and identify significant facts. Instead of trying to start a draft of an assignment, use writing as a way of recording and prompting critical thinking.

Writers use a number of prewriting techniques. Depending on the assignment, you may find one method more helpful than others. Although usually taught as separate methods, these prewriting strategies should not be viewed as a set of rigid procedures. Writers often blend several methods when thinking about a topic.

Prewriting Strategies

Brainstorming

Brainstorming takes many forms. Often writers start with an idea and begin making lists. The goal is to let one idea trigger another, as in a psychologist's free association exercise:

    cars
    new cars/SUVs
    gas mileage
    Middle East politics/oil/need for big cars?
    traffic jams
    commute to work
    potholes
    freeway
    original freeway plan of 1960s/current traffic
    traffic delays/stress/trapped in crowded system
    *freeways designed to make life easier 10 years ago have trapped people
    in an obsolete system with no alternatives*

Starting with "cars," the writer has moved through a series of ideas until she hit on a topic for a short essay, the crowded freeway system.

- Brainstorming can help you get started when you feel lost for a topic because you can easily jump from one idea to another. Even the most general or abstract starting point can identify a topic appropriate for an upcoming assignment.

Brainstorming is not limited to finding topics for academic assignments. When you know what you want to say, you can use targeted brainstorming to identify details needed to create an effective document. If you are writing an e-mail to apply for a job you saw posted on the Internet, you can use brainstorming to generate a list of details you might want to include in a cover letter and resume:

Assistant Manager – Coffee Nation

Two years' experience at Pablo's Café
Supervised four employees in manager's absence
Accounting and business courses related to retail
Completed restaurant management course UW-Whitewater
Fully familiar with Coffee Nation's products & services
Effective at motivating and training staff
Good at customer relations—helped Pablo's build repeat business
Get references from Pablo, Lucy Perez, Ted Weinstein

- Targeted brainstorming triggers ideas you might overlook if you simply start writing.

Asking Questions

Another method that sparks critical thinking is to ask questions. Write as many questions about your subject as possible. Don't pause to answer them, just list as many questions as you can:

Why do I hate commuting?
How long does it take me get home on a good day?
A bad day?
Why does it take so long?
When were the freeways designed?
Why are they so congested?
Why are there no other fast routes?
Why don't we have bus or rail service to suburbs?
How much will fixing the freeway cost?
Can new lanes be added?
Will the congestion make people lose desire to live in
suburbs and want to move back downtown?

- Asking questions forces you to think rather than simply observe. It is a useful method to test assumptions because questions ask for proof. If you list an idea such as "high school math was a waste" you simply record an opinion. Forcing yourself to ask questions like "Was high school math a waste?" or "Why do I feel high school math was a waste?" prompts a more thoughtful response.

- Posing questions can quickly identify topics requiring further research.

Freewriting

In freewriting you record your thoughts, ideas, impressions, and feelings without stopping or pausing to edit for spelling, grammar, punctuation, or even logic. Don't confuse freewriting with writing a rough draft of an essay—it is a method of discovering ideas. Freewriting is not unlike talking to yourself. It has no direction; it can skip from one topic to another without rational transitions; it may contain contradictory statements. Freewriting produces "running prose," like the tape recording of a rambling telephone conversation. The goal is to sketch out ideas as fast as you can.

Sit down with a piece of paper or at a computer and start writing. Some experts suggest writing nonstop for at least five minutes. If you can't think of anything to write, draw O's and X's or type gibberish. The main thing is to keep the process going until you can think of something to say. Let one idea remind you of another. Remember, there are no bad ideas.

Having spent a frustrating afternoon locked in bumper-to-bumper traffic on the expressway, a student came home and rapidly recorded her thoughts for an upcoming comparison essay:

The expressways built in the 1960s were supposed to liberate us from traffic jams. An early brochure my dad has shows the neat ribbons of conrete stretching in a planned set of spokes from the center city to the suburbs. "From Center City to Centerville in 15 minutes" (mayor's quote). And so the inter-urban trolleys were scrapped and their rails torn out. Bus routes were dropped and the freeways were built. And maybe for a few years people cokuld actually comute from Brookfield to downtown in fifteen minutes. x x x x x x x x x x x x x x x

But no one could forsee the endless suburban sprawl of malls, subdidivisons, industrials parks not to mention the new airport. By the 1980s the expressways were busy, bythe 90s clogged, and now there hopless. Downtown housing is eiter undesirable or unaffordable. Middleclass people have to live in the suburbs. But the jobs remain downtown. So with two parents working and kids attending separate schools families have two, three, even four cars, all clogging the espressays.

In 1940 it probably took a guy forty-five minutes to get from rural Centerville to City Hall on a bumpy two lane county road. Now on the expressway it takes just as long on a six lane potholed freeway system nearly the end of its fifty year lifespan.

They say it will cost almost a billion dollars and three years to fix the potholes, upgrade the bridges, and redo the crumbling ramps. When it is all done it will take an hour to get form Centerville to City Hall, except maybe the ride will be smoother. Like a lot of people who live in the suburbs and work downtown I feel condemned. I wish there was another option. At least on a train I could read or take a nap instead of wasting my time crawling at 10mph past signs warning me the speed limit is 70.

- Freewriting allows one idea to trigger another without your worrying about making logical connections.
- Freewriting can help you overcome writer's block. Having the freedom to write anything, even meaningless symbols, can help you avoid feeling that you have to produce flawless prose whenever you write.
- If writing complete sentences becomes time-consuming, just list key words or make notes. List or cluster ideas to save time. Don't feel obligated to write in complete sentences.

Clustering

Clustering is a visual method of prewriting. Instead of writing down ideas in whole sentences or generating lists, you map or sketch out ideas to establish patterns and relationships:

Freeways

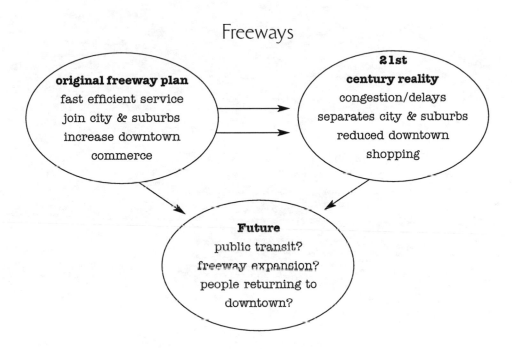

- Clustering assists writers who are visually oriented. Some people find it easier to think critically by placing ideas in columns or charts to show relationships, dramatize advantages and disadvantages, or explore causes and effects.

Remember, you can easily blend different techniques. You might begin by brainstorming, then freewrite to explore a certain idea, next pose some questions to identify areas that need research, and then use clustering to contrast opposing ideas.

Writing Exercise

Select one of the topics below and explore it using one or more methods of prewriting.

cell phones	drunk driving laws	talk shows	online dating
worst job	Iraq	high school bullies	video games
teen fashions	athletes as role models	euthanasia	racial profiling
singles bars	diets	airport security	Internet stalking
credit cards	car insurance	death penalty	child support

Critical Reading

> *If reading is to accomplish anything more*
> *than passing time, it must be active.*
> Mortimer Adler

In most college courses you read for knowledge, highlighting key terms, dates, facts, and theories that may appear on upcoming tests. When you read for pleasure, you probably don't take notes at all. You allow yourself to be taken into the writer's world, focusing on a story's characters and plot. Reading a magazine or newspaper article to learn about stocks or a new diet, you skim through familiar material to concentrate on new information.

Reading in a writing class is different. Few instructors are likely to "test" you on the content of the articles they assign. Rather, they expect you to examine an article to appreciate *how* it is written—how the writer presents and supports a thesis, organizes details, uses logic, selects words, and addresses the needs and concerns of readers.

READING WITH A WRITER'S EYE

When most people see a movie they allow themselves to be drawn into the story, to enjoy the action, laugh at jokes, or feel compassion for a character in crisis. But a film student watching the same movie studies how the director uses lighting, editing, and camera angles to create a scene. A drama student observes how an actor delivers a line or uses a gesture to establish a character.

As a composition student you need to read with a "writer's eye." Reading gives you the opportunity to watch other writers at work. When you read, note the way writers use words, form sentences, and develop paragraphs. Study how they limit topics, present ideas, address controversial issues, and indicate transitions. Read to discover techniques you can use in your own assignments:

- How did the author limit the subject?
- How did the writer arouse interest in the topic?

- What sentence opens the essay?
- What details did the writer include, and what details did he or she omit?
- How did the author present background information?
- What audience is the writer addressing?
- Where did the writer place the thesis statement?
- What kind of support is used?
- How did the writer organize ideas?
- How does word choice affect the tone and style?
- What thought, image, question, or fact did the author choose for the conclusion?

READING CRITICALLY

Critical reading takes place in stages. At first glance, it might seem to be a long process, but in fact, following these steps can maximize your time and help you focus on the most important elements of anything you read, including the essays in this text.

First Reading

1. **Look ahead and skim selections.** Do not wait until the night before a class discussion to read assignments. Check your syllabus and skim through upcoming readings to get a general impression. Often, if you think about the authors and their topics, you can approach the essay more critically.
2. **Study the head note and introduction.** Consider the author, the issue, and what you already know about the subject. Note the original source of the essay. What type of readers does the writer seem to be addressing?
3. **Suspend judgment.** Try to put your personal views aside as you read. Even if you disagree with the author's choice of topic, tone, or opinion, read the essay objectively. Remember, your goal is to understand *how* the writer states his or her point. Even if you reject an author's thesis, you can still learn useful techniques.
4. **Consider the title.** Titles often provide clues about the author's attitude toward his or her subject. Does the title label the essay, state a thesis, pose a question, or use a creative phrase to attract attention?
5. **Read the entire work.** Complete the entire essay in one sitting if you can. Do not pause to look up an unfamiliar word at this stage. Instead, try to get the "big picture."
6. **Focus on understanding the writer's main point.** If possible, summarize the writer's thesis in your own words.

7. **Jot down your first impressions.** What do you think of this work? Do you like it? If so, why? If you find it dull, disturbing, or silly, ask yourself why. What is lacking? How did the author fail in your eyes?

Put the essay aside, allowing it to cool. If possible, let two or three days pass before returning to the assignment. If the assignment is due the next day, read the selection early in the day and then turn to other work or run an errand, so you can come back to it with a fresh outlook.

Second Reading

1. **Review your first impressions.** Determine if your attitudes are based on biases or personal preferences rather than the writer's ability. Realize that an essay that supports your views is not necessarily well written. If you disagree with the author's thesis, try to put your opinions aside to objectively evaluate how well the writer presented his or her point of view. Don't allow your personal views to cloud your critical thinking. Appreciating an author's writing ability does not require you to accept his or her opinions or values.
2. **Read with a pen in your hand.** Make notes and underline passages that strike you as important, memorable, interesting, funny, odd, or disturbing. Reading with a pen will prompt you to write, to be an active reader rather than a passive consumer of words.
3. **Look up unfamiliar words.** Paying attention to words can increase your vocabulary and enhance your appreciation of connotations.
4. **Analyze passages you found difficult or confusing during the first reading.** In many instances a second reading can help you understand complex passages. If you still have difficulty understanding the writer's point, ask why. Would other readers also have problems comprehending the meaning? Could ideas be stated more directly?
5. **Review any questions at the end of the selection.** Considering the following questions can help you focus on a closer, more analytical reading of the work. The questions are arranged in three groups:

    Understanding Meaning:
    What is the writer's goal?
    What is the thesis?
    What audience is the writer addressing?
    What is the author trying to share with his or her readers?

    Analyzing Strategy:
    How effective is the title?
    How does the writer introduce the essay?

What evidence supports the thesis?
How does the writer organize ideas?
Where does the author use paragraph breaks?
What role does the writer play? Is the writer's approach subjective or objective?
How does the writer address possible objections or differing opinions?
How does the writer conclude the essay?
Does the author use any special techniques?

Evaluating Language:
How does the writer use words?
What does the language reveal about the intended readers?
What connotations do the words have?
How do the words establish the writer's tone?

6. **Summarize your responses in a point or two for class discussion.** Consider how you will express your opinions of the essay to fellow students. Be prepared to back up your remarks by citing passages in the text.

7. **Most importantly, focus on what this essay can teach you about writing.** How can this writer's style, way of organizing ideas, or word choice enrich your own writing? Though you may not wish to imitate everything you see, you can learn techniques to broaden your personal composing style.

8. **Think of how writers resolve problems you have encountered.** If you have trouble making an outline and organizing ideas, study how the essays in this book are arranged. If your instructor returns papers with comments about vague thesis statements and lack of focus, examine how the writers in this book generate controlling ideas.

Before Class Discussion

1. **Before class discussion of an assigned essay, review the reading and your notes.** Identify your main reactions to the piece. What do you consider the essay's strongest or weakest points?

2. **Ask fellow students about their reactions to the writing.** Determine if their responses to the writer's thesis, tone, approach, and technique match yours. If their reactions differ from yours, review your notes to get a fresh perspective.

3. **Be prepared to ask questions.** Ask your instructor about unfamiliar techniques or passages you find confusing.

Read the following essay by Scott Simon and note how he presents and supports his point of view:

SCOTT SIMON

Scott Simon is a war correspondent and reporter, but he is best known to listeners of National Public Radio as the host of "Weekend Edition with Scott Simon."

Why Even Pacifists Support This War

OVERVIEW: *This essay appeared shortly after the September 11, 2001, terrorist attacks against the World Trade Center and the Pentagon. As you read Simon's argument, consider if subsequent events have altered the thoughts and emotions the attacks produced. Is the idea of a war against terrorism as popular now as it was in late 2001? Why or why not?*

<u>Pacifists often commit the same mistake as generals: They prepare for the last war, not the next one.</u>

Many of the peace activists I have seen trying to rouse opposition to today's war against terrorism remind me of a Halloween parade. They put on old, familiar-looking protest masks—against American imperialism, oppression and violence—that bear no resemblance to the real demons haunting us now.

Pacifism has never been exactly popular. But when I became a Quaker as an adolescent in the late 1960s, pacifism seemed to offer a compelling alternative to the perpetuity of brute force. Mahatma Gandhi had overthrown an empire, and Martin Luther King had overturned a racial tyranny with nonviolent marches, fasts and boycotts that were nervy, ennobling and effective.

Pacifism seemed to offer a chance for survival to a generation that had been stunted by the fear of nuclear extinction.

I worked as a war reporter, but I never saw a conflict between this and being a Quaker. If my reporting was sometimes drawn more to human details than to the box-score kind of war coverage, those details struck me as critical to explaining war. I never covered a conflict—whether in Central America, the Caribbean, Africa or the Middle East—that seriously shook my religious convictions.

<u>In fact, most conflicts seemed to prove how war was rotten, wasteful and useless. El Salvador's civil war killed 70,000 people over nine years.</u> It

Margin labels:
1
Introduction
2

3
appeal of
pacifism

4

5
Simon's
roles as
Quaker and
war reporter

6

was hard to see how the political compromise that ended the conflict could not have been reached after just six months.

But in the 1990s, I covered the Balkans. In Sarajevo, Srebrenica and Kosovo, I confronted the logical flaw (or perhaps I should say the fatal flaw) of non-violent resistance: All the best people can be killed by all the worst ones.

I had never believed that pacifism had all the answers; neither does militarism. About half of all draft age Quakers enlisted in World War II, believing that whatever wisdom pacifism had to give the world, it could not defeat the murderous schemes of Adolf Hitler and his cohorts.

It seems to me that in confronting the forces that attacked the World Trade Center and the Pentagon, American pacifists have no sane alternative now but to support war. I don't consider this reprisal or revenge, but self-defense: protecting the world from further attacks by destroying those who would launch them.

Some peace activists, their judgment still hobbled by shock, seem to believe that the attacks against New York and Washington were natural disasters: terrible, unpredictable whirlwinds that struck once and will not reoccur.

This is wrong. We know now that there has been an ongoing violent campaign aimed at bringing down diverse nations, with none being more gloriously speckled than the United States. People who try to hold certain American policies or culture responsible are trying to decorate the crimes of psychotics with synthetic political significance.

In 1933, the Oxford Student Union conducted a famous debate over whether it was moral for Britons to fight for king and country. The exquisite intellects of that leading university reviewed the many ways in which British colonialism exploited and oppressed the world. They cited the ways in which vengeful demands made of Germany in the wake of World War I had helped to kindle nationalism and fascism. They saw no moral difference between Western colonialism and world fascism.

The Oxford Union ended that debate with this famous proclamation: "Resolved, that we will in no circumstances fight for king and country."

Von Ribbentrop sent back the good news to Germany's new chancellor, Hitler: The West will not fight for its own survival. Its finest minds will justify a silent surrender.

In short, the best-educated young people of their time could not tell the difference between the deficiencies of their own nation, in which liberty and democracy were cornerstones, and a dictatorship founded on racism, tyranny and fear.

And what price would those who urge reconciliation today pay for peace?

17   Should Americans impose a unitary religious state, throw women out of school and work and rob other religious groups of their rights so that we have the kind of society the attackers accept? Do pacifists really want to live in the kind of world that the terrorists who hit the World Trade Center and Pentagon would make?

18   Pacifists do not need any lectures about risking their lives to stop wickedness. Quakers resisted slavery by smuggling out slaves when even Abraham Lincoln tried to appease the Confederacy. Pacifists sneaked refugee Jews out of Germany when England and the U.S. were still trying to placate Hitler. Many conscientious objectors have served bravely in gritty and unglamorous tasks that aided the U.S. in time of war.

19   But those of us who have been pacifists must admit that it has been our blessing to live in a nation in which other citizens have been willing to risk their lives to defend our dissent.

20   The war against terrorism does not shove American power into calls on America's military strength in a global crisis in which peaceful solutions are not apparent.

21   Only American (and British) power can stop more killing in the world's skyscrapers, pizza parlors, embassies, bus stations, ships and airplanes. Pacifists, like most Americans, would like to change their country in a thousand ways. And the blasts of Sept. 11 should remind American pacifists that they live in that one place on the planet where change—in fact, peaceful

Conclusion   change—seems most possible.

22   It is better to sacrifice our ideals than to expect others to die for them.

E-WRITING: Exploring Writing Resources Online

The Internet provides an ever-growing range of information about reading. Using a search engine like Google or Alta Vista, enter the terms "reading strategies," "critical reading," and "reading techniques" to locate useful information.

InfoTrac® College Edition

For additional resources go to InfoTrac College Edition, your online research library, at http://infotrac.cengagelearning.com.

1. Enter the terms "reading strategies" and "critical reading" in the Subject Guide.
2. Enter the terms "reading skills," "improving reading comprehension," and "reading techniques" using Keywords.
3. Review online articles from current issues of major magazines and newspapers to practice reading skills.
4. Print copies of selected articles for future rereading and review.

STRATEGIES FOR CRITICAL READING

As you read selections in the text, consider these questions:

1. **What is the writer's goal?** Even writers exploring the same topic, such as describing an event or comparing two people, have different intentions. What is the purpose of the essay—to raise questions, motivate people to take action, change readers' perceptions?

2. **What is the thesis?** What is the writer's main idea? Is the thesis explicitly stated, developed throughout the essay, or only implied? Can you state the thesis in your own words?

3. **What evidence does the writer provide to support the thesis?** Does the writer use personal observations, narratives, facts, statistics, or examples to support his or her conclusions?

4. **How does the writer organize the essay?** How does he or she introduce readers to the topic, develop ideas, arrange information, conclude the essay? How does the writer use modes, such as comparison, process, and definition?

5. **Who are the intended readers?** What does the original source of the document tell you about its intended audience? Does the writer direct the essay to a particular group or a general readership? What terms or references are used? Are technical or uncommon terms defined? What knowledge does the writer seem to assume readers already possess?

6. **How successful is the writing in context?** Does the writer achieve his or her goals while respecting the needs of the reader and the conventions of the discipline or situation? Are there particular considerations that cause the writer to "break" the rules of "good writing"? Why?

7. **What can you learn about writing?** What does this writer teach you about using words, writing sentences, developing paragraphs? Are there any techniques you can use in future assignments?

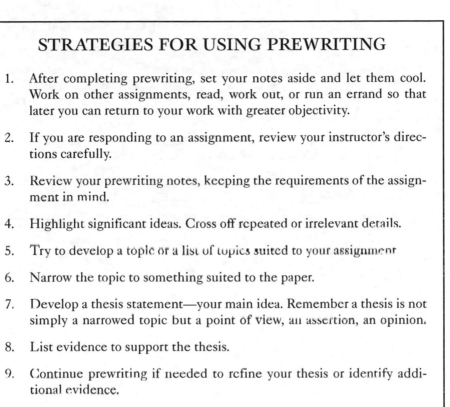

STRATEGIES FOR USING PREWRITING

1. After completing prewriting, set your notes aside and let them cool. Work on other assignments, read, work out, or run an errand so that later you can return to your work with greater objectivity.

2. If you are responding to an assignment, review your instructor's directions carefully.

3. Review your prewriting notes, keeping the requirements of the assignment in mind.

4. Highlight significant ideas. Cross off repeated or irrelevant details.

5. Try to develop a topic or a list of topics suited to your assignment

6. Narrow the topic to something suited to the paper.

7. Develop a thesis statement—your main idea. Remember a thesis is not simply a narrowed topic but a point of view, an assertion, an opinion.

8. List evidence to support the thesis.

9. Continue prewriting if needed to refine your thesis or identify additional evidence.

10. Create an outline to guide the writing of your first draft.

E-WRITING: Exploring Critical Thinking Online

The Internet presents a range of sources dedicated to critical thinking, ranging from sites maintained by academic organizations to those created by individual teachers posting information for their students.

1. Enter *"critical thinking"* as a search term in a general search engine such as Yahoo, Alta Vista, or Google to locate current websites dedicated to critical thinking.

2. Locate the online version of a national or local newspaper and review recent editorials. Can you detect any lapses in critical thinking? Do any editorials rely on hasty generalizations, anecdotal evidence, faulty comparisons, circular reasoning, or borrowed authorities?

3. For more dramatic examples of discovery errors in critical thinking, use search terms to locate sites about controversial topics. Review their arguments for lapses in critical thinking. Do you think these errors are accidental or deliberate?

4. To learn more about a specific problem in critical thinking, use one or more of the
    following as search terms:

    | coincidence | anecdotal evidence | post hoc | circular reasoning |
    | red herrings | guilt by association | hasty generalizations | fact and opinion |

 ## InfoTrac® College Edition

For additional resources go to InfoTrac College Edition, your online research
library, at http://infotrac.cengagelearning.com.

1. Enter "critical thinking," "logical fallacies," "hasty generalizations," "guilt by
    association," and "fact and opinion" as search terms.

2. Review several online articles on controversial topics for errors in critical thinking.

Analyzing Images

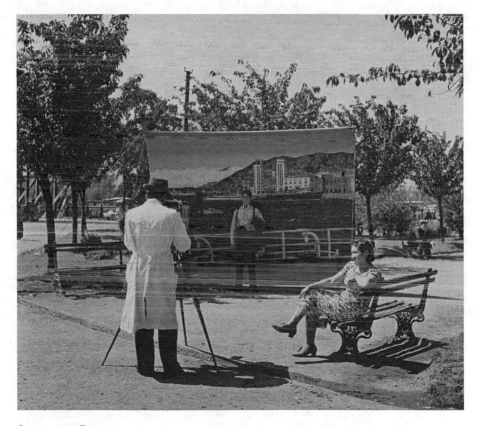

Image vs. reality

© Hulton-Deutsch Collection/Corbis

A picture is worth a thousand words.
Chinese Proverb

We increasingly communicate in images. We are bombarded daily with advertisements in newspapers and magazines, on television and billboards. College textbooks, which thirty years ago consisted of only text, now feature graphs and photographs on nearly every page. Websites, once blocks of words, now include streaming video. Satellites allow journalists to broadcast from remote parts of the world. Cable news networks provide images of breaking events twenty-four hours a day. The personal computer and desktop publishing allow students and small business owners to develop sophisticated multimedia presentations rivaling those created by major corporations.

Visual images are effective because they command attention. They are presented without comment or used to support a written statement. Sometimes an image serves only to grab attention or arouse curiosity, prompting people to pause to read a message.

Photographs, Film, and Video

Photographs, film, and video are compelling. There is an impression that "the camera does not lie." A written description of a person or a place never seems as objective or as accurate as a photograph. The camera, we believe, hides nothing. It tells the whole truth. It leaves nothing out. People writing reports about a car accident can exaggerate or minimize the damage, but a photograph, we believe, will provide us with irrefutable evidence. But visuals can be highly subjective and often misleading. They require careful analysis to determine their meaning and reliability.

The impression a photograph or video makes is shaped by a number of factors: perspective and contrast, context, timing and duplication, and manipulation.

Perspective and Contrast

How large is a group of a hundred? How tall is a twenty-story building? The impression we get of events, objects, and people depends on perspective, the angle and distance of the camera and the subject. A hundred protesters photographed in close-up will look like an overwhelming force. Fists raised, faces twisted in emotion, lunging toward the camera, they can appear

The image as icon. Elvis autographs photographs for fans.

© Bettmann/Corbis

all-powerful and unstoppable. Photographed from a distance the crowd can seem small against a landscape of multistory buildings or acres of empty pavement. In contrast to large fixed objects, their protest can appear futile and weak. If ordinary people going about routine business are shown in the foreground, the protesters, in contrast, may appear abnormal, ephemeral, even pathetic. A twenty-story building in a suburban neighborhood of two-story structures will loom over the landscape. Located in midtown Manhattan, dwarfed by skyscrapers, the same structure will seem undersized, less formidable, even homey in contrast. A luxury car photographed in front of a stately country home can appear as a desirable symbol of style, elegance, and taste. Parked next to a migrant farm worker's shack, the same car can appear oppressive, a symbol of tasteless greed, exploitation, and injustice. A mime shown entertaining small children will look wholesome, joyful, and playful. Posed next to a homeless man taking shelter in a cardboard box, a mime will look irrelevant, useless, even offensive.

Charles Lindbergh, 1927

© Bettmann/Corbis

An individual can appear large or small, weak or powerful, depending on perspective. In the photo above, Charles Lindbergh is shown in close-up. His face fills the frame. No other people, structures, or objects detract from his larger-than-life presence. In addition, he is photographed wearing his flight helmet and goggles, emblems of his famous 1927 transatlantic flight. His clear eyes look upward as if gazing to the horizon and the future. This photograph depicts a human being as powerful, in command of his environment. It is the type of image seen in movie posters, postage stamps, official portraits, and celebrity stills. Shown in isolation, any subject can appear dominant because there is nothing else to compare it to.

In contrast to Lindbergh's picture, the photograph of James Dean in Times Square (next page) is shot from some distance. Unlike Lindbergh, Dean is not shown in isolation but within an environment. Though he is at the center of the photograph, his stature is diminished by the urban landscape.

James Dean in Times Square, 1955.

© Dennis Stock, 1955/Magnum

Tall buildings rise above him. The iron fence on the right restricts his freedom of movement. In addition, the environment is hostile—dark, cold, and wet. Dean is hunched forward, his collar turned up against the wind, his hands buried in his pockets against the cold. The picture creates an image of brooding loneliness and alienation, suited to Dean's Hollywood image as a loner and troubled rebel.

The impression created of Lee Harvey Oswald (next page) is greatly shaped by perspective. In the press photo taken shortly after his arrest, Oswald looks weak, subdued, cowardly. He is literally cornered, shown off-center on the edge of the frame. Though he is the subject of the photograph, he is

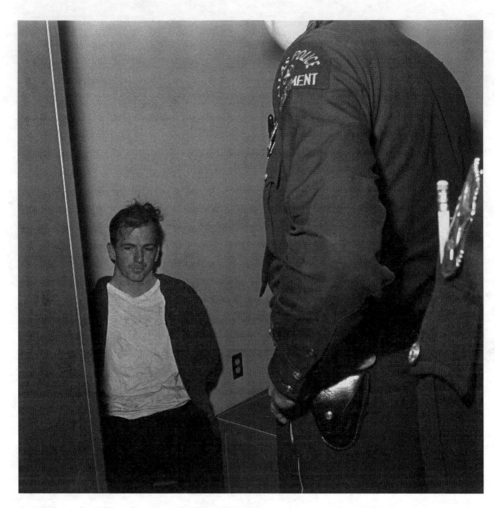

Lee Harvey Oswald under arrest, Dallas, 1963

© AP

markedly smaller in relation to the officers. The angle of the camera distorts the relative sizes of the figures so that the uniformed men in the foreground are oversized, their power and authority emphasized. The officer's badge appears larger than Oswald's head. The room is blank and featureless. Clearly handcuffed and still disheveled from his arrest, Oswald is depicted as a disarmed menace, an assassin rendered harmless.

Context

Photographs and video images are isolated glimpses of larger events. A camera captures a split second of reality, but it does not reveal what happened before or after the image was taken. The photograph of a baseball player hitting a home run shows a moment of athletic triumph, but it does not reveal the player's batting average or who won the game. A single striking image may distort our impressions of a larger event.

Motion picture and video cameras offer us a window onto the world, bringing world events into our homes—but it is a narrow window. During the hostage crisis in Iran in 1979, for example, television cameras continually showed violent demonstrations outside the American embassy, creating the impression that the entire nation was swept by a wave of anti-Americanism. American journalists, however, reported that only a block away they could walk through crowded streets and chat with passersby without incident. Aware of the power of image, protest groups around the world stage demonstrations for maximum media exposure.

Watching an evening of cable network news creates the illusion that you are being informed about world events. In thirty minutes you see a conflict in the Middle East, a White House spokesperson, a senator commenting on the economy, a high-speed car chase in San Diego. But cable news is highly limited to covering visual stories. More complicated stories may not provide gripping visuals or require too much explanation to make good television. Stories that break in developed countries within easy reach of media crews receive more coverage than events that occur in remote areas. Conflicts in the Middle East and Northern Ireland that claim a few hundred lives a year receive more coverage than a genocidal rebellion that kills hundreds of thousands in Rwanda.

Juries have acquitted people caught on videotape buying drugs or engaged in violent assaults. Whereas the public often only sees a dramatic segment, juries are often shown a videotape in its entirety. Defense attorneys place the tape in context by providing additional information about the people and events depicted. By raising doubts, they can persuade a jury to rethink what it has seen, questioning the tape's meaning and reliability.

Visual Connotations

Like words, images have connotations. They create emotional responses. Politicians are interviewed with flags and bookshelves in the background to demonstrate patriotism and indicate knowledge. Campaign commercials show candidates with their families, visiting the elderly, shaking hands with firefighters, or visiting veterans to link themselves with positive images. Ads and commercials will use provocative images of sex and violence to arrest people's attention. Book covers and movie posters only vaguely associated with World War II often feature a large swastika because it is a symbol bound to attract attention.

Certain images become icons, symbols of an event, culture, attitude, or value. Reproduced in books, films, or murals, and T-shirts, they serve to communicate a message with a single image. Marilyn Monroe's upswirled skirt symbolizes sex. The flag raising at Iwo Jima and the mushroom cloud rising above Hiroshima came to express the victory and horror of the Second World War. The photograph of two African-American athletes raising gloved fists at the Olympic Games became an icon of Black Power. The World Trade Center has become an international symbol of terrorism. Often the icon takes on a meaning of its own, so that fiction can become reality. Although John Wayne never served in the military, his picture is often hung in Pentagon offices because his Hollywood image expresses values embraced by the military.

Timing and Duplication

Timing and duplication can enhance an image's impact and distort perceptions. If two celebrities meet briefly at a crowded special event and photographs of them shaking hands are widely reproduced over several months it can create the impression they are close friends. The two figures become a single image repeatedly imprinted on the public, few recognizing that they are simply seeing the same moment from different angles. Stalin, Roosevelt, and Churchill only met on a few occasions during World War II, but the continual reproduction of photographs of them together helped create the image of the Big Three as a solid alliance against Hitler. Cable news reports of a suicide bombing, a shooting spree, or car chase will recycle scenes over and over, often creating an exaggerated sense of their significance.

Manipulating Images

Just as court painters often depicted royalty in flattering poses without blemishes, photographers and filmmakers can use lighting, perspective, and contrast to alter perceptions of reality. Short actors can be made to

President Wilson and General Pershing. A retoucher has partially erased a figure walking behind the two famous men, altering the perception of a historical event. Frequently, negative or distracting images are removed from pictures to enhance their effect.

© TimePix.

seem taller on screen by lowering cameras or placing taller people in the background. Makeup and lighting can magnify or diminish facial features, improving someone's appearance. Even candid images can be carefully selected to show a subject in a positive light. Portraits and photographs of Kaiser Wilhelm and Joseph Stalin camouflaged the fact that both men had one arm noticeably shorter than the other. Wishing to project power and authority, both leaders wished to disguise their physical disability. Although most Americans knew that President Roosevelt had been stricken with polio, few were aware how severely handicapped he actually was. The media did not release films of him in movement. Photographs and newsreels showed him standing or seated. The fact that he often had to be lifted out of cars or carried up steps was not made public. Although suffering from a painful back injury and Addison's disease, President Kennedy projected an image of youth and vigor by being shown in athletic contexts, playing touch foot-ball, swimming, or boating.

Photographs and film can be edited, revised, cut, and altered after the fact. A group photo can be reduced to focus on a single person. People and objects can be added or removed to alter the record of actual events. Leon Trotsky was once a powerful Soviet leader, often photographed standing next to Lenin. Wishing to obliterate his rival's role in the Russian Revolu-tion, Stalin had thousands of pictures retouched to remove Trotsky from group photographs.

Today with computer technology, images can be easily digitally removed and inserted. Photographs, motion pictures, and videos now have an increas-ing power to create their own reality that may exaggerate, minimize, or distort actual events.

Gender and Cultural Issues

Images, like language, affect our perceptions. Historically, images have reflected prevailing attitudes and biases. Words like *policeman, mankind, mailman,* and the universal use of *he* as a single pronoun gave English a distinct sexist stance. Historically, photographs focused on male activities, actions, and behaviors, with women generally appearing as family members or sex objects. Photographs taken of minorities often reflected and generated stereotyped views, so that African Americans were often photographed in subservient, patronizing, or comic roles. Advertising has historically pre-sented women as sexual objects or in a secondary role to men. Automobile ads show men standing next to or driving a car but show women draped across the hood as a kind of ornament. Soap ads depict men taking showers, whereas women are posed lying in tubs. As gender roles change, popular culture and advertising alter our perceptions of men and women.

Perception and Analysis

Our analysis of images is shaped by our perceptions, both personal and cultural. A photograph taken in Iran depicts a male professor lecturing female seminary students from behind a screen. To Western eyes, this image can seem a shocking example of oppression and exclusion. To many Iranians, the image of women studying Islam represents inclusion and empowerment.

Social change reflected by a clash of traditional gender images. Makeup and jewelry are decidedly feminine, in stark contrast to the masculine hard hat.

© SuperStock.

Strategies for Analyzing Visual Images

1. **Examine the image holistically.** What does it represent? Does it convey a message? What is your initial reaction?
2. **Consider the nature of the image.** Is this a professional portrait or a candid press shot? Was this video taken at a prepared ceremony or a spontaneous event? Were people, images, or objects deliberately posed to make a statement?

In Iran, a male professor lectures female students from behind a screen

© Lise Sarfati/Magnum

3. **Examine perspective.** Is the subject depicted in close-up or at a distance? Does the subject appear in control of the environment or does the background clash or dominate the frame?

4. **Analyze contrasts and contexts.** Is the background supportive, neutral, or hostile to the subject? Does the image depict conflict or harmony?

5. **Examine poses and body language of human figures.** How are human figures depicted? What emotions do they seem to express?

6. **Look for bias.** Do you sense the photographers were trying to manipulate the people or events depicted, casting them in either a favorable or negative light?

7. **Consider the larger context.** Does the image offer a fair representation of a larger event or an isolated exception?

8. **Review the image for possible manipulation.** Could camera angles or retouching have altered what appears to be a record of actual events?

9. **Consider the story the image seems to tell.** What is the thesis of this image? What visual details or symbols help tell the story?

4

Developing a Thesis

> *Come out with your subject pointed.*
> *Take a stand, make a judgment of*
> *value, make a thesis.*
> Sheridan Baker

WHAT IS A THESIS?

Good writing has a clear purpose. An essay is never "about" something. Whether the topic is global warming, your first job, a high school football coach, or *A Streetcar Named Desire*, your writing should make a point or express an opinion. The *thesis* is a writer's main or controlling idea. A *thesis statement* presents the writer's position in a sentence or two and serves as the document's mission statement. *A thesis is more than a limited or narrowed topic—it expresses a point of view. It is a kind of declaration, summarizing your purpose.*

Topic	Narrowed Topic	Thesis Statement
gun control	handgun ban	*The city's proposed handgun ban will not prevent gang violence.*
computer crime	consumer fraud on Internet	*Consumers will resist shopping on the Web until credit card security is assured*
campus housing	rehabbing dorms	*Given the demand for more on-campus housing, the fifty year-old men's dorm should be renovated.*
terrorism	cyberterrorism	*Federal security agencies must take steps to protect the Internet from cyberterrorism.*

Everything you write should have a thesis, not just essays that state an argument about a social or political topic. Without a strong thesis, a narration or description can become a collection of unrelated facts. Although a description may not have a thesis statement you can underline, the writing will have a focus, a purpose, a controlling idea.

ELEMENTS OF A THESIS STATEMENT

Effective thesis statements share common characteristics:

They are generally stated in a single sentence. This statement forms the core of the paper, clearly presenting the writer's point of view. Writing a thesis statement can be a critical part of the prewriting process, helping you move from a list or cluster of ideas to a specific paper. Even if the thesis statement does not appear in your final paper, writing this sentence can help focus your ideas and direct your writing.

Thesis statements express an opinion, not a topic. What distinguishes a thesis statement from a topic is that it does not announce a subject but expresses a viewpoint. The statement "There is a serious shortage of campus parking" describes a problem, but it does not express the writer's opinion. "Shuttle bus service should be expanded to alleviate the campus parking problem" serves as a thesis statement, clearly asserting the writer's position on the subject.

Thesis statements limit the topic. Part of the job of a thesis statement is to focus the paper, limiting the scope of the writer's area of concentration. "Television is bad for children" states an opinion, but the subject is so broad that any essay would probably be limited to a list of superficial observations. A thesis such as "Television action heroes teach children that violence is an acceptable method of resolving conflicts" is limited enough to create a far more engaging paper.

Thesis statements indicate the kind of support to follow. Opinions require proof. "Because of declining enrollment, the cinema course should be canceled" indicates a clear cause-and-effect argument based on factual evidence, leading readers to expect a list of enrollment and budget figures.

Thesis statements often organize supporting material. The thesis statement "Exercise is essential to control weight, prevent disease, and maintain mental health" suggests the body of the paper will be divided into three segments.

Effective thesis statements are precisely worded. Because they express the writer's point of view in a single sentence, thesis statements must be accurately phrased. General terms such as *good, bad, serious, significant* weaken a thesis. Absolute statements can suggest the writer is proposing a panacea. "Deadbolt locks should be installed in all dorm rooms to *prevent crime*" implies that a single mechanism is a foolproof method of eradicating all crime. "Deadbolt locks should be installed in all dorm rooms to *deter break-ins*" is far more specific and easier to support.

LOCATING THE THESIS

To be effective, thesis statements must be strategically placed. The thesis statement does not have to appear in the introduction but can be placed anywhere in the essay:

Placing the thesis at the opening provides the essay with a strong opening, clear direction, and an outline of the supporting evidence. However, if the thesis is controversial, it may be better to open with supporting details and confront readers' objections before formally announcing the thesis. An essay that opens with the statement "We must legalize heroin" might easily be dismissed by people thinking the writer must be naive or insensitive to the pain of addiction, the spread of AIDS, and other social problems stemming from drug abuse. However, if the essay first demonstrated the failure of current policies and argued that addiction should be treated as a medical rather than a legal issue, more readers might be receptive to the writer's call for legalization.

Placing the thesis in the middle of the essay allows the writer to introduce the subject, provide support, raise questions, and guide the reader into accepting a thesis that is then explained or defended. However, placing the thesis somewhere within the essay may weaken its impact because reader attention is strongest at the opening and closing paragraphs. Writers often highlight a thesis statement in the middle of an essay by placing it in its own paragraph or using italics.

Placing the thesis at the end allows the writer to close the essay with a strong statement. Delaying the thesis allows the writer to address reader objections and bias, providing narratives, examples, and statistics to support the conclusion. However, postponing the thesis will disappoint some readers who want a clear answer. Delaying the thesis can suggest to some readers that the writer's position cannot stand on its own and depends on a great deal of qualification.

EXPLICIT, EVOLVING, AND IMPLIED THESES

Although textbooks suggest that every essay should have an easily identifiable thesis statement, a sentence you should be able to locate and underline, this is not always the case. Most writers present explicit thesis
statements, while others use a series of sentences to develop their opinions. In some instances, the writer's thesis is not formally stated but only
implied.

Explicit Thesis Statements

Alan M. Dershowitz opens his essay "The 'Abuse Excuse' Is Detrimental
to the Justice System" with a boldly stated, explicit thesis statement:

> The "abuse excuse"—the legal tactic by which criminal defendants claim a
> history of abuse as an excuse for violent retaliation—is quickly becoming a
> license to kill and maim.

Advantages

1. An explicit thesis statement is clear and concise. The writer's purpose is
   stated directly so that readers will not be confused.
2. An explicit thesis can be used to make a strong opening or closing
   statement.
3. A concise, strongly worded statement is easily understood, so even a casual
   reader will quickly grasp the writer's main idea.

Disadvantages

1. Explicit thesis statements can present a narrow interpretation or solution
   to a complex situation or problem. In many instances a developing or implied thesis gives the writer greater freedom to discuss ideas and address
   possible objections.
2. Because they are so direct and easily understood, explicit theses can easily
   alienate readers with differing opinions. A developing thesis allows the
   writer to explain or qualify his or her opinions.

*Explicit theses are best used in writing in the modes of argument and persuasion,
comparison, and division and classification.*

Evolving Thesis Statements

In "Grant and Lee," Bruce Catton compares the two Civil War generals who met at Appomattox Court House to work out terms for the South's surrender. But instead of stating his thesis in a single sentence, he develops his controlling ideas in a series of statements:

> They were two strong men, these oddly different generals, and they represented the strengths of two conflicting currents that, through them, had come into final collision.

After describing the life and social background of each general, Catton expands his thesis:

> So Grant and Lee were in complete contrast, representing two diametrically opposed elements in American life. Grant was the modern man emerging; beyond him, ready to come on the stage, was the great age of steel and machinery, of crowded cities and a restless burgeoning vitality. Lee might have ridden down from the old age of chivalry, lance in hand, silken banner fluttering over his head. Each man was the perfect champion of his cause, drawing both his strengths and his weaknesses from the people he led.

Catton concludes his essay with a final controlling statement:

> Two great Americans, Grant and Lee—very different, yet under everything very much alike.

Advantages

1. An evolving thesis allows a writer to present readers with a series of controlling ideas, allowing them to absorb a complex opinion point by point.
2. An evolving thesis can be useful in presenting a controversial opinion by slowly convincing readers to accept less threatening ideas first.
3. An evolving thesis can help a writer tailor ideas to suit different situations or contexts. An evolving thesis can also be organized to address separate reader objections.

Disadvantages

1. Because the statements are distributed throughout an essay, they can appear "scattered" and may have less impact than a single direct sentence.

2. Evolving theses can make a writer appear unsure of his or her points, as if he or she is reluctant to state an direct opinion.

Evolving thesis statements are best suited for complex or controversial subjects. They allow the writer to address an issue piece by piece or present a series of arguments.

Implied Thesis Statements

In describing Holcomb, Kansas, Truman Capote supplies a number of facts and observations without stating a thesis. Although no single sentence can be isolated as presenting the controlling idea, the description is highly organized and is more than a random collection of details:

> The village of Holcomb stands on the high wheat plains of western Kansas, a lonesome area that other Kansans call "out there." Some seventy miles east of the Colorado border, the countryside, with its hard blue skies and desert-clear air, has an atmosphere that is rather more Far Western than Middle West. The local accent is barbed with a prairie twang, a ranch-hand nasalness, and the men, many of them, wear narrow frontier trousers, Stetsons, and high-heeled boots with pointed toes. The land is flat, and the views are awesomely extensive; horses, herds of cattle, a white cluster of grain elevators rising as gracefully as Greek temples are visible long before a traveler reaches them.

Having carefully assembled and arranged his observations, Capote allows the details to speak for themselves and give readers a clear impression of his subject.

Advantages

1. An implied thesis allows the writer's images and observations to represent his or her ideas. Implied thesis statements are common in descriptive and narrative writing.
2. An implied thesis does not dictate an opinion but allows readers to develop their own responses.
3. An implied thesis does not confront readers with bold assertions but allows a writer to slowly unfold controlling ideas.

Disadvantages

1. Writing without an explicitly defined thesis can lead readers to assume ideas unintended by the writer. Capote's description of a small town may

provoke both positive and negative responses, depending on the readers' perceptual world.

2. Writing that lacks a clear thesis statement requires careful reading and critical thinking to determine the writer's purpose. A strong thesis sentence at the opening or closing of an essay makes the author's goal very clear.

Implied thesis statements work best when the writer's evidence is so compelling that it does not require an introduction or explanation. Writers also use an implied thesis to challenge readers by posing an idea or presenting a problem without suggesting an interpretation or solution. Although you may not provide a clear thesis statement when writing a description or telling a story, your essay should have a clear purpose, a direction. A thesis statement, though it may not appear on the page, can prevent an essay from becoming a list of random facts or a chain of unrelated events.

STRATEGIES FOR DEVELOPING THESIS STATEMENTS

1. **Develop a thesis statement while planning your essay.** If you cannot state your goal in a sentence or two, you may not have a clear focus regarding your purpose. Even if you decide to use an implied thesis, a clearly worded statement on your outline or top of the page can help keep your writing on track.

2. **Write your thesis statement with your reader in mind.** The goal of writing is not only to express your ideas, but also to share them with others. Choose your words carefully. Be sensitive to your readers' perceptual world. Avoid writing biased or highly opinionated statements that may alienate readers.

3. **Make sure that your thesis statement expresses an opinion.** Don't confuse making an announcement or a factual statement with establishing a thesis. Review the wording of the statement to see if it includes action verbs. Readers should be directed to take action, change their ideas, or alter their behavior.

4. **Determine the best location for your thesis.** If you believe that most of your readers will be receptive to your views, placing the thesis at the opening may be appropriate. If your position is controversial or depends on establishing a clear context of support, delay your thesis by placing it in the middle or at the conclusion.

Continued

5. **Make sure your thesis matches your purpose.** Persuasive arguments demand a strongly worded thesis statement, perhaps one that is restated throughout the essay. If your position is complex, you may wish to develop it by making partial thesis statements throughout the essay. If you are not motivating your readers to take specific action, you may wish to use an implied thesis. State your observations or evidence and permit readers to develop their own conclusions.

6. **Test your thesis.** It is not always easy to find people willing to read a draft of your essay, but you can usually find someone who will listen to a sentence or two. Ask a friend or acquaintance to consider your thesis statement. Is it precise? Does it seem logical? What kind of evidence would be needed to support it? Are there any words or phrases that seem awkward, unclear, or offensive? If your thesis statement seems weak, review your prewriting notes. You may need to further limit your topic or choose a new subject.

7. **Avoid making simple announcements or presenting narrowed topics.** The most common errors writers make in developing thesis statements include simply announcing the subject of a paper or presenting a narrowed topic:

ANNOUNCEMENT:	My paper is about racial profiling. Snowboarding is a popular sport.
NARROWED TOPIC:	Police departments have been accused of racial profiling. Snowboarders are regarded as outlaws by traditional skiers.
IMPROVED THESIS STATEMENTS:	Police departments must develop methods to combat crime and prevent terrorism without resorting to racial profiling. Snowboarders and traditional skiers must learn to respect each other on the slopes.

E-WRITING: Exploring Thesis Statements Online

You can use the Internet to learn more about developing thesis statements.

1. Using a search engine like Alta Vista, Yahoo, or Google, enter "thesis statement" as a term and review the range of sources. You may wish to print out websites you find helpful.

2. Locate one or more newspapers online and scan through a series of recent editorials. Select a few articles on topics you are familiar with and examine the thesis statements. Which sentence summarizes the editorial's main point or assertion? Where is it placed? Are the thesis statements explicit, evolving, or implied? Are they carefully worded?

InfoTrac® College Edition

For additional resources go to InfoTrac College Edition, your online research library, at http://infotrac.cengagelearning.com.

1. Enter the search term "thesis statements" in the Subject Guide or Keyword.

2. Search for online articles about controversial topics such as terrorism, abortion, gun control, affirmative action, privacy, censorship, or a current scandal to locate articles and editorials. Select three or four articles and analyze them:

- What is the article's thesis? Can you restate it in your own words?

- Is the thesis stated in a single sentence or is only implied?

- Where did the author place the thesis? How does its location affect the way people will read the article?

- Does the thesis do more than state an opinion? Does it introduce support, limit the topic, address possible objections?

5

Supporting a Thesis

By persuading others, we convince ourselves.
Junius

WHAT IS SUPPORT?

Whether your thesis is explicitly stated or only implied, it must be supported with evidence. Readers will share your views, appreciate your descriptions, understand your stories, accept your solutions, change their opinions, or alter their behavior only if you provide sufficient proof to convince them. The type of evidence you select depends on context—your goal, your reader, the discourse community, and the nature of the document. Most people associate *evidence* with persuasive or argumentative writing, but all writers, even those composing personal essays or memoirs, provide support for their ideas.

A student arguing for a new computer system would provide factual support to create a convincing argument:

> *The college must improve its computer system.* This semester four hundred students did not receive mid-term grades because of a computer breakdown. The college e mail system, which is critical to the distance learning department, malfunctioned for two weeks, preventing students from electronically submitting research papers. The eight-year-old system simply does not have the speed and capacity needed to serve the faculty, students, and administration. Students were told two years ago that online registration would save the college money and make it possible to sign up for courses from home. But this service has been postponed for another year because the computers can't support it. If the college is to attract students, maintain its programs, and offer new services, it must upgrade its computers.

The same student writing a personal narrative would use supporting details to paint a picture, set a mood, and express a feeling:

I spent two years in Paris and hated it! Most people raise their eyebrows when I say that, but it is true.

My Paris was not the Paris shown in the movies or the Paris seen by tourists. I lived with my mother in a cramped high-rise built for low-income workers. My Paris was a noisy, dark two-room apartment with bad heat, banging pipes, and broken elevators. The hallways were filled with trash and spattered with graffiti. Neighbors blasted us night and day with bad rock music. Punks and druggies harassed my mom every time she left for school. I could not wait for her to finish her degree so we could move back to New Jersey. I lived in Paris for two years and never saw the Eiffel Tower.

Prewriting can identify the kind of support best suited to your task.

Writers verify their theses using a variety of types of evidence, ranging from personal observations to statistics. Because each type of evidence has limitations, writers generally present a blend of support, supplementing personal observations and analogies with statistics and quotations.

Personal Observations

Personal observations are descriptive details and sensory impressions about a person, place, object, or condition. Writers can support a thesis or controlling idea by supplying readers with specific details. The thesis "Westwood High School must be renovated" can be supported with detailed observations about leaking roofs, faulty wiring, broken elevators, and defective plumbing. Similarly, a personal description of your hometown might include observations about its neighborhoods and residents so that readers will understand your attitudes.

Advantages

1. Personal observations can be powerful if they are carefully selected and well organized. To be effective, writers must choose words carefully and be aware of their connotations.
2. By adding human interest and personal narratives, personal observations can be used to balance objective facts, allowing the writer to inject himself or herself into the writing.

Disadvantages

1. Because they are chosen by the writer, personal observations are biased. They often require outside evidence such as facts, statistics, or testimony in order to be convincing.
2. Personal observations may be inappropriate in objective reports. Because of this, writers often include material they observed without using first-person references such as "I" or "me."

Personal Experiences

Like personal observations, accounts of your own life can be convincing support. As a college student, you have great authority in discussing higher education. A veteran's comments about the military are likely to have greater credibility than those of a civilian. A single working mother is an authority on daycare. A patient's account of battling a serious disease can be as persuasive as an article by a physician or medical researcher.

Advantages

1. Personal experiences can be emotionally powerful and commanding because the writer is the sole authority and expert.
2. Personal experiences are an effective support in descriptive and narrative writing.
3. Individual accounts can humanize abstract issues and personalize objective facts and statistics.

Disadvantages

1. Personal experience, no matter how compelling, is only one person's story. As with personal observations, personal experience can be bolstered with the introduction of outside evidence such as expert testimony, facts, and statistics.
2. Unless presented carefully, personal experience can seem self-serving and can weaken a writer's argument. Before including your own experiences, consider if readers will think you are making a personal appeal, asking readers to accept ideas or take actions that primarily benefit only you.

Examples

Examples are specific events, persons, or situations that represent a general trend, type, or condition. A writer supporting the right to die might relate the story of a single terminally ill patient to illustrate the need for legal euthanasia.

Advantages

1. Specific cases or situations can illustrate an issue and humanize a complex or abstract problem. They often make effective introductions.
2. Examples can be used to demonstrate facts and statistics, which tend to be static lists.
3. Examples allow you to introduce narratives that can make a fact-filled paper more interesting and readable.

Disadvantages

1. Examples may be misleading or misinterpreted, so they must be representative. For instance, a single mugging does not prove that a crime wave is sweeping a college campus. To be effective, examples should illustrate something larger. Avoid selecting isolated incidents or exceptions to a general condition. Stating that your 90-year-old great-grandfather has smoked cigarettes for 75 years without ill effect does not prove that smoking is harmless.
2. Because they are highlighted, examples can sometimes be distorted into being viewed as major events instead of illustrations. Another danger is that they can create false generalizations and overlook complex subtleties. Examples can be placed in context with statistics or a disclaimer:

    Mary Smith is one of five thousand teachers who participated in last year's strike. Though some of her views do not reflect the opinions of her colleagues, her experiences on the picket line were typical.

Facts

Facts are objective details that are either directly observed or gathered by the writer. The need to renovate a high school could be demonstrated by presenting evidence from inspection reports, maintenance records, and a manufacturer's repair recommendations.

Advantages

1. Facts provide independent support for a writer's thesis, suggesting that others share his or her conclusions.
2. Facts are generally verifiable. A reader who may doubt a writer's personal observations or experiences can check factual sources.

3. Because of their objectivity, facts can be used to add credibility to personal narratives.

Disadvantages

1. Facts, like examples, can be misleading. Don't assume that a few isolated pieces of information can support your thesis. You cannot disprove or dismiss a general trend by simply identifying a few contradictory facts. Citing a list of celebrities who dropped out of high school does not disprove the value of education.
2. Facts, in some cases, must be explained to readers. Stating that "the elevator brakes are twenty years old" proves little unless readers understand that the manufacturer suggests replacing them after ten years. Lengthy or technical explanations of facts may distract or bore readers.

Testimony (Quotations)

Testimony, the observations or statements by witnesses, participants, or experts, allows a writer to interject other voices into his or her document, whether in the form of direct quotations or paraphrases.

Advantages

1. Testimony, like factual support, helps verify a writer's thesis by showing that other people share his or her views and opinions.
2. Testimony by witnesses or participants provides a human dimension to facts and statistics. Comments by a victim of child abuse can dramatize the problem, compelling readers to learn more and be willing to study factual data.
3. Expert testimony, usually in the form of quotations, enhances a writer's credibility by indicating that highly respected individuals agree with his or her thesis.

Disadvantages

1. Comments by people who observed or participated in an event are limited by the range of their experiences. An eyewitness to a car accident sees the crash from one angle. Another person, standing across the street, may report events very differently.
2. Witnesses and participants interpret events based on their perceptual worlds and may be less than objective.

3. Expert testimony can be misleading. Don't take quotes out of context. Don't assume that you can impress readers by simply sprinkling a paper with quotations by famous people. Statements by experts must be meaningful, relevant, and accurate.

Analogies (Comparisons)

Analogies compare similar situations to demonstrate the validity of the thesis. The thesis "AIDS prevention programs will reduce the incidence of infection" can be supported by pointing to the success of similar programs to combat venereal disease or teenage pregnancy.

Advantages

1. Analogies can be useful for introducing new ideas by comparing them to things readers find familiar or understandable.
2. Comparisons can help counter alternative theses or solutions by showing their failures or deficiencies in contrast to the writer's ideas.

Disadvantages

1. Analogy is a weak form of argument. Because no two situations are exactly alike, analogy is rarely convincing in itself. Arguing "heroin should be legalized because Prohibition failed to curb demand for beer" fails to distinguish between the chemical properties of opiates and alcohol and between their relative social acceptance.
2. Comparisons depend on readers' perceptual worlds. Suggesting that an urban planner's design should be adopted because it will transform a city's business district into another Fifth Avenue assumes readers find Fifth Avenue desirable.

Statistics

Statistics are factual data expressed in numbers. They can validate a writer's thesis in dramatic terms readers can readily appreciate. However, you must be careful because, although statistics represent facts rather than an opinion, they can be very deceptive. The statement "Last year the number of students apprehended for possessing cocaine tripled" sounds alarming until you learn the arrests went from one to three students at a university with an enrollment of 30,000. Numbers can be used to provide strikingly different perceptions. Suppose the state of California pays half a million welfare recipients $800 a month. A proposal to increase these benefits by two percent can be reported as representing $16 a month to the poor or $96 million a year to taxpayers. Both figures are accurate, and one can easily imagine which numbers politicians might use to support or reject the proposal.

STRATEGIES FOR USING STATISTICS

In gathering and presenting statistics, consider these questions:

1. **Where did the statistics come from?** Who produced the statistics? Is the source reliable? Statistics about the safety of nuclear power plants released by utility companies or antinuclear organizations may be suspect. If the source might be biased, search for information from additional sources.

2. **When were the statistics collected?** Information can become obsolete very quickly. Determine if the numbers are still relevant. For example, surveys about issues like capital punishment can be distorted if they are conducted after a violent crime.

3. **How were the statistics collected?** Public opinion polls are commonly used to represent support or opposition to an issue. A statement such as "Ninety percent of the student body think Dean Miller should resign" means nothing unless you know how that figure was determined. How many students were polled—ten or a thousand? How were they chosen— at an anti-Miller rally or by random selection? How was the question worded? Was it objective or did it provoke a desired response? Did the polled students reflect the attitudes of the entire student body?

4. **Are the units being counted properly defined?** All statistics count some item—drunk driving arrests, housing starts, defaulted loans, student dropouts, teenage pregnancies, AIDS patients. In some cases confusion can occur if the items are not precisely defined. In polling students, for instance, the term *student* must be clearly delineated. Who will be counted? Only full-time students? Undergraduates? Senior citizens auditing an elective art history course? This is particularly a problem in the social sciences. Unless there is a set definition of *alcoholic* or *juvenile delinquent*, comparing studies will be meaningless.

Continued

5.   **Do the statistics measure what they claim to measure?** The units being counted may not be accurate indicators. Comparing graduates' SAT scores assumes that the tests accurately measure achievement. If one nation's air force is 500 percent larger than its neighbor's, does it mean that it is five times as powerful? Counting aircraft alone does not take engine quality, pilot skill, natural defenses, or a host of other factors into account.

6.   **Are enough statistics presented?** One statistic may be accurate but misleading. The statement that "80 percent of Amalgam workers own stock in the company" makes the firm sound employee-owned—until you learn that the average worker has half-a-dozen shares. Ninety percent of the stock could be held by a single investor.

7.   **How are the statistics being interpreted?** Numbers alone do not tell the whole story. If one teacher has a higher retention rate than another, does it mean he or she is a better instructor or an easy grader? If the number of people receiving services from a social welfare agency increases, does it signal a failing economy or greater effort and efficiency on the part of an agency charged with aiding the disadvantaged?

Advantages

1.   Statistics can distill a complex issue into a single dramatic statement: One out of three American children grows up in poverty; each cigarette takes seven minutes off a smoker's life; 21,000 instances of domestic violence are reported every week.
2.   Statistics can be easily remembered and repeated to others. Readers may be unable to remember lengthy paragraphs or sophisticated reasoning but can easily recall a statistic and share it with others.

Disadvantages

1.   Because they are often misused, statistics are often distrusted by readers. Whenever you quote statistics, be prepared to explain where you obtained them and why they are reliable.
2.   Although statistics can be dramatic, they can quickly bore readers. Long lists of numbers can be difficult for readers to digest. Statistics can be made easier to understand if presented in graphs, charts, and diagrams.

Because each type of evidence has limitations, writers usually present a blend of personal observations and testimony, statistics and examples, or facts and analogies.

DOCUMENTING SOURCES

No matter how dramatic, evidence is not likely to impress readers unless they know its source. There are different documentation styles for citing sources, such as MLA (Modern Language Association) and APA (American Psychological Association) formats. Documentation, usually mandatory in research papers, is useful even in short essays. Even informal notations can enhance your credibility:

According to a recent Newsweek poll, 50 percent of today's freshmen plan to own their own business.

Half of today's freshmen plan to open to their own businesses someday (Newsweek, March 10, 2003).

STRATEGIES FOR USING EVIDENCE: CRITICAL THINKING CHECKLIST

Use these questions to evaluate the evidence you have assembled to support your thesis.

1. **Is the evidence suited to your thesis?** Review the writing context to determine what evidence is appropriate. Personal observations and experiences would support the thesis of an autobiographical essay. However, these subjective elements could weaken the thesis of a business report. The thesis "My aunt taught me the meaning of courage" can be supported by personal observations and narratives. But a thesis such as "America must protect itself from the threat of biological terrorism" demands expert testimony, statistics, and factual data to be convincing.

2. **Is the evidence accurate?** It may be possible to find evidence that supports your thesis, but are these quotations, facts, and statistics accurate? Are they current? Figures that were relevant in 1998 may be irrelevant today. Quotations taken out of context can distort the writer's original intent. Statements made by experts in the past may have been retracted in light of more recent events or research.

Continued

---

3. **Are the sources reliable?** Evidence can be gathered from innumerable sources but not all proof is equally reliable or objective. Many sources of information have political biases or economic interests and only produce data that support their views. If you are writing about the safety of nuclear power, you may wish to avoid taking all your information from either utility companies or antinuclear organizations. In gathering information about minimum wage, you might wish to balance data from labor unions and antipoverty groups with government statistics and testimony from business owners.

    In some instances, reliable and objective evidence is difficult to obtain. Highly partisan and controversial issues generate a great deal of information, much of it produced to support a particular viewpoint. You can persuade readers to accept your thesis if you balance sources and openly state that some evidence may be biased and subject to alternative interpretations.

4. **Is sufficient evidence presented?** In order to convince readers, you must supply enough evidence to support your thesis. A few isolated facts or quotations from experts are not likely to be persuasive. A single extended example might influence readers to accept your thesis about a close friend or relative but would not likely alter their views on issues such as immigration, recycling, divorce laws, or public schools. Topics such as these require facts, statistics, and expert testimony.

    Examine your thesis carefully to see if it can be separated into parts and determine if you have adequate proof for each section:

    The university should offer more Internet courses to increase enrollment.

    - This thesis suggests the current enrollment is unacceptable and must be increased. Is there enough factual support to document this view?
    - Internet courses are offered as a proposed solution. Are sufficient data offered to indicate their success in attracting new students?
    - Does the essay document why Internet courses are a better vehicle for increasing enrollment than alternative proposals such as advertising existing courses, expanding night school offerings, or creating new classes?

Continued

5. **Is the evidence representative?** To be intellectually honest, writers have to use evidence that is representative. You can easily assemble isolated facts, quotations taken out of context, and exceptional events to support almost any thesis. Books about UFOs, the Bermuda Triangle, and assassination conspiracies are often laden with unsupported personal narratives, quotations from questionable experts, and isolated events.

   If you can support your thesis only with isolated examples and atypical instances, you probably should question your conclusions.

6. **Is the evidence presented clearly?** Although evidence is essential to support your thesis, long quotations and lists of statistics can be boring and counterproductive. Evidence should be readable. Outside sources should blend well with your own writing.

   Read your paper out loud to identify awkward or difficult passages.

7. **Does the evidence support the thesis?** Finally, ask yourself if the evidence you have selected really supports your thesis. In listing personal observations, collecting statistics, or searching for quotations, it is easy to be led astray from your original goal. Before including a particular piece of evidence, test it against your thesis.

   If your evidence does not directly support your thesis, you may wish to review your prewriting notes and consider revising your thesis statement.

 E-WRITING. Exploring Thesis Support Online

You can use the Internet to learn more about supporting a thesis.

1. Using a search engine like Alta Vista, Yahoo, or Google, enter terms such as "supporting a thesis," "critical thinking evidence," "evaluating evidence," "essay support," and "essay evidence" to locate current sites of interest.

2. Locate resources about specific types of evidence online or in your library's databases by using "statistics" and "personal testimony" as search terms.

3. Search newspapers and journals online and select a few articles and editorials. After identifying the thesis, note how the authors present supporting evidence.

4. Ask instructors in your various courses for websites to locate useful sources in various disciplines.

InfoTrac® College Edition

For additional resources go to InfoTrac College Edition, your online research library, at http://infotrac.cengagelearning.com.

1. Enter the search terms "thesis support," "supporting a thesis," "statistics," "using statistics," "analyzing evidence," and "using evidence" in the Subject Guide or Keyword.

2. Search for online articles about controversial topics such as terrorism, abortion, gun control, affirmative action, privacy, censorship, or a current scandal to locate articles and editorials. Select three or four articles and analyze their use of support:

- What kind of evidence does the writer use—facts, examples, personal experience, or statistics? Does the writer depend on one type or does he or she blend various kinds of evidence?

- Does the writer seem to use evidence fairly and accurately, or do statistics and quotations appear to be taken out of context?

- Does the author explain the source of his or her support?

- Does the writer appear to present biased sources or fail to address alternative interpretations?

- How effectively does the evidence support the thesis?

- Does the author make any errors in critical thinking?

6

Improving Introductions and Conclusions

Good opening paragraphs . . . nearly always share one characteristic: they make a commitment to the reader. For the rest of the essay, the writer's chief concern should be to meet that commitment, to carry out that contract.
Maxine Hairston

A conclusion is the place for a good presentation, not a poor one. It is a reader's last impression of a work, and it should be strong, forceful, convincing, and final.
H. J. Tichy

The most important paragraphs in anything you write are the first and last. Whether reading an e-mail, business letter, or twenty-page research paper, people pay the greatest attention to the beginning paragraph. As they read, their concentration slowly ebbs as they try to absorb more and more information. If the document is fairly long, boredom and fatigue can lead readers to skim or even skip entire pages. Towards the end of the paper, readers slow down and focus on the writer's final points.

Understanding how people read can help you organize ideas. The most significant points should be placed at the opening or closing of whatever you write. Information placed in the middle is more likely to be overlooked.

The opening paragraph should introduce the topic, arouse reader interest, provide background information, and prepare readers for what follows. Too often, however, students begin essays with paragraphs that simply announce the topic, include needless background detail, or make bland and obvious statements:

My paper is about property taxes. Property taxes are an important economic issue today. People are leaving this state because they are too high. This is hurting Wisconsin.

STRATEGIES FOR IMPROVING INTRODUCTIONS

You can make introductions stronger by using a number of techniques to create openings that command interest and engage readers, encouraging them to pay attention to the rest of the document.

Use a Title

Weak introductions often simply announce the topic of an essay. A well-written title can state what the paper is about, pose a question to arouse reader interest, or state a thesis:

Wisconsin's Crippling Property Taxes
Should We Lower Property Taxes?
It Is Time to Lower Property Taxes

Because the title has announced the topic, your first sentence can open the paper with a more significant statement.

Open with a Thesis Statement

If your paper has a clear thesis, you can open an essay by directly stating what you want your readers to understand:

Wisconsin must lower property taxes to prevent a massive loss of revenue needed to improve education and finance welfare reform.

Begin with a Fact or Statistic

One goal of an introduction is to grab readers' attention by alerting them to a problem or issue by presenting an impressive fact:

In 2002 more than two hundred small businesses left Wisconsin to relocate in other states to escape excessive property taxes.

Use a Quotation

A memorable quotation can both attract attention and establish credibility by introducing the words of someone readers recognize, admire, or respect:

Addressing shareholders last December, Janet Hernandez stated, "After thirty years in Milwaukee, our firm cannot compete because of high property taxes."

Avoid opening an essay with a quotation by a famous person like George Washington or Martin Luther King, Jr. unless it directly relates to your purpose.

Open with a Short Example or Narrative

You can demonstrate your thesis, dramatize a problem, and arouse interest by relating a brief story:

In 1919 there were few jobs open for black veterans. Frank Washington opened a small repair shop that grew into a company that employed nearly a hundred people until his grandson was forced to close this month because of high property taxes.

Make sure the narrative remains brief and clearly relates to the purpose of your essay.

Delete General and Obvious Ideas

Often a rough draft will retain elements of the writer's prewriting. Writers frequently begin by noting general or abstract ideas before developing a focused topic. Sometimes students retain this background train of thought in the opening of a paper:

Many states face economic problems. Wisconsin is no exception. Wisconsin has high property taxes. These taxes are driving individuals and corporations to leave the state.

Once you have developed a topic and thesis, you can delete this background information. Readers don't necessarily have to know what led you to select this topic. You can begin with a strong statement that directly involves the reader with your main idea:

Wisconsin's high property taxes are driving individuals and corporations to leave the state.

Prepare Readers for What Follows

If you are developing your essay using a mode such as division, classification, comparison, or cause and effect, you can explain your approach so readers know what to expect in the rest of the essay and can follow your train of thought:

> Wisconsin's property taxes must be lowered for three reasons.

> For over a hundred years Wisconsin has funded its community colleges, public schools, and county services through property taxes. Today, however, these taxes have become so high that they are becoming a drag on the state's economy.

Delete Minor Details

Students frequently open essays with insignificant facts, such as dates and addresses, that add little meaning:

> It was January 15, 2003. The governor met with several business leaders at the Adler Hotel at 700 North Broadway. He explained it was time to address the issue of reforming property taxes.

You can improve the impact of an introduction by highlighting key events, ideas, and actions. Eliminate minor details or place them within other sentences. Avoid using several sentences to express a simple fact:

> In January 2003 the governor met with several business leaders and explained it was time to reform property taxes.

STRATEGIES FOR IMPROVING CONCLUSIONS

A short paper does not require a summary of what readers have just read. If you write a five-hundred-word essay that explains three ways to combat global warming, you don't need a final paragraph that begins, "In conclusion, there are three ways to combat global warming," especially if this paragraph only repeats your introduction. A longer or more complicated paper, however, may benefit from a final summary of your main points.

Some essays will not need a conclusion at all. A comparison paper that explains the difference between two subjects can simply end with a final point about the second topic. A division essay outlining three treatments for depression can conclude with the last item. Unless you have a final point or recommendation, that paper does not need a general summary, since that will add nothing new to the paper.

Although not every essay requires a separate conclusion, there are several ways to make sure your essay ends on a strong point.

End with a Thesis Statement

In addressing a controversial subject, you might not wish to risk alienating readers by stating an idea they may disagree with until you present evidence that supports your point of view or raises questions about commonly held opinions. Sometimes, the best place to state the thesis is at the end of an essay. Concluding with the thesis leaves readers with your most powerful statement:

> Our state must lower property taxes to maintain revenue growth, encourage entrepreneurs to launch new business ventures, and prevent the loss of jobs.

End with a Question

A final question can encourage readers to consider what they have just read:

> If we refuse to lower property taxes, are we willing to lose hundreds of businesses and thousands of jobs?

End with a Call to Action

A persuasive essay can be made stronger if it concludes with a call to action, directing readers to do something. Readers can feel disappointed or frustrated if you outline a problem but offer no method of helping to solve it. After presenting evidence, you can encourage readers to take action:

> If we want to keep more businesses and jobs from leaving the state, we must lower property taxes. Contact your state representatives this week and tell them to support Senator Gaylord's proposal.

End by Encouraging Readers to Think About the Topic

In some cases you may not have a recommended plan of action for readers to take, but you want to encourage them to consider your topic, think about its potential, or conduct additional research:

> Republicans and Democrats offer conflicting views of what we should do about property taxes. Voters will have to make a decision this fall that will

determine the future of this state. Consider how taxes affect your business, your job, your future.

End with a Memorable Image, Quotation, or Statistic

One way to get readers to consider your ideas is to leave them with something they will be able to remember and quote to others. Select one fact or quotation that makes a strong impression:

> People who think that lowering taxes is always a Republican issue should remember Nancy Sanchez's speech before the annual Democratic dinner, when she stated, "Taxes should raise funds needed to improve the quality of life in our state, not sabotage our economy."

Because introductions and conclusions are important, pay special attention to your first and last paragraphs while revising and editing. You may find it easier to craft the opening paragraph and final point after you have fully developed the body of the essay.

 E-WRITING: Exploring Introductions and Conclusions Online

You can use the Internet to learn more about writing introductions and conclusions.

1. Using a search engine like Alta Vista, Yahoo, or Google, enter terms such as "essay structure," "writing introductions," "writing conclusions," "opening paragraphs," and "effective conclusions" to locate current sites of interest.

2. Review an e-mail you have sent recently. How effective is your first sentence? Does it announce the subject or explain the purpose of your message? Does the last line make a strong statement or direct the reader to take specific action? Could your introductions and conclusions be improved?

 InfoTrac® College Edition

For additional resources go to InfoTrac College Edition, your online research library, at http://infotrac.cengagelearning.com.

1. Enter the search terms "essay structure," "writing introductions," and "writing conclusions" to locate articles of interest.

2. Review a series of online articles from newspapers and news magazines. How do writers develop introductions that grab attention, announce the topic, and prepare readers for the body of the text? How do they end articles? What makes a final paragraph memorable?

7

Conducting Research

> *The research paper is, in the fullest sense, a
> discovery and an education that leads you
> beyond texts, beyond a library, and encourages
> you to investigate on your own.*
> Audrey J. Roth

WHAT IS RESEARCH?

The words *research paper* on a syllabus can instill anxiety and dread. Perhaps you found writing term papers in high school a frustrating and time-consuming chore. Even if you received good grades in the past, you may feel wholly unprepared for the level of work expected in college. For most students research papers imply endless hours spent locating sources, photocopying articles, downloading databases, taking notes, selecting facts, organizing quotations, writing, and rewriting—all while trying to remember when to use endnotes.

Your ability to write effective research papers will greatly determine your success in college. In some courses the research project accounts for more than half the final grade. Instructors assign research papers because, unlike objective tests, they measure your ability to solve problems, apply knowledge, gather evidence, and interpret data.

Learning how to write a good research paper will not only improve your academic performance but also sharpen the critical thinking skills needed in most careers. Although few people write traditional research papers once they leave college, almost every professional uses the same methods to produce annual reports, market studies, product evaluations, proposals, and letters. Executives, administrators, attorneys, entrepreneurs, and scientists must base their decisions and recommendations on information. The ability to locate accurate sources, evaluate evidence, and interpret findings is essential for success in any field.

Common Misconceptions

Before undertaking a research paper, it is important to understand what a research paper is *not*. Many students work very hard collecting material and writing pages of text only to receive low grades because the paper they produce fails to meet the instructor's requirements. Even students who do well on research papers often make the project more burdensome and time-consuming than needed.

A research paper is not a summary of everything you can find about your topic. The goal in writing a research paper is not to present a collection of facts and quotations "about" a topic but to state a clear thesis supported by evidence. Although it is important to survey information, using twenty sources instead of ten will not necessarily improve the quality of your paper. The goal of a research paper is to present carefully selected evidence that supports your thesis.

A research paper does not simply repeat what others have written. A research paper is more than a string of related quotations and summaries. It is important to qualify evidence, to critique the quality and quantity of the sources you select. Research writers not only collect evidence but also evaluate and interpret it. The focus of a research paper is your thesis and commentary—not pages of text you have cut and pasted from the Internet.

A research paper does not merely support a preconceived point of view. Honest research begins with a topic or question. You should only reach a conclusion and develop a thesis after carefully examining the evidence. Taking the ideas of others out of context to support your position on abortion or the death penalty is not research.

A research paper does not include the ideas of others without documentation. Including the ideas and words of others in your text without attribution is plagiarism. Whenever you add facts, quotations, and summaries of outside sources, you must identify them.

CONDUCTING RESEARCH: AN OVERVIEW

Writing a research paper can be made less intimidating and less arduous if you break the process into key steps:

- Understand the scope of the assignment.
- Select an appropriate topic.
- Conduct preliminary research.
- Limit the topic and develop a working thesis.
- Create a timeline.
- Collect and evaluate relevant evidence.

Understand the Scope of the Assignment

Some instructors assign topics for research papers, but most professors provide students with directions or guidelines, allowing them to select topics. Students may be required to use a certain number of sources, present evidence in a specific manner, or address a particular issue:

Write an eight- to ten-page research paper using APA documentation that compares past and present treatments of a common psychological disorder. Your sources must include at least two professional interviews.

Analyze a critical theme, character, or technique used by the author of one of the works we have studied in this class. Do not summarize the work or repeat what you may have presented in your oral report. Your paper should be six to eight pages long, include a minimum of three electronic sources, and documented in MLA style.

Select a noted trial, Supreme Court decision, or scandal and examine its lasting impact on the law, American institutions, or perceptions of justice. Your paper should be ten pages long and documented in APA style.

- **It is important to fully understand all the requirements of an assignment and refer to them throughout the process.** Perhaps the most common mistake students make is failing to address the needs of the assignment. Once you begin looking up sources and examining data, you can be easily led astray and write an interesting paper that fails to meet the instructor's requirements. The psychology student writing about schizophrenia may be impressed by some recent medical articles and write a thorough research paper outlining genetic factors. Though well written and properly documented, if it fails to draw a comparison between past and present treatments and does not include interviews, the paper may be wholly unacceptable.
- **Ask your instructor for clarification of any points you find confusing.** If your instructor does not supply handouts, take careful notes to record specific requirements and directions. If your instructor does not assign topics, you may wish to ask for suggestions. Ask your instructor which topics to avoid.
- **Make copies of any instructor handouts or notes and keep them next to your computer or in your purse or briefcase for quick reference.** Refer to these guidelines when visiting the library or searching the Internet. Make sure your research remains focused on sources that address the needs of the assignment.

Select an Appropriate Topic

The first step in writing a research paper is selecting a topic or topics. Until you begin collecting evidence, you may not be sure if the subjects you start with are workable. Often, subjects that you might find interesting at first become unmanageable because sources are lacking or too numerous to handle.

STRATEGIES FOR SELECTING A TOPIC

1. **Select a topic that matches the assignment.** If your instructor requires you to include personal interviews, you may find it difficult to locate people who can provide insights on highly specialized issues. You may find local mental health professionals or volunteers who can tell you about depression, addiction, or common mental illnesses. But it may be difficult to locate anyone with knowledge of bimodal processing.

2. **Select a topic that interests you.** If you don't really care about your subject, you may find it difficult to sustain a long research effort. If you choose a topic that you have little knowledge about, you will have to conduct extensive background research. Brainstorm to discover if your existing knowledge and experiences apply to the assignment. Discuss possible topics with your instructor or friends and ask for suggestions.

3. **Consider your long-term goals.** Writing a research paper offers an opportunity to explore issues and subjects related to personal and career goals. Many doctoral dissertations and business proposals began as research projects. In addition to fulfilling a course requirement, your research may help shape your career goals or locate information you can use in your job or business. Make sure that your personal interests do not conflict with the goals of the assignment—refer to the instructor's guidelines to keep your project on track.

4. **Select a topic that is flexible.** Until you begin researching, you cannot tell how much information is readily available. Think of your topic as an accordion, something that may have to be compressed or expanded.

Continued

5. **Be willing to alter or reject topics.** Your first topic is only a starting point. If you find it difficult to work with, drop it and select another. Do not feel obligated to stick with something unless required by your instructor. Use prewriting techniques like clustering, brainstorming, and asking questions to develop new approaches to your topic.

6. **Select more than one topic to start.** At this point no decision is final. Until you begin investigating ideas, you may not know if a topic will be suitable. If you are unsure which topic to pursue, sketch out two or three for preliminary research.

Topics to Avoid

- **Topics that rely on a single source.** Research papers coordinate information from several sources. If you select an event covered in one news story or a process explained by a single set of instructions, you will not be able to achieve a major goal of a research paper. Check with your instructor if you are interested in a topic with only a single source.
- **Highly controversial topics—unless you can develop a new approach.** It is unlikely you can write anything about capital punishment or abortion that has not already been stated— unless you look at the issue from a unique perspective. You might research murder rates, comparing states with or without the death penalty, or examine Buddhist views of abortion. Controversial subjects may be difficult to research because many sources can be biased. Discuss your topic with your instructor and ask for recommended approaches or alternative subjects.
- **New topics.** Events or issues that have just happened may be difficult to research because little has been published except news reports and fragmentary comments. A quick Internet search might locate the amount of reliable material currently available.
- **Topics lacking credible sources.** Conducting research about UFOs, psychic phenomena, and alternative medicine can be difficult because sources may be anecdotal and unscientific. Avoid "conspiracy"-related issues. By their nature, these topics resist objective investigation. A reference librarian can suggest sources or a new topic.
- **Popular topics.** As when writing about a controversial topic, it may be difficult to find something new to say about an issue many students have written about. Popular issues may be hard to research because many of the books may already be checked out of the library.
- **Topics difficult to narrow or expand.** Until you begin discovering sources, you will not know how complex your task will be. If you select a topic that resists alterations, you may be forced to reject it in favor of a more manageable subject.

Conduct Preliminary Research

Once you have selected a topic or topics, you are ready to explore your subject. Your goal at this point is not to locate specific sources for your research paper but to survey the field of knowledge, get a sense of the discipline, identify schools of thought, and research trends, areas of conflict, and new discoveries.

STRATEGIES FOR CONDUCTING PRELIMINARY RESEARCH

1. **Review textbooks.** Textbooks generally offer brief overviews of subjects, but they also often include endnotes, bibliographies, and footnotes that can direct you to books and articles about specific issues.

2. **Survey encyclopedia articles.** A good encyclopedia will present background information that may help you get a fuller view of your subject. Online and CD versions have a search feature that allows you to type in keywords to generate a list of related articles.

3. **Review specialized encyclopedias, dictionaries, and directories.** A general encyclopedia such as *The Encyclopedia Britannica* can offer only brief commentaries on subjects and will not include minor people, events, or subjects. The reference room of your library will likely have specialized encyclopedias. The *Britannica Encyclopedia of American Art*, for example, might offer a multipage article about an artist not even mentioned in general encyclopedias.

4. **Review indexes, databases, and abstracts.** Available in print, online, or on CD-ROM, these are valuable tools in conducting research. Databases list articles. Many provide abstracts that briefly summarize articles, usually in a single paragraph. Still other databases are especially useful because they include the entire article in addition to abstracts. If the complete text is available, you may download and save it to a disk for later reading and note taking. Skimming abstracts allows you to quickly review a dozen articles in the time it would take to locate a journal and find a single article. Abstracts not only list the source of the full article but also indicate its length and special features such as photographs or tables. Sources like *Chemical Abstracts*, *Psychological Abstracts*, and *Criminal Justice Abstracts* provide summaries in specific disciplines. Many libraries

---

Continued

subscribe to online services, such as InfoTrac College Edition, that list articles from thousands of general, business, and scholarly newspapers, journals, and magazines.

Consult a librarian for assistance in identifying those articles for which the database includes the complete text. By their nature, abstracts of articles have limited usefulness. Full-text articles, on the other hand, will be invaluable after you've left the library.

Also, ask a librarian if you can access the library's databases from a remote site (for example, at home, in your dorm room, or from a laptop with Internet connection). This convenience provides countless advantages. Note: If this option is available, you'll likely need a current user name and password to gain access.

5. **Conduct an Internet search.** In addition to specific databases such as InfoTrac College Edition, you can use a number of popular search engines such as Alta Vista, Yahoo!, or Google to search for sources on the Internet. Each of these engines or search tools can access millions of sites. These tools offer Web guides that organize sites by categories such as "arts and humanities," "education," or "news and media." You can also enter key words to generate specific lists.

Students unfamiliar with conducting Internet searches are often frustrated by the overwhelming list of unrelated "hits" they receive. Entering Martin Luther King, Jr. may generate thousands of sites about Billy *Martin, Martin Luther,* and *King* George III.

Search engines usually provide tools to refine your search.

- Check the spelling of your search terms, especially names.
- Make the search words as specific as possible.
- Follow the search engine's directions to narrow your search. It will give you specific ways to include or exclude terms in your search.
- Internet searches may locate home pages of sites with numerous sources and direct links to related sites.
- You can find the latest update for a Web page by entering **javascript:alert(document.lastModified)** in the Internet Explorer address box.
- If you find it difficult to locate useful sources, ask a reference librarian for assistance.

E-RESEARCH ACTIVITY: Exploring Preliminary
Research Online

Explore the research sources available at your library or through online databases.

1. Determine which catalog system your library uses. Use the card catalog or computer catalog to look up *Lord of the Rings*. What is the novel's call number? Where is it located in the library?

2. Examine the list of online databases available in your library.

3. Search a business database for a company you have worked for or done business with (such as Taco Bell, Coca-Cola, Home Depot, Bath and Body, or Proctor and Gamble).

4. Use the Medline database to generate a list of articles about a medical problem you or a family member have experienced (for example, carpal tunnel syndrome, diabetes, or arthritis).

5. Use a general database like Reader's Guide, InfoTrac, or Infoseek to obtain a list of recent articles on one or more of the following topics:

caffeine	federal witness protection program
Alzheimer's disease	high-definition television
the Patriot Act	Hubble Space Telescope

6. Using one of the articles you identified in Research Activity 5, save the file to a disk and then print a hard copy of the first page of the text.

7. Send the file you created in Research Activity 6 as an e-mail attachment to your own e-mail address for later retrieval. This method might be necessary if you locate an article on a database but have no way to save it to your disk (perhaps you've forgotten it or it has become corrupted).

8. Use a search engine like Lycos, Yahoo!, Google, or Alta Vista to search for websites about one or more of the following topics:

Parkinson's disease	scuba diving
Sandra Day O'Connor	Yellowstone National Park
dive sites in the Florida Keys	automobile child restraint seats

Follow the search engine directions to limit your search and reduce the number of irrelevant sites.

A Note on Conducting Preliminary Research

Remember, your goal at this point is to simply survey the field and get an overall feel for your subject. Don't get bogged down with details or allow yourself to become overwhelmed by the complexity or number of sources.

- Determine if there is sufficient material on your subject to work with.
- Look for ways of limiting your topic.

- Identify patterns in the data—conflicting points of view, clusters of related articles, key figures or authors, current theories, or research trends.
- Allow sources to direct you to new topics or new approaches to your subject.

Continually refer to your instructor's guidelines to keep your search on track.

Limit the Topic and Develop a Working Thesis

After surveying the field of knowledge, you can consider whether your topic is worth pursuing. If you cannot find enough material or if the sources are too diverse or scattered, you may wish to consider a new subject. In most instances, the preliminary material you have located may help you further limit your topic:

Orwell's *1984*
Loss of Freedom Predicted by Orwell in *1984*
Role of Technology in Orwell's *1984*
Orwell and the Loss of Nature in *1984*

Famous Trials
Role of Media in High Profile Trials
Leopold and Loeb Case
Role of the Press in the Leopold and Loeb Case

Asking questions can help target your paper and prevent you from simply summarizing the work or the ideas of others:

What effect does the loss of nature have on humanity in *1984*?
Did media coverage affect the outcome of the Leopold and Loeb case?

At this point you may be able to develop a working thesis, a starting point for your research paper. Although it may be general and subject to change, the working thesis moves beyond a narrowed topic or question to make a tentative statement:

Orwell considered contact with nature essential to individual liberty.
Excessive media coverage influenced the outcome of the Leopold and Loeb case.

A working thesis is a tentative statement subject to change. It is a tool to guide your research; keep an open mind and be willing to alter your opinion.

Create a Timeline

In writing an essay examination, it is important to keep your eye on the clock to prevent running out of time and leaving critical questions unanswered. Similarly, when you begin a long research project, it is important to carefully budget your time and resources. In developing a long paper, make sure you devote enough time for each stage in the writing process. Don't spend six weeks gathering materials and try to write, revise, edit, and proofread a ten-page paper over a weekend.

- **Note the due date and work backward to create a schedule allowing sufficient time for each stage in the writing process.**

May 10	Paper due
May 5	Target date for completion
May 1	Final draft prepared for final editing and proofreading
April 25	Second draft completed
April 15	First draft completed for revision and rewriting
April 10	Final outline completed, final thesis
April 5	Research completed and sources selected
March 15	Topic narrowed, working thesis, and research initiated
March 10	Topic selected and preliminary research started
March 5	Research project assigned

- **Chart your progress on a calendar to keep on track.**
- **Establish cutoff dates for major stages in the process.** If you cannot find enough material by a fixed date, talk with your instructor and consider changing topics. If you find too much material, narrow your topic.
- **Don't allow the research stage to expand past a specific date.** Keep the scope of the assignment and the length of the paper in mind to guide the quantity of material you collect. Online databases and the Internet can make research seem almost unlimited. Stay focused on your topic and the professor's instructions.

Collect and Evaluate Relevant Evidence

The type of evidence you will need to support your thesis will depend on the discipline, the topic, and the scope of the assignment. In most instances you will use *secondary sources*—expert opinions, statistics, printed interviews, historical documents, critical interpretations, and experimental results found in books, in magazines, and online. A literary paper will focus on a story or novel, biographical material about the author, and critical interpretations. An economics paper on a recent market trend may examine stock market statistics and comments by experts.

Computerized Catalogs

Most libraries use electronic catalogs that list their holdings of books, magazines, videos, and other sources. The exact instructions for using a computer will vary slightly. Most systems provide onscreen directions to locate specific works by their author or title. If you do not have a particular source in mind, you can enter a subject or topic:

Leopold and Loeb

LIST OF ITEMS   12 ITEMS MATCH YOUR SEARCH

ITEM	-AUTHOR-	TITLE	
1	Bellak, Leopold, 1916–	The schizophrenic syndrome, Leo	1967
2	Busch, Francis X	Prisoners at the bar: an accou	1952
3		Compulsion [videorecording]	1995
4	Darrow, Clarence, 1857–	Clarence Darrow pleas in defen	1926
5	Darrow, Clarence, 1857–	The plea of Clarence Darrow in	1924
6	DeFord, Miriam Allen 18	Murderers sane and mad	1965
7	Geis, Gilbert	Crimes of the century: from Leo	1998
8	Higdon, Hal	The crime of the century	1975
9	Levin, Meyer, 1905–	Compulsion—New York, Simon	1956
10	Loeb, Leo, 1869–	The venom of Heloderma	1913
11	McKernan, Maureen	The amazing crime and trial	1924
12	Vaughn, Betty Ann Erick	The forensic speaking in the	1948

By highlighting or entering the number of the source, you can access specific information about it:

AUTHOR	Higdon, Hal
TITLE	The crime of the century: the Leopold and Loeb case/ by Hal Higdon. —New York: Putnam, c 1975 (AA C8080)
LOCATION	College Library Main Book Collection 3rd Floor West, Room 3191
CALL NO.	HV6245 H46

STATUS	Not checked out
FORMAT	380 p., [8] leaves of plates: ill; 24cm
NOTES	Includes index
	Bibliography: 0. 368
	ISBN: 0399114912
	OCLC NUMBER: 01801383

Many computerized catalogs are linked to other libraries so you can search for sources located at other campuses or in local public libraries.

Locating Periodicals

Libraries refer to magazines and journals as *periodicals* or *serials*. You can locate a magazine or a newspaper in the catalog or *serials holding list*. But this will simply explain where *Newsweek* or the *New York Times* is located in the building, either in bound volumes or on microfilm. To find which articles and issues to search for, you have to consult specific databases. Databases list articles under key words. The *MLA Bibliography*, for instance, lists articles about literature and authors:

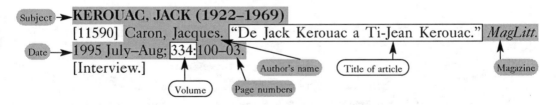

Fiction
[11590] Oates, Joyce Carol; Dauzat, Pierre-Emmanuel, translator. "Au bout de la route." *MagLitt*. 1995 July–Aug; 334: 96–99.

Letters
[11591] "Letters from Jack Kerouac to Ed White, 1947–68." *MissR*. 1994; 17(3): 107–60 [Includes letters (1947–1968) to White, Ed.]

Prose/Some of the Dharma
[11592] Sampas, John, foreword; Stanford, David, ed. and introd. *Some of the Dharma*. New York, NY: Viking; 1997. 420pp. ISBN 0-670-84877-8 [And poetry. Edition.]

SELECTING AND EVALUATING SOURCES

Database and Internet searches may provide you with hundreds, even thousands, of sources. Before you begin printing or photocopying, consider the type and number of sources needed. Without planning a list, you may waste a great deal of time collecting sources that may be interesting but unsuited to your paper.

STRATEGIES FOR SELECTING AND EVALUATING SOURCES

1. **List the types of sources needed to support your working thesis.** Review the assignment, instructor's directions, your preliminary research, and your working thesis to develop a list of needed sources:

    Working Thesis:
    Orwell considered contact with nature essential to individual liberty.
    > Sources needed:
    >> Orwell's attitudes toward nature
    >> Orwell's view of technology
    >> Biographical commentary on Orwell's views
    >> Letters, essays, journals showing Orwell's views of nature and human liberty

    Working Thesis:
    Excessive media coverage influenced the outcome of the Leopold and Loeb case.
    > Sources needed:
    >> Background/summary of Leopold & Loeb case
    >> Biographical information of principal figures in Leopold and Loeb case
    >> Description of press in Chicago in 1920s
    >> Actual 1924 newspaper accounts
    >> Assessment of effects of press on judge's decision

    For a ten-page paper, you may need only one or two biographical sources, not five or six. Make sure you select enough sources for each item on your list.

Continued

2. **Collect a variety of evidence.** If you are writing a paper about the home-less, you may wish to balance personal accounts with statistics and expert opinions. A paper about *Native Son* might benefit from sources from African American history or accounts of contemporary race relations in ad-dition to critical studies of the book and biographies of Richard Wright.

3. **Avoid collecting needless or repetitive data.** The Internet has made it possible to access thousands of documents. Although it is important to grasp the sweep and range of material about your subject, avoid printing more items than you need for your paper.

   - Select the most useful sources, briefly noting similar articles for con-firmation.
   - Refer to the assignment and your working thesis to keep your re-search focused.
   - Skim books and long documents by examining tables of contents and indexes to measure their usefulness before checking them out.

4. **Select reliable sources.** Recognized publishers, magazines, and estab-lished databases such as MLA, West Law, and Psychological Abstracts are edited by professionals who follow established standards. Articles appearing in the *New England Journal of Medicine*, the *Harvard Law Review*, or *Nursing* have been reviewed by physicians, attorneys, and nurses. On the other hand, small presses and individual websites may produce material based solely on rumor, anecdotal observation, and facts taken out of context. Do not assume that all the books in the library or sites found on the Internet are of equal value.

   - Books can be evaluated by checking reviews, many of which are available online. You can also examine the author's use of sources. Does the book include a bibliography? Does the author provide endnotes and support his or her conclusions with facts, quotations, or statistics? Is the author's biography available in *Who's Who* or other databases? Does the author seem biased?
   - You can get a sense of the quality of a magazine by reviewing other issues and examining the editorial staff. Determine the audience for the magazine. Publications designed for general readers like *Reader's Digest* or *People* will have a different purpose and tone than profes-sional journals in law or medicine.
   - Verify information you find on the Web by seeking confirming arti-cles on established databases. Examine the author or publisher of the Web site. Is it a professional organization, university, or govern-ment agency? Or is it a small, amateur, or personal site? Does the in-formation seem biased or objective?

Continued

5. **Verify controversial conclusions.** A book or website might offer a striking piece of evidence or make a dramatic conclusion. Before using this material, consider the source. Was the book published by a recognized publisher? Did the article come from a biased publication? Did you find this website using an established database like InfoTrac or Medline or by searching the Web with a general search engine like Yahoo! or AltaVista?

   - Review other books, articles, or material presented by this source.
   - Read a periodical's editorial page for signs of obvious bias. Even the tone of a publication's advertising can indicate whether the source is biased or objective.
   - Select keywords from the material and search established databases for confirmation.
   - Ask a reference librarian or your instructor to assist you in evaluating sources.

6. **Distinguish between fact and opinion.** In evaluating sources it is important to separate factual data from interpretation and analysis. The author of a book, magazine article, or website might accurately report a change in oil prices but present a highly personal and subjective interpretation or prediction.

7. **Examine sources for lapses in critical thinking.** Remember that all the books, articles, and studies you discover were created by human beings who, despite their degrees or expertise, may be biased or mistaken.

   - Do not assume that everything you read is accurate or true.
   - Facts may be misrepresented, conclusions misguided, and alternative interpretations ignored.

EVALUATING ONLINE SOURCES CHECKLIST

As you gather material from sources, consider these points:

✔ **Authorship:** Does the site mention the author or webmaster? This information is often noted at the bottom of the site's home page, but does not always appear on internal pages. Does the author or webmaster include his or her e-mail address? An e-mail to the author or webmaster might yield valuable insights.

Continued

✔ **Credibility:** If you are able to identify the site's author, can you also determine if he or she has significant knowledge about the topic? Does the site have a scholarly basis, or does it merely provide someone's personal opinion? Has it been updated recently?

✔ **Objectivity:** Does a reputable organization sponsor the site? Is this organization likely to be impartial in its examination of the information? Does the organization stand to gain from persuading you to accept its position? Do you detect inflammatory language that reveals bias or prejudice?

✔ **Purpose:** Can you determine the site's intended purposes? Is the site designed to present all available evidence? Does it seem to take a side? Is the site intended to inform readers or to sell a product or service?

✔ **Audience:** Are readers expected to have an opinion prior to visiting the site? Are readers encouraged to form an opinion based solely on the information presented? Or is further investigation invited via links to related sites?

✔ **Language:** Is the information presented in a manner that allows virtually any reader to understand it? Is specialized jargon included? Does its presence have a negative effect on the presentation or the general reader's comprehension?

✔ **Presentation:** Has the site been planned and designed well? Is it easy to navigate? Are the links active, current, and relevant? Does the text reflect that careful planning has been devoted to it, including thorough proofreading? But don't allow impressive graphics, sound, and video to substitute for accuracy in the information.

✔ **Critical Thinking:** Do you detect errors in critical thinking such as hasty generalizations, dependence on anecdotal evidence, faulty comparisons, false authorities, or attacking personalities?

STRATEGIES FOR OVERCOMING PROBLEMS WITH RESEARCH

Students frequently encounter common problems in conducting library research.

1. **There are no sources on the topic.** If your library and Internet search fails to yield sufficient results, review the subject and search words you are using.

    - Check the spelling of your keywords. Failing to enter words and numbers correctly will thwart an Internet or database search.
    - Check a thesaurus for synonyms.
    - Review the Library of Congress Subject Headings for alternative search terms.
    - Review textbooks, encyclopedias, and other reference sources for search terms.
    - Ask a reference librarian or your instructor for suggestions.

2. **There are sources about the subject but none are related to your specific topic or working thesis.** If you are analyzing the role of the mother in *Death of a Salesman*, you may find numerous articles on the play or Willy Loman but nothing on his wife. You do not have to find articles that exactly march your topic or thesis. Since one of the goals of a research paper is originality, your thesis may address unexplored territory. You can still use related or background sources. Biographies of Arthur Miller might yield insights into the attitudes represented by Linda Loman. Critical commentaries may provide views about the Loman family that relate to Linda's role in the play.

    - Pointing out the lack of sources can be crucial in demonstrating the value of your paper and the uniqueness of your approach.

3. **Sources present conflicting findings or opinions.** Experts often disagree. Biographers and historians evaluate people and events differently. Scientists dispute theories and present different interpretations of data. Economists argue whether tax cuts would stimulate or slow the economy.

    - As a student you are not expected to resolve conflicts among experts, but you should report what you find.
    - On the basis of your evaluation of the evidence, you may side with one group or alter your thesis to conclude that at present it is impossible to make a definitive statement.

Continued

4. **There are several books and articles, but they present the same information or refer to a common original source.** If you discover that the five books you have selected about teenage suicide or a person's life present virtually the same material, select the most representative, relevant, or best-written book.

- Although you may select only a single source, it is important to comment on the consistency of expert opinion.

5. **The only available sources are fragmentary, biased, outdated, inaccurate, or unprofessional.** In some instances the only available sources will lack substance or quality. A controversial historical incident may have produced a rash of inflammatory editorials, biased newspaper accounts, or subjective memoirs by adversaries.

- Ask your instructor if you should consider changing your topic.
- Consult a reference librarian for alternative sources.
- As a researcher you are not responsible for the lack of evidence or the quality of sources you can locate—but you should comment on the limited value of existing evidence.

TAKING NOTES

Traditional textbooks suggest that you record notes on index cards. By placing a single fact or quotation on a single card, you can easily shuffle and reorder them when you develop an outline. However, most students now photocopy or print pages and highlight selected passages. Others will scan text directly onto a computer disk. Yet another option is to download and save full-text articles from databases. Then you may minimize photocopying costs and conserve paper by printing hard copies of only the sections you consider necessary. Better yet, you can save money and trees by highlighting (in bold or an alternate color) useful passages in the file (so they are visible on the computer monitor) for later reference in your research paper.

Whatever method you use to record information from outside sources, it is essential to accomplish three tasks:

1. **Accurately record information you will need to cite the source.**
   Books: author's full name, full title of book (including any subtitle), publisher, place of publication, and year.

   - If a publisher lists several cities, choose the first location listed.
   - Note editions, translators, editors, or forewords.

Articles: author's full name, full title of article (including any subtitle), full title of the magazine or newspaper, edition, volume, pages, and date.
Motion pictures: title, director, studio, city, year of release.
Videotape: title, director, production company, city, date of production or original broadcast.
Electronic sources: author's (or editor's) full name, title of website or document, sponsoring organization, date of last update, date you accessed the source, the exact Internet address.

- If you photocopy pages from a book or magazine, write the information directly on the copies for future reference.
- When printing out websites, make sure that the address appears on the printed version. If not, record the information on your printout.

2. **Double-check your notes for accuracy.** If you take notes rather than photocopy a source, make sure that you have properly copied facts, numbers, and names. Always include the page number. Understand the difference between quoting and paraphrasing sources:

Original text:

When Robert Moses began building playgrounds in New York City, there were 119. When he stopped, there were 777. Under his direction, an army of men that at times during the Depression included 84,000 laborers reshaped every park in the city and then filled the parks with zoos and skating rinks, boathouses and tennis houses, bridle paths and golf courses, 288 tennis courts and 673 baseball diamonds.

Robert A. Caro, The Power Broker

Student notecard: full direct quotation

Robert A. Caro, <u>The Power Broker</u>. New York: Vintage, 1975
"When Robert Moses began building playgrounds in New York City, there were 119. When he stopped, there were 777. Under his direction, an army of men that at times during the Depression included 84,000 laborers reshaped every park in the city and then filled the parks with zoos and skating rinks, boathouses and tennis houses, bridle paths and golf courses, 288 tennis courts and 673 baseball diamonds." Pg. 7

Student notecard: partial direct quotation using ellipsis (. . .) to show omitted text

---

Robert A. Caro, <u>The Power Broker</u>. New York: Vintage, 1975
"When Robert Moses began building playgrounds in New York
City, there were 119. When he stopped, there were 777. Under
his direction, an army of men . . . reshaped every park in the
city. . . ." Pg. 7

- In deleting details, make sure that your notes accurately reflect the meaning of the original text. Do not take quotations out of context that alter the author's point of view.

Student notecard: Paraphrase, putting text into your own words

---

Robert A. Caro, <u>The Power Broker</u>. New York: Vintage, 1975
Robert Moses increased the number of New York City playgrounds from 119 to 777. During the Depression as many as
80,000 workers restored every city park, embellishing them
with zoos, playgrounds, and hundreds of tennis courts and
baseball diamonds. Pg. 7

Even though the student is not copying Robert Caro word for word, he or she will have to cite Caro in the research paper to acknowledge the source of the statistics.

3. **Label research materials.**
   - Make sure that you print or photocopy all the material needed. To save paper, some library printers do not automatically print the last page of an article. Make sure your copies are complete.
   - Clip or staple articles to prevent pages from becoming mixed up.
   - Label, number, or letter your sources for easy reference. You may find it useful to write notecards for some or all of your sources so they can be easily arranged on your desk.

4. **Organize database files.**

- Consolidate files you've downloaded from databases and make a back-up disk.
- As a quick and easy reference, consolidate abstracts of the articles to form a single file that provides an overview of the items you've identified as potentially useful.

RESEARCH CHECKLIST

As you conduct your research, consider these questions:

✔ Do you fully understand the needs of the assignment? Do you know what your instructor expects in terms of topic, content, sources, and documentation?

✔ Have you narrowed your topic sufficiently to target a search for sources?

✔ Has your preliminary research given you a global view of the field? Can you detect trends or patterns in the research, prevailing theories, or conflicts?

✔ Have you developed a flexible working thesis to guide your research?

✔ Have you explored database and online sources as well as books and print articles?

✔ Are you keeping the final paper in mind as you conduct research? If you sense your paper expanding beyond its target length, narrow your topic.

✔ Does the material you select accurately and fairly represent the wider spectrum of research material, or are you taking material out of context to support a preconceived thesis?

✔ Are you recording the data needed to document your sources in the final paper?

If you have difficulties locating material, ask your instructor or reference librarian for assistance.

E-WRITING: Exploring Research Sources Online

You can use the Internet to understand more about conducting research.

1. Using a search engine like Alta Vista, Yahoo, or Google enter terms such as "conducting research," "using library sources," "evaluating Internet sources," and "locating library sources."

2. Search the Internet for online library catalogs. Simply by entering names such as "Chicago Public Library" or "Harvard University" may lead you to an online catalog.

3. Analyze your college's online library catalog. Search for a specific book or magazines location. Use the Subject search to locate information on topics you have discussed in some of your courses. What links does your college library offer? What other sources are available for future research assignments?

InfoTrac® College Edition

For additional resources go to InfoTrac College Edition, your online research library, at http://infotrac.cengagelearning.com.

1. Select a topic you have recently discussed in one of your courses and enter it as a search term. Study the subdivisions and locate a range of articles that provide additional information about this topic.

2. Enter the name of your hometown, employer, or college as a search term to locate current articles.

8

A Brief Guide to Documenting Sources

WHAT IS DOCUMENTATION?

Many of the papers you will write in college require documentation—*a systematic method of acknowledging borrowed words and ideas*. Academic disciplines, publications, and professions have specific methods of documenting sources. When assigned a documented paper, make sure you understand the system your instructor expects.

Why Document Sources?

Whatever their discipline or topic, writers document outside sources for three main reasons:

1. *To avoid charges of plagiarism*
   Plagiarism (derived from the Latin word for "kidnapping") refers to stealing or using the words, ideas, or artistic work of others without giving them credit. Some students find it difficult to believe that copying a few paragraphs from *The World Book* or using statistics found on a website can be considered a "crime." But using sources without credit is a theft of intellectual property. Most colleges have strict policies against plagiarism. Instructors routinely fail students who plagiarize papers. Many universities expel students who submit plagiarized assignments. Charges of plagiarism have ruined the careers of famous scholars and diminished the reputation of political figures. Hollywood studios, screenwriters, novelists, rock singers, and rap stars have been sued for stealing ideas, words, or lyrics of other artists. As a writer, you can protect yourself from charges of plagiarism by noting outside sources. *Accurate documentation clearly distinguishes your work from that of others so no one can accuse you of cheating.*
2. *To support a thesis*
   Citing sources not only protects you from charges of cheating but also makes your writing more effective. To convince readers to accept your

thesis, it is important to provide them with evidence. In court, lawyers prove cases by presenting eyewitnesses, expert testimony, and exhibits. As a writer, you can persuade readers to accept your point of view if you provide proof. *The more controversial your thesis, the more readers will demand supporting evidence from credible sources.*

3. *To help readers learn more*
    Your citations not only protect you from plagiarism and strengthen your argument but also show readers where they can obtain additional information, by listing relevant periodicals, books, and websites.

When to Document?

Students are often confused about what they have to document.

What Not to Document

First, you do not have to document all the sources you use. Even if you look up something in an encyclopedia or a website, you do not have to note its use if the information belongs to what researchers call "the realm of common knowledge":

1. *Common expressions or famous quotations*
    You don't need to list the Bible or your edition of Shakespeare if you simply check the wording of a quotation by Jesus or Hamlet. If you refer to statements readers are familiar with, such as Martin Luther King, Jr.'s "I have a dream" or John F. Kennedy's "Ask not what your country can do for you—ask what you can do for your country," you don't have to note their original source. *Less familiar statements, especially controversial ones, must be documented.*

2. *Common facts not subject to change and available in numerous sources*
    You don't have to list the *Encyclopedia Britannica* as a source if you use it to look up where George Washington was born, when *Death of a Salesman* opened on Broadway, when Malcolm X died, or the height of Mount Everest. General facts such as these are not subject to change and are readily available in hundreds of books, almanacs, biographies, textbooks, and Web sites. No one will accuse you of stealing information that is considered standard and widely known by millions of people. *Facts subject to change or dispute, such as the population of Denver, the number of people on death row, or income tax regulations, must be documented.*

What to Document

In almost every other case, you must acknowledge the use of sources:

1. *Direct quotations*
   Whenever you copy word-for-word the spoken or written words of others, you must use quotation marks or block paragraphs to distinguish it from your own text, and you must indicate its source.

2. *Indirect quotations or paraphrases*
   Even if you don't copy information but restate the author's ideas in your own words, you must acknowledge the source. Changing a few words in a quotation or summarizing several pages in a paragraph does not alter the fact that you are making use of ideas and information from another source. Although you don't use quotation marks, you need to indicate that you have borrowed from an outside source.

3. *Specific facts, statistics, and numbers*
   Facts will only be acceptable to readers if they know where they came from. If you state, "Last year eighteen innocent men were sentenced to death for crimes they did not commit," readers will demand the source of this number.

4. *Graphs, charts, photographs, and other visual aids*
   Indicate the source of any visual aid you reproduce in your paper. If you create your own graphics based on statistics, you must indicate where the numbers originated.

Using Quotations

Direct quotations should be used sparingly. Remember, the goal of your paper is to express your own thoughts and opinions, not present a collection of other people's ideas. There are times, however, when direct quotations can be powerful additions to your essay.

Use direct quotations:

1. When presenting a significant statement by an authority or eyewitness.
2. When the statement is unique or memorable.
3. When the idea expresses conflicts with the mainstream of thought or common knowledge.
4. When the original statement is well-written and more compelling than a paraphrase or summary.
5. When readers may doubt a controversial point of view or question that a certain person made the statement.

Direct quotations have to be integrated into the text of an essay in a clear, sensible manner and be documented. (These examples use MLA format; for APA use of quotations, see Using APA Documentation).

1. Indicate short direct quotations (1–4 lines) by placing them in quotation marks followed by a parenthetical citation:

    According to Lester Armstrong, "The university failed to antici-pate the impact of state budget cuts" (17).

    Indicate long direct quotations (over 4 lines) by placing them in indented paragraphs without quotation marks. Indent ten spaces on the left side and introduce with a colon:

    According to Lester Armstrong, higher education suffered greatly during the recession:

    > The university failed to anticipate the impact of state budget cuts. As a result, construction on the new stadium was halted. Twenty-five administrators were laid off. Plans to expand the computer labs, bilingual programs, and adult night school were scrapped. The library budget was slashed by 24%, and two daycare centers were closed. The century-old Main Hall, which was scheduled for an extensive refurbishing, was given only cosmetic repairs and painting. (17)

2. Link direct quotations with your text. Avoid isolated quotations:

    Incorrect

    Children are greatly affected by violence on television. "By the time a child graduates from high school, he or she has witnessed over 18,000 homicides on television" (Smith 10). Young people come to view violence, even murder, as reasonable methods of re-solving conflicts.

    Blend direct quotations into your text by introducing them:

    Revised

    Children are greatly affected by violence on television. "By the time a child graduates from high school," Jane Smith notes, "he or she has witnessed over 18,000 homicides on television" (10). Young people come to view violence, even murder, as a reasonable method of resolving conflict.

3. You may edit quotations to eliminate redundant or irrelevant material. Indicate deleted words by inserting *ellipsis* (three spaced periods) in square brackets:

Original Text

George Washington, who was heading to New York to confer with his leading advisors, agreed to meet with Franklin in Philadelphia on June 10th.

Edited Quote

As Sanger notes, "George Washington [. . .] agreed to meet with Franklin in Philadelphia on June 10th" (12).

Deletions should only remove unneeded information; they should not alter the meaning of the text by removing qualifications or changing a negative statement into a positive one. It is unethical to alter a quotation, "We should, only if everything else fails, legalize drugs" to read, "We should [. . .] legalize drugs."

4. Insert words or other information to prevent confusion or avoid grammatical errors. For instance, if a direct quote refers to a Frank Bush by his last name and you are concerned readers will confuse him with President Bush, you may insert his first name, even though it does not appear in the original text.

Original Text

Hoping to ease tensions in the Middle East, Bush called for UN peacekeepers to patrol the West Bank.

Quotation

"Hoping to ease tensions in the Middle East, [Frank] Bush," according to *Newsweek*, "called for UN peacekeepers to patrol the West Bank" (14).

If you delete words or phrases, you may have to insert words to prevent a grammar error:

Original Text

Poe and other writers of his generation were influential in shaping a new, truly American literature.

Quotation

According to Sydney Falco, "Poe [. . .] [was] influential in shaping a new, truly American literature" (64).

Using Paraphrases

Paraphrases are indirect quotes. You must document your use of sources, even when you do not copy the text word-for-word. If you read two or three pages of a history book and summarize its points in a single paragraph, document your use of that source. Although you did not directly reproduce any words or sentences, the ideas you present are not your own and should be documented:

Original Text

More than 10,000 of New York's 29,000 manufacturing firms had closed their doors. Nearly one of every three employables in the city had lost his job. An estimated 1,600,000 New Yorkers were receiving some form of public relief. Many of those fortunates who had kept their jobs were "underemployed," a euphemism for the fact that they worked two or three days a week or two weeks a month—or, if they worked full time, were paid a fraction of their former salaries; stenographers, earning $35 to $40 per week in 1928, were averaging $16 in 1933; Woolworth's was paying full-time salesladies $6 per week.

Robert Caro, *The Power Broker* 323–24

Paraphrase

The Depression devastated New York City. A third of the manufacturers shut down operations, and over a million and half New Yorkers were on relief. Those with jobs saw their hours cut and their salaries slashed (Caro 323–24). Conditions in Chicago, Los Angeles, and San Francisco were similar.

Parenthetical references should be placed immediately after the paraphrased material at an appropriate pause or at the end of the sentence.

Using MLA Documentation

The MLA style, developed by the Modern Language Association, is the preferred documentation method used in language and literature courses. In the MLA system, outside sources are listed alphabetically at the end of the paper in a Works Cited list and parenthetical citations are placed after direct quotations and paraphrases. For complete details refer to *The MLA Handbook for Writers of Research Papers*, 6th edition, by Joseph Gibaldi.

Building a Works Cited List

List all sources you refer to under the title *Works Cited* at the end of your paper. Items should be alphabetized by authors' last names or the first significant word of titles if no author is listed.

Sample formats

Book by a single author:
Smith, John. *The City.* New York: Putnam. 2002.

Book by two authors:
Smith, John, and Naomi Wilson. *The New Suburb.* New York: Western. 2001.
    (Only the first author is listed last name, first name.)

Book with more than three authors:
Smith, John, et al. *Urban Housing.* Chicago: Chicago UP, 2000.
    (University Press is abbreviated as UP)

Work in an anthology:
Miller, Arthur. "Death of a Salesman." *American Literature* 1945–2000. Ed. Keisha Sahn
    and Wilson Goodwin. New York: Dial. 2001. 876–952.

Encyclopedia article:
"Miller, Arthur." *The World Book.* 1998 ed.
    (Volume and page numbers are not needed in familiar references)

Periodical article with a single author:
Smith, John. "Urban Planning Today." *American Architect* 25 Oct. 1999: 24–29.

Newspaper article without an author:
"Mideast Crisis Boils Over." *Washington Post* 22 May 2002: A5+.
    (If an article starts on one page, then skips to others, list the first page with a plus sign)

Television program:
"Oil Boom." Narr. Morley Safer. *Sixty Minutes.* CBS. WCBS, New York. 27 Jan. 2002.
    (Include both network and local station with date of broadcast)

Online article:
Wilkins, Robert. "Reflections on Milton." *Michigan Literary Review* 9.2 (1998).
    22 Feb. 2002 <http://www.umichigan.edu/english/litreview.html>.
    (Include both date of access and full electronic address)

Non periodical article on CD-ROM
"Albania." *The Oxford Encyclopedia of Education.* 3rd ed. CD-ROM.
   Oxford: Oxford UP, 2001.
E-mail
Hennessey, Richard. "Re: Urban Planning Conference." E-mail to Sean Brugha. 22 June 2001.
   (Provide name of writer, title of message in quotation marks, recipient, and date)

Intext Citations

As you include direct quotations and paraphrases in your paper, cite their use with parenthetical notations. These citations should be brief but accurate. If you mention an author or source in your text, you only need to add a page number:

> Winston Hachner has noted, "The Internet has provided us with a dilemma of choice" (874).
>
> *(Note: Place the period after the parenthetical citation)*

If you do not mention the source, include the author's last name or title with page numbers:

> The Internet has given us more choices than we can process (Hachner 874). The sheer volume of information can overwhelm, confuse, and strangle businesses accustomed to defined channels of communication ("Internet" 34–35).

Sources without page references do not require parenthetical notes if cited in the text:

> During a <u>Sixty Minutes</u> interview in 2002, Randall Pemberton argued, "A terrorist attack in cyberspace can cripple our economy."

You can avoid long, cumbersome parenthetical notes by citing titles or several authors in the text:

> As stated in the <u>Modern Directory of Modern Drama,</u> "August Wilson has emerged as one of the nation's most powerful dramatic voices" (13). Jacobson and Marley view him as a dominant force in shaping the country's perceptions of the African-American experience (145–146).

Using APA Documentation

The APA style, developed by the American Psychological Association, is the preferred documentation method used in social sciences, including psychology, sociology, political science, and history. In the APA style, outside sources are listed alphabetically at the end of the paper in a References list and parenthetical citations are placed after direct quotations and paraphrases. For complete details refer to the *Publication Manual of the American Psychological Association*, 5th edition.

Building a References List

List all sources you refer to under the title *References* at the end of your paper. Items should be alphabetized by authors' last names or the first significant word of titles if no author is listed.

Sample formats

Book by a Single Author:
Smith, J. (2002). *The city.* New York: Putnam Press.
   (Only authors' last names and initials listed; only first word and proper nouns in title are capitalized)

Book by Two Authors:
Smith, J., & Wilson, N. (2001). *The new suburb.* New York: Western Publishing.
   (Both authors listed by last name, initial.)

Book with More Than Six Authors:
Smith, J., Wilson, S., Franco, W., Kolman, R., Westin, K., Dempsey, F., Parkinson, J., et al. (2000). *Urban housing.* Chicago: Chicago University Press.

Chapter in an Edited Book:
Miller, A. (2001). Depression in the adolescent male. In J. P. Meyers, J. Reed, & R. Rank (Eds.), *The psychology of youth: Problems and solutions* (pp. 87–99). New York: The Dial Press.
   (Quotation marks not used in titles of articles and chapters)

Encyclopedia Article:
Depression. (1998). In *The world book* (Vol. 13, pp. 324–325). Chicago: World Book.

Periodical Article with a Single Author:
Smith, J. (1999, October 25). Urban planning today. *American Architect, 63,* 24–29.

Newspaper Article without an Author:
Mideast crisis boils over. (2002, May 22). *The Washington Post,* pp. A5, A8, A14, A26–A27.
   (If an article starts on one page, then skips to others, list all pages)

Television Program:
Paulus, G. (Executive Producer). (2002, January 27). *The mind* [Television broadcast]. New York: WNET.

Online article:
Wilkins, R. (1998, March). Reflections on depression. *Michigan Science Review, 9,* 116–123.
    Retrieved October 23, 2001, from http://www.umichigan.edu/science/scireview.html
    (Include both date of access and full electronic address)

Corporate or organizational Web site without dates:
New York City Health Department. (n.d.). *Bioterrorism.* Retrieved May 12, 2002, from
    http://www.nychd.org/bioterrorism.html
    (Cite specific pages where possible rather than home pages)

Article on CD-ROM
Albania. (2001). *Oxford Encyclopedia of Education* (3rd. ed.) [CD-ROM].
    Oxford: Oxford University Press.

E-mail
E-mail and personal communication are not included in References but are listed within the text by
referring to the writer and date.
    (R. Hennessey, personal communication, June 22, 2001)

Intext Citations

When you include quotations and paraphrases in your paper, cite their use
with parenthetical notations listing author and year. These citations should
be brief but accurate:

> Hachner (2002) has noted, "The Internet has provided us with a
> dilemma of choice" (p. 12).
>   *(Note: Place the period after the parenthetical citation)*
> Wellman (2000) compares two common therapies for treating de-
> pression.
>   *(Note: No page references cited for paraphrases)*

For sources without authors, include the first few words of the titles in the
text or a parenthetical citation:

> The *Psychology Year in Review* (2002) presents new theories on ad-
> diction. A recent article reveals a genetic predisposition to narcotic de-
> pendence ("Genetic Maps," 2002).
>   *(Include only years even if day and month are available)*

If a work has three, four, or five authors, cite all authors by only last names
in the first reference:

> Bodkin, Lewis, Germaine, and Neimoller (2001) dispute commonly
> held views of addiction.

In subsequent references, cite only the first author:

> Bodkin et al. (2001) found no single factor in determining predisposition to alcoholism.

For works with six or more authors, cite only the first author in first and subsequent references:

> Bryant et al. (2001) analyzed census figures to determine demographic changes.

STRATEGIES FOR AVOIDING COMMON PROBLEMS

1. *Use outside sources sparingly.* A good essay is not a collection of quotations and paraphrases. The focus of your paper should be your thesis, supporting ideas, and commentary. Avoid using long direct quotations that can be summarized in short paraphrases. *The fact that you find many interesting sources in the library or on the Internet does not mean that you should include everything you find in your paper. Be selective.*

2. *Take careful notes and collect documentation information when you locate valuable sources.*
   Make sure you copy direct quotations carefully word for word and do not distort their meaning by taking ideas out of context. Place direct quotations in quotation marks. If you photocopy a book or periodical, make sure you record the author's name and all publication information needed to document the sources. If you print an article from the Internet, make sure you record the full website address and the date.

3. *Select sources carefully.* Avoid sources that appear biased, outdated, or poorly presented. Remember that all books, periodicals, and Web sites were created by human beings who may be misinformed or prejudiced. Avoid basing your entire paper on a single source. Do not assume that all sources are of equal value. Use critical thinking skills to measure the significance of the sources you locate.

Continued

4. *Comment on the quality and quantity of sources.* Let readers know the results of your research. If sources are limited, outdated, or fragmentary, explain this situation to readers. If you find conflicting evidence or theories, objectively summarize the differences and justify your decisions in selecting sources. Don't assume direct quotations can speak for themselves. Don't insert sources into your essay without commenting on their value and demonstrating how they support your thesis.

5. *Clearly distinguish your ideas from those of others.* Accurate documentation, transitional statements, and paragraph breaks can help readers understand which ideas are solely yours and which ideas originate from outside sources.

6. *Blend quotations and paraphrases into your text to avoid awkward shifts.* There should be smooth transitions between your ideas and those of others.

7. *Be sure to use the documentation system your instructor expects.*

9

Writing the Research Paper

*A good research paper is actually the result or
culmination of many rough drafts.*
Jeanette A. Woodward

WHAT IS A RESEARCH PAPER?

The research paper is the standard method of demonstrating your skills in
many college courses. Collecting data, assembling quotations, finding
evidence, and developing a thesis are essential to laying the groundwork for
your paper. But before you plunge into working with sources and making
citations, it is important to take three preliminary steps:

1. **Review the needs of the assignment.** If you have not examined the
    instructor's requirements recently, refresh your memory. Study any hand-
    outs or notes you may have made.

    - Do you fully understand what is expected in terms of topic, content,
      sources, and format? If you are unsure, talk with your instructor.
    - Do your working thesis, sources, and notes fit the scope of the assign-
      ment? Should some sources be discarded? Should other avenues of re-
      search be pursued?

2. **Take a global look at your sources and notes.** Review the full scope of
    what your research has revealed. Consider the whole body of evidence you
    have discovered, including those items you examined but did not select.

    - What have you learned about the subject? Have you uncovered infor-
      mation that leads you to further narrow your topic or refine the thesis?
    - Do sources contradict or disprove your assumptions? Should you re-
      think your point of view?
    - What do the sources reveal about the state of knowledge about your
      topic? Is there consensus or conflict? Are there patterns in the evi-
      dence?
    - How reliable are the sources? Are they based on a careful reading of
      the subject, thorough research, and controlled experiments, or are
      they biased and /or do they rely on anecdotal data?

- Are there sources that can be grouped together, such as articles by experts who share the same opinion or similar statistics? Can some sources be considered duplicates?
- Can you prioritize sources? Which are the most important?
- How can critical thinking help you analyze the value of what you have located?

3. **Reshape your paper by reviewing your topic, examining the evidence, and refining the working thesis.**

REFINE YOUR THESIS AND DEVELOP AN OUTLINE

After examining your sources, refine the thesis. You may have limited the original topic and need to develop a thesis that addresses the new focus of your paper. In writing shorter papers, you may have needed only a brief plan or list of ideas to guide the first draft. But in writing a research paper, it is useful to develop a full outline to organize your ideas and sources.

Working Thesis

Orwell considered contact with nature essential to individual liberty.

Revised Thesis

Winston Smith's humanity and individual autonomy are stunted not only by the brutality of Oceania and the ever-present Thought Police, but by his lack of contact with nature.

Working Outline

A working outline is a rough guide to direct your first draft. Because it is not likely to be read by anyone other than yourself, it does not have to follow any particular format. Use it as a blueprint to organize your main points and sources.

I Intro—Conventional readings of *1984*

    A Simes quote

    B Wolzheck quote

    C Janeson quote

    D Goodman quote

II Transition/Thesis—Important Role of Nature Overlooked

III Unnatural/Artificial Life in Oceania

    A "Golden Country Dream" quote (<u>1984</u> p. 29)

    B Smith and Julia in nature

    C Nature and sexual passion—(<u>1984</u> quote p. 105)

IV Nature as Orwell's Moral Gold Standard

    A Sandison quote

    B Letter to Henry Miller quote (<u>Collected Essays</u> 4:80)

 V Orwell's Lack of Faith in Technology

    A Electricity quote (<u>Road</u> p. 84)

    B Bugs quote (<u>Road</u> p. 71)

VI Orwell's Doubts about Progress

    A Pleasure Spots quote (<u>Collected Essays</u> 4:80)

    B Radio quote (<u>Collected Essays</u> 4:80)

VII Conclusion

    A Sandison quote (p. 10)

    B Final Point—1984 relevant for 21st century

Along with an outline, develop a time line to chart your progress. Make sure you budget enough time for each stage of the writing process, including revising and editing.

STRATEGIES FOR DEVELOPING AN OUTLINE

1. **Write a clear thesis statement.** The thesis is the mission statement of your paper. It should provide a clear focus for the paper and direct your first draft.

    - Use the thesis statement as a guide for selecting outside sources.

2. **Write an outline in light of your thesis and the needs of the assignment.** Make sure that your outline addresses the goals of the paper and the instructor's requirements.

Continued

3. **Don't expect that your sources will neatly fall into place like pieces of a puzzle.** In many instances, the evidence you find may be fragmentary and lead in different directions. Outline your ideas and observations, weaving into the text those sources that confirm your point of view.

4. **Use sources to support your views; don't simply summarize them.** An outline forms a skeleton or framework for the first draft. Indicate where you will place source material such as quotations, facts, or statistics.

   - Do not feel obligated to include all the sources you have located.

5. **When writing an outline, leave ample space for alterations.**

6. **Label your sources for easy reference.** You may wish to develop a shorthand reference for each source, labeling sources A, B, C or giving them descriptive names to guide your outline.

7. **Separate longer sources for use in multiple places.** If you have located a long quotation, do not feel obligated to place it in a single block of text. Instead, you may select two or three sections and distribute them throughout the paper.

   - When separating longer passages, make sure you do not distort the source's meaning by taking ideas out of context.

8. **Design an introduction that announces the topic, sets up the thesis, and prepares readers for the direction of the paper.** Because research papers can be long and complex, it is important to give readers a road map, an explanation of what will follow.

   - An introduction can present the thesis, provide a rationale for the methods of research, or comment on the nature of sources. Your introduction might explain that you will compare two writers, use public opinion polls to track attitudes on race, or limit the discussion of Nixon's presidency to his domestic policies.

   - Introductions can be used to address research problems, commenting on the lack of reliable data or conflicting opinions. Introductions can also include a justification of your approach that anticipates reader objections.
   - As with writing any paper, you will probably come up with new ideas while writing the draft. After revising the body, you may wish to rewrite the opening and closing.

Continued

9. **Organize the body by using the modes of organization.** Clear structure plays an important role in making your paper readable and convincing. Without a clear pattern of organization, your paper may become a confusing list of quotations and statistics.

    - Use modes, such as *comparison* and *division*, to organize evidence.
    - Use transitional statements and paragraph breaks to signal changes in direction.

10. **Craft a conclusion that ends the paper on a strong point rather than a simple summary of points.** Although it may be useful to review critical points at the end of a long paper, the conclusion should leave the reader with a memorable fact, quotation, or restatement of the thesis.

WRITING THE RESEARCH PAPER

Your goal in writing the first draft, as with any paper, is to get your ideas on paper. Using outside sources, however, complicates the writing process. Students often make common errors in approaching the evidence they have collected.

STRATEGIES FOR USING SOURCES

1. **Avoid simply reporting on what you found.** The quotations, facts, and statistics you have selected should support your point of view. Avoid what some writers call the "string of pearls" effect of simply patching together outside sources with little original commentary or analysis:

    When it first opened on Broadway, *Death of a Salesman* had a great impact on audiences (Stein, 19). According to Sally Lyman, "The play captured the hidden anxiety coursing through postwar America" (17). Another critic, Timothy Baldwin, stated, "This play made the audience face its greatest fear—growing old" (98). Fred Carlson said that he walked out of the theater shaken and deeply moved (23).

    - Although outside sources may be interesting and worth quoting or paraphrasing, *your* ideas, interpretations, and arguments should form the basis of the paper.

Continued

2. **Explain any lack of sources.** If you select a new, unknown, or uncommon subject, there may be few sources directly supporting your thesis. Although readers might be impressed by your argument, they may question why you have not supported your ideas with evidence. An instructor may question if you thoroughly researched your topic. Commenting on the lack of sources can both demonstrate the uniqueness of your approach and justify the lack of outside sources:

   Critics of *Death of a Salesman* have concentrated on the male characters, examining Willy Loman's dreams, his relationship to Biff, his sons' conflicts. Of 125 articles published in the last four years about this play, none focus on the essential role of Linda Loman, who serves as the axis for the male conflicts in the play.

3. **Summarize conflicting opinions.** One of the responsibilities of a researcher is to fairly represent the available body of evidence. If respected authorities disagree, you should explain the nature of the controversy:

   Scientists debate whether this disorder is hereditary. Yale researchers Brown and Smith cite the British twin study as evidence of a genetic link (35–41). However, both the American Medical Association and the National Institutes of Health insist the small numbers of subjects in the twin study do not provide sufficient evidence to support any conclusions (Kendrick 19–24).

4. **Indicate if sources represent widely held views.** Often you will find that sources present similar views or interpretations. If you find four or five sources that present the same information, you may wish to select the source that is the most thorough, most recent, or best written. You can emphasize the significance of this source by mentioning that its ideas are shared by others:

   Nearly all experts on teenage suicide support Jane Diaz's observation that low self-esteem, stress, and substance abuse are the principal contributing factors to the current rise in adolescent suicide (Smith 28; Johnson 10–15; King 89–92).

5. **Comment on the quality as well as quantity of your sources.** Not all sources have equivalent value. Sources may be inaccurate, biased, or based on limited evidence. If you conduct research on controversial issues or events, you may find little reliable material. If you are unable to

Continued

determine which source is closest to the truth or which study is accurate, inform your readers of the dilemma you face:

> Although the 1908 railroad strike received national attention, few major newspapers offered more than superficial reports. Sensational accounts of lynching, rape, and murder appeared in New York and Chicago tabloids. The radical *Torch of Labor* blamed the deaths of two strikers on a plot engineered by Wall Street bankers. The conservative *Daily World* insisted union organizers were bent on overthrowing the government. Most sources, however, do agree that Red Williams played a critical role in organizing a labor protest that ultimately weakened the emerging Transport Workers Union.

GUIDELINES FOR USING DIRECT QUOTATIONS

Direct quotations give power and authority to your research paper by introducing the words of others just as they were written or stated. But to be effective, direct quotations have to be carefully chosen, accurately presented, and skillfully woven into the text of your paper.

1. **Limit use of direct quotations.** Avoid reproducing long blocks of text, unless direct evidence is essential for accuracy or emphasis. In many instances, you can summarize and paraphrase information.

   - Use direct quotes when they are brief, memorable, and so well stated that a paraphrase would reduce their impact. Avoid using direct quotes when you can accurately restate the information in a documented paraphrase.
   - **Remember, the focus of a research paper is *your* ideas, observations, and conclusions, not a collection of direct quotations.**

2. **Link direct quotations into your commentary.** Avoid isolating quotations:

   Faulty:

   Television advertising exploded in the Fifties. "Advertising agencies increased spending on television commercials from $10 million in 1948 to $2 billion in 1952" (Smith 16). These revenues financed the rapid development of a new industry.

   Revised:

   Television advertising exploded in the Fifties. According to Kai Smith, "Advertising agencies increased spending on television commercials from $10 million in 1948 to $2 billion in 1952" (16). These revenues financed the rapid development of a new industry.

Or

Television advertising exploded in the Fifties, with advertising agencies increasing spending "from $10 million in 1948 to $2 billion in 1952" (Smith 16). These revenues financed the rapid development of a new industry.

3. **Introduce block quotes with a complete sentence followed by colon:** The Quiz Show Scandal of the 1950s shook public confidence in the new medium. The idea that the highly-popular shows were rigged to ensure ratings infuriated and disillusioned the public:

    > NBC received thousands of letters and telephone calls from irate viewers who felt cheated. Although the public readily accepted that Westerns and soap operas were fictional, they believed that the teachers and housewives who appeared on shows like "Twenty-One" were "real people" like themselves. Having followed their favorite contestants week after week, loyal viewers strongly identified with people they considered genuine. Learning that all the furrowed brows and lipbiting were choreographed, they felt duped. (Brown 23)

4. **Provide background information to establish the value of direct quotations.** Bibliographical entries at the end of your paper may explain a source but do not help readers understand its significance:

    Faulty:
    President Roosevelt showed signs of declining health as early as 1942. Sheridan noted, "His hands trembled when writing, he complained of headaches, and he often seemed unable to follow the flow of conversation around him" (34–35).

    Revised:
    President Roosevelt showed signs of declining health as early as 1942. George Sheridan, a young naval aide who briefed the White House during the Battle of Midway, was shocked by the President's condition. Sheridan noted, "His hands trembled when writing, he complained of headaches, and he often seemed unable to follow the flow of conversation around him" (34–35).

5. **Indicate quotations within quotations.** Although most writers try to avoid using direct quotations that appear in another source, sometimes it cannot be avoided. You can easily indicate a quote within a quote with (qtd. in):

Original Source
From Sandra Bert's *The Plague* (page 23)
The medical community of San Francisco was overwhelmed by the sudden increase in AIDS cases in the early 1980s. Tim Watson, a resident at the time, said, "It was like being hit by a tidal wave. We went home every night absolutely stunned by the influx of dying young men."

Research Paper quoting Tim Watson:
Within a few years the number of AIDS cases, especially in the Bay Area, exploded. Physicians were shocked by the influx of patients with untreatable infections. "It was like being hit by a tidal wave," Watson remembered (qtd. in Bert, 23).

6. **Accurately delete unneeded material from quotations.** You can abbreviate long quotations, deleting irrelevant or unimportant details by using ellipsis points (. . .). Three evenly spaced periods indicate words have been deleted from a direct quotation:

Original:
The governor vetoed the education bill, which had been backed by a coalition of taxpayers and unions, because it cut aid to inner city schools.

James Kirkland

Shortened quotation using ellipsis points:
Kirkland reported that "the governor vetoed the education bill . . . because it cut aid to inner city schools."

- Use a period and three ellipsis points (four dots. . . .) to indicate deletion of one or more full sentences.
- Avoid making deletions that distort the original meaning. Do not eliminate qualifying statements:

Original:
Given the gang wars, the failure of treatment programs, the rising number of addicts, I regretfully think we should legalize drugs until we can find better solutions to the problem.

—Mayor Wells

Improper use of ellipsis points:
At a recent press conference, Mayor Wells stated, "I . . . think we should legalize drugs . . ."

7. **Use brackets to insert words or indicate alterations.** In some instances, you may have to insert a word to prevent confusion or a grammatical error.

Original:

George Roosevelt [no relation to the President] left the Democratic Party in 1935, troubled by the deepening Depression. Roosevelt considered the New Deal a total failure.

—Nancy Stewart

Brackets enclose inserted word to prevent confusion:

As the Depression deepened, many deserted the Democratic Party, seeking more radical solutions to the worsening economy. According to Stewart, "[George] Roosevelt considered the New Deal a total failure."

Original:

Poe, Whitman, and Ginsburg are among some of America's greatest poets.

—John Demmer

Brackets enclose altered verb:

Demmer states that "Poe . . . [is] among some of America's greatest poets."

STRATEGIES FOR CITING SOURCES

Many students find citing sources one of the challenging aspects of writing a research paper. Mastering the details of accounting for each source can be frustrating. It is important to understand that documenting where you obtained information for your paper serves three key purposes:

1. **Citations prevent allegations of plagiarism.** Plagiarism occurs when you present the facts, words, or ideas of someone else as your own. Students often find it difficult to believe that copying something out of *The World Book* for a term paper can be considered a crime, but plagiarism has serious consequences. In many colleges students who submit a plagiarized paper will automatically fail the course. In some schools, students will be expelled. Outside of academics, plagiarism (often called "copyright infringement") has ruined the careers of politicians, artists, and executives. Prominent columnists and writers have been fired from newspapers and magazines for using the ideas of others without acknowledging their original source. Hollywood studios have been sued by artists who claim ideas from their rejected screenplays were used in other films.

   • Accurate documentation protects you from plagiarism by clearly labeling borrowed ideas.

Continued

2.   **Citations support your thesis.** Attorneys arguing a case before a judge or jury present labeled exhibits to prove their theory of a case. As a researcher, you support your thesis by introducing expert testimony, facts, case histories, and eyewitness accounts. Like an attorney, you have to clearly identify the source for evidence for it to be credible. A paper about crime that draws upon statistics from the FBI and studies from the Justice Department will be more credible than one relying only on personal observations and opinions.

   •   The more controversial your thesis, the more readers will demand supporting evidence.

3.   **Citations refer readers to other sources.** Citations not only illustrate which ideas originated with the writer and which were drawn from other sources, but they also alert readers to where they can find more information. Through your citations, readers may learn of a biography or a Web site offering additional evidence.

Exceptions to Citing Sources

You do not need to use citations for every fact, quotation, or idea you present in your paper:

1.   **Common expressions or famous quotations.** Famous sayings by people such as Shakespeare, Jesus, or Benjamin Franklin (for example, "To err is human" or "I am the resurrection") do not have to be cited, even when presented as direct quotes. If you are unsure, ask your instructor.

2.   **Facts considered in the "realm of common knowledge."** You do not have to provide a citation if you referred to a source to check a fact that is readily available in numerous sources. You do not have to cite *The Encyclopedia Britannica* if you used it to find out where Arthur Miller was born or when North Dakota became a state. No one will accuse you of stealing facts that are commonly known and not subject to change or interpretation.

In almost every other instance, however, you have to acknowledge the use of outside material:

1.   **Direct quotations.** Whenever you quote a source word for word, you must place it in quotation marks and cite its source.

2. **Indirect quotations or paraphrases.** Even if you do not copy a source, but state the author's ideas in your own words, you must cite the source. Changing a few words or condensing a page of text into a few sentences does not alter the fact that you are using someone else's ideas.

3. **Specific facts, statistics, and numbers.** Data will be credible and acceptable only if you present the source. If you state, "Last year 54,450 drunk drivers were arrested in California," readers will naturally wonder where you obtained that number. Statistics make credible evidence only if readers trust their source.

4. **Graphs, charts, and other visual aids.** Indicate the source of any graphic you reproduce.

   - You must also cite the source for information you use to create a visual display.

STRATEGIES FOR REVISING AND EDITING RESEARCH PAPERS

1. **Review the assignment, thesis, and working outline.**

2. **Examine your draft for use of sources.**

   - Does the draft fulfill the needs of the assignment?
   - Does the text support the thesis?
   - Is the thesis properly placed? Should it appear in the opening or the conclusion?
   - Are enough sources presented?
   - Is there any evidence that should be included or deleted?
   - Do you provide enough original commentary, or is your paper merely a collection of facts and quotes?

3. **Read the draft aloud.**

   - Does the paper have an even style and tone? Are there awkward transitions between sources and your commentary?

4. **Revise the introduction and conclusion.**

5. **Edit for mechanical and spelling errors. Make sure your paper follows the appropriate style for documenting sources.**

DOCUMENTATION STYLES

Writers document their use of outside sources with one of several methods. The MLA and APA formats are commonly used in the humanities and social sciences. Both methods provide guidelines for placing parenthetical notes after quoting or paraphrasing outside sources and listing them at the end of the paper. Traditional textbooks suggest recording each source on a note card so they can be easily shuffled and placed in alphabetical order. If you are writing on a computer, you may find it easier to scroll down and enter each source as you refer to it.

THE MLA STYLE

The MLA style, created by the Modern Language Association, is used in language and literature courses. Parenthetical notes listing the author or title and page numbers are inserted after quotations and paraphrases. At the end of the paper all the sources are alphabetized on a "Works Cited" page. For full details about using the MLA style, consult Joseph Gibaldi's *MLA Style Manual and Guide to Scholarly Publishing*, second edition, or *MLA Handbook for Writers of Research Papers*, sixth edition.

STRATEGIES FOR WRITING PARENTHETICAL NOTES

Parenthetical notes usually include an author's last name and a page number. If no author is listed, titles—sometimes abbreviated—are used. To keep the notes as brief as possible, the MLA format does not precede page numbers with *p.*, *pp.*, or commas. The parenthetical note is considered part of the sentence and comes before the final mark of punctuation. Notes should be placed as close to the source as possible without interrupting the flow of the text.

1. **Parenthetical notes include author and page number.** A direct quotation from Ralph Ellison's novel *Invisible Man* is indicated with a parenthetical note placed after it:

    The novel's unnamed character calls himself invisible because society does not recognize him as a human being. He defends his

    Continued

retreat from society, realizing that many would view his decision as a sign of irresponsibility. "Responsibility," he argues, "rests on recognition, and recognition is a form of agreement" (Ellison 14).

2. **Parenthetical notes include only page numbers if the author is clearly identified in the text:**

Sheila Smitherin praised Ellison's novel, stating that modern black literature "was born on the pages of *Invisible Man*" (32).

3. **If two or more sources are cited within a sentence, notes are inserted after the material that is quoted or paraphrased:**

Smith stated that the novel "exposed the deep-rooted racism society was unwilling to confront" (34), leading one columnist to argue that the book should be taught in every high school (Wilson 12–13).

4. **Long quotations are indented ten spaces without quotation marks:**

The Group Theater revolutionized American drama. According to Frank Kozol, the members tried to create something then unseen on the New York stage:

> Clurman and his followers wanted to create a new kind of theater. They not only wanted to produce new, socially relevant plays, but create a new relationship between playwright and cast. It would be a collective effort. Designed to be a theater without stars, actors lived together and shared living expenses. They were infused with the revolutionary spirit of the times. The Group Theater soon launched the career of Clifford Odets, whose plays were among the most poignant depictions of life during the Great Depression. (Taylor 34–35)

Notice that the parenthetical note appears outside the final punctuation of the last sentence.

STRATEGIES FOR WRITING A WORKS CITED PAGE

List all sources you have cited on a separate sheet at the end of your paper, titled "Works Cited." If you include works you have read for background but not actually cited, title the page "Works Consulted."

- Arrange the list of works alphabetically by the author's last name or first significant word of the title if no author is listed:

  Jones, Wilson. Chicago Today. New York: Putnam, 2002.
  "A New Look for Toronto." Toronto Magazine Fall 2003: 21.

- For sources with more than one author, alphabetize by the first author's last name:

  Zinter, Mary, and Jan Ames. First Aid. New York: Dial, 2002.

- Begin each citation even with the left margin, and indent subsequent lines five spaces. Double-space the entire page. Do not separate entries with additional spaces:

  Abrams, Jane. "Rebuilding America's Cities." Plain Dealer [Cleveland] 21 Jan. 2002: A11.
  Brown, Gerald. The Death of the Central City: The Malling of America. New York: Macmillan, 2003.

- If more than one source is used for an author, alphabetize the works but list the author's last name only once, substituting three hyphens for the name in subsequent citations:

  Keller, Joseph. Assessing Blame. New York: Columbia UP, 2003.
  ---. Quality Control. New York: Miller, 2000.

GUIDELINES FOR LISTING SOURCES IN WORKS CITED AND PARENTHETICAL NOTES

Books

1. Write the author's last name, first name, then any initial. Copy the name as written on the title page. "C. W. Brown" would appear as:

    Brown, C. W.

    Omit any degrees or titles such as Ph.D. or Dr.

2. State the full title of the book. Place a colon between the main heading and any subtitle. Underline all the words and punctuation in the title, except for the final period.

    Brown, C. W. <u>Sharks and Lambs: Wall Street in the Nineties</u>.

3. Record the city of publication, publisher, and date of publication. If the book lists several cities, use only the first. If the city is outside the United States, add an abbreviation for the country. If an American city may be unfamiliar, you can include an abbreviation for the state. Record the main words of the publisher, deleting words like "publishing" or "press" (Monroe for Monroe Publishing Company). Use the initials "UP" for "University Press." End the citation with the last year of publication.

WORKS CITED ENTRY FOR BOOK WITH ONE AUTHOR:

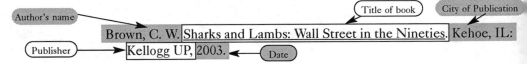

PARENTHETICAL NOTE:
(Brown 12)

Book with Two or Three Authors

WORKS CITED ENTRY:
Smith, David, John Adams, and Chris Cook. <u>Writing On-line</u>. New York: Macmillan, 2000.

PARENTHETICAL NOTE:
(Smith, Adams, and Cook 23–24)

Books with Four or More Authors

WORKS CITED ENTRY:
Chavez, Nancy, et al. <u>Mexico Today</u>. New York: Putnam, 2003.
PARENTHETICAL NOTE:
(Chavez et al. 87)

Book with Corporate Author

WORKS CITED ENTRY:
National Broadcasting Company. <u>Programming Standards</u>. New York: National Broadcasting
    Company, 2002.
PARENTHETICAL NOTE:
(National Broadcasting Company 112)

To avoid a cumbersome parenthetical note, you can mention the author or title in the text:

According to the National Broadcasting Company's <u>Programming Standards</u>, "No single
executive should be able to cancel a program" (214).

Book with Unnamed Authors

WORKS CITED ENTRY:
<u>New Yale Atlas.</u> New York: Random. 2003.
PARENTHETICAL NOTE:
(<u>New Yale</u> 106)

Book with Multiple Volumes

WORKS CITED ENTRY:
Eisenhower, Dwight. <u>Presidential Correspondence</u>. Vol. 2. New York: Dutton, 1960. 6 vols.
PARENTHETICAL NOTE:
(Eisenhower 77)

If you cite more than one volume in your paper, indicate the number:

(Eisenhower 2: 77)

Book in Second or Later Edition

WORKS CITED ENTRY:
Franklin, Marcia. <u>Modern France</u>. 3rd ed. Philadelphia: Comstock, 1987.
PARENTHETICAL NOTE:
(Franklin 12)

Work in an Anthology

WORKS CITED ENTRY:
> Ford, John M. "Preflash." <u>The Year's Best Fantasy</u>. Eds. Ellen Datlow and Terri Windling. New
> York: St. Martin's, 1989. 265–82.

PARENTHETICAL NOTE:
> (Ford 265–66)

Note: If you include more than one work from the same anthology, list the
anthology in the Works Cited section separately under the editors' names
and list individual entries in a shortened form:

> Ford, John M. "Preflash." Datlow and Windling 265–82.

Book in Translation

WORKS CITED ENTRY:
> Verne, Jules. <u>Twenty Thousand Leagues Under the Sea</u>. Trans. Michel Michot. Boston: Pitman,
> 1992.

PARENTHETICAL NOTE:
> (Verne 65)

Book with Editor or Editors

WORKS CITED ENTRY:
> Benson, Nancy, ed. <u>Ten Great American Plays</u>. New York: Columbia UP, 2002.

PARENTHETICAL NOTE:
> (Benson 23)

The preceding parenthetical note would be used to cite Benson's comments.

Book with Author and Editor

WORKS CITED ENTRY:
> Gissing, George. <u>Workers in the Dawn</u>. Ed. Jason Day. London: Oxford UP, 1982.

PARENTHETICAL NOTE:
> (Gissing 78)

Book in a Series

WORKS CITED ENTRY:
> Swessel, Karyn, ed. <u>Northern Ireland Today</u>. Modern Europe Ser. 3. New York: Wilson, 2003.

PARENTHETICAL NOTE:
> (Swessel 34)

Republished Book

WORKS CITED ENTRY:
Smith, Jane. <u>The Jersey Devil</u>. 1922. New York: Warner, 2002.
PARENTHETICAL NOTE:
(Smith 23–25)

Periodicals

Newspaper Article

WORKS CITED ENTRY: (Title of article)   (Title of newspaper)   (Date)   (Page number)

Chavez, Maria. "The Hispanic Century." New York Times 12 Mar. 2003: A13.

(Author's name)

PARENTHETICAL NOTE:
(Chavez)

Note: If an article has only one page, page numbers are not included in parenthetical notes.

Magazine Article

WORKS CITED ENTRY:
Janssen, Mary. "Iran Today." <u>Time</u> 25 Mar. 2003: 34+.

Note: If an article appears on nonconsecutive pages, list the first page followed by a "+" sign.

PARENTHETICAL NOTE:
(Janssen 38)

Scholarly Article

WORKS CITED ENTRY:
Grant, Edward. "The Hollywood Ten: Fighting the Blacklist." <u>California Film Quarterly</u> 92.2
(2002): 14–32.
PARENTHETICAL NOTE:
(Grant 21–23)

Newspaper or Magazine Article with Unnamed Author

WORKS CITED ENTRY:
  "The Legacy of the Gulf War." <u>American History</u> 12 Mar. 2003: 23–41.
PARENTHETICAL NOTE:
  ("Legacy" 25)

Letter to the Editor

WORKS CITED ENTRY:
  Roper, Jack. Letter. <u>Chicago Defender</u> 12 Jan. 2002, sec. B: 12.
PARENTHETICAL NOTE:
  (Roper)

Other Print Sources

Encyclopedia Article with Author

WORKS CITED ENTRY:

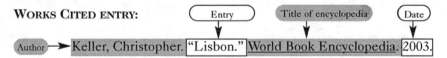

Note: Provide edition number if given.

PARENTHETICAL NOTE:
  (Keller)

Note: Page numbers are not used with works in which articles are arranged alphabetically.

Encyclopedia Article with Unnamed Author

WORKS CITED ENTRY:
  "Lisbon." <u>Columbia Illustrated Encyclopedia</u>. 2002.
PARENTHETICAL NOTE:
  ("Lisbon")

Pamphlet with Author

WORKS CITED ENTRY:
Tindall, Gordon. <u>Guide to New York Churches</u>. New York: Chamber of Commerce, 1998.
PARENTHETICAL NOTE:
(Tindall 76–78)

Pamphlet with Unnamed Author

WORKS CITED ENTRY:
<u>Guide to New York Museums</u>. New York: Columbia U. 2003.
PARENTHETICAL NOTE:
(<u>Guide</u> 176–82)

The Bible

WORKS CITED ENTRY:
<u>The Holy Bible: New International Version</u>. Grand Rapids: Zondervan, 1988.

Note: Titles of sacred texts are not underlined, unless they are specific editions.

PARENTHETICAL NOTE:
(Mark 2:4–9)

Nonprint Sources

Motion Picture

WORKS CITED ENTRY:

Note: You may wish to include names of performers or screenwriters if they are of special interest to readers. These names should be inserted between the title and the distributor.

Television Program

WORKS CITED ENTRY:
"The Long Goodbye." <u>Law and Order</u>. Dir. Jane Hong. Writ. Peter Wren. Perf. Rita Colletti, Diane Nezgod, and Vicki Shimi. NBC. WTMJ-4, Milwaukee. 12 May 2003.

Videotape or DVD

WORKS CITED ENTRY:
Colonial Williamsburg. Prod. Janet Freud. Videocassette. Amer. Home Video, 1996.

Note: You may include information about the director, performers, or screenwriters if these are important for readers. These names should be inserted between the title and the distributor.

Live Performance of a Play

WORKS CITED ENTRY:
All My Sons. By Arthur Miller. Dir. Anita Dayin. Lyric Theater, New York. 10 May 2003.

Speech

WORKS CITED ENTRY:
Goode, Wilmont. "America in the Next Century." Chicago Press Club. 12 Oct. 2003.

Personal or Telephone Interview

WORKS CITED ENTRY:
Weston, Thomas. Personal interview. 21 May 2003.

In the preceding citation, you would substitute "Telephone" for "Personal" if the interview was conducted by telephone.

Parenthetical Notes for Nonprint Sources

Because nonprint sources do not have page numbers and often have long titles, parenthetical notes can be cumbersome. Most writers avoid inserting citations by mentioning the source within the text:

Multiple personality disorder was featured in a recent episode of Law and Order.

In Gone With the Wind special effects were used to re-create the burning of Atlanta.

Interviewed in the fall of 2003, Laura Dornan suggested that many critics failed to see the feminist theme in her play.

Electronic Sources

CD-ROM

WORKS CITED ENTRY:

"Understanding Macbeth." Master Dramas. CD-ROM. New York: Educational Media, 2002.

E-mail

WORKS CITED ENTRY:

Ballard, Morton D. "Rental Cars." E-mail to Germaine Reinhardt. 21 May 2003.

Electronic Journal

WORKS CITED ENTRY:

Smith, Perry. "Truman Capote and Kansas." Phoenix 2.7 (2003). 15 Sep. 2003 <http://www.
englishlit.com/hts/phoenix/index>

Article from Online Newspaper

WORKS CITED ENTRY:

"Long Day's Journey Into Night Production Disappointing." New York Times on the Web 17 Mar.
2003. 22 Apr. 2003 <http://www.nytimes.com/aponline/a/ ap play.html>.

Reference Database

WORKS CITED ENTRY:

The Emerald Project: Irish Literature from 1500–2000. 2000 Boston University. 21 Oct. 2000
<http://www/bostonuniv/emerald/>.

Electronic Texts

Many books are available online. Because they lack page numbers, mention
the title within the text to avoid long parenthetical notes.

WORKS CITED ENTRY:

Gissing, George. Demos. London, 1892. The Electronic Text Center. Ed. Jacob Korgman.
Aug. 2002. U of Michigan Library. 5 Mar. 2003 <http//etext.lib.michigan.edu/cgibin/
browsemixed?ed5gisgeor5revolution&utopia/archive/eng>.

Web Pages

Web pages vary greatly. In general, include the name of the person or organization that created the site, the title (if there is not a title, you can use a description, such as the one used in the next entry), the date of creation or most recent update, the date of access, and the URL.

WORKS CITED ENTRY:

Chicago Irish Center. Home page. 5 Apr. 2003. 10 May 2003 <http://www.chi.irish.cent.org>.

Discussion Group Posting

WORKS CITED ENTRY:

Baker, Jordan. "Golf Today." Online posting. 2 Mar. 2003. Professional Sports Discussion List. 15 Mar. 2003 <http://www.prosports.com/posting/>.

Synchronous Communication

To cite a posting from forums such as MOO, MUD, or IRC, include names of speakers, a description of the event, the date, the name of the forum, date of access, and telnet address:

WORKS CITED ENTRY:

Gladkin, Dorcas. Melville discussion of "Biblical Symbolism in Moby Dick." 19 Oct. 2000. MediaMOO. 1 Nov. 2000 <telnet://www.litcafe/homepages/smith/melville.html>.

FTP

To cite material retrieved by FTP (file transfer protocol), include the uniform resource locator, date of creation, date of access, and electronic address:

WORKS CITED ENTRY:

"Hamlet Act I." The Electronic Shakespeare Project. Ed. Nancy Hamilton. 22 Sept. 2000. U. of Iowa. 12 Oct. 2000 <ftp://hamlet.engl.ui.edu/pub/hamlet>.

Gopher

To cite information retrieved by Gopher, include the uniform resource locator, date of creation, date of access, and electronic address:

WORKS CITED ENTRY:

Simes, David. "Understanding Orwell's Vision." 22 Jul. 2003. 13 pp. 7 Aug. 2003 <gopher://h-net. ukw.edu/oo/orwell/internet-cit>.

Linked Sources

MLA does not provide a method of citing hypertext links, but the following format allows readers to follow your search:

WORKS CITED ENTRY:
Trainer, Lois. "F. Scott Fitzgerald." Online posting. 4 Aug. 2003. Ansaxnet. 10 Oct. 2000 <http://www.amlit/edu>. Lkd. <http://www.yalelit.edu/biography>.

SAMPLE RESEARCH PAPER USING MLA STYLE
(with Cover Page and Formal Outline)

No page
number

centered
one third
down from
p of page

er's name

The Role of Nature in

Orwell's 1984

by

Gordon Comstock

Course
number,
rofessor's
name,
date

English 102

Professor Brandeis

10 May 2004

Note: If your instructor does not request a separate cover page, the first page of your paper should include the title and your name:

Comstock 1

Gordon Comstock

English 102

Professor Brandeis

10 May 2004

The Role of Nature in

Orwell's 1984

Last name
with
lowercase
Roman
numeral
used for
outline page
numbers

Outline

Thesis statement: Winston Smith's humanity and individual autonomy are stunted not only by the brutality of Oceania and the ever-present Thought Police, but by his lack of contact with nature.

I. Most commentators view Orwell's last novel as a grim account of perverted Socialism and the abuse of technology.

II. Most readers have overlooked the role of nature in 1984. Winston Smith's lack of contact with nature robs him of his humanity.

III. Smith rebels against both the dictatorship of Big Brother and the artificiality of his environment.

    A. Smith lives in a London of shabby houses and soulless concrete towers.

    B. Food and fiber in Oceania are artificial and dehumanizing.

IV. Smith escapes this world only in dreams of a pasture he calls "The Golden Country."

    A. The dream provides a background for a sexual encounter.

    B. Winston Smith experiences a similar landscape in reality when he travels into the country with Julia.

        1. Nature provides Smith and Julia with inspiration and comfort.

        2. Smith and Julia can only enjoy sex in a natural setting, away from society.

V. Smith realizes the Party controls its citizens by separating them from reality.

VI. Nature was Orwell's "moral gold standard."

    A. Orwell did not share the Left's faith in scientific progress.

    B. Orwell sensed that even benign uses of technology designed to make life more comfortable had sinister implications.

        1. Artificial environments eliminated contact with nature.

        2. Controlled environments allowed for manipulation and deadened thought.

VII. Orwell viewed contact with nature as essential for society to be just, humane, and decent. 1984 remains relevant in the twentyfirst century of cyberspace and "virtual" realities.

Last name,
age number

itle (1" from
op of page)
Introduction
Review of
critical views
ing selected
direct
quotations

Transition
Comment on
the lack of
critical
sources on
this theme
Thesis

Summary of
novel
focusing on
student's
thesis

Block
quotation

The Role of Nature in Orwell's 1984

Most commentators view Orwell's last novel as a grim account of perverted Socialism, a vision of a society dominated by Big Brother, a god-like
Stalin figure. "Orwell was looking backward, not forward," David Simes argues, "seeing the future as a Nazi state with nuclear weapons" (16–17).
Nancy Wolzheck offers the view that "Orwell saw the centralization of power
as the enemy of human individuality and liberty" (192). "The principal
theme of 1984," Edward Janeson writes, "is the corruption of political
power" (181). Wilson Goodman asserts, "Orwell's novel reveals the horror of
totalitarianism coupled with inhuman uses of technology" (18–19).

But most readers have overlooked a central element in 1984, the role of
nature. Winston Smith's humanity and individual autonomy are stunted not
only by the brutality of Oceania and the ever-present Thought Police, but by
his lack of contact with nature.

Orwell's protagonist Winston Smith rebels not only against the brutal
dictatorship of Big Brother but the artificiality of the world created by the
Party. Smith lives in a London of shabby nineteenth-century houses and
soulless concrete towers. He moves through a realm of artificial structures
and windowless cubicles devoid of nature. Food and fiber in Oceania bear little resemblance to natural products; they are manufactured from synthet-
ics. Smith survives on a diet of processed foods and imitation coffee. He
only has a childhood memory of lemons, a fruit he has not seen in thirty
years. Omnipresent telescreens simultaneously bombard him with propa-
ganda and record his every move. In this artificial world, Smith's natural
instincts for comfort, companionship, and freedom are demeaned and crim-
inalized. Sex, the most natural instinct in humans, has been oppressed and
sullied so that Smith's only contacts with women since his divorce have
been with prostitutes.

In 1984. Smith escapes this grim world only in his sleep, when he
dreams of what he calls the "Golden Country":

> It was an old, rabbit-bitten pasture, with a foot track wandering
> across it and a mole-hole here and there. In the ragged hedge on the
> opposite side of the field the boughs of the elm trees were swaying

very faintly in the breeze, their leaves just stirring in the dense
masses like women's hair. (29)

This conventional bit of countryside becomes the setting for eroticism. A
dream girl runs toward Smith, tossing aside her clothes in disdainful ges-
tures "belonging to the ancient time" (29).

Smith encounters this dream landscape when he and Julia slip from
London to escape the ever-present telescreens that track their every movement and prevent them from consummating their illegal relationship. Meeting in the country, they enter a rabbit-bitten pasture with leaves like
"women's hair." Like the girl in the dream, Julia sheds her Junior Anti-Sex
League sash in defiance. Smith and Julia can only enjoy sexual intimacy
apart from civilization, in the wild where their passion is not blunted by social restraint. This freedom is difficult to maintain in the city, forcing them
to hole up like criminals in a dingy room to escape detection.

Nature provides Smith and Julia with inspiration and comfort, vitalizing
their sexual instincts. Nature allows them to feel that their biological urges
are wholesome and fundamental, elements linking them to the apolitical

Selected use
of direct
quotations

world of flowers and birds. Smith wants to feel not "merely the love of one
person" but "the animal instinct, the simple undifferentiated desire" which
will "tear the Party to pieces" (105). Nature gives Smith the spirit to rebel,
to energize elements of humanity the Party seeks to eradicate, sully, and
trivialize.

Smith realizes that his alienation, his sense of superfluousness is caused
not only by political oppression but by his separation from nature. The Party
achieves its power not only through surveillance, censorship, and torture,
but by distorting natural law. During Smith's interrogation, O'Brien insists

Direct
quotation of
dialogue

that " 'the stars are bits of fire a few kilometers away. We could reach them
if we wanted to. Or we could blot them out' " (219). By altering people's concept of nature, the Party assumes all power. Separated from reality, the citizen of Oceania is enveloped in the artificial, managed world of the state, with
no independence.

Nature, according to Alan Sandison, was Orwell's "moral gold standard"
(10). Nature was an essential part of Orwell's judgment. Writing to Henry

Ellipsis
indicating
deleted
words

Miller, whose books he admired, Orwell chided Miller for wandering off "into
a kind of reverie where the laws of ordinary reality were slipped just a little
but not too much" (Collected Essays 4:80). Orwell added, ". . . I have a sort

of belly-to-earth attitude and always feel uneasy when I get away from the ordinary world where grass is green, stones hard etc." (4 : 80).

Orwell saw the loss of nature as the inevitable result of mechanical progress. Technology was the major tenet of the ideologies of Orwell's pre-environmentalist era. Mussolini drained the Pontine marshes; Hitler constructed the autobahn; Stalin erected huge hydroelectric dams. Orwell, unlike most Socialists of his generation, did not share the Left's faith in scientific progress. He even doubted the role of electricity, the pet project of Lenin and Stalin, in making the world better. He viewed electricity as a *Ellipsis used* "queer spectacle . . . showering miracles upon people with empty bellies. . . . *to delete* Twenty million people are underfed but literally everyone in England has ac- *unnecessary* cess to a radio" (Orwell Road 84). *details*

In The Road to Wigan Pier, Orwell decried the slums he saw in Depression-era Britain. He was also distressed by the fact that the poor were deloused before being allowed to move into new low-income housing. "Bugs are bad," he noted, "but a state of affairs in which men will allow themselves to be dipped like sheep is worse" (71).

Orwell found something insidious and dangerous even in the most benign uses of technology. Writing in 1946, he criticized the proposed development of postwar "pleasure spots" in the same way he denounced the "hygiene" in public housing. The planned resorts he read about in "slick magazines" would be comprised of artificial lagoons, heated swimming pools, sunlamps, and glass-covered tennis courts. Examining the characteristics of such artificial playlands, Orwell saw many of the same elements he would later depict in harsher terms in 1984:

Block
quotation

1. One is never alone.
2. One never does anything for oneself.
3. One is never within sight of wild vegetation or natural objects of any kind.
4. Light and temperature are always artificially regulated.
5. One is never out of the sound of music.

(Collected Essays 4:80)

Orwell found the music to be particularly disturbing and the most important standard ingredient of the modern artificial environment:

Block
quotation
with
ellipsis

Its function is to prevent thought and conversation, and to shut out any natural sound, such as the song of birds or the whistling of the wind, that might otherwise intrude. The radio is already consciously used for this purpose by innumerable people. In very many English homes the radio is literally never turned off, though it is manipulated from time to time so as to make sure that only light music will come out of it. I know people who will keep the radio playing all through a meal and at the same time continue talking just loudly enough for the voices and the music to cancel each other out. . . . The music prevents the conversation from becoming serious . . . while the chatter of voices stops one from listening attentively to the music and thus prevents the onset of that dreadful thing, thought. (Collected Essays 4:80)

Orwell drew on his observations of the radio in middle class English homes to envision the telescreens of Oceania.

1984 exaggerated trends Orwell saw taking place around him. The danger to humanity was not only totalitarian governments but science and technology. The growing artificiality of life, whether inspired by tasteless commercialism or state planning, threatens human individuality and ability to make rational judgments about the world. In a natural environment all men and women are equal in their response to the world. In the artificial universe created by technology the individual can only respond to an environment created by other humans, a world designed to curtail thought, deceive, and control.

Orwell saw nature as an essential ingredient in any society that wishes to be just, humane, and decent. "Man only stays human," Orwell argued, "by preserving large patches of simplicity in his life" (Collected Essays 4:80). Modern inventions, though they make life easier and more comfortable under the best circumstances, can have severe consequences on the individual and "weaken his consciousness, dull his curiosity, and, in general, drive him nearer to the animals" (Collected Essays 4:81). As Alan Sandison notes in The Last Man in Europe, "the greatest moral danger Orwell can envision for a man is that he should be denied contact with the ordinary world where grass is green, stones hard" (10).

1984 then remains a relevant novel. Orwell's vision of a Stalinist nightmare state may no longer seem compelling, but his observations about the growing artificiality of life and the need for humans to maintain contact Conclusion   with nature are perhaps more pertinent in the twenty-first century world of cyberspace and "virtual" realities.

Comstock 5

Works Cited

Goodman, Wilson. <u>Orwell's Dark Vision</u>. New York: Columbia UP, 1992.

Janeson, Edward. "Power and Politics in <u>1984</u>." <u>Modern Fiction Studies</u>.
    May 1999: 179–90.

Orwell, George. <u>The Collected Essays, Journalism and Letters of George
    Orwell</u>. Ed. Sonia Orwell and Ian Angus. Vol. 4. New York: Harcourt,
    1968. 4 vols.

---. <u>1984</u>. 1949. New York: New Amer. Lib., 1961.

---. <u>The Road to Wigan Pier</u>. New York: Berkley, 1967.

Sandison, Alan. <u>The Last Man in Europe</u>. London: Macmillan, 1974.

Simes, David, ed. <u>British Authors 1900–1950</u>. Oxford: Oxford UP, 1987.

Wolzheck, Nancy. "Orwell Under Fire." <u>Time and Tide</u>. 10 May 2001.
    12 Oct. 2003 <http://www.timeandtide.com>.

Heading
centered
rst line flush
with left
margin, then
indented

APA STYLE

Most courses in the social sciences, including anthropology, education, political science, psychology, and sociology, follow the rules for documentation created by the American Psychological Association. For full details,
consult the American Psychological Association's *Publication Manual of the
American Psychological Association*, fifth edition.

STRATEGIES FOR WRITING
PARENTHETICAL NOTES

In APA documentation parenthetical notes are placed after material
requiring documentation, and all sources are recorded in a References list at
the end of the paper.

- **Parenthetical notes include author, year of publication, and, for direct quotes, page numbers.** Most sources are identified by the author's
  name and the year of publication. Page numbers are usually omitted from
  paraphrases but are always included in direct quotations. The information may be placed in a single note or distributed throughout the text:

  Smith (2003) suggested that multiple personality disorder was more common than
  previously reported.

Continued

It has been suggested that multiple personality disorder is more common than previously believed (Smith, 2003).

Based on recent studies, Smith (2003) asserts that "multiple personality disorder is more common than previously reported" (p. 321).

- **Multiple parenthetical notes indicate more than one source.** If two or more sources are cited within a sentence, notes are inserted after the material quoted or paraphrased:

Johnson (2002) stated that the study "revealed that Chicago schools were adequately staffed" (p. 43), leading Renfro (2003) to reject the teachers' union proposal.

- **For the first text reference, list up to five authors' names:**

Johnson, Hyman, Torque, and Kaiser (2003) observed that computers enhance student performance.

Note: With multiple authors in a parenthetical cite, use an ampersand (&; Johnson, Hyman, Torque, & Kaiser, 2003).

- **For the first reference of a citation with six or more authors, list the first author's name and "et al." (and others):**

Johnson et al. (2003) examined computer education in Chicago, New York, El Paso, and Philadelphia.

- **List corporate and group authors in full initially; then abbreviate:**

Computers are valuable in teaching higher mathematics (Modern Education Council [MEC], 2002). Textbook publishers now include online support for individual tutoring (MEC, 2002).

- **Assign letters (a, b, c) to indicate use of more than one work by an author with same year of publication:**

Kozik (2002a) studied students in Chicago bilingual classes and later reviewed the performance of an English immersion program in San Diego (2002b).

- **Alphabetize multiple sources and separate with a semicolon:**

Several reports suggest that noise pollution can directly contribute to hypertension (Jones, 1997; Smith, 2002).

- **Web sites can be mentioned within the text:**

Chinese educators have attempted to expand Internet access for university students, particularly in the fields of engineering and medicine. Their efforts can be documented by examining Peking University's World Wide Web site at http://www.upkng.eng.edu.

STRATEGIES FOR WRITING A REFERENCES PAGE

List all the sources you have cited on a separate sheet at the end of your paper titled "References" (center the word References and do not italicize it or place it in quotation marks). If you include works you have read for background but not actually cited, title the page "Bibliography."

- **Arrange the list of works alphabetically by authors' or editors' last names, followed by initials. If no authors are listed, alphabetize by the first significant word of the title:**

  Jones, W. (2002). *Chicago today.* New York: Putnam.
  A new look for Toronto. (2003, Fall). *Toronto Magazine*, 21.

- **For sources with more than one author, alphabetize by the first author's last name and list subsequent authors by last names and initials:**

  Zinter, M., & Ames, J. (2002). *First aid.* New York: Dial.

- **Begin each citation even with the left margin, then indent subsequent lines five spaces. Double-space the entire page. Do not separate entries with additional spaces:**

  Abrams, J. (2002, January 21). Rebuilding America's cities. *Cleveland Plain Dealer*, pp. 1, 7, 8.
  Brown, G. (2003). *The death of the central city: The malling of America.* New York: Macmillan.

- **If more than one source from a given author is used, list the works in chronological order and repeat the author's name:**

  Brown, G. (2003). *The death of the central city: The malling of America.* New York: Macmillan.
  Brown, G. (2000). *Hope for renewal.* New York: Putnam.

GUIDELINES FOR LISTING SOURCES IN REFERENCES AND PARENTHETICAL NOTES

Books

- Write the author's last name, first and subsequent initials:

  Brown, C. W.

- Place the year of publication in parentheses, followed by a period and one space.
- Italicize the full title of the book. Place a colon between the main heading and any subtitle. Capitalize only the first word in the title and any subtitle and any proper nouns or adjectives within the title:

  Brown, C. W. (2003). *Sharks and lambs: Wall Street in the nineties.*

- Record the city of publication and publisher.

  Brown, C. W. (2003). *Sharks and lambs: Wall Street in the nineties.* New York: Kellogg Press.

Note: Do not shorten or abbreviate words like "University" or "Press."

PARENTHETICAL NOTES:

Brown (2003) stated . . .
(Brown, 2003)
(Brown, 2003, pp. 23–25)

Book with Two or Three Authors

REFERENCES ENTRY:

Smith, D., Johnson, A., & Cook, F. D. (1989). *Writing for television.* New York: Macmillan.

PARENTHETICAL NOTES:

First note:
Smith, Johnson, and Cook (1989) stated . . .

Subsequent notes:
Smith et al. (1989) revealed . . .

First note:
(Smith, Johnson, & Cook, 1989)

Subsequent notes:
(Smith et al., 1989)

Book with Corporate Author

REFERENCES ENTRY:

National Broadcasting Company. (2002). *Programming standards*. New York: National Broadcasting Company.

PARENTHETICAL NOTES:

According to the National Broadcasting Company's *Programming Standards* (2002), "No single executive should be able to cancel a program" (p. 214).
(National Broadcasting Company [NBC], 2002, p. 214)

Book with Unnamed Author

REFERENCES ENTRY:

New Yale Atlas. (2003). New York: Random House.

PARENTHETICAL NOTES:

According to the *New Yale Atlas* (2003) . . .
(*New Yale Atlas*, 2003, p. 106)

Book with Multiple Volumes

REFERENCES ENTRY:

Eisenhower, D. (1960). *Presidential correspondence*. (Vol. 2). New York: Dutton Books.

PARENTHETICAL NOTES:

Eisenhower (1960) predicted . . .
(Eisenhower, 1960, p. 77)

Book in Second or Later Edition

REFERENCES ENTRY:

Franklin, M. (1987). *Modern France* (3rd ed.). Philadelphia: Comstock Press.

PARENTHETICAL NOTES:

Franklin (1987) stated . . .
(Franklin, 1987, p. 12)

Book in Translation

REFERENCES ENTRY:

Verne, J. (1992). *Twenty thousand leagues under the sea* (M. Michot, Trans.). Boston: Pitman Press.

PARENTHETICAL NOTES:

Verne (1992)
(Verne, 1992, p. 65)

Book with Editor or Editors

REFERENCES ENTRY:
Benson, N. (Ed.). (2002). *The absent parent.* New York: Columbia House.
PARENTHETICAL NOTES:
According to Benson (2002) . . .
(Benson, 2002)

Book with Author and Editor

REFERENCES ENTRY:
Gissing, G. (1982). Effect of sunlight on circadian rhythms. In J. Day (Ed.), *Workers in the dawn*
(pp. 45–94). London: Oxford University Press.
PARENTHETICAL NOTE:
(Gissing, 1982, p. 78)

Republished Book

REFERENCES ENTRY:
Smith, J. (2002). *The Jersey devil.* New York: Warner Books. (Original work published 1922)
PARENTHETICAL NOTES:
Smith (2002) observes . . .
(Smith, 2002, pp. 12–13)

Periodicals

Newspaper Article

REFERENCES ENTRY:
Chavez, M. (2002, August 15). The Hispanic century. *The New York Times*, pp. 2A, 8A–9A.

Note: List all page numbers, separated by commas.

PARENTHETICAL NOTES:
Chavez (2002) states . . .
(Chavez, 2002, p. 8A)

Magazine Article

REFERENCES ENTRY:
Janssen, M. (1997, January/February). Iran today. *Foreign Affairs, 64*, 78–88.
PARENTHETICAL NOTES:
Janssen (1997) notes . . .
(Janssen, 1997, pp. 80–82)

Scholarly Article

REFERENCES ENTRY:
Grant, E. (2002). The Hollywood ten: Fighting the blacklist. *California Film Quarterly, 92,* 112–125.

PARENTHETICAL NOTES:
Grant (2002) observes . . .
(Grant, 2002, pp. 121–123)

Newspaper or Magazine Article with Unnamed Author

REFERENCES ENTRY:
The legacy of the Gulf War. (2000, October). *American History, 48,* 23–41.

PARENTHETICAL NOTES:
In "The Legacy of the Gulf War" (2000) . . . ("Legacy," 2000, pp. 22 24)

Note: For parenthetical notes, use shortened titles in quotation marks.

Letter to the Editor

REFERENCES ENTRY:
Roper, J. (1997, June 12). Why the proposed bond won't pass. [Letter to the editor]. *Chicago Defender,* p. B12.

PARENTHETICAL NOTES:
According to Roper (1997) . . .
(Roper, 1997, p. B12)

Other Print Sources

Encyclopedia Article

REFERENCES ENTRY:
Keller, C. (2003). Lisbon. In *Encyclopedia of Europe* (Vol. 8, pp. 232–233). New York: Wiley.

PARENTHETICAL NOTES:
Keller (2003) reports . . .
(Keller, 2003, p. 232)

Encyclopedia Article with Unnamed Author

REFERENCES ENTRY:
Lisbon. (2002). In *Columbia illustrated encyclopedia* (Vol. 10, p. 156). New York: Columbia University Press.

PARENTHETICAL NOTES:
In "Lisbon" (2002) . . .
(Lisbon," 2002, p. 156)

Pamphlet

REFERENCES ENTRY:
Tindall, G. (Ed.). (2002). *Guide to New York churches*. New York: New York Chamber of
Commerce.

PARENTHETICAL NOTES:
Tindall (2002) noted . . .
(Tindall, 2002, pp. 34–36)

Nonprint Sources

Motion Picture

REFERENCES ENTRY:
Scorsese, M. (Director). (1995). *Casino* [Motion picture]. United States: Universal.

PARENTHETICAL NOTES:
Scorsese (1995) depicts . . .
(Scorsese, 1995)

Television Program

REFERENCES ENTRY:
Hong, J. (Producer). (1997, May 12). *Women at work*. [Television broadcast]. New York: Public
Broadcasting Service.

PARENTHETICAL NOTES:
According to Hong (1997) . . .
(Hong, 1997)

Videotape

REFERENCES ENTRY:
Freud, J. (Producer), & Johnson, K. (Director). (1996). [Videotape]. *Colonial Williamsburg*. New
York: American Home Video.

PARENTHETICAL NOTES:
Freud and Johnson (1996) . . .
(Freud & Johnson, 1996)

Speech

REFERENCES ENTRY:
Goode, W. (2003, October 12). *America in the next century.* Address before the Chicago Press Club, Chicago, IL.

PARENTHETICAL NOTES:
According to Goode (2003) . . .
(Goode, 2003)

Electronic Sources

E-mail

Because e-mail is not recorded in archives and not available to other researchers, it is mentioned in the text but not included in the list of references. Treat it as a personal communication—mentioned in the text only, as follows:

PARENTHETICAL NOTE:
Medhin (personal communication, March 1, 2002) suggested . . .
Medhin (personal communication, March 1, 2002)

CD-ROM

REFERENCES ENTRY:
MedNet, Inc. (2002). *Directory of mental disorders* [CD-ROM]. New York: Author.

PARENTHETICAL NOTES:
MedNet (2002) states . . .
(MedNet, 2002)

Electronic Journal

REFERENCES ENTRY:
Smith, P. (2002, March 2). Help for homeless promised. *Psychology Journal.* Retrieved January 25, 2003, from http://www.psychojourn./hts/index

Note: Because the content of websites can change, it is important to list the date you retrieved the information.

PARENTHETICAL NOTES:
According to Smith (2002) . . .
(Smith, 2002)

Article from Online Newspaper

REFERENCES ENTRY:
Gulf war syndrome: Diagnostic survey reveals dangerous trend. (2003, March 11). *New York Times*. Retrieved December 15, 2003, from http://www.nytimes.com/aponline/ap-gulf.html

Note: Do not end the entry with a period if the last item is a URL.

PARENTHETICAL NOTES:
In "Gulf War" (2003) . . .
("Gulf War," 2003)

Database

REFERENCES ENTRY:
Criminal Justice Network. (2002). *Capital cases and defense funding.* Retrieved May 4, 2003, from telnet freenet.crimjus.ca. login as guest, go index (2003, June 23).

PARENTHETICAL NOTES:
According to "Capital Cases" (2002) . . .
("Capital Cases," 2002)

Electronic Texts

REFERENCES ENTRY:
Weston, T. (1989). *The electronic teacher.* Retrieved May 25, 2000, from Columbia University, the Education Server website: http://www.edserv.edu/index.html

PARENTHETICAL NOTES:
Weston (1989) points out . . .
(Weston, 1989)

Web Pages

REFERENCES ENTRY:
Regis, T. (2003, January 5). Developing distance learning. [In *Regis*. Retrieved October 27, 2003, from http://regis.devel/home/distlearng/toc.html

PARENTHETICAL NOTES:
Regis (2003) suggests . . .
(Regis, 2003)

Synchronous Communication

To cite a posting from newsgroups, online forums, and electronic mailing lists, include author's name, post date, message subject line, "Message posted to" followed by the URL.

REFERENCES ENTRY:
> Goring, D. (2003, May 12). Seminar discussion on alcoholism. Message posted to
> Telnet://www.drugabuse.parc. edu:8888

PARENTHETICAL NOTES:
> Goring (2003) indicates . . .
> (Goring, 2003)

FTP

REFERENCES ENTRY:
> Divak, T. (2002). *Cocaine addiction and pregnancy.* Retrieved March 25, 2003, from ftp://
> addiction.sources.com library/article/drugs/c8.txt

PARENTHETICAL NOTES:
> Divak (2002) records . . .
> (Divak, 2002)

Gopher

REFERENCES ENTRY:
> Simes, D. (2003). Understanding Orwell's vision. *English.* Retrieved May 16, 2003, from
> gopher://h-net.ukw.edu/ oo/orwell/internet-cit

PARENTHETICAL NOTES:
> Simes (2003) states . . .
> (Simes, 2003)

SAMPLE RESEARCH PAPER USING APA STYLE
(with Abstract)

Shortened title
and page
number

Heading
centered and
double-spaced

Feeding Frenzy:
Journalism and Justice in
the Leopold and Loeb Case
Sean O'Connell
Criminal Justice 201
May 10, 2004

Abstract

No paragraph
indent

Current popular opinion suggests that recent high profile legal proceedings
have been adversely affected by excessive and sensational media coverage.
These cases, many argue, have set dangerous precedents which will cause
lasting harm to American justice. The 1924 trial of Leopold and Loeb indicates that this is not a new concern. A careful analysis of the role of journalism in what was called "the crime of the century" reveals the media may
have undue influence in individual cases but have little lasting influence on
the criminal justice system.

Feeding Frenzy:
                            Journalism and Justice in
                            Leopold and Loeb Case

Introduction   The twentieth century ended with a flurry of highly publicized crimes and
trials—the Menendez case, the O. J. Simpson trial, the Jon Benet Ramsey investigation, and the impeachment of President Clinton. In each instance, the
media made instant celebrities of suspects and witnesses. Driven by fame or
money, even minor figures became household names, publishing books and
appearing on talk shows. Commentators continually lamented that justice
was being perverted by media attention, that televised trials were turning
lawyers into actors and trials into a kind of theater. Justice, many argued,
was being irrevocably damaged.

An earlier case, however, reveals that this phenomenon is not new. In
the spring of 1924 two young men committed a crime that made them nationally known celebrities and sparked a firestorm of media attention, which
Direct   many at the time insisted "damaged justice forever" (Harrison, 1924, p. 8).
quotation
with author,
year,
page number   The "Crime of the Century"

On May 21, 1924, Jacob Franks, a wealthy Chicago businessman, received news that his fourteen-year-old son had been kidnapped. A letter
signed "George Johnson" demanded ten thousand dollars and gave Franks
detailed instructions on how to deliver the ransom. Desperate to save his
Paraphrase   son, Franks complied with the kidnapper's request, but before he could de-
with   liver the money, he learned his son had been found dead. Less than twelve
author and
year   hours after the abduction, a workman discovered the naked body in a ditch
on the outskirts of the city (Arkan, 1997).

The killing of Bobby Franks created a national sensation. Rumors circu-
lated that the kidnapper had been a jealous teacher or a disgruntled employee or customer of one of Jacob Franks' enterprises. Because the body
had been stripped, many speculated that the killer had been a sexual per-
vert (Higdon, 1974).

The press seized upon the story, printing numerous accounts of the police investigation. One paper offered readers a cash prize for submitting the
best theory of the case and was swamped with thousands of letters (Higdon,
1974). The police soon had a strong lead. A pair of glasses had been discovered near the body. Though common in appearance, the frames had a newly

Video listed by
title and year

patented hinge. The eyeglasses were quickly traced to a neighbor, nineteen-year-old Nathan Leopold ("Born Killers," 1998).

Nathan Leopold explained he had probably dropped the glasses while leading a birding class a few days earlier. At the time of the crime, he claimed to have been driving with a friend named Richard Loeb and two girls they had picked up in Jackson Park. At first, investigators found Leopold's story believable (Leopold, 1958). Leopold and Loeb seemed unlikely criminals. Like Bobby Franks, they were sons of millionaires; Richard Loeb's father was vice-chairman of Sears & Roebuck. They were gifted students, both having completed college at eighteen. Leopold spoke numerous languages and had become a nationally recognized ornithologist ("Born Killers," 1998). Brought in for questioning, Richard Loeb initially corroborated Leopold's alibi, claiming they spent May 21st with girls they picked up in Jackson Park (Higdon, 1974).

State's Attorney Robert E. Crowe remained unconvinced and continued his investigation. On May 31st, after a long interrogation, Richard Loeb gave a detailed confession, admitting that he and Nathan Leopold were solely responsible for the murder of Bobby Franks. There was no doubt about their guilt. They led police to where they had disposed of the victim's clothing and the lagoon where they had dumped the typewriter used to write the ransom letter (Arkan, 1997). Satisfied he had an airtight case, Richard E. Crowe announced to the press, " I have a hanging case " ("Born Killers," 1998). The stunned Loeb family asked the most famous lawyer of the era, Clarence Darrow, to save their son's life (Leopold, 1958).

The arrest of two wealthy young men, their total lack of remorse, rumors of homosexuality, and the appearance of Clarence Darrow in the case created a media firestorm.

The Chicago Press of the 1920s

At the time of the Franks kidnapping, Chicago had six daily newspapers, including two Hearst publications known for sensational headlines (Higdon, 1974). Newspapers of the era were highly competitive. Attorney and journalism professor David Evans (personal communication, April 2, 2000) notes, "Newspapers in those years were eager to capitalize on crime, sex, and violence to boost sales and increase their advertising rates based on circulation."

Personal
interview,
cited fully in text
but not included
on References
page

Competition led journalists and newspapers to engage in illegal practices. Reporters, whose salaries and bonuses were tied to sales, impersonated police officers to obtain leads, stole documents, and bribed officials for information (Evans, 2000). Major Chicago dailies engaged in brutal circulation wars, hiring gangsters to terrorize newsdealers and newsboys from rival papers. The commuter who stopped at a newstand to purchase a *Herald and Examiner* might be beaten by a thug working for *The Chicago Tribune* (Higdon, 1974; Evans, 2000).

Feeding Frenzy

The Leopold and Loeb case presented the Chicago press with an unparalleled opportunity for sensationalism. For many the case represented the moral degeneration of American youth. The 1920s was an era of youthful rebellion, marked by flappers, speakeasies, and open discussions of sex. Prohibition was widely violated, leading millions of Americans to associate with bootleggers and fuel the growing criminal empires of gangsters like Al Capone (Bergreen, 1994).

The Chicago papers had given great press coverage to the gangland killings of the era. But unlike the crude turf battles of the "beer wars," the Leopold and Loeb case gave reporters new avenues to exploit. They quickly dubbed the case a "Thrill Killing," a crime motivated by something darker and more sinister than simple greed (Evans, 2000). After Leopold and Loeb were arrested, Chicago papers reported extensively on their privileged status and their total lack of remorse. *The Chicago Daily News* referred to the defendants as "jealous actors" who "taunted" each other as reporters watched ("Leopold and Loeb," 1924, p. 4). Stories commented on the stylish dress and demeanor of the two young men, who smoked cigarettes and gave impromptu press conferences. Stating the crime had been an experiment, Nathan Leopold told *The Chicago Daily News*, ". . . it is as easy to justify such a death as it is to justify an entomologist impaling a beetle on a pin" ("Leopold and Loeb," 1924, p. 4).

These stories inflamed the public. Crowds demanded the young men be hanged. Commentators across the country saw the pair as symbols of a corrupt generation without moral consciousness.

The "Trial of the Century"

Despite their confessions, Leopold and Loeb pleaded not guilty. Their attorney, Clarence Darrow, an outspoken opponent of the death penalty, took the

Feeding Frenzy 6

case to put capital punishment on trial. Sensing the hostile mood of the jury and cognizant of the crowds milling outside the courthouse demanding the killers be put to death, Darrow changed the plea to guilty (Higdon, 1974).

Darrow's Strategy

Convinced that a jury would not only convict his clients but demand the death penalty, Darrow wanted to avoid a trial. By entering a plea of guilty, Darrow would be able to address the judge directly. He believed he would have a better chance to convince a single individual to spare his clients' lives. A jury, Darrow knew, would make a collective decision. A judge, however, would bear individual responsibility for sending two teenagers to the gallows ("Born Killers," 1998).

Darrow did not consider pleading Leopold and Loeb not guilty by reason of insanity, because this would have required a jury trial. He did, however, argue to Judge Caverly that mental illness should be considered a mitigating factor. He argued that Leopold and Loeb should be imprisoned for life rather than executed (Higdon, 1974).

Press Coverage

The hearing before Judge Caverly became a media circus. Each day thousands of people mobbed the courthouse, hoping to obtain a seat in the courtroom. Admiring women sent flowers to Leopold and Loeb. A despondent man offered to be hanged in their place. A young woman offered to perjure herself, claiming to be one of the girls Leopold and Loeb had picked up in Jackson Park. *The Chicago Tribune,* which owned a radio station, briefly urged readers to demand that the hearing be broadcast over the new medium. Reporters stole a medical report from Darrow's office and printed intimate details about the defendants' sex lives (Higdon, 1974).

When Darrow called psychiatrists to testify on behalf of his clients, William Randolf Hearst offered Sigmund Freud an undisclosed sum to travel to Chicago to comment on the defendants' mental state. Freud declined, but less reputable "experts," including phrenologists, offered opinions to the press. Diagrams of Leopold and Loeb's brains appeared in the paper with arrows pointing to facial features revealing propensities for falsehood and unnatural sexual appetites (Evans, 2000).

Feeding Frenzy 7

Angered by the crime, the public was outraged by the idea that the killers would be let off because they had unhappy childhoods. Widely viewed as spoiled rich kids, Leopold and Loeb received little sympathy in the press. Hundreds of ministers wrote Judge Caverly arguing that they should be put to death. Arguing before the judge, State's Attorney Crowe echoed sentiments expressed in dozens of editorials (Evans, 2000). Having called over a hundred witnesses, Crowe felt confident he had made a compelling case for the death penalty.

Darrow's Use of the Press

Sensing that Judge Caverly would be influenced by community opinion, Darrow sought to defuse some of the negative publicity. Numerous reporters had claimed that Darrow was being paid a million dollars, inflaming public resentment against the affluence of his clients ("Born Killers," 1998; Evans, 2000). Darrow encouraged the fathers of Leopold and Loeb to release a statement to the press asserting that his fee would be determined by the Illinois Bar Association and that their goal was only to secure life imprisonment for their sons. Darrow employed primitive sampling techniques to measure the public mood. He directed pollsters to ask randomly selected men in the Loop if they believed Leopold and Loeb should be executed. Before release of the statement, sixty percent favored the death penalty. After release of the statement, sixty percent agreed that life imprisonment would be a suitable punishment (Higdon, 1974).

According to Evans (2000), the most significant element of Darrow's strategy was an eloquent twelve-hour closing argument against the death penalty. Quoting the Bible, legal scholars, and great works of literature, he delivered a compelling oration. He stressed the youth of the defendants, arguing that in any other case few would see a life sentence for an eighteen-year-old as lenient. After three weeks of deliberating the case, Judge Caverly shocked the press by sentencing Nathan Leopold and Richard Loeb to life plus ninety-nine years. Despite the severity of the sentence, editorials across the country considered the decision a gross injustice. Edna Harrison (1924) wrote a stinging denunciation of Judge Caverly:

> Nowhere has justice been more blinded than in this city. It is an outrage that perversion, kidnapping, and murder have been rewarded.

Parenthetical note including two sources

Indented block quotation

Feeding Frenzy 8

The science of psychology reduced crime to an ailment and killers to patients. This case has damaged justice forever. (p. 8)

The Lasting Influence

The fact that the "outrage" occurred in 1924 illustrates the high profile case made no lasting impact on routine criminal investigations and legal proceedings. David Evans (2000) has argued that the case of Leopold and Loeb, like the sensational trials of the 1990s, had no lasting effect on justice:

Thousands of trials, both fair and unfair, followed the Leopold and Loeb case. In most instances media attention has had little impact on judges and juries. The insanity plea is rarely used and rarely successful. Psychiatric arguments about diminished capacity have become routine but have not significantly altered the rate of convictions or the severity of sentences, which have steadily become longer.

The case of Leopold and Loeb indicates clearly that excessive media coverage may alter the outcome of a particular sensational trial but has no significant influence on the criminal justice system.

Feeding Frenzy 9

REFERENCES

Heading
centered

Entries begin
flush with
left margin

Arkan, J. (1997). *Leopold and Loeb.* Retrieved April 10, 2000, from chicago.crime.com library/article/trials/c15.txt

Bergreen, L. (1994). *Capone: The man and the era.* New York: Touchstone.

Born killers [Television series episode]. (1998). In C. Meindel (producer), *In search of history.* New York: The History Channel.

Harrison, E. (1924) *The case of Leopold and Loeb.* Chicago: Dearborn.

Higdon, H. (1974). *The crime of the century.* New York: Putnam.

Leopold, N. (1958). *Life plus 99 years.* Garden City: Doubleday.

Leopold and Loeb. (1924, June 2). *The Chicago Daily News,* pp. 1–4.

RESEARCH PAPER CHECKLIST

Before submitting your research paper, review these questions:

✔ Does your research paper have a clearly stated thesis?

✔ Do you provide sufficient evidence to support your thesis?

✔ Does the paper focus on your ideas and commentary or does it only summarize other sources?

✔ Do you comment on the quantity and quality of the evidence you have found?

✔ Does the opening introduce the subject, present the thesis, or explain your research method?

✔ Does the conclusion end the paper on a strong point?

✔ Does the paper follow the appropriate style for citing sources?

✔ Questions for your instructor:

- Is my topic acceptable?
- How many sources do I need?
- Does my paper need an outline?
- Which documentation style is required?

E-WRITING: Exploring Research Writing Online

You can use the Internet to understand more about writing research papers.

1. Using a search engine like Alta Vista, Yahoo, or Google enter terms such as "writing research papers" and "evaluating research papers."

2. Use a search engine to locate sites for the Modern Language Association (MLA) and the American Psychological Association (APA). Note their directions for documenting sources.

InfoTrac® College Edition

For additional resources go to InfoTrac College Edition, your online research library, at http://infotrac.cengagelearning.com

1. Search for articles in technical and academic magazines and note how writers use documentation to support their points of view. How important is documenting sources in persuading readers? Does the appearance of a works cited page or end-notes give a document more authority?

2. Use search terms like "MLA" and "APA" to locate articles about documentation.

10

Global Warming

*The sooner we start doing something about global
warming the better, because by the time that
everyone agrees that global warming has started, it
could be too late to do much about it.*
–S. George Philander

*Allocating allowable emissions according to a
"polluter pays" principle also poses a moral
dilemma. Should current generations bear moral
responsibility for actions taken by their forebears?
Alternatively, should our children and grandchildren
be forced to live in a world marred by the
consequences of significant global warming?*
–Fen Osler Hampson and Judith Reppy

*One day, our models will make sense of all the
existing data, and scientists will tease new data
from yet unknown sources. When that happens,
global warming may turn out to be real; it may
even turn out to be man-made. In that case, then
maybe we will have to shoulder the enormous
burden the warming lobby wants us to take on now.*
–Dolly Setton

*We must abandon the old mindset that demands
an oil-based economy, not just because it sparks
wars and terrorism, but because the future of life
on earth depends on leaving it behind.*
–Mark Lynas

The Disappearing Glaciers

The glaciers in Glacier National Park are disappearing. The area covered
by glaciers has declined 70 percent since 1850. The Grinnell Glacier,
which once spread over 576 acres, now covers less than 200 acres. The
shrinking Grinnell Glacier is one of only fifty mountain glaciers left in the
park. In 1850 there were a hundred and fifty. Scientists estimate that the last
remaining glaciers may vanish by 2030.

Melting glaciers are just one indicator of long-term climate change. In the summer of 1990, oystermen in Delaware Bay began finding more and more empty shells in their nets. The oysters had been killed by a parasite that thrives in warmer waters. Oyster hauls dropped 90 percent. Tree rings in Alaska reveal that their growth was fairly constant for a hundred years but diminished in the last two decades, in theory because of warmer and drier summers. Rising ocean temperatures have destroyed coral reefs in the South Pacific. Melting polar ice is causing sea levels to rise, threatening low-lying cities like New Orleans and Venice with floods and erosion. In Antarctica ice shelves thousands of years old have crumbled, causing sections the size of Rhode Island to break off and drift out to sea.

The Candle and the Bell Jar

In England in the 1770s Joseph Priestly, a Unitarian minister and scientist, conducted a series of experiments using a bell jar. He placed a candle under the jar and observed the flame flicker out. A mouse placed under the bell jar suffocated. Both the candle and the mouse consumed something in the air they needed to survive. Priestly also noticed that if he placed a sprig of mint under the bell jar, the candle could be relit. If placed under the bell jar with the mouse, the small plant would keep the animal alive. Whatever vital element in the atmosphere of the jar consumed by the candle and the mouse was restored by the mint. Priestly had discovered a basic natural process. Animals and burning fuels consume oxygen and emit carbon dioxide. Plants absorb carbon dioxide and release oxygen.

Tim Appenzeller uses Priestly's bell jar to explain how human activity is changing the Earth's climate:

> The world is just a bigger jar. Tens of billions of tons of carbon a year pass between land and the atmosphere: given off by living things as they breathe and decay and taken up by green plants, which produce oxygen.... Compared with these vast natural exchanges, the few billion tons of carbon that humans contribute to the atmosphere each year seem paltry. Yet like a finger on a balance, our steady contributions are throwing the natural cycle out of whack. The atmosphere's carbon backup is growing: Its carbon dioxide level has risen by some 30 percent since Priestly's time. It may now be higher than it has been in at least 20 million years.

For 200 years human industry has poured hundreds of billions of tons of carbon into the atmosphere from factories, trains, automobiles, aircraft, power plants, and furnaces. The natural "sinks" that absorb carbon dioxide—oceans, soils, and plants—do not have the capacity to offset this amount of added emissions. In addition, human activity has reduced sinks through deforestation, road construction, and urban sprawl, intensifying the imbalance. The excess carbon dioxide in the atmosphere traps heat like the glass roof of a greenhouse, raising the temperature on Earth. As early as 1896, the Swedish chemist Svante Arrhenius, noting the growth of industrialization and increasing use of fossil fuels, predicted that carbon dioxide emissions would increase, raising the Earth's temperature several degrees.

GLOBAL WARMING FACT SHEET

Principal greenhouse gases	carbon dioxide, methane, nitrous oxide, ozone, chlorofluorocarbons, hydrofluorocarbons, and perfluorinated carbons * 70% of global warming is attributed to carbon dioxide * 33% of U.S. emissions comes from transportation (motor vehicles, trains, and airplanes)

Countries with highest greenhouse gas emissions with share of world total		
United States	19.9%
China	9.9
Japan	5.1
Germany	3.8
United Kingdom	2.4
Indonesia	1.0

Average yearly per capita carbon dioxide emissions		
United States	12,100 lbs
Canada	9,900
Australia	8,800
Russia	7,150
Germany	7,150
United Kingdom	6,050
Japan	4,736
France	4,125
China	500

Percentage of increase in carbon dioxide caused by burning fossil fuels	75%

Continued

Percentage of increase in carbon dioxide caused by changes in land use	25%	
Increase in carbon dioxide concentration in parts per million	1900	299 ppm
	1959	316
	2002	373

Sources: CNN; Environmental Protection Agency; International Council for Local Environmental Initiatives; Victor Miguel Ponce, San Diego State University

Global Warming and Social Justice

Reducing carbon emissions poses not only technical but also economic challenges, especially for undeveloped countries. Environmentalists agree that carbon dioxide emissions must be lowered—but how should reductions be measured: by a per capita formula, by a percentage of a country's gross domestic product, or by current emission levels? Fen Osler Hampson and Judith Reppy argue that solutions to global warming have a direct effect on poverty and social justice:

> If we ask all countries to reduce emissions by the same percentage, we may condemn Third World countries to perpetual poverty because they would have to forgo the use of hydrocarbons in their economic development (and because they cannot afford the substitutes now available). Alternatively, if we adopt a per capita measure for allocating emission reductions, rich countries would bear the brunt of the burden.

Africa contributes relatively little to global warming but will likely suffer the most from the effects of climate change. Increased droughts, floods, and erosion have damaged crop yields and fishing, displacing rural populations who then move to cities that have among the worst air quality in the world. Economic development requires electricity and transportation. Africa's coal power plants and its fleet of older motor vehicles release much more carbon than their counterparts in developed countries.

Sprigs of Mint

As Joseph Priestly discovered 200 years ago, plants absorb carbon dioxide. In the 1970s, China began a program of planting millions of trees to control erosion and flooding. Scientists calculate that the new forests had a secondary effect on climate, absorbing millions of tons of carbon. The Kyoto climate treaty also encourages nations to plant new forests. The realization of the value of forests may put pressure on countries to limit clear-cutting forests, especially South America's rain forests, which absorb much of the world's carbon dioxide.

Even millions of new trees, however, cannot absorb all the carbon dioxide produced by industry and transportation. Consumers, corporations, and governments will have to use less energy and reduce emissions from industrial production. A third of carbon dioxide emissions comes from burning fossil fuels used in transportation, primarily motor vehicles. But getting the owners of the world's 750 million cars and trucks to switch to alternative vehicles may take decades.

Lingering Doubts

Although the majority of world scientists believe global warming is occurring, there are skeptics. Some question if warming is actually taking place, citing measurements of actual cooling in certain locations. Climate change has not been uniform or consistent. In the 1970s, for example, glaciers actually expanded during abnormally cold winters and cool summers. Some scientists argue that pollution can have a cooling effect since particles in the air reflect sunlight away from the Earth. In 2001 *Newsweek* reported the difficulty in measuring and predicting climate change:

> Scientists began reporting a few years ago that aerosols cool the atmosphere, but recently there's been equally convincing evidence that they can have the opposite effect. James Hanson, a climate scientist at NASA's Goddard Space Laboratory in New York, found that soot particles embedded in snow absorb the sun's energy and radiate heat, which may explain why temperatures have risen more at the poles than at the equator. Other scientists have found that soot in the atmosphere can either absorb heat or reflect sunlight, depending on the shape of the particles.

Some researchers agree global warming is occurring but question if it is caused by natural cycles or the sun's intensity rather than human activity.

Because steps to curb global warming will be costly and could cause a loss of jobs and productivity, many economists and business leaders insist that conclusive scientific evidence has to be presented before nations take aggressive action. Pointing to the steady temperature drops recorded at California's Mount Wilson Observatory since 1918 and satellite data showing only minor temperature increases in the atmosphere, Dolly Setton argues that "the Earth's temperature could be, for all we know, waxing and waning independent of human actions or omissions."

Researchers who believe global warming is taking place disagree about its severity, since climate change will have unpredictable effects. As winters shorten, more land will be covered with plant life, which absorbs carbon, offsetting or delaying future warming. Climate change may change ocean currents and cause some parts of Northern Europe to become colder.

The Global Challenge

Concerns about climate change, coupled with the desire to free industrialized economies from dependence on Middle Eastern oil, will continue to spur debate on developing new energy sources and greater conservation. Changing an economy based on fossil fuels will be costly and may threaten the prosperity of nations and individuals, but as evidence mounts pointing to dire economic costs of climate change, difficult decisions will have to be made.

Before reading these entries, consider these questions.

Do people know enough about science to understand global warming? To make sensible decisions about the climate, people have to analyze scientific data and evaluate conflicting interpretations. Do enough citizens have knowledge about scientific principles to make intelligent decisions about environmental issues?

Are politicians willing to address global warming? The effects of global warming are not always identifiable or immediate and require costly remedies. Addressing climate change will likely take billions of dollars and may affect economic growth. Are politicians, who traditionally get elected by promising to cut taxes, expand the economy, and create jobs, able to convince voters to support measures to reduce pollution?

Do most people ignore global warming because they feel they can do nothing about it?   Because the worst scenarios about global warming will not take place until 20 or even 50 years from now and deal with abstract concepts like climate, do people feel helpless? What can be done to encourage people to support environmental policies and change their lifestyles to reduce energy consumption?

Must global warming solutions be linked to immediate economic costs or benefits to work?   If tax policies encouraged use of alternative fuels, energy conservation, and reforestation, would consumers and industry make needed changes? Could, for instance, tax breaks encourage greater use of solar power? Could cities and towns subsidize planting trees on abandoned lots and farmland? Should the government fund research in alternative fuels or give substantial tax incentives for car makers and car buyers to stimulate production of hybrid vehicles?

Is global warming used for political reasons?   As you read about global warming, notice if writers use the issue of climate change for ideological reasons. Do people who criticize capitalism, development, or industry use global warming to attack the free enterprise system? Do some business leaders dismiss evidence of global warming because reducing emissions will be costly?

WRITING ABOUT GLOBAL WARMING

Global warming can stimulate a number of responses that can be useful topics for writing assignments.

Critical Thinking and Prewriting

Global warming could change life on this planet. Climate changes may alter weather patterns, causing greater soil erosion, droughts, floods, and reduced agricultural yield. Developed countries may have to spend billions of dollars to cope with global warming, while poorer nations may endure more pollution, famines, and political instability. Critical thinking can help identify and develop topics.

Getting Started: Exploring Ideas

1. What will it take to assemble enough evidence to convince political and business leaders to take action? If we wait until crop yields begin to fail and rising sea levels threaten major cities, will it be too late to reverse climate change?

2. Will the role of the United States in the 21st century be determined in part by its actions or lack of actions regarding climate change? Because the United States emits the most greenhouse gases, will smaller countries resent the United States if they feel it is not doing enough? Why would a country like Sweden or Denmark make costly investments to clean their industries if their efforts are cancelled out by an American lack of action?

3. Will global conflicts intensify as Third World countries suffer the effects of climate change without having reaped the benefits from the industrialization that caused it?

4. What will actually motivate nations to move away from fossil fuels—concerns about the environment, fears of shortages and rising prices, or political instability and terrorism in the Middle East?

5. Do people really care about the environment? Why are SUVs, large homes, and jet travel so popular? Are consumers willing to change their lifestyles to reduce carbon emissions?

6. Can global warming stimulate economic growth by creating demand for energy efficient products, new production methods, and development of new fuels?

Strategies for Writing about Global Warming

Define key terms.
Before writing about global warming, make sure you clearly understand basic scientific terms and words like *emission* and *sinks* used in discussions of climate change.

Focus on a specific pollution source.
Instead of attempting to comment on pollution in general, concentrate on a particular industry, greenhouse gas, or geographical region. You could write about power plants, methane gas emitted by livestock, or the growing fleet of older automobiles in Africa.

Examine the importance of "sinks" in climate change.
Most writers discuss carbon emissions rather than absorption. Can the loss of rain forests be as important a factor as auto exhaust in causing climate change? Should more countries follow China's example of planting millions of acres of trees?

Determine the level of public awareness and concern.
Do immediate concerns about terrorism, deficits, war, jobs, health care, and Social Security overshadow an issue like global warming that is abstract and hard to assess?

Discuss how individual consumers can make a difference.
Provide realistic options for people who want to do something on the personal level to combat climate change.

Examine the status of international treaties.
The United States did not sign the Kyoto accords. Other developed nations have made agreements to reduce emissions but insist on loopholes to ensure economic growth. Focus on one agreement, or discuss how different nations have responded to international calls for mandatory regulations.

Discuss the importance of grassroots organizations in stimulating change.
The civil rights movement caused government, corporations, and institutions to change hiring policies. The women's movement forced society to make reforms. Will it take a grassroots movement of voters and consumers to convince government and industry to make substantial efforts to reduce climate change?

WRITING IN THE MODES

You may find that selecting a particular mode is an effective way of examining a topic, organizing ideas, and shaping an essay.

Narration
1. Relate a specific event that made you aware of climate change.
2. Write a narrative concerning your awareness of global warming. When did you first become aware of the issue? What evidence do you consider important in shaping your opinion on the matter?
3. Explain the history of a product or industry that causes or alleviates climate change. Why has solar power not replaced fossil fuels? Will concerns about global warming renew support for nuclear power?

Description
1. Describe any personal observations you have made regarding climate change. Have you noticed warmer winters and hotter summers in your region? Have farmers, hunters, or fishermen reported changes in the environment?

2. Describe people's attitudes about global warming. Do your fellow students, neighbors, and coworkers see it as a serious problem?
3. Describe problems the international community has in reaching agreements on reducing emissions.

Definition
1. Select a term used in climate change and provide a full definition supported with details. What is a *sink*? Is the term *global warming* misleading since climate change might actually cause some parts of the Earth to grow colder?
2. Define the U.S. role in climate change. Should it become the leader in promoting new fuels and conservation measures?

Example
1. Select one or more examples that illustrate the level of public concern about climate change. Consider, for example, the popularity of hybrid vehicles and SUVs.
2. Provide one or more examples of consumer behavior that either contributes to or reduces greenhouse gas emissions.

Comparison and Contrast
1. Compare climate change to other hazards that require substantial investment. During the Cold War the public was willing to devote billions to defense spending and construction of fallout shelters. Residents of low-lying regions have voted for bond issues to pay for levees to prevent floods. Can an abstract danger like global warming prompt the same sacrifice? Will politicians and environmentalists have to demonstrate the dangers of climate change to influence public opinion?
2. Compare the arguments of those who believe global warming is occurring to those who insist the evidence is not conclusive. Are their arguments based on logic, research, and reasoning? Does one side seem more credible? Why?
3. Compare two alternative sources to fossil fuels, such as solar cells or hydrogen.

Division and Classification
1. Use division to explain different sources of greenhouse gas emissions.
2. Use division to explain possible remedies to global warming.
3. Classify predictions of climate change from least to most severe.
4. Classify remedies for global warming from the least expensive or most practical to the most expensive or most difficult.

Process

1. Create a set of instructions to guide the average consumer in reducing energy use and greenhouse gas emissions.
2. In a short essay, explain how global warming occurs. You may wish to focus on a particular pollutant or industry.

Cause and Effect

1. Outline the principal causes for climate change.
2. Explain the reasons why the United States did not sign the Kyoto accords.
3. Explain how global warming will affect a particular region of the country, a specific industry, or a certain group of people.
4. Detail the results of environmentalists' efforts to raise awareness of global warming. How effective have they been?

Argument and Persuasion

1. Develop a persuasive essay expressing your views on how the federal government should respond to climate change. Should it fund more research to determine if global warming is taking place, or should it require power plants to reduce emissions? Should gasoline taxes be raised to discourage consumption and tax breaks given for development of alternative fuels?
2. Write an essay that supports or opposes a particular government policy that deals with the environment.
3. Respond to one or more of the readings in this chapter by agreeing or disagreeing with the writers' conclusions.

STUDENT PAPER

Planting a Tree

When my dad was in second grade his teacher gave each child a small sapling to celebrate Arbor Day. He planted the foot-high maple in the backyard. Forty years later it is still there in my grandmother's backyard. Now, of course, it is a huge tree, strong enough to hold a tire swing. During those forty years, of course, my dad has owned maybe eight or nine cars, flown in jet planes a hundred times, built two houses, and, of course, helped ruin the environment every time he dialed up the thermostat, turned on the TV to watch a ball game, and drove me to school in our SUV.

Now it sounds like I am being harsh to my father. But he is just a symbol. We do a million things in our lifetime to heat up the planet we live on by using fossil fuels. Maybe we do a little to offset this by recycling, riding our bikes instead of using the car, and just maybe planting a tree.

The problem with global warming is that it affects all of us, and we feel helpless even though all of us are part of the problem. We can escape some problems. You don't have to worry about Social Security or healthcare costs if you make and invest enough money to pay for your own retirement and insurance. You can send your kids to private schools and buy a house in a gated community to escape the problems of the cities. But you can't make your part of the atmosphere cleaner or cooler. Global warming can flood cities, ruin crop yields, increase poverty, and set back economic development. Our kids' futures may be in jeopardy.

Many of our political leaders talk about the environment but are afraid to really do anything. They are afraid that by supporting a treaty that mandates a reduction in our pollution, it will hurt the economy. People who lose their jobs or watch their stocks take a dive this year are not going to be thinking about saving the planet for future generations. And there is an army of global warming deniers out there to fuel their anger.

But there are things we can do besides worry. Americans produce maybe thirty to fifty times more carbon a year than a person in the Third World. Our energy consumption is heating up the planet. Each of us can help a little every day by consuming less and using fuel more wisely. It sounds simplistic, but the actions of millions of Americans greatly affect the planet we all live on. If we are unwilling to change our lifestyles, we can hardly expect the billions of people in Asia and Latin America who aspire to own cars and bigger houses to be any more responsible.

Industry always responds to consumer demand. If we demand hybrid cars, recycled products, and energy-saving appliances, companies will respond. And maybe we can get school kids, farmers, and homeowners to plant more than one tree in their lifetime. There's some empty land behind our cabin up north. Each time we go up there for a weekend I plan to plant a tree. Maybe it's just a token gesture, like turning out a light here and there. But since we are all part of the problem, we can also all be part of the solution.

Understanding Meaning

1. What is the student's thesis? Can you state it in your own words?
2. Why, according to the student, do people feel helpless about global warming?
3. What solutions does the student suggest people take to deal with climate change?
4. How significant is the title?

Evaluating Strategy

1. How does the student use the example of his or her father to demonstrate the problem of global warming?
2. What evidence does the student use to support the thesis? Is it sufficient?
3. Is the essay well organized? Would you arrange any paragraphs differently?
4. How effective is the conclusion?

Appreciating Language

1. Is the tone and style of the essay suited to a college course? Are there any words or phrases you would delete or replace?
2. Does any essay about climate change have to define what is meant by *global warming* to prevent confusion?
3. Should the student define what he or she means by the phrase *global warming deniers*? Should it be defined, or do you think readers will understand what the student means?

Writing Suggestions

1. Write a brief essay that supports or opposes one or more ideas the student presents in the essay. Do you think Americans have to serve as role models for the rest of the world? Do people feel helpless about climate change?
2. *COLLABORATIVE WRITING.* Discuss this essay with other students and develop a list of three or four things individuals can do to reduce emissions. What habits have to change? What choices should consumers make?

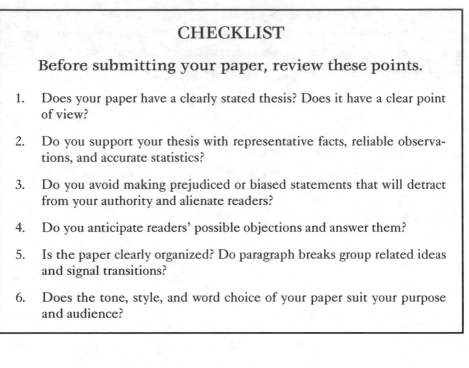

CHECKLIST

Before submitting your paper, review these points.

1. Does your paper have a clearly stated thesis? Does it have a clear point of view?

2. Do you support your thesis with representative facts, reliable observations, and accurate statistics?

3. Do you avoid making prejudiced or biased statements that will detract from your authority and alienate readers?

4. Do you anticipate readers' possible objections and answer them?

5. Is the paper clearly organized? Do paragraph breaks group related ideas and signal transitions?

6. Does the tone, style, and word choice of your paper suit your purpose and audience?

Companion Website

See **academic.cengage.com/english** for information on planning, organizing, writing, and revising essays.

E-Reading: InfoTrac College Edition
http://www.infotrac-college.com

For Further Reading
E–Readings Online

Search for articles by author or title in InfoTrac College Edition after entering your user name and password.

Tim Appenzeller, *The Case of the Missing Carbon*
Planting new forests may soak up billions of tons of carbon and help moderate climate change.

Fred Geterl, *The Devil Is in the Clouds*
Cloud studies reveal the complexities of determining climate change because "soot in the atmosphere can either absorb heat or reflect sunlight, depending on the shape of the particles."

US Today Magazine, *Is Europe about to Freeze?*
Climate change could alter ocean currents so that, while much of the world becomes warmer and drier, Northern Europe could become as cold as Alaska.

Adam Piore, *A Hot Zone for Disease*
Rising temperatures can lead to rising rates of infectious diseases that affect both humans and animals.

David Stipp, *The Pentagon's Weather Nightmare*
Climate changes will strain resources, destabilize governments, and create national security risks.

 If you have access to *Comp21*, click on Themes, then click on Global Warming.

11

DANIEL A. LASHOF

Daniel A. Lashof received his BA from Harvard University in 1980 and completed his PhD at the University of California-Berkeley in 1987. He is a senior scientist and director of the global warming project for the Natural Resources Defense Council. He has taught environmental science as an adjunct professor at the University of Maryland and has published several articles on climate change.

Earth's Last Gasp?

CONTEXT: *Lashof argues in this 1997 article for USA Today that the burning of fossil fuels (principally coal, oil, and natural gas) creates an excess of carbon dioxide, "a gas that traps heat like the glass panes of a greenhouse." This greenhouse effect is resulting in the gradual warming of the Earth's temperature. Over time, this will have a disastrous effect on global ecology and even threaten the continuation of human life itself. Although Lashof contends that scientists agree on these facts, politicians have been cautious about taking the necessary actions to prevent further harm to the environment.*

1   ". . . Entrenched special interests, such as the coal and oil industries, can be expected to use every tool at their disposal to fight sensible climate policies, regardless of the broad-scale benefits for the economy and the environment."

2   When coal, oil, and natural gas are burned to generate electricity, drive automobiles, run factories, and heat homes, the atmosphere is polluted with carbon dioxide, a gas that traps heat like the glass panes of a greenhouse. Scientists have been observing the buildup of carbon dioxide and other so-called greenhouse gases in the atmosphere for decades with increasing inter est and concern. Yet, the problem of human-induced global climate change, or global warming, didn't emerge onto the public agenda until 1988, when a string of unusually hot weather, coupled with the Congressional testimony of NASA scientist Jim Hansen proclaiming "a high degree of confidence" that humans already were changing the Earth's climate, garnered headlines around the country.

3   During the following four years, a string of record temperatures and high-profile reports kept global warming in the headlines. This intense period of publicity and diplomatic activity culminated in the Earth Summit at Rio de Janeiro in June, 1992, where 150 nations signed the Rio Climate Treaty, committing themselves to preventing "dangerous" interference with the climate system.

"Earth's Last Gasp?" by Daniel A. Lashof from USA TODAY, May 1997.

4   A combination of factors conspired to move global warming off the front pages following the Earth Summit. Media coverage and Congressional concern seem to be driven more by how hot it was last summer in the eastern U.S. (less than one percent of the planet's surface) than by long-term global warming trends and considered scientific opinion. When particles injected into the stratosphere by the Mt. Pinatubo volcanic eruption in the Philippines in June, 1991, temporarily cooled global temperatures by about 0.5° C, this apparently took the heat off policymakers as well.

5   Recently, though, the climate issue has made a comeback. By the end of 1994, the Pinatubo plume almost completely had settled, and global temperatures returned to record levels in 1995, just as climate models had predicted at the time of the eruption. Meanwhile, an international panel involving around 2,500 scientists from 130 countries quietly had been preparing an updated assessment of climate change. When the Intergovernmental Panel on Climate Change (IPCC) adopted its final report in the fall of 1995, it made headlines around the world for the conclusion that "the balance of evidence suggests a discernible human influence on global climate." Thus, the consensus of the international scientific community confirms Hansen's testimony, which had helped to launch climate change as a public issue seven years earlier. The panel report also included the following:

6   *Rapid climate change.* The average rate of warming over the next century probably will be greater than any seen in the last 10,000 years if global warming pollution is not controlled. Extrapolating from a wide range of scenarios for future pollutant emissions and the scientists' range of uncertainty about how the climate will respond to a given change in greenhouse gas concentrations, global mean temperature is projected to rise by 1.8 to 6.3° F between 1990 and 2100.

7   *Death and disease.* More than 500 deaths were caused by an intense heat wave that struck the midwestern U.S. in the summer of 1995. Although it is not possible to attribute this (or any other) particular event to global climate change, that is the type of event projected to become more frequent due to global warming. A study of Dallas, Tex., by researchers at the University of Delaware projects that the number of heat-related deaths would rise from an average of 20 per year currently to 620–1,360 per year in the middle of the next century. More outbreaks of infectious diseases, such as malaria and dengue fever, are foreseen as well. A Dutch study estimates that, by the middle of the 21st century, climate change could induce more than 1,000,000 additional malaria deaths per year.

8   *Battered coasts.* Global sea levels are expected to rise by one and a half feet during the next century. This will erode beaches, wipe out many

wetlands, and allow storm surges to penetrate farther inland. In cities such as New Orleans, La., and Galveston, Tex., an increase in sea level will mean shoring up seawalls and dikes in order to prevent flooding. In many areas, protection will not be practical and retreat from the shoreline will be the only viable option.

9   *Floods and droughts.* As a result of global warming, more precipitation would come from intense storms and less from gentle drizzles, increasing the risk of storm damage and flooding. At the same time, warmer temperatures would reduce the amount of water stored in mountain snowpacks and dry soils more rapidly, making drought more likely, especially in the mountain, West, and mid-continental areas.

10   *Insurance crisis.* The string of hurricanes, storms, and floods over the last few years has caused billions of dollars in property damage, depleting insurance industry reserves and threatening major companies with bankruptcy. Before 1980, there had been no individual events that caused insured losses over $1,000,000,000; since then, there have been more than a dozen weather-induced billion-dollar catastrophes. Although burgeoning property values in vulnerable areas are a major factor in the heightened losses, claims have risen as a percentage of insured values. There is great concern in the insurance industry that the frequency of extreme weather events could be increasing. Hurricane Andrew, with $20,000,000,000 in insured losses, combined with other recent catastrophes to put nine U.S. insurance companies out of business. It easily could have been much worse—had Andrew struck just 20 miles to the north, damages would have been $75,000,000,000. The insurance industry has taken note of these risks and is beginning to call for pollution cuts.

11   *Ecological havoc.* The ecological implications of climate change will be more subtle than a hurricane, but may be no less significant. According to the World Wildlife Fund, numerous endangered species currently confined to reserves or small pockets of intact habitat could be pushed over the edge to extinction as suitable climate zones shift out from under protected areas. Migration of alpine species upslope has been reported, and some of these species soon could be pushed off mountaintops. Widespread forest dieback—a condition in woody plants whereby peripheral parts are killed—could occur as projected rates of global warming shift climate zones toward the poles as much as 10 times faster than trees can disperse. In the ocean, measurements of zooplankton abundance off the coast of California show an 80% decline over the last 40 years associated with warmer surface water temperatures and reduced transport of nutrients from deeper layers of the ocean.

12   None of this is to suggest that the exact consequences of unabated climate change can be predicted. Nor would it be responsible to assert that the Chicago heat wave, Texas drought, Alaska forest fires, or any other individual extreme event definitely could be the result of greenhouse gas emissions. Nevertheless, the dimensions of the global warming threat are clear and it would be equally irresponsible to ignore the risk that there is a connection. While we can hope that the climate problem turns out to be less severe than current projections indicate, if we choose not to respond, it is equally likely that things will be worse.

Understanding Meaning

1. The article provides a clear explanation of the greenhouse effect. According to Lashof, what first caused this environmental threat to get wide public attention?
2. Whom does Lashof blame for the fluctuation in American attention paid to global warming over the years?
3. Who comprised the IPCC? What was its major finding?
4. Some authors have predicted dire effects from global warming; others predict no effect at all. Where does this author fall on that spectrum?
5. *CRITICAL THINKING.* Look at paragraph 7, "Death and Disease." Various studies predict that heat-related deaths will rise drastically by the middle of this century. Does Lashof seem to suggest that nothing would be done during that time period to counteract the deadly effect of the increasing heat on human health?

Evaluating Strategy

1. Is the essay easy to follow?
2. What does Lashof do in the second paragraph to help nonexperts understand his subject?
3. Why does Lashof not provide sources for his specific factual information?

Appreciating Language

1. Analyze the play on the words *heat* and *hot* in paragraph 4. Does Lashof make such use of wordplay elsewhere?
2. Based on the language in this article, what would you assume about the audience of *USA Today*? How has this prominent scientist adapted his

language for his audience? Is it "reader friendly"? If you have read other essays on global warming, how does this one compare?

Writing Suggestions

1. Explain in an essay what most surprised you in the summary of the report from the IPCC. Were there effects of global warming that you had never thought of or read about before?

2. *COLLABORATIVE WRITING.* Exchange with a classmate a piece you wrote in response to Writing Suggestion #1 above. Respond in writing to the piece you receive, answering these two questions: Is there a thesis statement that clearly sums up what the essay is about? Is there detailed support for that thesis?

12

S. GEORGE PHILANDER

S. George Philander (1942–) received a BS from the University of Cape Town in 1963 and his PhD from Harvard University in 1970. A professor and researcher in meteorology, Philander has published several books about global warming, including Is the Temperature Rising?: The Uncertain Science of Global Warming *(1998) and* Our Affair with El Niño: How We Transformed an Enchanting Peruvian Current into a Global Climate Hazard *(2004).*

A Global Gamble

CONTEXT: *Philander argues that there is a scientific consensus concerning the reality, causes, and dangers of global warming. The only questions are what to do about it and how soon action should be taken. "It is as if we are in a raft," he writes, "gliding smoothly down a river toward dangerous rapids and a waterfall, and are uncertain of the distance to the waterfall." At the very least, Philander believes, we should try to reduce carbon dioxide by making greater use of public transportation and by driving more fuel-efficient vehicles.*

1   The debate about global warming is a debate about the outcome of a gamble. We are betting that the benefits of our industrial and agricultural activities will outweigh the possible adverse consequences of an unfortunate by-product of our activities, an increase in the atmospheric concentration of greenhouse gases that could lead to global warming and global climate changes. Some experts warn that we are making poor bets, that global warming has started and that disasters are imminent. Others assure us that the chances of global warming are so remote that the outcome of our wager will definitely be in our favor. The impasse is disquieting because the issue is of vital importance to each of us; it concerns the habitability of our planet. How long will it be before the experts resolve their differences? How long before we must take action?

2   Some people falsely believe that global warming is a theory which has yet to be confirmed. They do not realize that scientists are in complete agreement that a continual rise in the atmospheric concentration of greenhouse gases will inevitably lead to global warming. The disagreements are about the timing and amplitude of the expected warming. It is as if we are in a raft, gliding smoothly down a river towards dangerous rapids and a waterfall, and are uncertain of the distance to the waterfall. If we know what

"A Global Gamble" by George Philander from TIKKUN, November 1999. Reprinted by permission of Tikkun.

that distance is then we can tackle the very difficult political matter of deciding on the appropriate time to get out of the water. But all scientific results have uncertainties, which lead to disagreements over plans for action. The result of such disagreements is usually the postponement of the political decision until more accurate scientific results are available—everyone knows that scientists should be capable of precise predictions—or until we are in sight of the waterfall.

3   We are reluctant to accept that some environmental problems are so complex that precise scientific predictions are impossible, that difficult political decisions are necessary in the face of scientific uncertainties. Consider the two main issues being debated: first, whether global warming is evident in the record of globally averaged temperatures to date; and second, whether the results from computer models of the Earth's climate are reliable.

4   We experience massive global warming each year as part of the regular seasonal cycle. From the winter solstice, December 21 onwards, the intensity of sunshine increases steadily. Temperatures, however, fluctuate considerably within seasons. Take, for example, the recent weather in Princeton, New Jersey. This past February, the temperature was so high that the forsythia started to bloom. The intensity of sunlight continued to increase thereafter, but March nonetheless brought some snow and even April was cool. Such fluctuations, known as the natural variability of our climate, can mask the transition from one season to the next, and they can also mask global warming associated with an increase in the greenhouse effect. That is why the unusually high temperatures of the early 1990s do not necessarily imply that global warming is under way. Similarly, should the next few years be unusually cold, it will not follow that the risk of global warming has receded. In the same way that we can not determine the transition from one season to the next by monitoring temperatures on a daily basis, so we can not determine the onset of global warming by monitoring temperatures on an annual basis.

5   To get at the bigger picture and alert us to global warming we have to rely on computer models that simulate the Earth's climate—just as we have to rely on a calendar to mark the change in seasons. The models reproduce many aspects of the climate realistically, but climate and global warming are such complex phenomena that the models fail to capture some features. Most members of the scientific community have sufficient confidence in the current models to accept the forecasts concerning future climate changes. A few critics focus on the models' flaws and cite those as the reasons for rejecting the models' results. These skeptics play a valuable scientific role by forcing a reexamination of assumptions made in the models,

thus contributing to their continual improvement. However, the inevitable attention paid to these critics in the press is unrelated to the merits of their scientific arguments. Furthermore, such critics often neglect to point out that, because of the inevitable flaws, the models are as likely to underestimate as to overestimate the severity of global warming.

6   When we consider how extreme the effects of global warming are likely to be, we ought to pay attention to the geologic record, which contains valuable information about climate changes in the past. That record provides abundant evidence that this planet's climate is sensitive to small perturbations. For example, slight changes in the distribution of sunlight on Earth can cause climate changes as dramatic as recurrent Ice Ages. In spite of this evidence concerning our climate's sensitivity to perturbations, we are proceeding with the creation of a huge disturbance: a doubling of the atmospheric concentration of carbon dioxide, a powerful greenhouse gas.

7   Still, some experts argue that, until the uncertainties in the scientific results are reduced, we should not implement any policies for fear that those policies will put our economy at risk. Implicit in such statements are assumptions in the form of models that predict how the economy will respond to certain policies. The uncertainties in such economic models are far greater than those in climate models. Economics depends on human behavior, and determining whether a certain policy will benefit or harm the economy is even more difficult than determining how greenhouse gases will affect the climate.

8   The sooner we start doing something about global warming the better, because by the time that everyone agrees that global warming has started, it could be too late to do much about it. By starting early we can take a gradual approach, finding out which policies work, which do not.

9   Any policy should be carefully monitored to be sure it satisfies two conditions: (1) it should result in a decrease in the atmospheric concentration of greenhouse gases, and (2) it should not adversely affect the economy. The results can be determined only after the policy has been in effect for a while. If it is successful, it should be continued; if not, we can try something else. We must avoid committing ourselves to grand plans that claim to solve the problem once and forever.

10   We can begin such a sensible plan on an individual level. Since the goal is to reduce the rate at which we inject carbon dioxide into the atmosphere, we should try to use less energy by using public transportation or driving fuel-efficient vehicles.

11   Every day, all of us—businessmen, politicians, military strategists— routinely make decisions on the basis of uncertain information, usually after

we have familiarized ourselves with the available facts. Scientists can provide us with the facts concerning global warming. It is our joint responsibility to make policy decisions on the basis of those facts.

Understanding Meaning

1. According to Philander, how is the debate about global warming like the debate about the outcome of a gamble?
2. Is global warming a certainty? Why is it so difficult to say whether it is or not?
3. What does Philander say about the relationship between global warming and the economy?
4. Does Philander feel that there is one solution that will solve the problem of global warming for all time? Explain.
5. *CRITICAL THINKING.* Philander states that some people "do not realize that scientists are in complete agreement that a continual rise in the atmospheric concentration of greenhouse gases will inevitably lead to global warming" (paragraph 2). Is that the same thing as their being in complete agreement that we are experiencing a continual rise in the concentration of such gases or that the rise is the result of actions by humans? Explain.

Evaluating Strategy

1. Explain how Philander uses the analogy of the river in paragraph 2 to explain global warming. What does it mean to "get out of the water"?
2. Which of his types of evidence is most easily understood by the nonscientist? Which is least easily understood?
3. Where in the piece does Philander make use of point-counterpoint types of argument ("Some people say this . . . but. . . .")? Why is it a good idea in argumentative writing to acknowledge opinions that do not agree with your own? Why not just ignore them?
4. What is Philander trying to accomplish in his last paragraph?

Appreciating Language

1. Explain how Philander uses the language of gambling to explain global warming.
2. What sort of ethos does Philander project through his use of language? Does he, for example, attack his opponents?
3. What is the tone of the piece? What attitude does Philander project about global warming?

Writing Suggestions

1. Philander is trying to convince his audience that it is necessary sometimes to act before there is scientific certainty that a disaster is coming. Can you think of examples where it simply makes sense to act even before scientists are sure? List a few examples.
2. *COLLABORATIVE WRITING.* Share your list with your group and come up with a master group list to share with the class. Does your list provide convincing evidence that Philander's argument is valid?
3. Write an essay in which you explain whether you feel we sometimes have to take action before there is scientific certainty that an event will occur. You may want to use ideas from your group or class discussion as examples.
4. Write an essay in which you argue that there are actions that will not in any way be a major inconvenience that individuals should take now to reduce the chances of the ill effects of global warming.

13

UN CHRONICLE

The UN Chronicle *is an official publication of the United Nations, which is headquartered in New York City.*

Global Warming Challenges African Development

CONTEXT: *The following report, which appeared in the December 2002 issue of the* UN Chronicle, *describes how air and water pollution are having a negative impact on economic development in Africa. Although the continent itself does not produce a significant amount of carbon dioxide, it is particularly vulnerable to the impact of global warming because of its extreme dependence on agriculture and its relative lack of antipollution technology.*

1 Sharp increases in air and water pollution, land degradation, droughts and wildlife losses are facing Africa unless urgent action is taken to deliver environmentally-friendly development, states a report released by the United Nations Environment Programme (UNEP). Growing populations, wars, high levels of national debt, natural disasters and disease have all taken their toll on the people and the rich natural environment of Africa in the past three decades. Over the coming three decades, new and emerging threats, including climate change, the unchecked spread of alien, introduced species, uncontrolled expansion of cities, and pollution from cars and industry, are likely to aggravate levels of poverty, environmental decline and ill-health.

2 Many African countries are attempting to address some of the root causes of environmental degradation through initiatives such as the New Partnership for Africa's Development (NEPAD). But a far bigger effort within and outside the continent is needed to steer Africa on a prosperous, environmentally-sustainable course. Actions include deeper cuts in its debt burden, a boost in overseas aid, the empowering of local communities, enforcing environmental agreements, introducing green and clean technologies, and allowing African countries fair access to international markets for their goods and services. Without this, Africa is unlikely to develop in a way that benefits its people, landscapes and wildlife, and ultimately the world, states the "Africa Environment Outlook," the most comprehensive and

authoritative assessment of the continent's environment ever produced, compiled by UNEP for the African Ministerial Conference on the Environment.

3   *Climate*. Africa's people are heavily dependent on rain-fed agriculture. Records from 1900 show that its annual rainfall has been decreasing since 1968, possibly as a result of global warming due to man-made emissions. There is also evidence that natural disasters, particularly drought in the Sahel, have become more common and severe. Droughts and floods are increasing pressure on fragile lands, leading to the displacement of people and wildlife, adding to increased soil erosion and the silting up of rivers, dams and coastal waters. There can also be severe economic consequences. In Uganda, record rains of 1997 destroyed 40 per cent of its 9,600-kilometre feeder road network. Between 1997 and 1998, a prolonged drought in Seychelles led to the closure of the Seychelles Breweries and the Indian Ocean Tuna Company.

4   Emissions of carbon dioxide, the main global warming gas, have risen eightfold in Africa since 1950 to 223 million metric tons. However, those are still less than the emissions of a developed country such as Germany or Japan. South Africa accounts for 42 per cent of these emissions, while Egypt, Nigeria and Algeria combined account for 35.5 per cent. Despite contributing very little to global greenhouse gas emissions, Africa is extremely vulnerable to the impacts of global warming as a result of its dependency on agriculture and lack of financial resources to offset these impacts.

5   The Gulf of Guinea, Senegal, Egypt, the Gambia, the eastern African coast and the Western Indian Ocean islands are at particular risk from rising sea levels. A one-metre rise would flood large areas of the Nile Delta, and the Egyptian city of Alexandria would be severely affected; a similar rise would swamp 70 per cent of Seychelles.

6   Meanwhile, significant extinction of plants and animals is anticipated over the coming decades, affecting rural livelihoods and tourism, if global warming continues unchecked. Hartebeest, wildebeest and zebra in South Africa's Kruger National Park, Botswana's Okavango Delta and Zimbabwe's Hwange National Park could be severely threatened by a predicted 5-per-cent drop in rainfall. Crop yields in some parts of southern Africa may fall by as much as 20 per cent. It is also predicted that malaria-carrying mosquitoes will spread to Namibia and South Africa over the coming decades, the "Outlook" states. Early warning systems on rainfall and drought have been established across the continent. Mechanisms agreed under the Kyoto Protocol, the legal instrument on climate change, could benefit Africa economically and socially by providing cleaner and greener energy sources and financial incentives to plant

carbon dioxide–absorbing trees. Fifty-two African countries are parties to the United Nations Convention to Combat Desertification and sixteen have now drawn up action plans aimed at improving land productivity, land rehabilitation and sustainable management of water resources.

7   *Air pollution.* Africa has the highest rate of urbanization in the world. That, alongside taxes that encourage dirty fuels, a sharp rise in import of often older model cars and outdated, inefficient industrial plants, is increasing levels of air pollution. The number of motor vehicles in northern Africa has nearly doubled in the past 10 to 15 years. In Uganda, eastern Africa, the number of road vehicles has quadrupled since 1971. Older cars emit up to twenty times more pollution than newer ones.

8   Health costs associated with vehicle emissions were among the factors costing Senegal the equivalent of 5 per cent of its gross domestic product. Tighter controls on the importation of cars from abroad, including a requirement that they not be older than five years, have been proposed there and could be a blueprint for other African countries. Egypt has introduced unleaded petrol, and South Africa has signed the United Nations Motor Vehicle Emissions Agreement.

9   In northern Africa, many cities experience levels of sulphur dioxide that are double the World Health Organization standard, especially where there are refineries and coal power stations. The use of wood as a fuel can increase the health risks for women and children at home. In the United Republic of Tanzania, for example, children under five who die from acute respiratory infections are three times more likely to have been exposed to the burning of such fuels.

10   Many countries have brought in air quality standards and regulations to control pollution, although a lack of resources makes enforcement difficult. Renewable energy schemes, e.g. wind, solar and waste-into-energy projects, are being introduced in some countries, such as Algeria, Morocco and Mauritius.

11   *Coastal and marine environments.* Africa's rich coastal and marine areas are under threat from pollution, over-harvesting of resources, erosion and the potential impacts of climate change, the report states. Indeed, an estimated 38 per cent of coastal ecosystems, such as mangrove swamps and coral reefs, are under threat from developments like ports and the growth of coastal settlements and their sewage discharges. Forty per cent of Nigeria's mangrove swamps, important fish nurseries, buffers against erosion-causing waves and sources of construction materials had already been lost by 1980. The damming of the Nile River at Aswan has reduced the level of nutrients so much that the sardine catch in the Nile Delta has slumped from

22,618 million tonnes in 1968 to under 13,500 million tonnes, and is still declining.

12   Over-harvesting of fish by local and foreign fleets is leading to a decline in stocks. Local supplies across most of Africa are forecast to decline over the next ten years as a result of insufficient resources, such as fishery patrol vessels, to enforce controls. Fish farming is unlikely to help as farmers are expected to focus on high-value species for export to places like Europe. But in Northern Africa, total catches of marine fish has climbed by 30 per cent since 1990 to about 1.1 million tonnes; however, its marine environment is at risk. In the Red Sea, pollution linked with insensitive tourism, dumping of wastes, and leaks and oil spills from ships is seen as a key threat.

13   In eastern Africa, as in many parts of Africa, sediment from coastal erosion clogs up and chokes important marine habitats, such as coral reefs, damaging their value for tourism and fisheries. Coastal erosion rates along some parts of western Africa, such as Togo and Benin, are now as high as 30 metres a year. The problem is aggravated by environmental degradation in the interior, including poor agricultural land use and felling of trees that stabilize soil during heavy rains.

14   In the western Indian Ocean islands, dynamite fishing, walking on coral reefs, recent high-sea temperatures and illegal use of nets are damaging the economically important reefs. In Mauritius, two-thirds of coastal residents discharge wastes into the sea, and in the Comoros there are no wastewater treatment works at all. Laws requiring environmental impact assessments before development have been introduced by many African countries, including Egypt, Gambia, Ghana, Kenya, Mauritius, Nigeria and South Africa.

15   Regional and subregional programmes and action plans, such as the UNEP Regional Seas Programme, are providing the framework for a more holistic management of Africa's coastal zones. Several important agreements and conventions have been created, including the Nairobi, Abidjan and Jeddah Conventions. However, there is a desperate need for more trained staff, finance, equipment, research, monitoring, surveillance and enforcement of regulations.

Understanding Meaning

1. According to this article, what factors have harmed the African continent and its people in the past three decades?
2. What new threats does the UNEP's report state are likely to add to poverty, environmental decline, and ill health over the next three decades?

3. The article makes it clear that what is currently being done to deal with the problem of environmental degradation is not enough. What else is needed?
4. What are some of the agricultural and economic effects that may have been caused by global warming? Why is Africa harmed more by climate change than other places even though it does not produce as much carbon dioxide?
5. Why does the report consider automobiles a danger to Africa's future? What does it say is being done to counter their negative impact?
6. What harm has already been done to Africa's coastal and marine environment?
7. *CRITICAL THINKING.* Why is it in the best interest of other nations to support efforts to keep Africa environmentally sound?

Evaluating Strategy

1. How convincing is the evidence the article presents as support?
2. Do you find the article's predictions about the future convincing? Why or why not?
3. What one sentence best summarizes the main idea?
4. *CRITICAL THINKING.* Is it possible for an author to include so many facts that it is difficult for the audience to know how to analyze and evaluate them? What could be done to help the author when there are a large number of facts to present?

Appreciating Language

1. Is the language in this article primarily objective or subjective? Does the author exhibit much of an emotional response to the devastation and suffering being described?
2. Does the vocabulary in the article make it hard to understand? Are there highly technical terms unfamiliar to those who are not specialists in the field?
3. What audience would you assume the piece is written for?

Writing Suggestions

1. Africa is far removed from the United States. How might the crisis affecting Africa impact our country? Write a short essay explaining how the United States can assist African nations to cope with both climate change and development.
2. Choose one of the three highlighted topics: climate, air pollution, or coastal and marine environments. Write a paragraph in which you explain

what has caused the problems, what the effects have been or might be, and what, if anything, is being done about the problems.

3.   *COLLABORATIVE WRITING.* Discuss this article with a group of other students. How can developed countries that have caused global warming tell poor countries how to manage their resources? Does it suggest a kind of arrogance, or hard-won wisdom? Should the United States, which produces the most emissions, have to take dramatic steps to reduce its use of fossil fuels before it can encourage African countries to save the environment? Write a statement of one or two paragraphs that reflect the views of your group. If your group has different viewpoints, consider drafting opposing statements.

14

FEN OSLER HAMPSON AND
JUDITH REPPY

Fen Osler Hampson and Judith Reppy are coeditors of Earthly Goods: Environmental Change and Social Justice *(1996). Hampson is professor of international affairs at Carlton University in Ottawa, Canada, and Reppy is professor of science and technology studies and acting director of the peace studies program at Cornell University.*

Environmental Change and Social Justice

CONTEXT: *Environmental issues raise special difficulties in the realm of political and ethical theory. To begin with, problems such as global warming do not respect national boundaries. Hence, any effective solution to such problems must be enforced internationally. Second, it is often difficult to balance the interests of nonhuman life (plants, animals, and entire ecosystems) against human interests. Who, for example, is to say that the continued existence of an endangered species is more important than a certain number of jobs in a specific industry? Finally, even if we can somehow determine what ought to be done and why, we must still decide how and by whom the social and economic costs are to be borne.*

1   The specter of global warming haunts Earth's future. In the next century, the world will experience climate changes on a global scale because of the build-up of greenhouse gases in the atmosphere from the burning of fossil fuels and the destruction of forests. Although the exact timing and magnitude of these changes cannot be predicted, they are likely to leave no country untouched. At the same time, deforestation and other human activities are leading to the extinction of many plant and animal species and a corresponding reduction in the planet's genetic stockpile.

2   What principles should guide our response to these undesirable consequences of human activity? A concern for social justice is central to devising an acceptable global response to environmental change and should be placed at the forefront of the international debate. Absent these moral concerns, we run the risk of devising environmental policies that will perpetuate inequity within and among societies and further damage the relationship between human society and the larger ecosystem. In short, ethical issues are not

"add-ons"—they are fundamental to framing the problems to be addressed and finding acceptable solutions. [. . .]

3   We need guidelines for moral reasoning about environmental change . . . but we also need to analyze the distribution of political and economic power and to think critically about the use of other sources of authority, such as scientific knowledge. The central question for social justice is: Who counts? Only after we have answered this question—and taken into account marginalized populations and respect for the ecosystem itself—can we begin to construct responsible solutions to the practical problems posed by climate change.

4   The issues of social justice arising from global environmental change are far more complex than generally conceded in ordinary political discourse. For example, scientists tell us that to avoid serious global warming global greenhouse gas emissions must be reduced by up to 60 percent of their current level.[1] This raises some difficult questions, however: What is a fair allocation of the costs of preventing global warming? Should emissions be divided up on a per capita basis, in proportion to present or future emission levels, according to level of gross domestic product, or by some other formula?

5   The answer to this question is not narrowly economic or technical. If we ask all countries to reduce emissions by the same percentage, we may condemn Third World countries to perpetual poverty because they would have to forgo the use of hydrocarbons in their economic development (and because they cannot afford the substitutes now available). Alternatively, if we adopt a per capita measure for allocating emission reductions, rich countries would bear the brunt of the burden. To achieve an overall emissions reduction of 20 percent, for instance, rich countries would have to reduce their emissions by much more than 20 percent to enable poor countries to increase their energy consumption. Allocating allowable emissions according to a "polluter pays" principle also poses a moral dilemma. Should current generations bear moral responsibility for actions taken by their forebears? Alternatively, should our children and grandchildren be forced to live in a world marred by the consequences of significant global warming?

6   If we knew that the physical and biological consequences of global warming would be small, the problem would not be important. Conversely, if we knew that the costs of disruption would be large, the moral imperative

---

[1] See, for example, M. C. MacCracken, "The Evidence Mounts Up," Nature 376 (1995): 645; and Intergovernmental Panel on Climate Change, *Climate Change 1992: The Supplementary Report to the IPCC Scientific Assessment* (New York: Cambridge University Press, 1992).

to take preventive action now would be great. The degree of uncertainty about the effects of global warming on ecological systems is considerable, however, and that about its possible economic and social consequences (and the ability of institutions to adapt to environmental change) is even greater. Thus, the real question is what to do when confronted with a problem that has so many uncertainties associated with it. But clearly, whatever choices we make, a "business as usual" ethic is unacceptable in dealing with a problem that has potentially global costs. [. . .]

7   Deciding whose preferences should receive attention or whose rights should have priority in devising just solutions to pressing environmental concerns is not easy. What does fairness mean in dividing responsibilities between rich and poor nations regarding problems like global warming, whose causes are uncertain and whose consequences may not be experienced for decades to come? How should societal procedures for addressing such ethical issues be structured?

8   At a deeper level, these ethical issues rest on our understanding of humanity's place in nature. Our judgment of good and bad, just and unjust, needs to be informed by a sense of our connection to the natural world. To the degree that we value the ecosystem for its own sake and not simply as an exploitable resource, we enter a new realm of ethical thinking—one in which justice is defined not only in terms of an equitable distribution of costs and benefits among humans but also in terms of the effects of human activities on the whole ecosystem. This means we can no longer treat the question of justice as separable from that of the environment itself.

Understanding Meaning

1. The purpose of some articles on global warming is to convince readers that it is inevitable or that its existence remains an uncertainty. What do these authors assume?
2. Do they offer evidence that a change in climate will occur? Is that their purpose? Explain.
3. The authors are concerned less with the specific scientific details of global warming than with the ethical issues. What are their broad ethical concerns?
4. *CRITICAL THINKING.* To what extent are human activities responsible for destructive or dangerous environmental change? How do human effects on a region compare, for example, with the effects of a hurricane or volcanic eruption?

Evaluating Strategy

1. How does this article's near absence of examples affect your view of its effectiveness?
2. Is there a reason the authors ask so many questions? Do they answer the questions they ask? Why or why not?
3. Does this essay focus primarily on the past, the present, or the future? What is the effect on the reader of that strategy?

Appreciating Language

1. What are some of the abstract words that keep this essay largely at the level of generalization?
2. Analyze the word choice in the first sentence. Why do the authors use the words *specter* and *haunt* in this context?
3. What tone do the authors use in talking about the environment? In other words, what does their attitude toward the environment seem to be?

Writing Suggestions

1. *COLLABORATIVE WRITING.* Work with your group to make a list of ethical issues related to the environment.
2. Choose an issue from the lists generated by your group and write an essay explaining its ethical dimensions.
3. If you choose to use electricity and other resources extravagantly, is there anything wrong with that if you can afford the bills? Should it become an ethical issue at all, or merely a matter of personal finance? Write a short statement summarizing your views.
4. If the technology is available to produce energy-saving engines, why are there still vehicles on the market that get extremely low mileage? How much should the government regulate what types of vehicles can be sold? Write a short essay that describes the role the government should have in controlling the automotive industry.

15

Fatherhood

From the wild Irish slums of the 19th-century eastern seaboard, to the riot-torn suburbs of Los Angeles, there is one unmistakable lesson in American history: A community that allows a large number of young men to grow up in broken families, dominated by women, never acquiring any stable relationship to male authority, never acquiring any rational expectations about the future—that community asks for and gets chaos.
–Daniel Patrick Moynihan

The decline of fatherhood is one of the most basic, unexpected, and extraordinary social trends of our time. Its dimensions can be captured in a single statistic: in just three decades . . . the percentage of children living apart from their biological fathers more than doubled. . . .
No one predicted this trend, few researchers or government agencies have mentioned it, and it is not widely discussed, even today. But the decline of fatherhood is a major force behind many of the most disturbing problems that plague American society: crime and delinquency; premature sexuality and out-of-wedlock births to teenagers; deteriorating educational achievement; depression, substance abuse, and alienation among adolescents; and the growing number of women and children in poverty.
–David Popenoe

Fathers are not expendable, disposable, unnecessary, or replaceable. They are vital to the future of their children.
–Patricia Fry

. . . the push for traditional nuclear
families remains strong, even if it means
bringing abusive dads back where
they can do more harm.
–Judith Davidoff

SEPARATE AND UNEQUAL

On July 29, 1967, President Lyndon Johnson appointed Illinois governor Otto Kerner to head the National Advisory Commission on Civil Disorders to investigate the causes of urban riots that had erupted across the United States. After seven months, the commission released the Kerner Report, which compiled evidence of a profound racial divide in education, employment, income, health care, and housing. The Kerner Report warned that the United States was "moving toward two societies, one black, one white—separate and unequal." For decades, social scientists, politicians, educators, and civil rights leaders invoked the phrase "separate and unequal" to advocate affirmative action, school desegregation, welfare reform, and stronger antidiscrimination laws in order to overcome a social divide that threatened to create a permanent underclass of American citizens.

Two Societies

Thirty years later, David Blankenhorn published *Fatherless America*, which predicted the United States was rapidly moving toward two societies, separate and unequal, based not on differences in race but in fatherhood:

> After the year 2000 . . . the United States will be a nation divided into two groups, separate and unequal. The two groups will work in the same economy, speak a common language, and remember the same national history. But they will live fundamentally divergent lives. One group will receive basic benefits— psychological, social, economic, educational, and moral—that are denied to the other group.
>
> The primary fault line dividing the two groups will not be race, religion, class, education, or gender. It will be patrimony. One group will consist of those adults who grew up with the daily presence and provision of fathers. The other group will consist of those who did not. By the early years of the next century, these two groups will be roughly the same size.

Throughout the second half of the twentieth century, divorce rates increased steadily, as did out-of-wedlock births, so that by the 1990s half of American children lived in homes without fathers. Fatherless children, Blankenhorn argued, are more likely to use drugs, drop out of school, engage in crime, and have difficulties leading meaningful adult lives. The problems caused by fatherlessness cut across lines of race, religion, and class. But unlike the riots of the 1960s, the crisis of fatherlessness had gone largely unnoticed.

A year later David Popenoe published "A World Without Fathers" in the *Wilson Quarterly*, which echoed Blankenhorn's findings, noting both the scope of fatherlessness and the collective unwillingness to recognize its ramifications. The consensus among social scientists, Popenoe stated, was that the "discord and conflict in the home prior to a divorce are more detrimental than a father's absence" and that "divorce is best for parents and children alike." Popenoe, like Blankenhorn, saw fatherlessness as a root cause of several social problems, especially delinquency:

> Having a father at home is no guarantee that a youngster won't commit a crime, but it appears to be an excellent form of prevention. Sixty percent of America's rapists, 72 percent of its adolescent murderers, and 70 percent of its long-term prison inmates come from fatherless homes. Fathers are important to their sons as role models. They are important for maintaining authority and discipline. And they are important in helping their sons to develop both self-control and feelings of empathy toward others.

Popenoe challenged the prevailing attitude that children do not necessarily require a biological father but strong, caring adults in their lives. His research indicated that children raised in homes without fathers are at greater risk of child abuse by both single mothers and their sexual partners. A Health and Human Services report concluded that single mothers were twice as likely as men to abuse their children. Another study showed that girls were thirty-three times more likely to be sexually abused in households with a stepfather or live-in boyfriend.

A growing number of social commentators began to share the view that problems of child poverty, youth violence, sexual assault, and domestic violence stem from what Blankenhorn called the "flight of males from their children's lives."

Where Are the Fathers?

In 2002, three small boys were found locked in a filthy basement in Newark. Deprived of food and water, they had been brutally abused by their mother and her male companions. One boy died. His twin and a younger brother, both malnourished and dehydrated, were hospitalized. The public, newspaper editorials, and politicians condemned New Jersey's Division of Youth and Family Services, which had failed to investigate allegations of child abuse. The governor pledged to reform state services. In examining the story, Jane Eisner, a Philadelphia reporter, observed something missing in the public outcry. Although people were quick to blame the mother and her accomplices and the state agency charged with supervising the family, no one appeared to hold the fathers accountable. Like 70 percent of the children born in Newark, two brothers did not have a father's name on their birth certificates. The father of the third brother was located living with another woman in another state. Although he had not seen his son in three years, he threatened to sue the state of New Jersey for failing to protect his child.

The Politics of Fatherhood

Concerns about fatherlessness began to influence public policy in the 1990s. Seeking to break the cycle of poverty and welfare dependency, the federal government scrapped its sixty-year-old AFDC program, replacing it with welfare-to-work that included time limits and work requirements. Single mothers on welfare were now expected to work to receive benefits. Welfare reform advocates also proposed confronting the problem of "deadbeat dads," or fathers who failed to pay child support. They estimated that over thirty billion dollars in child support payments had gone uncollected.

A number of states instituted fatherhood initiatives designed to help men who don't live with their children find jobs so they can pay child support. Some delinquent fathers were given the option of participating in programs or going to jail. Like requiring mothers to work, fatherhood programs would, advocates claimed, improve the lives of children, reduce state welfare budgets, and impress on men the legal consequences of paternity.

Critics of these fatherhood programs questioned the validity of research on fatherlessness, maintaining that children could benefit from adult role models other than biological fathers. Some families, they insisted, were better off without the presence of an alcoholic or abusive father. Other critics believed that the idea of a "fatherhood crisis" rested on assumptions that men failed to support their families out of irresponsibility, overlooking the fact that many fathers of children on welfare were low-income themselves. A report by the Urban Institute showed that the majority of fathers who had jobs were earning an average of seven dollars an hour. A third would qualify for food stamps after paying child support. Fatherhood programs appeared to blame social problems like crime and delinquency on moral failings rather than poverty and low wages. "Like workfare," Judith Davidoff argued, "the crackdown on 'deadbeat dads' does not deal with the underlying issue of poverty. In fact, it may exacerbate the problem." In some states, men labeled "deadbeat dads" have been barred from contact with their children, weakening, rather than strengthening, family bonds.

The emphasis on fatherhood has troubled women's organizations that support efforts to reduce the number of delinquent fathers but question the underlying motives of the fatherhood movement. Many fatherhood programs that have received state funding are faith-based operations that stress traditional family values. Feminists have argued that the goal of these organizations is to make men not only take greater responsibility for their children but also assume leadership roles in families, reinforcing traditional gender stereotypes that justify male supremacy and undermine women's independence.

Looking to the future, David Popenoe believes that fatherhood, though essential to family unity and social stability, has to be reconciled with changes in society and gender identity:

> The father's role must also be redefined in a way that neglects neither historical models nor the unique attributes of modern societies, the new roles for women, and the special qualities that men bring to child rearing.

Before reading these entries, consider these questions:

What is a father?   How do you define a *father*? Is he a man who impregnates a woman, a man who provides financial support, or a live-in parent? DNA testing has been used to identify paternity and require men to pay support for a child conceived in a single sexual encounter. On the other hand, husbands who have used DNA tests during divorce proceedings to prove that an unfaithful wife had borne another man's child have been ordered to pay child support, because judges argued that biology alone does not constitute fatherhood.

What social forces have changed the roles of fathers?   Which forces have had the greatest impact on changes in fatherhood—divorce, the sexual revolution, welfare and welfare reform, poverty, or an increasingly mobile society?

How have male attitudes about assuming responsibility for their children changed? Do men seem less concerned about taking responsibility for the children they father than in the past? Are there fewer social pressures to marry when a relationship results in pregnancy?

What role does popular culture play in changing attitudes toward fatherhood?   Do sitcoms that depict fathers as hapless losers, dramas that highlight domestic violence and divorce, and soap operas that romanticize extramarital affairs weaken the public's image of fatherhood? How many television shows and movies have you seen that present strong, caring fathers?

Has government support of single-parent families had the effect of making fathers feel less responsible for their children's well-being? Welfare-to-work programs direct single mothers to find job training or employment. More corporations offer flexible schedules and day care services to accommodate working mothers. As a result, do some men feel they do not need to support their children?

WRITING ABOUT FATHERHOOD

The subject of fatherhood can trigger a number of responses that can be useful topics for writing assignments.

Critical Thinking and Prewriting

What is your image of a father? What is the reality of fathers in your own family? What do children need from fathers? What do women expect from the fathers of their children? Is fatherlessness a real crisis? Is a two-parent family an ideal? Can a noncustodial divorced father be as effective in raising his children as a live-in father can be?

Getting Started: Exploring Ideas

1. Has the women's movement changed our view of fatherhood? Because the struggle for women's rights has often been seen as a liberation from

paternalism, has it led society to question the importance of fatherhood? Does even the term *fatherhood* suggest traditional or conservative values?

2. Has legalized abortion led some men to take less responsibility for birth control or children they conceive? Because women have a choice to abort an unwanted child, can the argument be made that if they continue the pregnancy, the child is their responsibility alone?

3. In traditional families, mothers stayed at home and fathers worked outside the home. Now that women work outside the home, participate in civic affairs, and serve in the military, can mothers provide the same advice, insight, and guidance as fathers? Are women today better equipped to parent children on their own?

4. Does a child need a connection to a biological father or simply to a male figure? Can a stepfather or uncle fill the role of a missing father?

5. Does the absence of a father lead children to question or resent their mothers? If they dislike their mother's discipline or authority, do they assume she drove away their fathers? If they were conceived in a casual sexual encounter, do they lose respect for their mothers when they reach adolescence, or are they at higher risk for repeating the pattern?

6. Does society have a double standard regarding parents? When the children of a single mother are discovered to be neglected or abused, should the absent father be held responsible as well?

7. Can fatherlessness be reduced by holding men accountable? How should teenagers who father children be treated?

Strategies for Writing about Fatherhood

Define *fatherhood*.
Establish a clear definition of what you consider *fatherhood*. What makes a man a father? What responsibilities do fathers have?

Use personal experiences or those of friends as support.
Review your own experiences with your father and comment on what he taught you. If you never knew your father, did you feel you were missing anything?

Examine the way popular culture depicts men and fatherhood.
Do movies and television programs emphasize fatherhood? Are Hollywood's male figures—cowboys, detectives, warriors, athletes, spies, and action heroes—usually bachelors without family ties? What does that imply about masculinity?

Compare the impact fathers or fatherlessness has on boys and girls.
Do boys and girls respond differently to the presence or absence of a father in their lives? Do boys need an adult male role model? Do girls who grow up fatherless assume that they, too, will become single mothers?

Consider the role women play in fatherhood.
Do more women today feel able to raise children on their own? Do women enter relationships with less of an expectation that the men in their lives will make a long-term commitment to them or their children?

Poll attitudes about fatherhood.
Poll coworkers, fellow students, and friends to get a sense of how people view fatherhood. Develop a set of questions asking if a man who gets a woman pregnant should be expected to marry her, how much of a man's income should be paid in child support, whether welfare programs should encourage marriage, or if the entertainment industry has diminished the status of fatherhood. To get a more accurate assessment of people's attitudes, avoid asking for yes or no answers. Instead, create clearly worded, unbiased statements, and ask people if they strongly disagree, disagree somewhat, have no opinion, agree somewhat, or strongly agree. You may wish to analyze the responses by gender, age, or marital status.

Examine the politics of fatherhood.
Do some people use concern about fatherhood to punish men, blaming them for being sexually promiscuous and failing to support the children they produce? Do others use concerns about fatherlessness to promote male supremacy? How do various feminist and women's organizations view fatherhood? Does blaming fathers ignore the economic causes for father-lessness and the failure to pay child support? Do liberals and conservatives have different policies regarding fatherhood?

WRITING IN THE MODES

Narration
1. Write about an event that influenced your concept of fatherhood. You might relate an incident with your own father or the father of a friend.
2. Use a personal experience or observation to relate how a single mother raised children or resolved a problem that traditionally called for action or advice from a father.

Description

1. Describe the qualities of a good father. Which of these are specifically related to being male? Which can be provided by a single mother or other adult in a child's life?
2. Describe the status of fatherhood among your peers in high school. How many of the students you knew lived with both parents, saw a divorced father on a limited basis, or had no contact at all with a father? Could you detect differences in their academic performance, maturity, self-esteem, or relationships with others?

Definition

1. Define what you consider the most important qualities of a father or father figure.
2. Define a *deadbeat dad*. Are unemployed men "deadbeats" if they fail to pay child support? Is a wealthy celebrity a "deadbeat dad" if he pays the mother of a child he fathered a hundred thousand dollars a year but refuses to visit or otherwise acknowledge his son or daughter?

Example

1. Use one or more examples of fathers who fit your definition of a good father, "deadbeat dad," or stepfather. Your examples may be personal, historical, or hypothetical.
2. Use one or more examples of successful families headed by a single mother. How did she overcome the problems of fatherlessness?

Comparison and Contrast

1. Compare male and female attitudes about fatherhood and child rearing.
2. Compare the parenting skills needed by live-in fathers and those who live apart from their children.

Division and Classification

1. Use division to explain different styles of fatherhood.
2. Explain different methods that single mothers can use to raise children without fathers.
3. Classify from best to worst the ways society and government can cope with fatherlessness.
4. Classify fathers from those who are the primary caregivers of children to those who have no involvement with their children.

Process

1. Describe step by step how state governments should address fathers who fail to pay child support.
2. Write a set of directions for fathers who wish to remain active in their children's lives following a divorce.

Cause and Effect
1.   Examine the effect of the various fatherhood movements. Do they help
     children's lives? Do some seek to reestablish male dominance in families?
2.   In your opinion, what is the major cause of fatherlessness? Support your
     argument with statistics and quotations from experts as well as your expe-
     riences and observations.

Argument and Persuasion
1.   Select one of the articles in this chapter, and write an essay that agrees or
     disagrees with one of its main points.
2.   Write an essay stating your opinion about government policies that currently
     stress marriage and punish "deadbeat dads." Do these policies recognize
     the importance of families and seek to strengthen them? Do they seek to
     shift attention away from the problems of poverty and unemployment by
     blaming personal conduct?
3.   Write an essay that addresses the problems caused by changes in family
     structure. Should government policies recognize the realities of father-
     lessness by providing more day care and financial support to low-income
     mothers, or should they try to reunite families by stressing marriage and
     encouraging men to live with their children?

STUDENT PAPER

Defining Fatherhood Down

What does it mean to be a father?

Hollywood gave us Judge Hardy coaching a pugnacious and
perpetually confused Mickey Rooney through the pangs of high school
and early romance. Later on, Ward Cleaver dispensed wisdom so
Wally and the Beav wouldn't be corrupted by the delinquent
machinations of Eddie Haskell. Ozzie, a middle-aged teenager in a
varsity sweater, could be expected to show up at the malt shop to
bond with Ricky and Dave. Bill Cosby portrayed a doctor who
managed to balance work and family so he was always available to
mold both sons and daughters with grace and humor. A father was a
man who lived with his wife and took care of his kids.

As the divorce rate began to increase in the 1960s and 1970s,
more and more fathers moved out. They began the generation of
"non-custodial" parents—fathers who saw their children every other

weekend and two weeks during the summer. Some of these fathers abandoned their children, others provided only intermittent attention and support, and some did the best job they could. But even the best of these men were part-time parents.

In the last twenty years the number of out-of-wedlock births has increased. A lot of males become fathers before they finish high school. It means little to them. Decades ago a boy who got a girl pregnant was pressured by family, friends, and clergymen to "do the right thing" and marry her. Many of these marriages failed, no doubt. But at least boys learned from the plight of others to connect fatherhood with marriage, with responsibility, with making a committed relationship with the mother.

Today there is no such pressure. There are plenty of role models of professional athletes and rock stars who father children without a thought of having any kind of a relationship with their children or the mothers except maybe a monthly check.

Over the summer I worked in a warehouse with two guys my age. We were all eighteen and would go for pizza after work. Sometimes we hit the beach and flirted with girls who worked on the boardwalk. Over the summer both of them casually mentioned they had kids. Ted had a son "somewhere back in Ohio," and Dujuan had a daughter who lived in San Jose with an ex-girlfriend he'd dated for less than a month. Neither one mentioned sending any of their pay to their children or said anything about visiting their kids. Plenty of places on the boardwalk sold toys, but neither of my friends ever looked at them. Neither of them ever referred to themselves as "fathers."

I enjoyed their company. Ted played guitar, spent Saturdays restoring a '68 Mustang with his cousin, and talked about studying engineering. Dujuan loved surfing, spent hours walking the beach and feeding the seagulls, and said he might like to go into real estate with his aunt someday. They were fun to hang out with and dependable employees. But the fact that they could so casually mention they were fathers began to bother me. Having a kid to them was like serving a hitch in the army or playing football in high school. It was just part of a mess they had with a girl in high school that had nothing to do with their futures.

This attitude is now common. We have defined the norm of fatherhood down from being a full-time parent to being a part-time parent to being a non-parent. Boys who grow up without fathers come to accept the idea that men have children and vanish. If they get a girl pregnant and give her some cash now and then and send the kid a toy for Christmas, they see themselves as fulfilling their obligations, doing more than their fathers ever did for them.

Some people blame this on legalized abortion. Some males take the attitude that if a girl gets pregnant she can have an abortion. If she decides to keep the child, she is opting to take on the responsibility. Some blame feminists for depicting males as oppressors and celebrating the ability of women to handle careers and raise kids on their own. It really does not matter who we blame. We all suffer by the dwindling role of fathers in society. It makes men even more likely to separate sex from any kind of commitment or relationship. It burdens women with the hard task of raising children alone. It places an emotional void in the lives of children, especially boys.

Thinking about this paper made me realize something else about Ted and Dujuan. In the three months I knew them, they never mentioned anything about their fathers.

Understanding Meaning

1. What is the student's thesis? Can you restate it in your own words?
2. What impact did the students' coworkers have on his understanding of how concepts of fatherhood have changed? How do you respond to his descriptions of the two eighteen-year-olds?
3. Does the student view media images of fathers as idealistic or unrealistic?
4. How important is the student's final comment?
5. *CRITICAL THINKING*. The student sees fatherhood as being "defined down." Do you believe that in contrast motherhood has been "defined up"? Are women expected to fulfill traditionally fatherly tasks, such as helping children with homework, being active in their sports, teaching them to drive, and introducing them to the workplace?

Evaluating Strategy

1. How effective is the opening paragraph? Do media images of fathers provide enough substance for a serious essay about fathers? Would the student, who appears to take fatherhood seriously, have been more effective if he discussed his relationship with his own father?

2. How does the student use comparison and contrast to develop the essay?
3. The student concludes the essay with an afterthought. Should this idea have been incorporated into the essay? Does making a statement like that draw attention to it, or simply make the essay seem like an undeveloped rough draft?

Appreciating Language

1. What words and phrases does the student use to describe his friends? Do you detect any bias?
2. How does the student define *father*?
3. What does the student mean by the phrase *defining fatherhood down*?

Writing Suggestions

1. Write an essay that agrees or disagrees with the student's statement that fatherhood is being "defined down."
2. *COLLABORATIVE WRITING.* Discuss this essay in a small group. Do you think young men, even teenage boys, should be encouraged to marry girls they impregnate? Why or why not? Record comments by the group and draft a one- or two-paragraph statement. If students have conflicting opinions, organize their responses using comparison and contrast or classification.

CHECKLIST

Before submitting your paper, review these points.

1. Does your paper have a clearly stated thesis? Does it have a clear point of view?

2. Do you support your thesis with representative facts, reliable observations, and accurate statistics?

3. Do you avoid making biased statements that will detract from your authority and alienate readers?

4. Do you anticipate readers' possible objections and answer them?

5. Is the paper clearly organized? Do paragraph breaks group related ideas and signal transitions?

6. Does the tone, style, and word choice of your paper suit your purpose and audience?

Companion Website

See **academic.cengage.com/english** for information on planning, organizing, writing, and revising essays.

E-Reading: InfoTrac College Edition
http://www.infotrac-college.com

For Further Reading
E–Readings Online

Search for articles by author or title in InfoTrac College Edition after entering your user name and password.

Patricia Fry, *Fathers in America—Yesterday, Today, and Tomorrow*
Industrialization and divorce have changed the pattern of fatherhood, but the role of fathers in their children's lives remains vital.

Garrison Keillor, *Daughter Dearest: The Little One Adores You Now, Dad, but Brace Yourself for the Next Chapter*
Contemplating his young daughter at play, Keillor realizes that it is "an act of optimism to bring a child into the world."

David Popenoe, *A World without Fathers*
To move toward "a more just and humane society," Popenoe argues, "we must reverse the tide that is pulling fathers apart from their families."

Martin Davis, *Turning the Hearts of Deadbeat Dads*
Charles Ballard, a former convict, heads a faith-based organization that seeks to reunite fathers with their abandoned children.

Judith Davidoff, *The Fatherhood Industry*
Driven by questionable evidence about the importance of fathers, current welfare policies push to maintain two-parent families "even if it means bringing abusive dads back to where they can do more harm."

Stephen Baskerville, *Is There Really a Fatherhood Crisis?*
The focus on fatherhood has led both liberals and conservatives to view restoring fathers to families as a remedy of social ills, creating policies that criminalize "deadbeat dads" but overlooking the fact that the most common reason men fail to pay child support is low pay and unemployment.

 If you have access to *Comp21*, click on Themes, then click on Fatherhood.

16

DAVID BLANKENHORN

David Blankenhorn (1955–) was born in Baumholder, Germany. He received a BA from Harvard University in 1977 and an MA from Warwick University in 1978. He is the founder and president of the Institute for American Values, a nonpartisan organization dedicated to research and education on family issues, and has published articles about the status of the American family in the New York Times, USA Today, Newsday, *and the* Los Angeles Times. *His book* Fatherless America: Confronting Our Most Urgent Social Problem *was published in 1995.*

Fatherless America

CONTEXT: *Before reading Blankenhorn's essay, consider your own attitudes toward fatherhood. In your experience, how important are fathers? Do children without fathers in their lives face greater risks than other children?*

1   The United States is becoming an increasingly fatherless society. A generation ago, an American child could reasonably expect to grow up with his or her father. Today, an American child can reasonably expect not to. Fatherlessness is now approaching a rough parity with fatherhood as a defining feature of American childhood.

2   This astonishing fact is reflected in many statistics, but here are the two most important. Tonight, about 40 percent of American children will go to sleep in homes in which their fathers do not live. Before they reach the age of eighteen, more than half of our nation's children are likely to spend at least a significant portion of their childhoods living apart from their fathers. Never before in this country have so many children been voluntarily abandoned by their fathers. Never before have so many children grown up without knowing what it means to have a father.

3   Fatherlessness is the most harmful demographic trend of this generation. It is the leading cause of declining child well-being in our society. It is also the engine driving our most urgent social problems, from crime to adolescent pregnancy to child sexual abuse to domestic violence against women. Yet, despite its scale and social consequences, fatherlessness is a problem that is frequently ignored or denied. Especially within our elite discourse, it remains largely a problem with no name.

4   If this trend continues, fatherlessness is likely to change the shape of our society. Consider this prediction. After the year 2000, as people born after 1970 emerge as a large proportion of our working-age adult population, the United States will be a nation divided into two groups, separate and unequal. The two groups will work in the same economy, speak a common language, and remember the same national history. But they will live fundamentally divergent lives. One group will receive basic benefits—psychological, social, economic, educational, and moral—that are denied to the other group.

5   The primary fault line dividing the two groups will not be race, religion, class, education, or gender. It will be patrimony. One group will consist of those adults who grew up with the daily presence and provision of fathers. The other group will consist of those who did not. By the early years of the next century, these two groups will be roughly the same size.

6   Surely a crisis of this scale merits a response. At a minimum, it requires a serious debate. Why is fatherhood declining? What can be done about it? Can our society find ways to invigorate effective fatherhood as a norm of male behavior? Yet, to date, the public discussion on this topic has been remarkably weak and defeatist. There is a prevailing belief that not much can—or even should—be done to reverse the trend.

7   When the crime rate jumps, politicians promise to do something about it. When the unemployment rate rises, task forces assemble to address the problem. As random shootings increase, public health officials worry about the preponderance of guns. But when it comes to the mass defection of men from family life, not much happens.

8   There is debate, even alarm, about specific social problems. Divorce. Out-of-wedlock childbearing. Children growing up in poverty. Youth violence. Unsafe neighborhoods. Domestic violence. The weakening of parental authority. But in these discussions, we seldom acknowledge the underlying phenomenon that binds together these otherwise disparate issues: the flight of males from their children's lives. In fact, we seem to go out of our way to avoid the connection between our most pressing social problems and the trend of fatherlessness.

9   We avoid this connection because, as a society, we are changing our minds about the role of men in family life. As a cultural idea, our inherited understanding of fatherhood is under siege. Men in general, and fathers in particular, are increasingly viewed as superfluous to family life: either expendable or as part of the problem. Masculinity itself, understood as anything other than a rejection of what it has traditionally meant to be male, is typically treated with suspicion and even hostility in our cultural discourse.

Consequently, our society is now manifestly unable to sustain, or even find reason to believe in, fatherhood as a distinctive domain of male activity.

10   The core question is simple: Does every child need a father? Increasingly, our society's answer is "no," or at least "not necessarily." Few idea shifts in this century are as consequential as this one. At stake is nothing less than what it means to be a man, who our children will be, and what kind of society we will become.

11   In addition to losing fathers, we are losing something larger: our idea of fatherhood. Unlike earlier periods of father absence in our history, we now face more than a physical loss affecting some homes. We face a cultural loss affecting every home. For this reason, the most important absence our society must confront is not the absence of fathers but the absence of our belief in fathers.

12   In a larger sense, this is a *cultural* criticism because fatherhood, much more than motherhood, is a cultural invention. Its meaning for the individual man is shaped less by biology than by a cultural script or story—a societal code that guides, and at times pressures, him into certain ways of acting and of understanding himself as a man.

13   Like motherhood, fatherhood is made up of both a biological and a social dimension. Yet in societies across the world, mothers are far more successful than fathers at fusing these two dimensions into a coherent parental identity. Is the nursing mother playing a biological or a social role? Is she feeding or bonding? We can hardly separate the two, so seamlessly are they woven together.

14   But fatherhood is a different matter. A father makes his sole biological contribution at the moment of conception—nine months before the infant enters the world. Because social paternity is only indirectly linked to bio logical paternity, the connection between the two cannot be assumed. The phrase "to father a child" usually refers only to the act of insemination, not to the responsibility for raising a child. What fathers contribute to their offspring after conception is largely a matter of cultural devising.

15   Moreover, despite their other virtues, men are not ideally suited to responsible fatherhood. Although they certainly have the capacity for fathering, men are inclined to sexual promiscuity and paternal waywardness. Anthropologically, human fatherhood constitutes what might be termed a necessary problem. It is necessary because, in all societies, child well-being and societal success hinge largely upon a high level of paternal investment: the willingness of adult males to devote energy and resources to the care of their offspring. It is a problem because adult males are frequently—indeed, increasingly—unwilling or unable to make that vital investment.

16   Because fatherhood is universally problematic in human societies, cultures must mobilize to devise and enforce the father role for men, coaxing and guiding them into fatherhood through a set of legal and extralegal pressures that require them to maintain a close alliance with their children's mother and to invest in their children. Because men do not volunteer for fatherhood as much as they are conscripted into it by the surrounding culture, only an authoritative cultural story of fatherhood can fuse biological and social paternity into a coherent male identity.

17   For exactly this reason, Margaret Mead and others have observed that the supreme test of any civilization is whether it can socialize men by teaching them to be fathers—creating a culture in which men acknowledge their paternity and willingly nurture their offspring. Indeed, if we can equate the essence of the antisocial male with violence, we can equate the essence of the socialized male with being a good father. Thus, at the center of our most important cultural imperative, we find the fatherhood script: the story that describes what it ought to mean for a man to have a child.

18   Just as the fatherhood script advances the social goal of harnessing male behavior to collective needs, it also reflects an individual purpose. That purpose, in a word, is happiness. Anthropologists have long understood that the genius of an effective culture is its capacity to reconcile individual happiness with collective well-being. By situating individual lives within a social narrative, culture endows private behavior with larger meaning. By linking the self to moral purposes larger than the self, an effective culture tells us a story in which individual fulfillment transcends selfishness, and personal satisfaction transcends narcissism.

19   In this respect, our cultural script is not simply a set of imported moralisms, exterior to the individual and designed only to compel self-sacrifice. It is also a pathway—indeed, our only pathway—to what the founders of the American experiment called the pursuit of happiness.

20   The stakes on this issue could hardly be higher. Our society's conspicuous failure to sustain or create compelling norms of fatherhood amounts to a social and personal disaster. Today's story of fatherhood features one-dimensional characters, an unbelievable plot, and an unhappy ending. It reveals in our society both a failure of collective memory and a collapse of moral imagination. It undermines families, neglects children, causes or aggravates our worst social problems, and makes individual adult happiness—both male and female—harder to achieve.

21   Ultimately, this failure reflects nothing less than a culture gone awry: a culture increasingly unable to establish the boundaries, erect the signposts, and fashion the stories that can harmonize individual happiness

with collective well-being. In short, it reflects a culture that increasingly fails to "enculture" individual men and women, mothers and fathers.

22   In personal terms, the end result of this process, the final residue from what David Gutmann calls the "deculturation" of paternity, is narcissism: a me-first egotism that is hostile not only to any societal goal or larger moral purpose but also to any save the most puerile understanding of personal happiness. In social terms, the primary results of decultured paternity are a decline in children's well-being and a rise in male violence, especially against women. In a larger sense, the most significant result is our society's steady fragmentation into atomized individuals, isolated from one another and estranged from the aspirations and realities of common membership in a family, a community, a nation, bound by mutual commitment and shared memory.

Understanding Meaning

1. What is Blankenhorn's thesis? Can you restate it in your own words?
2. Why, in Blankenhorn's view, is fatherhood declining in the United States?
3. What does Blankenhorn see as the main social implications for millions of children who grow up without fathers?
4. How does fatherhood change men and their behavior? Do you agree with Blankenhorn's statement that "men are inclined to sexual promiscuity and paternal waywardness"?
5. *CRITICAL THINKING.* Could the role of fatherhood be analyzed by studying children separated from their fathers for extensive periods of time, as during World War II? If the children of veterans who spent years overseas grew up with more or fewer problems than children of the same era whose fathers stayed at home, would that support or contradict Blankenhorn's thesis? Why or why not?

Evaluating Strategy

1. What support does Blankenhorn present to support his thesis?
2. How can a writer stress the importance of fatherhood without implying that single mothers cannot effectively raise children? How does Blankenhorn address single mothers?
3. *BLENDING THE MODES.* Where does Blankenhorn use comparison and cause and effect to construct his argument?

Appreciating Language

1. How do you define *fatherlessness*? At what point does a noncustodial father become an *absentee* father?
2. What does Blankenhorn mean by the term *decultured paternity*?
3. How would you characterize the tone and style of this essay? Would it alienate any readers? Why or why not?

Writing Suggestions

1. Write a short essay about how the presence or absence of a father affected your life or the life of a friend or relative. Do these experiences support or contradict Blankenhorn's argument?
2. Write your own definition of fatherhood.
3. *COLLABORATIVE WRITING.* Discuss Blankenhorn's essay in a small group. Do you agree or disagree with his views of fatherhood? Draft a short response that addresses one or more of Blankenhorn's points. If students disagree, consider drafting opposing viewpoints.

17

JANE EISNER

Jane Eisner began her career with the Philadelphia Inquirer *as a reporter in the mid-1980s. She has subsequently held the positions of City Hall bureau chief, foreign correspondent, and editorial page editor. She began writing a regular column for the* Inquirer *in 2000.*

Where Are the Fathers?

CONTEXT: *In this 2003 article, Eisner writes about a scandal in the New Jersey Division of Youth and Family Services, which had lost track of three children who were abused by their mother and her male companions. While most of the media blamed the abusers and the state agency responsible for supervising the children's care, Eisner asks, "Where are the fathers?"*

1   Columns like this I don't want to write. I don't want to think about the lives of children like the three boys imprisoned in a Newark, N.J., basement, left to scrounge for air, food and water, left to die in filthy isolation by family members entrusted with their care.

2   Suffering at the hands of one's parent must be the worst torture for a child. Allowing a child to die of neglect is the worst indictment of society. No one can be excused.

3   New Jersey's Division of Youth and Family Services is reeling from a body blow of bad publicity, as well it should. Caseworkers closed the book on Melinda Williams' three boys last year without investigating allegations of the abuse that eventually led to the horrific death of 7-year-old Faheem Williams. His twin and a younger half-brother, trapped in that basement for who knows how long, are recovering from starvation and dehydration in a New Jersey hospital. The psychological damage caused by such cruelty surely won't be known for some time.

4   How state officials charged with protecting the lives of endangered children could lose track of Williams' three boys—and, it turns out, 277 others—is mind-boggling. Gov. James E. McGreevey's pledge to address his government's many failures in these cases can't be realized a moment too soon.

5   But to blame this tragedy only on overworked caseworkers and bureaucratic ineptitude misses the fundamental problem. And that's why, despite my revulsion, I had to write this column.

6   Because somebody's got to ask: Where are the fathers?

7   How is it that Melinda Williams, by all accounts a mentally ill substance abuser in and out of jail, could be left to parent these children by herself?

8   How have we created a culture that makes it so easy for men to father children they take no share in raising? Why are women who can't provide for children having them anyway?

9   Why are so many assuming that only the state has failed here?

10   As David Blankenhorn, a founder of the National Fatherhood Initiative, wrote in an Internet posting on Sunday: "In all of the coverage of this terrible story—chronic abuse and neglect of the children, the multiple problems of the children's mother, a 'friend' of the mother who sexually abuses one of the children, another boyfriend who discovers one of the children dead, and the complete, sickening failure of the relevant state agencies over a number of years to protect these children—hardly a word has been mentioned about the role of fatherlessness.

11   "It's as if the fact is an elephant in the room that we hardly need to mention."

12   And yet mention it we must. At this point in the investigation, there's no way to prove that fatherlessness led to this death and endangerment.

13   But the national data clearly point to this fact: Child abuse is more likely when the father is absent. One example of many: In a longitudinal study of 644 families, children living with a single parent were two times more likely to be physically abused than children living with both parents.

14   Fathers, especially married fathers, provide protection, stability and good role models. Sure, there are abusive fathers—but children are far more likely to be hurt by an unrelated male living with their mother than by the person who provided half their genetic makeup.

15   Yet the state responsible for protecting the Williams' boys doesn't even know who the father is for the dead Faheem and his brother Raheem. As with nearly 70 percent of the children born in Newark, the twins' father was not named on their birth certificates.

16   Why is that space allowed to remain blank?

17   The father of 4-year-old Tyrone Tyson Hill has surfaced in Vermont, unemployed, living with a woman nearly half his age, and threatening to sue the state of New Jersey for failing to protect his child. Tyrone Hill never married Melinda Williams and hasn't seen his son in three years.

18   Hill has a lot of nerve blaming the state when he himself has shown so little interest in his son.

19   Where are the fathers? True, there's no guarantee that the presence of their real father or fathers would have saved those poor boys. Some fathers are better left absent.

20   But we will never do right by our children if we don't even ask the question.

Understanding Meaning

1. According to Eisner, in what sense is New Jersey's Division of Youth and Family Services responsible for the tragedy? In what sense is the mother?
2. What evidence does Eisner provide to suggest that the absence of fathers is no longer considered unusual?
3. One of the fathers received some media attention. How valid does Eisner feel his charge is against the Division of Youth and Family Services?
4. *CRITICAL THINKING.* Is this the kind of tragedy that can be prevented solely by government action, or does it require a change in cultural values and social behavior?

Evaluating Strategy

1. Eisner starts by saying this is not the kind of article she wanted to write. What effect does this have on readers?
2. Eisner discusses the responsibility of the mother and the state agency while questioning the fathers' role. Would her article be more effective if she simply blamed the missing fathers? Why or why not?
3. How does Eisner use quotes by David Blankenhorn to support her observations?
4. Eisner poses rhetorical questions such as, "Where are the fathers?" and "Why are women who can't provide for children having them anyway?" Do you find those questions effective? Why or why not?

Appreciating Language

1. How would you describe the tone and style of the article? Is it suited for a newspaper? Why or why not?
2. What words or phrases suggest to you that this is a personal opinion piece rather than a news story?

Writing Suggestions

1. Write an essay explaining why fathers are held less responsible for their children than are mothers. Had children being raised by their fathers been abused, would more people hold absentee mothers accountable?
2. Write an essay about a similar tragedy that you have heard about. Do these scandals, which often command a lot of brief media attention, ever lead to substantial reforms?
3. *COLLABORATIVE WRITING.* In a small group, discuss this article and the commonly repeated saying, "It takes a village to raise a child." In your view, what does this statement mean? Does it suggest that parenting requires community support? Or does it sound like an excuse for parents who expect government agencies to provide for their children? Develop a statement reflecting the views of the group. If students have different points of view, create opposing statements.

18

BRAD STETSON

Brad Stetson (1963–) was born in California and completed his PhD at the University of Southern California. Since 1993 he has served as director of the David Institute, a social research organization in Tustin, California. His books include Challenging the Civil Rights Establishment *(1993),* Pluralism and Particularity in Religious Belief *(1994), and* Human Dignity and Contemporary Liberalism *(1998).*

Fatherlessness Is Born of the "Choice" Culture

CONTEXT: *In this article, published in Human Life Review in 1996, Stetson argues that the pro-choice position on abortion has undermined the importance of fatherhood. Women can legally terminate a pregnancy; the father of the child has no say whether his child is even born. If the child is born, men who don't wish to be fathers may resent the woman for not having had an abortion.*

1   It is now generally acknowledged that there is a crisis of fatherlessness in this country. Whether deadbeat dads, absent dads, or men who have never accepted paternity for their children, many American men have unilaterally decided that their acts of sexual intercourse do not in any way obligate them morally to the offspring that may result.

2   There has of late been a spate of detailed sociological studies document-ing the personal and social destructiveness of this trend. Few, though, have broached the obvious but politically incorrect possibility that the withering of American fatherhood is significantly related to the social ethos erected the past three decades to support the culture of "choice." If we consider the psy-chological effects on men of our culture saturation with the principle of "choice," it's not hard to understand why men are becoming "pro-choice" about fatherhood.

3   The ethical imperative of "my body, my choice" has meant that women can decide whether or not to give birth once they become pregnant. But this principle—that personal, bodily acts (like sexual intercourse) only require one's moral commitments if one wants them to—has not stayed confined to the narrow preserve of abortion rights. Its prominent repetition through the years has caused it to become installed in the public consciousness as an

"Fatherlessness Is Born of the 'Choice' Culture" by Brad Stetson, first appeared in THE HUMAN LIFE REVIEW, Spring 1996. Reprinted by permission of Brad Stetson.

all-purpose—but very low grade—ethical touchstone for determining what one's moral duties are. So, women choose whether to become mothers, or more accurately, whether to give birth to the children they conceive. They choose whether to become mothers in the social sense. But men do not choose to become fathers. In fact, women—through electing either to obtain or not to obtain an abortion—choose for men whether men will become fathers and whether men will be legally obligated to pay, over the course of nearly two decades, a substantial amount of money in child support.

4   The one-sidedness of this decision power is patent. Men's objections to it—which are rare because of the de rigueur assent to "choice" and the intimidating feminist scorn which awaits any objection—are met with the retort, "Don't have intercourse if you're not ready to accept the duties of a father." But the same logic, "Don't have intercourse if you're not ready to accept the duties of a mother," does not apply to women. They are allowed to choose whether or not to be a parent. Since men know that the women they've impregnated could just as easily obtain an abortion as give birth to the child, they reason that if she forgoes the abortion—and they do not wish to assume the varied and sustained obligations of fatherhood—then the women should have sole responsibility for the child. Why should I be responsible, a man thinks, when she could have had an abortion? If she wants to choose to be a mother, that's fine for her, but she should not be able to influence my social and economic future by choosing for me whether I am to be a father. My body, my choice. So fatherhood, and the obligations attendant to it, are optional. Men have learned from the culture of "choice" that children's interests can permissibly be subjugated to their own personal desires, should the two conflict. Thus, our cultural enthroning of "choice" communicates to fathers, as it does to mothers, that children need not really be our top priority.

5   But beyond fomenting fatherlessness, "choice" has also worked to disengage men from their offspring, since their offspring don't socially become their offspring unless the women want them to. Hence, some men are psychologically ill-prepared to participate in raising their children once they are born because they suspended the development of a parental sense within themselves, obviously not wanting to experience the pain of having emotionally embraced their child only to lose him or her to abortion. Indeed, the sustained uncertainty that the possibility of abortion presents can even subtly turn a man's offspring into a menace in his own eyes as its potential demise becomes the source of considerable anxiety. This uncertainty, plus the powerful cultural ascendancy of "a woman's right to choose," demotivates men from seeking to encourage the formation within themselves of emotional and

psychological ties to their children. A man is understandably hesitant to embark down the existentially profound road of fatherhood if he is unsure—and utterly powerless to establish—that his child will actually be born.

6   I'm reminded of the neo-Marxist/eco-feminist man I knew in graduate school who informed me with genuine elation and humble joy that his fiancee (who was also manning the barricades) was pregnant. When I saw him a week later, his ashen face and seething rage underlined the anguish he said he felt at learning that his fiancee had just aborted their unborn child. He, like so many men today, learned that the law of "choice" is a great wall separating him from his nascent children. Of course, had he not wished to be a father, this wall would have become a passageway to the abandonment of his most profound purpose as a man. How tragic it is that what is thought to be the empowerment of women—"choice"—at the same time discourages men from entering into fatherhood, and so contributes to the profound social corrosion wrought by fatherlessness.

Understanding Meaning

1. What is Stetson's thesis? Can you state it in your own words?
2. In paragraphs 4 and 5, Stetson suggests links between legalized abortion and the "crisis of fatherlessness." What are the connections that he sees?
3. Does Stetson see a double standard in legalized abortion?
4. *CRITICAL THINKING*. Do you agree with Stetson's premise that men don't choose to be fathers but, because of legalized abortion, that women choose for them? If abortion were illegal, would some men simply invent other excuses for not taking responsibility for their children?

Evaluating Strategy

1. What is Stetson's strategy in organizing the opening two paragraphs?
2. Where does Stetson shift his focus from the parents to the effect of this debate on the children?
3. *BLENDING THE MODES*. How effective is the final narrative? Does a human interest story add impact to Stetson's argument? Why or why not?

Appreciating Language

1. How would you characterize the general tone and style of Stetson's article? What audience does it seem suited to?

2.   What meaning does Stetson give to the word *choice*? Does Stetson imply something negative about this word when applied to abortion? If a woman chooses to have an abortion, is she making other "choices" as well?
3.   Explain Stetson's references to walls and passageways in the last paragraph.

Writing Suggestions

1.   Write an essay that agrees or disagrees with Stetson's position that fatherlessness is born from the "'choice' culture." Could it be that abortion causes men to avoid responsibility, or are some abortions caused by men who refuse to take responsibility?
2.   *COLLABORATIVE WRITING.* In a small group, discuss whether you think that the partner of a pregnant woman should have the right to prevent her from having an abortion. Are there any circumstances that should supercede the woman's right to determine if she wants to terminate a pregnancy? Draft a statement reflecting the view of the group. If students have different opinions, use comparison or classification to organize responses.

19

SUSAN J. MILLER

Susan J. Miller grew up in a poor neighborhood in New York City, where her father worked as a window dresser. Fascinated with jazz, he met many notable musicians, some of whom became family friends. He was also a heroin addict. Miller wrote about her relationship with her father in the memoir Never Let Me Down *(1998).*

My Father's Other Life

CONTEXT: *In this excerpt from* Never Let Me Down, *Miller recounts memories of her father, who "by his own admission . . . came to parenthood ignorant of love and acquainted only with hate."*

1 One night, at an hour that was normally my bedtime, I got all dressed up, and my mother and father and I drove into New York, down to the Half Note, the jazz club on Hudson Street. I was thirteen, maybe fourteen, just beginning teenagehood, and had never gone anywhere that was "nightlife." I had heard jazz all my life, on records or the radio, my father beating out time on the kitchen table, the steering wheel, letting out a breathy "Yeah" when the music soared and flew. When they were cooking, when they really swung, it transported him; he was gone, inside the music. I couldn't go on this trip with him, but I thought I could understand it. It seemed to me that anyone could, hearing that music. Bird, Diz, Pres, Sweets, Al, Zoot. It was my father's music, though he himself never played a note.

2 I knew the players, for about the only friends my parents had were musicians and their wives. They fascinated me: their pants with black satin stripes, their battered horn cases. When I was a little kid, I'd lie in bed listening to them talk their hip talk in the next room. I knew I was the only kid in our white neighborhood to be overhearing words like "man" and "cat" and "groove," and jokes that were this irreverent and black. I knew they were cool and I loved it.

3 At the Half Note that night, the three of us walked through the door, and the owner appeared, all excited to see my father, and in the middle of this smoky nightlife room, he kissed my hand. This was real life, the center of something. We sat down. In front of us, on a little stage, were Jimmy Rushing, a powerful singer, and two sax players, Al Cohn and Zoot Sims,

"My Father's Other Life" by Susan J. Miller. Appeared originally in GRANTA, Number 47 and later in HARPER'S, August 1994.

whom I'd known all my life. And there was a whole roomful of people slap-ping the tables, beating out time, breathing "Yeah" at the great moments, shaking their heads, sometimes snapping their fingers, now and then burst-ing out with "Play it, man," or "Sing it." When the break came, Zoot sat down with us and ate a plate of lasagna or something and didn't say much except for these dry asides that were so funny I couldn't bear it. And there was my dad: these men were his friends, his buddies. They liked the things about my father that I could like—how funny he was, uncorny, how unsen-timental, how unafraid to be different from everyone else in the world.

4   As a child, I didn't know that my father and many of the musicians who sat with their wives in our living room, eating nuts and raisins out of cut-glass candy dishes, were junkies. It wasn't until I was twenty-one, a college senior, that my father told me he had been a heroin addict, casually slipping it into some otherwise unremarkable conversation. The next day, my mother filled in the story. My father had begun shooting up in 1946, when my mother was pregnant with my brother, who is nineteen months older than me. He stopped when I was around thirteen and my brother was fifteen.

5   I never suspected a thing. Neither did my brother. We never saw any drug paraphernalia. There was a mysterious purplish spot in the crook of my father's elbow, which he said had something to do with the army. His vague explanation was unsatisfactory, but even in my wildest imaginings I never came near the truth. In the Fifties, in the white, middle- and working-class communities where we lived, no one discussed drugs, which were synony-mous with the utmost degradation and depravity. My parents succeeded in hiding my father's addiction from us, but as a result, we could never make sense of the strained atmosphere, our lack of money, our many moves. The addiction was the thread that tied everything together, but we didn't know that such a thread existed, and so decisions seemed insanely arbitrary, my mother's emotions frighteningly hysterical. She was terribly depressed, sometimes desperate. I regularly found her sitting, eyes unfocused, collapsed amid the disorder of a household she was too overwhelmed to manage.

6   My father was from Brighton Beach, Brooklyn, and earned his living dressing windows in women's clothing stores in and around New York City. Being a window dresser was a touch creative, but most importantly it meant he didn't have to fit in; all he had to do was get the job done. He was a man of socially unacceptable habits. He was fat, he picked his teeth, he burped, he farted, he bit his nails until he had no nails and then he chewed his fingers, eating himself up. He was a high-octane monologuer, a self-taught high-school dropout who constantly read, thought, and talked politics and culture, gobbling up ideas, stuffing himself as fast as he could—with everything.

7   By the time I was in college my father was taking amphetamines, LSD, mescaline, peyote, whatever he could get. I would receive long letters from him, written when he was coming down from an acid or mescaline trip. Often he tripped alone in the living room of our New Jersey apartment, awake all night, listening to records, writing and thinking while my mother slept. I read pages of his blocky, slanted printing, about how the world is a boat and we are all sinking. Usually I threw them away without finishing them, scanning his stoned raps in front of the big, green metal trash can in the college mail room, picturing him in the living room with the sun rising, wired up, hunched over the paper, filling up the page, wanting me to know all the exciting things he had discovered. Part of me wanted to hear them and love him—and indeed did love him for taking the acid, for taking the chance. But another part shut down, unable to care.

8   He would not have been a good father even if he hadn't been an addict. By his own admission, he came to parenthood ignorant of love and acquainted only with hate.

9   My mother told me about my grandmother Esther, the wicked witch of Brighton Beach. According to my mother, my grandmother despised men. She lavished attention on her daughter, my father's only sibling. She dealt in machinations, lies, and deceptions, feeding the fires of hate between father and son, sister and brother. When my father did well in school, his mother scorned him. She tore up a citation he'd won—and then spat on it. She never kissed him, except on the day he went off to boot camp. His mother and my mother, then his young wife, were standing on the platform, saying good-bye. Seeing the other mothers tearfully embracing their sons, his mother was shamed into touching hers: she pecked his cheek.

10   My father only once told me a story about himself and his mother. I was in college at the time. The two of us were driving on the highway on a beautiful, clear, cold winter day. My father was behind the wheel. Fourteen years earlier, in 1956, his father had died in the hospital while my father and his mother, Esther, were visiting him. My father took Esther home to Brooklyn, where she asked him for a favor. There were some terms in her will she wanted to review. Would he read it out loud to her? (Even in Yiddish my grandmother was illiterate.) My father was tired and upset and somewhat puzzled that his mother wished to go over her will on the night of her husband's death, but he agreed. The will turned out to be simple: Esther's house and savings were to go to Sarah, her daughter. Then he heard himself, the fly in the web, reading: And to my son, Sidney, I leave nothing, because he is no good.

11   My father stared at the road ahead.

12   Why, I cried, would she have you read that to her? What did you do?

13   My father's voice was tired and bitter. She wanted to see what I would do, he said; she wanted to watch my reaction. Ma, I said, I gotta go home now. I'm tired and it's late. I didn't want to show her how bad I felt, I didn't want to give her the satisfaction. I didn't care about the money. Let my fucking sister have the money. But why did she have to write that sentence? Why did she have me read it?

14   My father started to cry. He had never cried in front of me. His hands loosened their grip on the wheel. The car began to drift into the opposite lane, across the white unbroken line.

15   Look out, I yelled. He grabbed the wheel and turned us toward safety. Look out, I yelled, and he did. Look out, I yelled, for what else could I have said?

16   In August 1988, my father was diagnosed with liver cancer, the result of chronic hepatitis, a disease associated with heroin addiction. The doctors predicted he would live for five months. He tried chemotherapy, ate a macrobiotic diet, enrolled in an experimental holistic treatment program. When I visited him in November, it was clear that things would not turn around.

17   My mother, who had stuck by him through everything, was still by his side. He was eager to share his latest revelation. A social worker in the treatment program had asked him what he would miss most when he died. He said: I told her that, yeah, sure, I'll miss my wife and my kids, but what I'll miss most is the music. The music is the only thing that's never let me down.

18   That the revelation would hurt us—my mother especially—never occurred to him. He never kept his thoughts to himself, even if it was cruel to express them. Neither my mother nor I said a word. The statement was the truth of him—not only what he said but also the fact that he would say it to us, and say it without guilt, without apology, without regret.

Understanding Meaning

1.   What first impression does Miller give readers about her father? How does he appear at the night club?
2.   How important was music in her father's life?
3.   How did Miller learn that her father was a heroin addict? What did learning about his addiction explain about the life her family led as she was growing up?
4.   What story did Miller's father tell her about his mother? Why do you think she related it to her readers?

5. Why does Miller believe her father would not have been a good parent even if he were not addicted to drugs?
6. *CRITICAL THINKING.* How did Miller react to her father's final revelation? How, in her view, did it sum up his life?

Evaluating Strategy

1. How does the opening scene establish Miller's father's obsession with jazz?
2. Miller includes stories about her father's childhood. What impact do they have in shaping his character and her opinion of him?
3. Miller tells readers that she usually discarded her father's letters before finishing them. Why does she include this fact?

Appreciating Language

1. What words and phrases does Miller use to describe her father? What do they reveal about her feelings toward him?
2. Miller uses words like *junkie, addict,* and *shooting up* to describe her father's addiction rather than *chemically dependent* or *victim.* What does this demonstrate about her attitude toward his drug use?

Writing Suggestions

1. Write about a single incident that revealed something important about one of your parents. How did their childhood make them the adult they became? Can you see a connection between their childhood and yours?
2. *COLLABORATIVE WRITING.* Discuss this essay with several students. What does it indicate about how a parent's addiction affects children? Record comments and draft a short paragraph summarizing student responses.

20

JOYCE CAROL OATES

Joyce Carol Oates (1938–) was born in Lockport, New York and received a BA from Syracuse University in 1960 and an MA from the University of Wisconsin in 1961. She is currently a professor at Princeton University. Oates is one of the most prolific writers in the United States, having published over fifty novels and short story collections, including Expensive People *(1967),* Wonderland *(1971),* Childworld *(1976),* Black Water *(1992) and* I'll Take You There *(2002).*

My Father, My Fiction

CONTEXT: *In this memoir, Oates discusses how her father influenced her life and her writing, recounting not only how he overcame poverty to support his family but also learned to fly a plane and play the piano.*

1   A November day, 1988, and I am sitting in my study in our house in Princeton, N.J., as dusk comes on, listening to my father playing the piano in another wing of the house. Flawlessly, he's moving through the *presto agitato* of Schubert's "Erl King," striking the nightmarish sequence of notes firmly but rapidly. There's a shimmering quality to the sound, and I'm thinking how the mystery of music is a paradigm of the mystery of personality: most of us "know" family members exclusive of statistical information, sometimes in defiance of it, in the way that we "know" familiar pieces of music without having the slightest comprehension of their thematic or structural composition. We recognize them after a few notes, that's all. The powerful appeal of music is inexplicable, forever mysterious, like the subterranean urgings of the soul, and so too the powerful appeal of certain personalities in our lives. We are rarely aware of the gravitational forces we embody for others, but we are keenly aware of the gravitational forces certain others embody for us. To say *my father, my mother* is for me to name but in no way to approach one of the central mysteries of my life.

2   How did the malnourished circumstances of my parents' early lives allow them to grow, to blossom, into the exemplary people they have become?—is there no true relationship between personal history and personality?—*is* character, bred in the bone, absolute fate? And what are facts, that we should imagine they have the power to explain the world to us? On the contrary, it is facts that must be explained.

HERE ARE FACTS:

3   My father's father, Joseph Carlton Oates, left his wife and son when my father, an only child, was 2 or 3 years old. Abandoned them, to be specific: they were very poor. Twenty-eight years later, Joseph Carlton reappeared to seek out his son, Frederic . . . arrived at a country tavern in Millersport, N.Y., one night about 1944, not to ask forgiveness of his son for his selfishness as a father, not even to be reconciled with him, or to explain himself. He had come, he announced, to beat up his son.

4   It seems that Joseph Carlton had heard rumors that Frederic had long held a grudge against him, wanted to fight him. Thus Joseph Carlton sought him out to bring the fight to him, so to speak. He'd been living not far away (which might mean, in those days, as close as 20 miles), totally out of contact with his ex-wife, my grandmother. But when the drunk, belligerent Joseph Carlton confronted Frederic, the one in his early 50's, the other a young married man of 30, it turned out that the younger man had in fact no special grudge against the older and did not care to fight him, though challenged.

5   "I couldn't bring myself to hit someone that old," my father says.

6   Joseph Carlton Oates and Frederic Oates are said to have resembled each other dramatically. But though I resemble both my father and my long-deceased grandfather, I never saw this grandfather's face, not even in a photograph. Joseph Carlton—of whom my grandmother would say, simply, whenever she was asked of him, "he was no good"—became one of those phantom beings, no doubt common in family histories, who did not exist.

7   Suppose Joseph Carlton Oates had not abandoned his wife and young son in 1916. Suppose he'd continued to live with them. It is likely that, given his penchant for drinking and for aggressive behavior, he might very well have been abusive to his wife and to my father, would surely have "beaten him up" many times—so infecting him, if we are to believe current theories of the etiology of domestic violence, with a similar predisposition toward violence. So abandoning his young family was perhaps the most generous gesture Joseph Carlton Oates could have made, though that was not the man's intention.

8   My father was born in 1914 in Lockport, N.Y., a small city approximately 20 miles north of Buffalo and 15 miles south of Lake Ontario, in Niagara County; its distinctive feature is the steep rock-sided Erie Canal that runs literally through its core. Because they were poor, my grandmother (the former Blanche Morgenstern) frequently moved with her son from one low-priced rental to another. But after he grew up and married my mother (the former Carolina Bush), my father came to live in my mother's

adoptive parents' farmhouse in Millersport; and has remained on that land ever since.

9   My mother has lived on this attractive rural property at the northern edge of Erie County, by the Tonawanda Creek, in the old farmhouse (built 1888) and then in the newer, smaller house in which my parents now live (wood frame, white aluminum siding and brown trim, built in 1961 largely by way of my father's efforts), virtually all her life. This is over 70 years: Carolina Bush was born Nov. 8, 1916, the youngest of a large farm family, given to her aunt as an infant when her father suddenly died and left the family impoverished. (Is "die" too circumspect a term? In fact, my maternal grandfather was killed in a tavern brawl.)

10   In time, Frederic and Carolina had three children: I was born in 1938 (on Bloomsday: June 16), my brother Fred ("Robin" for most of our childhood, thus to me Robin forever) was born in 1943, my sister Lynn (who has been institutionalized as autistic since early adolescence) in 1956.

11   The generation that preceded my parents' is vanished, of course. First-generation Americans, many of them; or immigrants from Hungary, Ireland, Germany. My father's mother, Blanche, whom I knew as Grandmother Woodside (she remarried after her early, dissolved marriage), the person whom of all the world I loved most after my parents, died in 1970, after a lengthy illness.

12   When his mother died, my father was deeply grieved, heartbroken; but according to my mother, he kept most of his sorrow to himself.

13   For both my parents their marriage is surely the supreme fact of their lives: they married young, seem never to have loved or been seriously involved with others. Yet when their 50th wedding anniversary rolled around in 1987 they chose to keep the date a secret and refused to celebrate.

14   (My father's wish, surely. He is the sort of man not inclined to "make too much of things." Which is no doubt what the composing of this memoir constitutes. When I was growing up, Daddy was conspicuously and often humorously bored with his birthday, and even more with Christmas; and from him, for better or worse, I seem to have inherited similar prejudices. Thoreau's remark "Beware of all enterprises that require new clothes" speaks eloquently to this temperament.)

15   Facts: the property my parents shared with my Bush grandparents was a small farm with a fruit orchard, some cherry trees, some apple trees, primarily Bartlett pears. My memories are of chickens, Rhode Island reds, pecking obsessively in the dirt . . . for what is a chicken's life but pecking obsessively in the dirt? Chicken duties (feeding, egg gathering) seem to have fallen within a specifically female province, meaning my Grandmother Bush, my mother and

me; fruit picking, especially the harvest of hundreds of bushel baskets of pears, fell to my father, when he wasn't working in Lockport at Harrison Radiator. For a brief fevered interim, there were pigs—pigs that broke free of their enclosure in the barn, and were desperately chased by my father, pigs that sickened and died, or, worse yet, were successfully slaughtered but somehow imperfectly cured, so that their meat, the point after all of so much comical despair, was inedible.

16   Now, decades later, nothing remains of the Bush farm. My childhood seems to have been plowed under, gone subterranean as a dream. The old house was razed years ago when the country highway was widened, the old barn was dismantled, all of the fruit orchard has vanished. *My* lilac tree near the back door, *my* apple tree at the side of the house, *my* cherry tree . . . long uprooted, gone. Fields once planted in corn, in potatoes, in tomatoes, in strawberries . . . gone. Looking at the property now from the road you would not be able to guess that it was once a farm.

17   I wonder if it is evident how painfully difficult it has been for me to write this seemingly informal memoir?—as if I were staring into a dazzling beacon of light, yet expected to see?

18   All children mythologize their parents, who are to them after all giants of the landscape of early childhood; and I'm sure I am no exception.

19   And yet . . . and *yet:* it does seem to me that my parents are remarkable people, both in themselves, as persons, "personalities," and as representatives and survivors of a world so harsh and so repetitive in its harshness as to defy evocation, except perhaps in art.

20   Though frequently denounced and often misunderstood by a somewhat genteel literary community, my writing is, at least in part, an attempt to memorialize my parents' vanished world; my parents' lives. Sometimes directly, sometimes in metaphor. Of my recent novels, "Marya: A Life" (1986) is an admixture of my mother's early life, some of my own adolescent and young-adult experience, and fiction: reading "Marya," as they read everything I write, they immediately recognized the setting—for of course it *is* the setting—that rural edge of Erie County just across the Tonawanda Creek from Niagara County, not far from the Erie Canal (and the Canal Road where Marya lives). The quintessential world of my fiction. "You Must Remember This" (1987) is set in a mythical western New York city that is an amalgam of Buffalo and Lockport, but primarily Lockport: the novel could not have been imaginatively launched without the Erie Canal, vertiginously steep-walled, cutting through its core. And though my father is not present in the fictional world of "You Must Remember This," his shadow falls over it; it's a work in which I tried consciously to synthesize my

father's and my own "visions" of an era now vanished. Felix Stevick is not my father except in his lifelong fascination with boxing and with what I consider the romance of violence, which excludes women; that conviction that there is a mysterious and terrible brotherhood of men by way of violence.

21   But it is in an early novel, "Wonderland" (1971), that my parents actually make an appearance. My beleaguered young hero Jesse stops his car in Millersport, wanders about my parents' property, happens to see, with a stab of envy, my young mother and me (a child of 3 or 4) swinging in our old wooden swing; and when my father notices Jesse watching he stares at him with a look of hostility. So I envisioned my father as a young man of 27— tall, husky, with black hair, intent on protecting his family against possible intrusion. "In such a way," thinks my fatherless hero, "does a man, a normal man, exclude the rest of the world."

22   Memory is a transcendental function. Its objects may be physical bodies, faces, "characteristic" expressions of faces, but these are shot with luminosity; they possess an interior radiance that transfixes the imagination like the radiance in medieval and Renaissance religious paintings— that signal that Time has been stopped and Eternity prevails. So, though we can't perceive "soul" or "spirit" first-hand, it seems to me that this is precisely the phenomenon we summon back by way of an exercise of memory. And why the exercise of memory at certain times in our lives is almost too powerful to be borne.

23   From a letter of my father's, written Oct. 8, 1988:

24   Your postcard asking about my history came the day after I phoned so I don't quite know how to give you what you want because I have no school records like you and Fred   all I can do is guess.

25   Born in Lockport 3/30/14. Parents separated when I was two or three years old. Started violin lessons in sixth grade (class instruction) then began private lessons with money earned peddling newspapers. My mother bought my violin for me otherwise I would have had to quit because the one I used in class belonged to the school. I played in the high school symphony orchestra as a freshman. My mechanical drawing teacher got me a job with Schine Theaters in Lockport in the sign shop working after school. At summer vacation I worked full time at the job and quit school in my second year. Worked at the theater until I was about 17 when the sign shop closed and I went into production advertising.

26   Got a job in local commercial sign shop when I was about 18 and bought a car. After about 4 years of this work I got a job at Harrison Radiator in the punch press department, and, thinking I had a steady job, I learned to fly, got married, then found myself laid off for extended periods so I had to continue

working at the sign shop until the second world war began when I was able to get transferred into the engineering tool room and learned the tool and die making trade, later on was able, after going to night school to learn trig and related subjects, started tool and die design. At about fifty years of age, I took piano lessons for about four years at which time I was operated on to remove herniated disc material and was out of commission for six months then worked about ten more years and retired. Took a course in stained glass as a hobby, a class in painting, then four years ago I started classes in English Literature and music at SUNY which I hope to continue for a few more years.

From my journal, May 20, 1986:

27   Last week, my parents' visit. And it was splendid. And it went by with painful swiftness. They arrived on Wednesday, left on Saturday afternoon, immediately the house is too large, empty, quiet, unused. . . . My mother brought me a dress she'd sewed for me, blue print, quite feminine one might say; long-sleeved, full-skirted. "Demure"—to suit my image.

28   Another family secret revealed, with a disarming casualness. Perhaps because of their ages my parents don't want to keep secrets? Not that they are *old* at seventy or seventy-one. My father told of how his grandfather Morgenstern tried to kill his grandmother in a fit of rage, then killed himself—gun barrel placed under his chin, trigger pulled, with my grandmother Blanche close by. My father was about fifteen at the time. They were all living in a single household evidently. . . . A sordid tale. Yet grimly comical: I asked what occupation my great-grandfather had, was told he was a gravedigger.

29   Family secrets! So many! Or, no, not so very many, I suppose; but unnerving. And I think of my sweet Grandmother Woodside who nearly witnessed her own father's violent suicide. . . . She had come home to find the house locked. Her father was beating her mother upstairs in their bedroom. Hearing her at the door, he came downstairs with his gun, and for some reason (frustration, drunkenness, madness?) he went into the basement and shot himself. Several times I said to my father, dazed, but you never told me any of this! and my father said, with the air of utter placidity. Didn't I?—I'm sure I did. This is a countertheme of sorts. The secret is at last revealed, after decades; but it's revealed with the accompanying claim that it had been revealed a long time ago and isn't therefore a secret. . . .

30   One of my most deeply imprinted memories of childhood is of being taken up in a small plane by my father: tightly buckled in the front seat of a two-seater Piper Cub as my father in the cockpit behind me taxis us along the bumpy runway of a small country airport outside Lockport. Suddenly,

the rattling plane leaves the ground, lifts above a line of trees at the end of the runway, climbing, banking, miraculously riding the air currents until the roaring noise of the engine seems to subside and we're airborne, and below is a familiar landscape made increasingly exotic as we climb. Transit Road and its traffic . . . farmland, wooded land, hedgerows . . . houses, barns, pastureland, intersecting roads . . . creeks and streams . . . and the sky opening above us oceanic, unfathomable.

31   My father has always been a happy, energetic, imaginative man, but never more so than when airborne, riding the waves of invisible currents of air. For what is flying your own plane but defying the laws of nature and of logic? Transcending space and time and the contours of the familiar world in which you work a minimum of 40 hours a week, own property in constant need of repair, have a family for whom you are the sole breadwinner? What is flying but the control of an alien, mysterious element that can at any moment turn killer—the air?

32   My father began flying lessons in 1935, when he was 21 years old, made his first solo flight in 1937, and, over the decades, logged approximately 200 hours of flying time. It was during the 1940's, especially after the end of World War II when Army Air Forces training planes came into private ownership, that he flew most frequently, on weekends, out of small country airports near our home. What a romance of the air! He took members of the family, including his very young daughter Joyce, up in Piper Cubs, Cessnas, Stinsons; he flew a sporty Waco biplane; the most powerful aircraft in his experience was a Vultee basic trainer, 450 horsepower, which was an Air Force trainer with a canopy, which flew at more than 10,000 feet. Intense excitement   unless it was something beyond excitement— has blurred my precise memory of the flight we once made, my father and me, in a 175-horsepower Fairchild primary trainer. I wore a helmet and goggles, but no parachute, for the very good reason that I wouldn't have known how to use a parachute.

33   Flying is safer than driving a car, my father has always insisted.

34   In these planes my father and his flying buddies performed loops, turns, split-S's, slow rolls, spins. Possessed of a brash sense of humor, as it might have been called, my father sometimes flew low to buzz friends' and neighbors' houses. Upon a number of daring occasions he flew gliders—if "flew" is the correct expression—borne up to 1,500 feet by a plane, then released. A few years ago when a West German film crew came to interview him and my mother in preparing a film on "Joyce Carol Oates" for German public television, the program director paid for renting a plane so that he could fly the director and a cameraman (in a Cessna 182 single-propeller

plane) over the terrain of my childhood: and it's as if, eerily, seeing this footage, I have come full circle, seeing again these exotic-familiar sights, my father in the cockpit.

35   How many times I've stared at a newspaper photograph, recently reprinted for novelty's sake in *The Lockport Union-Sun and Journal*, of 60 employees of Department 11, Press Room, of the Harrison Radiator Division, Washburn Street plant, Aug. 11, 1941. There, in the second row, looking not just young, but boyish, coltish, dramatically handsome, with a thick springy head of black hair, is my father, Frederic Oates.

36   My father, 27 years old.

37   At which time my mother would have been 24, and I 3.

38   So long ago!—in another lifetime, it seems; and irretrievable.

39   I have been speaking of my father's avocational life, his "personal" life, but most of the actual hours of his (waking) life were spent at work. For 40 years he was an employee of Harrison Radiator of Lockport, N.Y.; since the early 1940's he was a dues-paying member of the United Automobile Workers of America. It has always seemed that Frederic Oates's temperament and intelligence might have better suited him for some sort of artistic or theoretical or even teacherly career, but, born in the circumstances in which he was, and coming of age during the Depression, he shared the collective fate of so many. Schooling even through high school was not an option.

40   (So when it is said of me that I am the first member of my family to graduate from high school, still less college, this is another misleading fact: only chance saved me and others of my generation from the work-oriented lives of our parents. At the time of this writing my father is a student at the State University of New York at Buffalo—the kind of deeply engaged "older" student whom professors, and I speak as one, dearly appreciate in their classes.)

41   In the old days at Harrison Radiator, as at all nonunion factories, plants, mills, shops, "sweatshops," it was not uncommon that workers might arrive for work in the morning only to be told cursorily that they weren't needed that day, and that there was no promise of when, or if, they might be needed again. Management owed nothing to labor; not even simple courtesy. A few weeks after I was born in 1938 my father reported to work and was told there was no work, some of the press room employees were laid off indefinitely. I have to wonder what a young husband tells his wife when he returns home so early in the day—what the words are, what the tone of voice. About all my father will say of such episodes is, "They were hard." He has never been a person given to self-pity, nor yet to a nostalgic reinvention of the past.

42   If there was anger it's long since buried, plowed under, to be resurrected in his daughter's writing, as fuel and ballast. *How to evoke that world, that America, rapidly passing from memory.*

43   One definite advantage of my father's shaky economic situation was that he developed a second career of sorts, i.e., sign painting, at which he was very good. (For decades, my father's signs were immediately recognizable in the area. I can "see" the distinctive style of their lettering even now.) And he acquired a habitude of busyness, a predilection for work, for using his hands and his brain, not so much in gainful employment as in useful employment; a trait everyone in my family shares. This is not puritanism, but something less abstract, perhaps even visceral: we love to work because work gives us genuine happiness, the positing and solving of problems, the joyful exercise of the imagination.

44   I spoke of anger, and, yes, it's a "class" anger as well, but I want to make clear that this is a personal anger, not one I have inherited from my family.

45   A few days ago, my husband and I took my parents for lunch on the Delaware River (they are visiting us here in Princeton for a week), to one of those "historic" inns for which the region is famous, and while we sat contemplating the antique furnishings of the Black Bass Inn—the tables in the dining room are made of old sewing machines—the subject turned to Harrison's, to the old days, in the 1930's. And after a while my mother said, as so often she sums up an era, and a theme, in a single succinct remark, "I guess we were poor, but it didn't seem that way at the time. Somehow, we always managed."

46   The old farmhouse in Millersport was razed in 1960, yet there is a dream of mine in which I wake yet again to find myself there, in my old room—the first of the countless rooms of my life. I open my eyes in astonishment to see the square half-window overhead, the child's bureau at the foot of my bed and the child's desk facing it and, through the doorway (no door, only a curtain), in the farthest right-hand corner of the living room the upright piano my father played and on which in time I would practice my piano lessons. A musical instrument is a mysterious thing, inhabiting a complex sort of space: it is both an ordinary three-dimensional object and a portal to another world; it exists as a physical entity solely so that it—and, indeed, physicality—can be transcended. Thus my father's old upright in that long-vanished living room inhabits its luminous space in my memory.

47   For nearly his entire life my father has played, and loved playing, the piano: classical music, popular music, Scott Joplin, jazz. He is a precise sight-reader of music but he can also play by ear and improvise, neither of which I can do; he is far more naturally musical than I, though I have inherited from

him a temperament that must be called "musical." People like us are always involved in music no matter what we're doing.

48   If we aren't actually sitting at the piano and playing, our fingers are going through the phantom motions of playing; if we aren't singing or humming out loud, we are singing or humming silently. We are captivated by Mozart, Chopin, Schubert, Beethoven, Bach, but just as readily by "St. James Infirmary," "As Time Goes By," one or another old Hoagy Carmichael tune. For people like us music is a matter of a pulsebeat, melody and rhythm and occasional lyrics, a constant interior beat in a counterpoint of sorts to the world's exterior beat. It must be a way of defining ourselves to ourselves, or perhaps it's purely pleasure, to no purpose. If from my father Frederic Oates I'd inherited nothing more palpable than a habit of singing to myself, I'd say this was more than enough.

49   So I sit listening to my father playing piano in another wing of the house—now he's playing Satie's elegant "Gnossiennes"—and I think these things. How to write a memoir of him? How even to begin? I spoke of mystery, and it's primarily mystery I feel when I contemplate my father, indeed, both my father and my mother. The quality of personality they embody, their unfailing magnanimity of spirit, is so oddly matched with their origins and with the harsh and unsentimental world out of which they emerged. I can bear a prolonged consideration of that world only in my writing, and there it is transmogrified as writing—as fiction. To consider it head-on, not as art but as historical reality, leaves me weak and bewildered.

50   If there is one general trait I seem to have inherited from both of my parents it's their instinct for rejoicing in the life in which they have found themselves. They remain models for me, they go far beyond me, I can only hope to continue to learn from them. *Happiness is a kind of genius*, Colete shrewdly observed, and in this genius my parents abound.

Understanding Meaning

1. What contradiction does Oates see in her father's life?
2. What are the main facts about her father's early life?
3. What does Oates admire about her father?
4. What does playing the piano and flying a plane reveal about Oates's father?
5. How did Oates depict her father in her novel *Wonderland*?
6. What does Oates find mystifying about her father's life?

7. *CRITICAL THINKING.* Consider Oates's observation that "all children mythologize their parents, who are to them after all giants of the landscape of early childhood. . . ." Do we ever see our parents as "people," or do they always loom over us larger than life? Do people with absent or dysfunctional parents have to "de-mythologize" them?

Evaluating Strategy

1. Oates begins and closes her essay describing her father playing the piano. How does she use this to help explain his life?
2. Oates introduces a great deal of factual detail about her father's life. Is this an important device in explaining her father? Why or why not?
3. Oates tells readers how she depicted her father in one of her novels. Why is this important? Does It explain what she wants the public to know about her father?

Appreciating Language

1. What words and phrases does Oates use to describe her father? How do they reveal her feelings toward him?
2. Oates uses the word *transcending* several times. Look this word up in the dictionary. How does it suit her thoughts about her father?
3. How does Oates distinguish "gainful employment" from "useful employment" to describe her father's dedication to work?

Writing Suggestions

1. Describe your father or another significant adult in your childhood and focus on a single activity you associate with this person. What did a job or hobby reveal about his or her values, personality, or attitudes?
2. *COLLABORATIVE WRITING.* Discuss this essay in a small group. Do you think it is inevitable that children "mythologize" their parents? Are parents always major forces in our lives? Record comments by the group and summarize them in a paragraph. If students have conflicting opinions, consider drafting opposing statements.

21

Gender Identity: Raising Boys and Girls

*As parents, we also have initiation rites
when our children recycle our own
experiences. It's only inevitable if we decide
boys will be boys and girls will be girls.
They will be unless we step in and create
new ways for them to feel strong and safe.*
–Ellen Goodman

*It's the way boys are masculinized and the
way girls are feminized that turns some of
them into bullies.*
–Marie Wilson

*I'd like to think that the future belongs to
the feminist who can respect her son the
career soldier and to the career soldier who
can respect his son the hairdresser.*
–Cathy Young

*When it comes to actually countering preju-
dices like sexism in the classroom, it goes
only one way, with girls being encouraged
to do traditionally male jobs while boys
continue to avoid and to demean jobs
traditionally done by girls.*
–Roxanne Stachowski

GENDER IN THE 21st CENTURY

Roxanne Stachowski never thought that she would face discrimination or harassment in high school, especially one that championed openness and diversity. When she enrolled in a technical theater class, however, she discovered that tasks were strictly divided along gender lines. Boys dominated lights, set construction, sound, and props. Female students were generally assigned to costume work, which boys held in low regard. Although she tried to be friendly, she was ridiculed and harassed, not only by male students but also by the few girls allowed to work alongside the boys:

> They were the girls deemed "masculine" enough to hang out with them and participate in their discrimination. These girls worked on the "masculine projects." What's worse, instead of helping to bridge the gap between myself and that group, these girls were just as prejudiced. The fact that the girls participated in their "all in good fun" derision encouraged the boys to believe that it wasn't a gender issue.

Writing about her experiences in *off our backs*, Stachowski observed that girls "who do 'boy' jobs may be accepted, but girls doing 'female' jobs continued to be disrespected and demeaned."

Stachowski's high school experience reflects how changing gender roles affect society, education policies, and parenting strategies.

New Arenas

Throughout the twentieth century, feminists challenged the traditional gender roles that limited women to marriage and a few female-dominated professions, such as teaching and nursing. Commenting on Take Our Daughters to Work Day, Anna Quindlen describes a photograph of her small daughter, gavel in hand, standing beside a female federal judge:

> Present at the revolution: that's what I feel every time I look at that photograph. Every time a girl plays Little League, every time a father assumes his daughter is as likely to go to college as his son, every time no one looks twice at a female cop or balks at a female surgeon, it's a moment in history, radical and ordinary at the same time.

Quindlen noted that today there are nearly 200 female federal judges. When she was her daughter's age, there were less than a dozen. Take Our Daughters to Work Day helps to introduce girls to greater opportunities and reshape their view of what it means to be female. Questioned about why boys should not also be taken to work by their parents, Quindlen referred to Eleanor Holmes Norton: "asked why there was no such day for boys, she said it was for the same reason there's no White History Month."

As girls and women have entered traditionally male arenas such as math, science, and sports, they have also engaged in typically male antisocial behaviors, namely alcohol and drug abuse and delinquency. A 2003 report in *Alcoholism & Drug Abuse Weekly* revealed that nearly 28 percent of high school girls smoke and 45 percent drink alcohol, with over half engaging in binge drinking. The dangers of smoking and drinking are far greater for adolescent females:

> Girls and young women are likelier than boys and young men to experience more adverse health consequences, such as greater smoking-related lung damage. Women are more susceptible to alcohol-induced brain damage, cardiac problems and liver disease, which occur more quickly and with lower levels of alcohol consumption than with males.

Most disturbing for many parents and adolescent counselors is the rapid increase in violence by girls and young women. While arrest rates for boys under eighteen rose 11 percent over a four-year period, the rate for girls increased 23 percent. Girls now commit one quarter of violent juvenile crime. Elizabeth Mehren, a *Los Angeles Times* reporter, studied the dramatic rise in female violence. Media depictions of cold-blooded female killers and female gangs suggested that girls were acting just like boys. Merhren's research reveals that female offenders, although increasing in number, differed from their male counterparts. Although often violent, girls were frequently victims of sexual abuse themselves:

> Gangster girls do make good copy and provide great pictures, but my research suggested that girl gangs are largely overrated. For the most part they represent a companionate activity—a way for girls to earn points with their gangbanger boyfriends—kind of like old-fashioned ladies' auxiliaries. . . .
>
> But the truth is that girls are even more likely to commit crimes in the course of running away, generally from abusive homes. That's the real story, the under-reported story, the one we too often miss altogether. . . . Intake studies in juvenile facilities show that 50 percent to 70 percent say they have been emotionally, physically or sexually abused. . . .

Calling the rise of female violence "the third wave" in the epidemic of violence in the United States, Dr. Howard Spivak told a symposium sponsored by the American Academy of Pediatrics, "Unless we do something about this, we are going to see girls going down the same path that we have seen men and boys going down for the past several decades."

Where the Boys Aren't

In the early 1960s women accounted for less than 5 percent of students in many medical colleges. In 2003, for the first time in history, more women than men applied to medical school. For supporters of women's rights, this represents one of several indicators of progress, women breaking stereotypes and entering traditionally male professions.

For some educators, however, these numbers document a disturbing decline in male academic performance. Boys are scoring lower on standardized tests in elementary school, especially in reading and writing skills. Boys are more likely than girls to be diagnosed with learning disabilities and placed in remedial or special classes. They are also less likely than girls to graduate from high school, and those who receive diplomas are less likely than girls to pursue higher education.

The gap between male and female achievement is widest in the African American community. In many urban school districts, more than half of African American male students drop out of high school, a much higher rate than for female students. Welfare reform now requires recipients to work or obtain job training to receive benefits. As a result, poor single mothers are more likely than their children's fathers to enter the workforce. Between 1980 and 2000, the number of African American men enrolling in college increased by 37 percent. The number of black women starting college increased by 70 percent. In some colleges, only 8 percent of black males who enter actually graduate. Nationwide, 70 percent of African Americans graduating college are female.

Parents of small boys and some educators believe that the current elementary school curriculum places males at a disadvantage. Writing for *Business Week*, Michelle Conlin observed that, "It may still be a man's world. But it is no longer, in any way, a boy's." Jennifer Bingham Hull, writing in *Parenting*, notes that kindergarten classes, which once emphasized games and physical play, have become more academic. More schools have day-long kindergarten with few or no recess periods for active play. Hull points out this shift is particularly bad for boys:

> In the past decade, research including such technology as brain imagery has confirmed that sex differences in kids are quite pronounced. With their less-developed fine motor skills, boys at age 5 may have more difficulty than most girls holding a pencil or buttoning a coat. They usually need larger spaces to move around, require more breaks, and have shorter attention spans (all perfectly normal for boys this age). They also learn differently from girls and do better when lessons use hands-on learning rather than verbal instructions, which girls are better at following.

Marcia Vickers detailed her son's experiences in a private kindergarten. Like many four-year-old boys, her son did not exhibit the fine motor skills found in girls his age. Too often, Vickers argues, small boys, who normally develop later than girls, are diagnosed as having developmental problems. Concerned parents, eager to have their children enrolled in elite private preschools, have created a "cottage industry" of therapists and special tutors who charge $135 an hour to teach preschool boys how to color within the lines or cut out shapes with scissors, skills they will naturally develop on their own, albeit at a later age than girls. The idea of labeling normal boys as having developmental problems that require professional intervention may have harmful results:

> If boys can't draw and color a bunny rabbit or cut simple shapes with scissors, they are subtly made to feel inferior. And a growing number of professionals believe that pressuring boys early only creates a sense of helplessness on their part. That can extend to how they feel about themselves and how they view school for many years.

Instead of viewing boys as challenged, schools should, in the view of Dr. Leonard Sax, an advocate of single-sex education, "be playing to boys' strengths, such as playing games, building forts out of blocks, kicking a soccer ball, rather than emphasizing their weaknesses."

The idea of single-sex classes is gaining support among a number of parents and educators who feel boys and girls benefit from activities that emphasize their different learning styles. Critics like Carolyn Kobosko, however, point out that boys and girls need to interact: "You need some girls to model the higher-level writing. And you need boys to model the math."

Most challenging of all for many parents is determining what constitutes masculine and feminine behavior in the 21st century. As Roxanne Stachowski noted, girls are supported when they enter traditionally male jobs, but males continue to look down on traditionally female tasks. When children do not conform to standard gender stereotypes, parents and psychologists wonder when or even if they should intervene. Nancy Kalish observes that parents are often troubled when their sons "don't act like boys":

> Through feminism and the burgeoning men's movement, we've blurred what used to be recognized as the line between male and female roles. Today, few adults would question a girl who would rather play with a soccer ball than with Barbie. But the issue isn't as simple for boys. Because while we may cheer for the young hero of the film *Billy Elliott* in his struggle to become a ballet dancer, some of us wouldn't eagerly applaud our own sons if they chose such a traditionally feminine pursuit.

Changing concepts of masculinity and femininity pose new challenges to parents, teachers, and therapists in determining how to help children achieve their greatest potential, when to correct potentially troublesome behaviors, and even how to identify those behaviors.

Before reading these entries, consider these questions.

Do attitudes about homosexuality shape our views of gender? Do parents worry that if their children show an interest in activities traditionally associated with the opposite gender that they may be gay or will be perceived as gay? Does this affect boys more than girls? Are young boys who take an interest in fashion or dance treated differently than young girls who play with toy trucks or talk about being police officers when they grow up?

How does the changing role of women affect their children? Many children today grow up in homes where mothers work in traditionally male-dominated professions. Does this naturally lead children to have a less rigid view of what it means to be "male" or "female"?

How do media images affect children's sexual identity? Does the popularity of professional sports on television lead boys to prize size and physical strength? Do television images of supermodels and teen actresses lead girls to focus on their appearance? Does the media provide positive images of people breaking gender stereotypes?

Do boys growing up in female-headed households have problems developing a male identity? Does the lack of a father's influence handicap boys' development? Do mothers feel confused or insecure about how to raise their sons without a male role model?

What role does peer pressure have in shaping children's view of gender? Does the desire to be part of an accepted group or avoid ridicule lead children to imitate the attitudes and behaviors of other children? What messages about gender do children receive from other children?

WRITING ABOUT GENDER

The issue of gender can generate a number of responses that can be useful topics for writing assignments.

Critical Thinking and Prewriting

Gender can spark emotional reactions and prompt you to repeat ideas you have read or heard about. Critical thinking can help identify and develop meaningful topics.

Getting Started: Exploring Ideas

1. What do you consider the most important factor in determining the way children acquire their views of gender—parents, peers, school curriculum, or popular culture?
2. What role does ethnicity play in gender roles? Do some cultures have strict views of the way men and women are expected to behave? Do children from certain ethnic or religious backgrounds have greater direction in how they should behave as they mature? Do they face problems when their values are challenged by a multicultural society that emphasizes diversity and questions traditional gender roles?
3. How much of gender differences are influenced by biology and how much by environmental forces? Are boys naturally more aggressive than girls? If left on their own, do boys engage in more competitive games than girls? Are girls naturally more drawn to form peer relationships?
4. Why are some boys falling behind in school? Has the emphasis on securing greater opportunities for girls led teachers and administrators to overlook the needs of male students? Does the emphasis on sports lead boys to take academic subjects less seriously? Are boys who exhibit normal energy too often labeled as having learning disabilities or behavioral problems?
5. Have gender roles changed more for girls than for boys? Are girls encouraged to pursue traditional male interests while boys are expected to remain the same? Are parents, peers, and teachers more likely to encourage a girl to become a doctor than a boy to become a nurse?
6. Has the stress on erasing gender differences led to a further devaluing of anything traditionally regarded as "female"? Because women are now attorneys, physicians, politicians, and business owners, do both men and women now regard homemaking, teaching, and nursing as less desirable pursuits? If a high school senior with good grades and prospects for college scholarships announces she would rather be a child-care provider or a beautician than go to law school, would her parents and teachers support or question her decision?
7. How can traditional gender roles be erased without creating confusion for children?

Strategies for Writing about Gender

Define key terms.
Establish a clear definition for words like *masculine, feminine,* and *gender.*

Distinguish between "roles" and "jobs."
Is a male nurse who manages health aides and other workers in a clinic or a female attorney who represents abused children challenging traditional gender roles or simply engaging in traditional male and female behavior with unconventional job titles?

Use your experiences and those of your friends and family as resources.
Personal experiences and observations can be used to examine gender issues. Because you may be writing about individual situations, consider supporting any conclusions with facts, statistics, and expert testimony.

Consider how age, income, education, ethnicity, religion, and region affect gender issues.
Are gender roles more rigid among some populations than others? How is gender identity different between rich urban and low-income rural populations? Are some religious denominations dedicated to erasing gender distinctions by ordaining women as ministers and using translations of the Bible that avoid sexist language? Do some religious denominations have fixed roles for men and women that are viewed as sacred and unchangeable?

Determine which gender has to make the greatest changes.
Do women face making more changes as they enter traditionally male fields? Do men only have to accept their presence? Can they ignore traditional female activities?

Poll friends, fellow students, coworkers, relatives, or family members.
Develop a few questions exploring opinions about gender and get as many people as you can to provide answers. Instead of simply asking questions requiring yes or no answers, consider giving people statements and asking them if they strongly disagree, disagree somewhat, have no opinion, agree somewhat, or strongly agree. Responses to these questions provide more precise assessments of people's attitudes.

Explore the changing aspects of gender by comparing the present with the past.
Compare the images of women on current television dramas, sitcoms, and soap operas with those of the 1950s or 1960s. Go to a library and study old issues of magazines like *Time* and *Life* to see how articles and advertisements depicted women in the past. What has changed? What remains the same?

Examine changes in language to reduce sexism.
Today, textbooks, English teachers, editors, and most politicians attempt to avoid sexist language such as using the male pronoun "he" to refer to nouns that could be male or female—*doctor, voter, consumer, citizen,* or *buyer.* Terms like *police officer, sales representative,* and *flight attendant* have replaced sexist terms like *policeman, salesman,* and *stewardess.* Compare old books and magazines with current ones to see how language has changed. Consider if these changes influence attitudes or perceptions.

WRITING IN THE MODES

You may find that selecting a particular mode is an effective way of examining a topic, organizing ideas, and shaping an essay.

Narration
1. Write a short essay recalling a conflict based on gender. Did someone ever assume you could not repair a car because you were female or cook because you were male?
2. Relate a childhood experience that shaped your view of your own gender. What messages were you given by parents, teachers, or older children about the way you were supposed to behave?
3. Explain how gender attitudes have either changed or remained the same over a period of time at your school, workplace, church, or social organization. Did men and women maintain traditional roles, or could you see a shift taking place?

Description
1. Write an essay in which you describe the characteristics of a person you met who challenged gender stereotypes. How was this person regarded by others?
2. Describe the gender roles in your high school. Did males and females have separate interests, behaviors, and activities? Did anyone defy traditional roles? How were students who attempted to cross gender lines treated by others?

Definition
1. Establish your definition of masculinity or femininity. Do you see these as genetic traits or as attitudes shaped by society? What roles are masculine or feminine?
2. Define the qualities needed by someone seeking to become president of the United States. In your opinion, could a woman exhibit these qualities and be elected? Why or why not?

Example

1. Discuss one or more examples of people who have challenged traditional gender roles. You can use historical, personal, or hypothetical examples.
2. Use one or more examples to explain how the role of women has changed in the last twenty years.

Comparison and Contrast

1. Polls continue to reveal a "gender gap" in voting patterns. Review recent articles and compare how women and men differ on certain issues. If more and more women are entering traditionally male professions, why is there still a gender gap?
2. Compare how men and women are depicted on television programs. You can focus on a single format, such as talk shows, soap operas, dramas, or situation comedies.
3. Contrast views of gender identification between those who see erasing distinctions between male and female as positive steps to reduce sexism and expand people's options and those who see it as a sign of social breakdown and disorder.

Division and Classification

1. Use division to explain the main factors that shape a child's notion of gender. What role do genetics, parental influences, peer pressure, and popular culture play?
2. Classify occupations or institutions from the most open to the least open to changes in gender roles. Which churches, corporations, political organizations welcome women assuming positions of leadership? Which resist change? Which reject women assuming power?

Process

1. Describe steps parents should take to help their sons and daughters develop confidence and strong identities in a society that is blurring the distinctions between what is considered male and female.
2. Describe the way parents and teachers should address differences in skill levels in boys and girls. Should adults try to find teaching methods that benefit both genders or engage boys and girls in separate learning activities?

Cause and Effect

1. Develop an essay that discusses the causes for gender roles. Why are some jobs, activities, and sports considered male and others considered female? Is it genetic, social, psychological, or cultural? For example, field hockey, which is considered a girl's sport in the United States, is played by men in India. In the United States, elementary school teachers were almost exclusively male until the Civil War, when women took over the jobs of teachers who joined the army.

2. Discuss the positive and negative effects of changing gender roles. Does it
    provide children with wider opportunities, or does it lead to confusion?

Argument and Persuasion

1. Develop an argument that supports or criticizes the idea of single-sex edu-
    cation in public schools. Should it be optional? Should only the first few
    grades be segregated by gender? Should classes remain integrated but
    boys and girls given different choices of learning activities?
2. Develop a persuasive essay suggesting how parents should deal with a
    child who exhibits behaviors associated with the opposite gender. If a
    four-year-old boy plays with dolls, wishes to be called by a girl's name,
    and expresses an interest in fashion, what should parents do? Should they
    try to redirect his energy into more masculine activities, ignore his behav-
    ior, encourage his interests, or seek professional help?
3. Write an essay that agrees or disagrees with one or more points made in
    one of the readings in this chapter.

STUDENT PAPER

Class, Not Gender

A lot is made about gender, let alone race, these days, but I think it
avoids the biggest difference in this country. It is a difference we don't
like to talk about because it sounds undemocratic. It is class. The big
difference is not male and female and no longer white and black. The
big difference between Americans is class.

I belong to a family split right along the fault lines. My mom has
two sisters. One got pregnant in high school, dropped out, and married
a cab driver. She lives in a flat in Canarsie. Hers is an Archie Bunker
world of bowling, beer drinking, Mets games, and high school football.
My mom's younger sister finished high school, went to Columbia, then
to law school. She married a stockbroker and lives in a town house in
SoHo. Her life is a world of gallery openings, sushi bars, martinis,
weekends at the Hamptons, and prep school soccer games.

At family gatherings, the relatives divide up, but not along gender
lines. No longer do the women gather in one room and talk about babies and recipes while the men talk about cars and football in another.

Now that both men and women work, the main topic of conversation is about jobs and retirement. In one room, people talk about overtime pay, Social Security, and union dues. In the next, conversation centers around tax shelters, billable hours, and expense accounts. The men and women who work on Wall Street and the men and women who drive cabs and wait tables have nothing in common. The women see different doctors, shop in different stores, and send their kids to different schools. The men play different sports, wear different clothes, and drive different cars.

Blue-collar men and women talk about their Chevys, their favorite TV characters, weekends at the beach, and where to find the best pizza in Queens. They speak the same language, though the men tend to swear a bit more. The Wall Streeters discuss their BMWs and Benzes, the latest Broadway show, their favorite cruise, and the newest carb-free café in the Village. There is only an uneasy alliance between the blue-collar guys and their upscale in-laws. My aunts and their daughters bear no sign of sisterhood, just a polite standoff. They seem to spend most of their time going over each other's hair and clothes.

The fact is for all the college courses on gender and diversity, we avoid the biggest, maybe the most troubling, division between us. I think it is because we are comfortable dealing with the other divisions. You are born with a race and a gender, and you don't change. If you are white, you grow up knowing you will never become black. If you are a female, you spend your whole life seeing men as the other, the opposite. But if you are poor, you hunger to be rich. If you are born rich, you fear becoming poor.

It is that idea of possible change that makes class hard to wrestle with. We all want to be rich, but we all can't make it. All the sensitivity and diversity training tells us that we should all be equal. And maybe because we like to feel we live in a democracy, we live in denial. Diversity is all about acceptance. We are supposed to accept the differences of black and white, male and female, Jew and gentile, gay and straight. But to accept a difference between rich and poor implies acknowledging social class as being normal, admitting that society has winners and losers. And that idea is uncomfortable for everyone to accept, both rich and poor.

Understanding Meaning

1. What is the student's thesis? Can you restate it in your own words?
2. How does class divide the student's family?
3. Why does the student feel that other divisions between people are easier to accept?
4. Why does the student believe that class is a far more important distinction than gender?

Evaluating Strategy

1. What evidence does the student use to support the thesis? Do you find it convincing?
2. The student includes several geographical references—Canarsie, Queens, the Hamptons, SoHo. Would readers outside of the New York area understand them? Should the student define or explain these if writing to a national audience? Why or why not?

Appreciating Language

1. How would you characterize the tone and style of this essay? Is it suitable for a college essay? Do terms like "blue-collar guys" seem inappropriate for an academic paper? Why or why not?
2. The student describes two divisions in the family. Do you detect any bias in word choices that suggests a preference for one group over the other?

Writing Suggestions

1. Write an essay that discusses another division between people besides class, race, or gender. How important are religious differences or regional distinctions? Are there forms of discrimination that are ignored by the media, government, and academics?
2. *COLLABORATIVE WRITING.* Discuss this essay with a group of students. Do they agree with the student's idea that we are reluctant to recognize class differences? Does this explain the fascination with rags-to-riches stories, lotteries, and television shows offering contest winners a million dollars? Record comments by the group in a statement. If students offer different points of view, consider using comparison or division to express their opinions.

CHECKLIST

Before submitting your paper, review these points.

1. Does your paper have a clearly stated thesis? Does it have a clear point of view?

2. Do you support your thesis with representative facts, reliable observations, and accurate statistics?

3. Do you avoid making prejudiced or biased statements that will detract from your authority and alienate readers?

4. Do you anticipate readers' possible objections and answer them?

5. Is the paper clearly organized? Do paragraph breaks group related ideas and signal transitions?

6. Does the tone, style, and word choice of your paper suit your purpose and audience?

 Companion Website

See **academic.cengage.com/english** for information on planning, organizing, writing, and revising essays.

 E-Reading: InfoTrac College Edition
http://www.infotrac-college.com

For Further Reading
E–Readings Online

Search for articles by author or title in InfoTrac College Edition after entering your user name and password.

Timothy F. Kirn, *Dangerous Trend: Violent Behavior by Girls*
Females are now responsible for 25 percent of violent crimes committed by adolescents.

David Hefner, *Where the Boys Aren't: The Decline of Black Males in Colleges and Universities Has Sociologists and Educators Concerned About the Future of the African American Community*
The gap in college attendance and graduation rates between African American males and females has increased dramatically, so that 70 percent of African Americans who earn bachelor's degrees are women.

David Klinghoffer, *Boyz II Men: Adolescent Culture Is Destroying the Lives of Boys and Girls in America*
Klinghoffer notes that "in the absence of adults, children construct for themselves a distorted simulation of adulthood, patched together from random sources: TV, movies, and their own fantasies."

Alcoholism & Drug Abuse Weekly, *Report: Girls Are More Vulnerable to Addiction*
Girls are smoking, drinking, and abusing drugs at younger ages and are more likely than boys to become addicted and suffer serious health consequences, even if they consume less than males.

Jennifer Bingham Hull, *The Lost Boys: Now That Kindergarten Has Become More Academic, It May Not Be the Best Learning Environment for Boys*
Sixty percent of five-year-olds attend all-day kindergartens, many with little or no recess time, but boys, who benefit from physical activity and exercise, perform poorly in sedentary classes.

Lynn Norment and Kevin Chappell, *How Parents Influence the Way Sons and Daughters View Their Dates, Spouses, and the World*
Fathers who overly protect their daughters and mothers who form strong bonds with their sons may be setting their children up for troubled adult relationships and failed marriages.

 If you have access to *Comp21*, click on Themes, then click on Gender Identity.

22

ANNA QUINDLEN

Anna Quindlen (1952–) graduated from Barnard College in 1974 and began working as a reporter in New York. After writing articles for the New York Post, *she took over the "About New York" column for the* New York Times. *In 1986 she started her own column, "Life in the Thirties." Her collected articles were published in* Living Out Loud *in 1988. She has written numerous op-ed pieces for the* Times *on social and political issues. In 1992 she received the Pulitzer Prize. The following year she published another collection of essays,* Thinking Out Loud: On the Personal, the Political, the Public, and the Private. *Quindlen has also written three novels,* Object Lessons *(1992),* One True Thing *(1994), and* Black and Blue *(1998).*

Horrors! Girls with Gavels!

CONTEXT: *In this column, published in* Newsweek *in 2002, Quindlen celebrates the tenth anniversary of Take Our Daughters to Work Day, an annual observance in which parents take their daughters to their place of employment. This ritual is meant to inspire girls to pursue a wide variety of careers previously dominated by men.*

1 Not long ago I spoke at a meeting sponsored by a company's women's networking group. Like most other American corporations, this one had a lot of women in entry-level jobs, a fair number of women in middle management and a few women in the top ranks, in a pyramid configuration that has become commonplace.

2 Commonplace, too, was the response of the majority males at the top to this particular evening event. It rankled, this meeting, closed to them in the same way the ranks of management had once been closed to their distaff counterparts. It rankled, even for one night. Apparently none of them saw it as a learning experience, the possibility of imagining for just a few hours what it had been like to be female for many, many years.

3 This immediately called to mind Take Our Daughters to Work Day, which comes around again at the end of this month in what is its 10th anniversary. It's amazing how the event has become an institution in only a decade, with thousands of companies and millions of girls participating. And it's amazing how, almost from its inception, the opponents were all over it, complaining that it sent a bad message about female victimhood,

that it was based on false research about girls and low self-esteem, above all that it was gender-biased, that the boys were not invited. The same people who weren't the least bit bothered when boys got the only decent school sports programs—or, for that matter, the entire Supreme Court—were flipping out about a bunch of 13-year-old girls eating in the corporate cafeteria for one afternoon.

4   "What will we tell the boys?" parents agonized. I never had a bit of trouble explaining: I just remind them that the Senate is still 87 percent male. Boys have issues and problems, too, but they're not the same as the ones girls have. We just don't start from the same place; otherwise it wouldn't be called "helping" when a man performs tasks in his own home, or "babysitting" when he looks after his own children. That's why the most famous remark about Take Our Daughters to Work Day is the one from Eleanor Holmes Norton; when asked why there was no such day for boys, she said it was for the same reason there's no White History Month.

5   Women still agonize over balancing work and family; lots of guys still assume they'll balance work and family by getting married. Boys don't have to be introduced to the office. They're old acquaintances. In a survey done for the Ms. Foundation for Women about changing roles, 61 percent of the respondents said they believe men and women are treated differently in the workplace. You can talk all you want about improved access for women now, but it's a recent development, and it still stops several steps from most executive suites.

6   That's not victimhood, it's history. And maybe that's what Take Our Daughters to Work Day has become, a living monument to recent history, to the peaks we've struggled up and the plateaus we're often stuck on. Some of the critics of the day insist darkly that it's part of the feminist agenda, which is always made to sound like a cross between a coven and a communist cell. (I prefer to think it is dedicated to justice, equality and comfortable shoes.) Ironic, isn't it; some of those up in arms about the program are women professionals who, if not for the very movement they decry, might have wound up plowing their ambition into casseroles and no-wax floors instead of punditry and sociological research.

7   There's a photograph from one Take Our Daughters to Work Day on my desk that sums it all up for me. The daughter is mine. She has a huge grin on her face, and a gavel in her hand, and standing behind her is a female federal judge. The judge is wearing a pink sweater; my daughter is wearing the judge's robes. And when I look at that picture I wonder if the judge and I were thinking the same thing, looking at that girl: that the chance of either of us hearing "woman" and "judge" in the same sentence

when we were her age was just about nil. Today there are 199 women judges in the federal system; when I was 11, there were three. Present at the revolution: that's what I feel every time I look at that photograph. Every time a girl plays Little League, every time a father assumes his daughter is as likely to go to college as his son, every time no one looks twice at a female cop or balks at a female surgeon, it's a moment in history, radical and ordinary both at the same time.

8   Critics say that we should talk to girls about their marvelous opportunities instead of taking them out of school and promoting that pesky "feminist agenda" once a year. Pooh. Gavels speak louder than words. Besides, kids are always getting pulled out of school to go to Monticello or chocolate factories or Six Flags. How come there's an uproar only when the field trip takes girls to a place in which girls were fairly recently unheard of, unwelcome? I remember fondly my daughter toddling around my office during the first Take Our Daughters to Work Day 10 years ago with a pencil in her fist, roaring, "I'm working!" whenever anyone tried to talk to her. There are girls now who are second-generation Takers, who went to work themselves when they were teenagers and are now inviting others. The Ms. Foundation for Women has found a group of those women who say that the event had a major impact on their lives, on the way they saw themselves and envisioned their futures. One day seems a scant investment for that sort of return.

9   But it will be a long time before we can truly judge the full effects of the program, just as it has taken us decades to appreciate the effects of the feminist revolution. The assumption of access based on ability and not on gender that seemed utopian when we were young has now become the guiding principle of the mainstream, even when it is honored only in the breach. Take Our Daughters to Work Day is as much about our successes as it is about our continued striving. How could it not be? Our successes have remade the world. Welcome to it, girls. The boys may complain. But that will teach you something, too.

Understanding Meaning

1. What visual image stands out for Quindlen as a symbol of Take Our Daughters to Work Day? Why is it a particularly meaningful image?
2. How much have things changed between her childhood and her daughter's?
3. Why exactly would anyone oppose women taking their daughters to work one day a year? Why does Quindlen not think there is a problem in having this yearly celebration for girls but not for boys?

4. Do you think that girls today feel that there are jobs that they are still not able to pursue? If so, what jobs or types of jobs?
5. *CRITICAL THINKING.* Does Quindlen appear to ignore the problems faced by African American and Hispanic males? Would a Take Your Son to Work Day benefit minority males, who are statistically more likely than white females to drop out of school and statistically more likely than white males to spend time in prison?

Evaluating Strategy

1. How effective is Quindlen's opening example?
2. Quindlen clearly favors women's rights. Is she biased or unfair to men? Explain.
3. How effective is Quindlen's discussion of the photograph in getting her idea across?

Appreciating Language

1. On a scale of informal to formal, how would you rate this essay?
2. Consider Quindlen's audience, the readers of *Newsweek*. Is her approach appropriate? Why or why not?
3. Quindlen makes a number of statements that have the power of a well-written punch line. Analyze one of these:

   - The same people who weren't the least bit bothered when boys got the only decent school sports program—or, for that matter, the entire Supreme Court—were flipping out about a bunch of 13-year-old girls eating in the corporate cafeteria one afternoon.
   - . . . the most famous remark about Take Our Daughters to Work Day is the one from Eleanor Holmes Norton, when asked why there was no such day for boys, she said it was for the same reason there's no White History Month.
   - Ironic, isn't it; some of those up in arms about the program are women professionals who, if not for the very movement they decry, might have wound up plowing their ambition into casseroles and no-wax floors instead of punditry and sociological research.
   - Every time a girl plays Little League, every time a father assumes his daughter is as likely to go to college as his son, every time no one looks twice at a female cop or balks at a female surgeon, it's a moment in history, radical and ordinary both at the same time.
   - Our successes have remade the world. Welcome to it, girls. The boys may complain. But that will teach you something, too.

Writing Suggestions

1. Choose one or more of the quotations from Quindlen listed in Appreciating Language #3 above to analyze and/or support or counterargue in an essay.
2. In many colleges and universities, there are still some majors that draw more males than females and others that draw more females than males. Do you see that as a problem? What do you see as the cause of the disproportion?
3. *COLLABORATIVE WRITING*. After you have drafted an essay in response to Writing Suggestion #1 or #2 above, exchange drafts with a classmate. Write a paragraph in response to the essay you read. Explain the strengths of the essay as well as anything that needs revision or elaboration.

23

ELLEN GOODMAN

Ellen Goodman (1941–) was born in Massachusetts and graduated from Radcliffe College. She worked for Newsweek *and the* Detroit Free Press *before joining the* Boston Globe *in 1967. Her column "At Large" has been widely syndicated since 1976. As an essayist and television commentator, Goodman has discussed feminism, changes in family life, sexual harassment, and male and female relationships. Her essays have been collected in several books, including* Close to Home *(1979),* At Large *(1981), and* Turning Points *(1979).*

Girls Will Be Girls. Unfortunately.

CONTEXT: *In this nationally syndicated column published in 2002, Goodman uses the term "really mean girls" to describe those who are adept at hurtful gossip and nasty conversation— usually meant to destroy the reputation of other girls or women. Goodman sees this often self-destructive hostility as a reaction to the general powerlessness women experience in a male-dominated culture.*

1   You have to hand it to Ally McBeal. In with the Zeitgeist, out with the Zeitgeist—and without ever gaining an ounce.

2   Oooh, was that mean? Well, never mind. Meanness is the point.

3   In the final episode of the series, everybody's favourite neurotic was driven out of town by a pack of 10-year old girls. Ally gave up her job, her friends, her apartment to rescue her daughter Maddie—product of a college egg donation—who was being tormented by classmates otherwise known as the RMGs: the really mean girls.

4   Does this final twist of the plot sound like something lifted from the latest media mania? It should. For the past several months, mean girls have been everywhere. On best-seller lists, on talk shows, in magazines. We've been inundated with anxiety about Alpha females, queen bees, girl bullies and RMGs on a rampage of "relational aggression."

5   Three years ago, right after the Columbine killings, everyone seemed to be worried about the schoolboy culture. Now suddenly everyone seems to be in a panic about the schoolgirl culture.

6   The fact that girls can be mean to each other has been designated "news." The power of girls to harm each other has been dourly and duly described as "on the increase." Ted Koppel even put this revelation on *Nightline*, proclaiming, "I am just fascinated by this."

"Girls Will Be Girls. Unfortunately." by Ellen Goodman from NATIONAL POST, May 25, 2002.

7   Frankly, I doubt that this is news to any woman past fourth grade.
Margaret Atwood described this girl world first and best in her novel *Cat's
Eye*. When Patricia O'Brien and I went to write about women's friendships
in *I Know Just What You Mean*, we saw that "cliques are to girls as bullies
are to boys." It's out there. But maybe there's a new, or at least revisionist,
subtext to this bad-girl news. See, girls aren't all empathic, they're also
vicious. See, girls aren't victims, they're perpetrators. See, girls don't lose
their voice at adolescence; it just turns to whisper campaigns. See, it isn't
just boys who are aggressive; so are girls. Girls just do it with words instead
of their fists.

8   Bingo. Boys and girls are the same. They may be awful, but they're
equally awful. Case closed.

9   I think it's useful to hold the adolescent culture up to the adult light.
But it's also useful to keep a little perspective.

10   When Rachel Simmons, author of *Odd Girl Out*, told Oprah that being
shunned was "meaner" than getting hit, I wanted a time out. Wasn't
Columbine worse than a cruel instant message? More to the point, this isn't
a contest. Sexism, if I remember Women's Studies 101, doesn't only affect
women. Both genders are pushed into narrow, constricting roles. And bullies, of the male or female persuasion, are the gender police.

11   Marie Wilson, president of the Ms. Foundation, notes that girls turn on
each other just as the boy-girl thing clicks in. They look at the world and
find that their mothers and other women aren't really in charge. If they can't
have power upward, she says ruefully, "they control downward." She adds,
"It's the way boys are masculinized and the way girls are feminized that
turns some of them into bullies."

12   Think of it as "informal initiation rites," says psychologist Carol
Gilligan, who's done seminal work on girls. In her new book, *The Birth of
Pleasure*, an elegant and powerful narrative that runs through mythology,
memoir and literature, Gilligan observes that boys begin this initiation as
young as five. "The cultural force driving this initiation surfaces in the
often brutal teasing and shaming of boys who resist or do not fit cultural
codes of masculinity."

13   At adolescence, she adds, girls "experience a similar initiation into
womanhood . . . manifest in the often vicious games of inclusion and exclusion." Gilligan has compared adolescent girls to "sheepdogs." When one
moves out of the pack, they herd her back in line. Girls are forced to toe the
line, especially in sexual behaviour and appearance.

14   But why, she asks skeptically, has the old-girl culture come into the
spotlight now? It's good to talk about what once felt shameful. But there's

no proof that the old-girl culture is stronger today. The "mean girls" media mania, says Gilligan, "gives it a feeling of inevitability. I don't think it is inevitable."

15   As parents, we also have initiation rites when our children recycle our own experiences. It's only inevitable if we decide boys will be boys and girls will be girls. They will be unless we step in and create new ways for them to feel strong and safe.

16   Ally McBeal's law firm always did seem like a bad high school. Now she ends her run by giving up to the RMGs. Too bad for her—and for her daughter—that she didn't stand and fight.

Understanding Meaning

1. What is Goodman's purpose in the essay?
2. What is the relationship between the TV show *Ally McBeal* and her main point?
3. A few years after the school shootings in Columbine, Goodman saw a shift in focus away from "the schoolboy culture" to "the schoolgirl culture." Does she seem to agree that the meanness of girls and boys is really about the same?
4. According to this article, how does the meanness of boys and girls differ?
5. *CRITICAL THINKING.* Do you feel that the mean treatment of girls by other girls is worse because of all the attention it has gotten from the media? Explain.

Evaluating Strategy

1. How does Goodman make use of the once-popular television show *Ally McBeal*? Why was she disappointed by the ending of the series?
2. How does she get across her idea that "Meanness is the point"?
3. Is Goodman's casual style appropriate, given her subject and audience? Why or why not?
4. Does Goodman really mean it at the end of paragraph 8 when she says, "Case closed"?

Appreciating Language

1. What is Goodman trying to suggest when she starts the second paragraph, "Oooh, was that mean?"
2. What is the effect of the parallel sentences at the end of paragraph 7 that all begin, "See . . ."?

Writing Suggestions

1. *COLLABORATIVE WRITING.* Discuss this essay in a small group. Have you seen depictions of RMGs—really mean girls—in movies and television shows? How have they been portrayed? Have they been used for humor or to expose a serious problem? Record the group's comments, and organize the responses by division or classification.
2. Write an essay describing really mean girls at the high school you attended. If they did not exist, was there another type that drew attention for causing problems? Were there male equivalents?
3. Write an essay analyzing the role of the media in shaping the behavior of high school students.

24

ELIZABETH MEHREN

Elizabeth Mehren is the New England bureau chief for the Los Angeles Times. *She is based in New England and is the author of* Born Too Soon: The Story of Emily, Our Premature Baby *(1991) and* After the Darkest Hour the Sun Will Shine Again: A Parent's Guide to Coping with the Loss of a Child *(1997).*

Girls and Juvenile Violence: Stories Rarely Told

CONTEXT: *An increasing number of girls are engaging in violent crime, and girls who run away from home are more likely than boys to commit crimes. But because the justice system is largely designed to deal with male offenders, it is not as well equipped to confront the special problems created by female criminals (such as giving birth while in custody). "When we report about crime," Mehren concludes in this 1998 article, "it is important that we remember the young ladies."*

> "The gangs, I loved them. The people in them were always laughing. Nobody ever told them what to do. I got like that too. Nobody could tell me nothing. . . . Every bad thing, I did it good. I was real good at being bad."
> —Nancy, 17 years old.
> "Girl Trouble: America's Overlooked Crime Problem," Elizabeth Mehren, the *Los Angeles Times*, 1996.

1   Recently I clipped another small article buried deep inside yet another regional newspaper. I added it to a bulging file I keep of such stories. "Girl, 15, Given 45 Years for Murder," it read, and then recounted a highly abbreviated tale of the youngest person ever convicted of murder in this young woman's home state, Rhode Island. Jessica Gonzalez was just 13 when she shot a 23-year-old single mother in the head in a dispute over a man. I couldn't help wondering where the "youngest killer" story would have been played if the murderer had been male.

2   This is no feminist tract: The sad, simple truth is that female juvenile violence is on the upswing. But in terms of news—and in terms of national policy—it has no credibility. Scholars, law enforcement specialists and, I am sad to say, journalists, just don't take this issue seriously.

"Girls and Juvenile Violence: Stories Rarely Told" by Elizabeth Mehren from NIEMAN REPORTS, Winter 1998.

3   Recent figures from the National Center for Juvenile Justice show a 23 percent increase over four years in the number of arrests for girls under 18. For boys, the figure is 11 percent. While the percentage of females under age 18 who break the law is growing, the number still remains relatively small. Also, while killers like Gonzalez are more common than ever, girls tend to be arrested for less serious offenses than boys. Nearly three-quarters of the 678,500 girls arrested in 1994—the most recent year for which FBI statistics are complete—were charged with nonviolent offenses. In short, the girls are bad, and there are more of them. But they're not bad enough, and there's not enough of them to draw the media's attention to their stories in any consistent way. How's that for a weird twist on equality?

4   I am fortunate to work for a newspaper, the *Los Angeles Times*, that often gives reporters large chunks of time to research major projects. Two years ago I spent nearly six months looking into the subject of girls in the juvenile justice system—or "bad girls," as the project became known for short. (Truth in disclosure requires that I mention that a recurring mantra I heard in reporting what became a prize-winning seven-part series was "There are no bad girls, just girls who do bad things.") I traveled to half-a-dozen states and made contact with people in a dozen more. I was shocked at the dearth of academic specialists who knew much about this subject, in contrast to the virtual cottage industry of experts that has developed around boys. But I was thrilled to meet some amazing people in the trenches, those working directly with young women who violate the law. These people became excellent sources in helping me to understand why these girls were where they are. In fact, most of them were dying to talk. They were all too aware of—and troubled by—the simultaneous severity and obscurity of the issue. Sometimes, I felt as though they'd been waiting for my call, waiting for someone from the media to show some interest.

5   I also spent time with girls in jail, in residential treatment facilities and in a variety of probation programs. I met with parents, boyfriends, victims, public defenders, district attorneys, school officials, psychotherapists and social workers, politicians, and—yes—the Girl Scouts. That hardy organization has an active program for girls and women in prison.

6   One of my first important encounters came following a session in Baltimore's juvenile court. Inside and out, the building has a Dickensian quality. A waiting room that lacks magazines, playthings for young children, wall decorations or even a drinking fountain is always filled to overflow capacity, so families are seen splayed around hallways, often holding hasty, way-too-public conferences with lawyers or probation officers. Kids in shackles are marched through hallways en route to court hearings. The

mother I met with looked like a star saleswoman for Century 21, and in fact that's what she was. A single mother of two daughters, she'd worked her way up from part-time receptionist. She told me that when the call came at four in the morning telling her that her younger daughter—the "good" daughter, the model-student daughter, the daughter who never even had a boyfriend, or anyway, not one that her mother knew about—was in custody for stealing a car, she was speechless. "Juvenile delinquency," she remembered thinking. "I thought that meant boys."

7   That, of course, is the prevailing opinion of most policymakers, not to mention most of us in the media. It is true that from time to time we go through a brief period of frenzied coverage about "the girl gang problem," as if bands of marauding females with tattoos and scary hair were about to take over the universe. Not likely. Gangster girls do make good copy and provide great pictures, but my research suggested that girl gangs are largely overrated. For the most part they represent a companionate activity—a way for girls to earn points with their gangbanger boyfriends—kind of like old-fashioned ladies' auxiliaries. Sure, they sometimes slice each other up, often relying on the razor blades they carry under their tongues or in their big hairdos. One teenager rolled up her T-shirt to reveal a midriff scarred like a patchwork quilt, the handiwork of an enemy who was at that moment confined to the same work camp, albeit not for that particular offense. With some pride, that girl told me she used a screwdriver, not a knife or a razor.

8   But the truth is that girls are even more likely to commit crimes in the course of running away, generally from abusive homes. That's the real story, the under-reported story, the one we too often miss altogether. The Baltimore real estate mother told me the trouble must have started when her daughter, then 11, was molested by an uncle. Then, in tears, she confided that she, too, was molested as a child—by her own mother. Intake studies in juvenile facilities show that 50 percent to 70 percent say they have been emotionally, physically or sexually abused—high end on sexual. Anecdotally, wardens and others inside girls prison units and the few female-specific facilities that exist for juveniles believe the figure to be far higher.

9   Efforts at rehabilitation generally follow a one-size-fits-all (or in this case, none) model. The juvenile justice system was, after all, designed for boys. Gender-specific treatment is rare. Not surprisingly, justice is meted out in a decidedly jagged fashion. Following the ever-popular theory that girls who commit crimes must be "crazy," middle- and upper-class girls are often shipped off to private mental health facilities—usually compliments of their parents' insurance policies. Some bureaucratic genius who was presumably paid by the syllable dreamed up the term "transinstitutionalization"

to describe this process. The rest of the girls who commit crimes such as assault and/or battery, grand theft or robbery, drug infractions or murder are shunted off to the same kind of dismal, revolving-door youth facilities that house male offenders. As with their male counterparts, their first jail sentence is seldom their last. This is why, parenthetically, the number of adult female offenders is also skyrocketing.

10   But girls come equipped with another set of complexities: their ovaries. When an incarcerated juvenile gives birth, almost universally, she is immediately separated from her child. Young mothers seldom receive special breaks when it comes to jail terms—nor, necessarily, should they. Still, the implications for yet another generation are daunting and, as reporters, our stories about these girls ought to occasionally explore the impact all of this will likely have on their children.

11   Some girls I interviewed boasted that they were just as bad as the boy next door. Some boys I talked to admitted they were afraid of girls who practiced the art of "banking"—walking in a tight little row and methodically taking down anyone who gets in the way. Boys also expressed admiration at how tough and bloodless girls were getting to be these days. These perspectives tear apart some of our gender stereotypes and they can provide leads to more nuanced coverage of juvenile violence today.

12   I heard many people within the juvenile justice system refer to girls as afterthoughts or "throwaways": invisible delinquents who are in the system—albeit a system that doesn't really know what to do with them. The sad fact is that, in terms of public awareness, they are all but invisible, too. I'm not trying to paint an alarmist picture, but today juvenile violence is, unfortunately, an increasingly equal opportunity experience. When we report about crime, it's important that we remember the young ladies.

Understanding Meaning

1. As a reporter, why did Mehren find the story of girls in the juvenile justice system an unusual one? How does the coverage of male juveniles involved in crime compare to that of female juveniles?
2. What is Mehren's purpose in the article?
3. When Mehren contacted authorities who deal most directly with delinquent girls, what was their attitude toward reporters?
4. According to these authorities, what background do many of the girls share? What happens to the children that these girls have in prison?
5. Which girls, according to Mehren, are more likely to get involved in crime other than gangster girls? Once convicted, how does social class enter into the sentencing?

6. What is Mehren's closing advice to her fellow journalists?
7. *CRITICAL THINKING.* Mehren reports that some of these girls get into trouble with the law once they run away from home. What other reasons might a teenage girl have for committing a crime?

Evaluating Strategy

1. What effect was Mehren trying to achieve by starting with two examples? What is her point about cases like the one in which a fifteen-year-old girl is sentenced to prison for forty-five years for murder?
2. How effective are Mehren's other examples?
3. Where does Mehren most directly sum up the thesis of her essay? (Remember that it may take more than one sentence.)
4. How relevant—and convincing—are Mehren's statistics?
5. Why is the quotation from the mother in paragraph 6 an important one?

Appreciating Language

1. Certain statements or expressions that Mehren includes in the piece have a sarcastic or ironic edge. Analyze these:

    *   "How's that for a weird twist on equality?" (paragraph 3)
    *   "Juvenile delinquency," she remembered thinking. "I thought that meant boys." (paragraph 6)
    *   "When we report about crime, it's important that we remember the young ladies." (paragraph 12)

2. One of Mehren's key statements is her reference to "the simultaneous severity and obscurity of the issue" (paragraph 4). What does she mean?
3. Explain what Mehren means in this statement that ends paragraph 11: "These perspectives tear apart some of our gender stereotypes and they can provide leads to more nuanced coverage of juvenile violence today."

Writing Suggestions

1. Choose an issue that you feel has received too little attention from the media, and explain in an essay what the issue is and why it is not more widely covered.
2. *COLLABORATIVE WRITING.* Discuss Mehren's essay with a group of other students. Ask each member to suggest reasons why girls engage in crime. Develop a paragraph summarizing your group's main ideas.

25

RONALD SCHACHTER

Ronald Schachter is a former high school English teacher who is now a freelance writer and developer of online curriculum, based in Newton, Massachusetts. He has published articles about education technology, teacher development, and school administration.

The Single-Sex Solution: Is There a Way That Separate Can Be Even Better Than Equal?

CONTEXT: *This article, published in* District Administration *in 2003, suggests that in our concern for gender equity we may have lost sight of the fact that young girls and boys learn best in different ways and under different conditions.*

1   Just before eight in the morning at Thurgood Marshall Elementary School in Seattle, some boys play a last-minute game of soccer on one side of the elongated playground. Girls jump rope in another section, and the two groups share the slides and a jungle gym at the far end of the yard. It's a typical scene that plays out daily in schoolyards across the country.

2   Principal Benjamin Wright checks his watch and then, looking and sounding like a tough football coach, loudly blows the whistle hanging from his neck. "Let's do this!" he yells.

3   Immediately, the dispersed students come toward him and get into tight lines separated according to their grade levels—and their gender. Thus begins a school day that is hardly typical, as the children march upstairs to single-sex classrooms in an educational experiment designed to improve student achievement and destined to raise controversy.

4   The Thurgood Marshall School is charging through its third year of separating classes by sex and—along with more than a dozen other schools around the country—is trying to demonstrate that single-sex public education can make a positive difference, especially to students in predominantly minority, low-income districts.

5   "We were at the bottom of the barrel. We were the worst school in the district," says Wright, who arrived at the school in 1998 and notes that the student population is almost 95 percent minority. "My philosophy is that

"The Single Sex Solution: Is There a Way That Separate Can Be Even Better Than Equal?" by Ronald Schachter from DISTRICT ADMINISTRATION, April 2003.

we have to meet each child where he or she is. Then we can do whatever it takes to make them successful. You can best do that if you isolate the sexes."

6   In Seattle's decentralized school district, Wright promoted his idea of separating the sexes, first in a fourth-grade pilot program and then for the entire school. Seattle's Superintendent of Public Schools Joseph Olchefske was listening.

7   "All of the work around the standards-based movement is built on the simple premise that it's the job of every school to see that every child achieves," Olchefske says. "If gender-based education works, it's incumbent on us to do it."

8   The early results argue that the new approach at Thurgood Marshall has worked, along with the more conventional reforms of longer school years and smaller class sizes that Wright also introduced. Scores on the WASL, the standardized state achievement test required of fourth graders, rose sharply in 2001 and 2002, the first two years of the single-sex program. For instance, in 2000, only 27 percent of the students in co-ed classes met the state standards for reading and 11 percent for math. The results in reading increased to 51 percent in 2001 and 60 percent in 2002. And while students showed a small decline in math for 2001, an impressive 45 percent met state standards in the following year.

Experiments are Multiplying

9   The single-sex movement that Wright and the Seattle Public Schools have joined has gained momentum during the past year from a Bush administration initiative to relax Title IX regulations and over the past decade from several prominent educational theories. Girls perform better, particularly in math and science—says one of these theories—if they are separated from their male counterparts. Another says that boys, especially those in the inner city at risk for dropping out, have their own set of learning needs that can best be addressed in an all-male environment.

10   These dual approaches play out in Thurgood Marshall's classrooms. The fourth-grade boys' and girls' classrooms stand side by side and mirror each other, right down to the bank of computers to one side, the brightly colored inspirational sayings on the walls, and the U-shaped arrangement of tables at which the students sit. The parallelism stops there.

11   "I really think the girls focus better without the boys," says fourth-grade teacher Casie Baddeley of her students. "They don't worry about doing things that the boys will make fun of. They know that the boys influence

them, and they really do have more confidence to speak for themselves when boys aren't there. Now it's to the point that even if there are boys in the room, the girls don't care. They have enough confidence to speak out and say what they feel."

12   Baddeley punctuates her teaching with comments aimed at reinforcing self-esteem and says that this new-found confidence extends to her girls' relationship to science and math. "The first activity I have every year is to have the girls draw a 'mathematician,'" she says. "And almost all of them will draw men. And we'll talk about, 'Why are none of your pictures of women?' And they say, 'I don't know.' Then I give them a mid-assessment. Some do men. But many do women, and they are drawing themselves."

It's Different for Boys

13   For the 19 boys next door in Linh Le's fourth-grade classroom, discipline is the name of the game, at least for starters. Today they are learning the science of what happens when a balloon filled with water is heated in a microwave oven. Le has her students move over to the microwave to view the experiment and adds firmly, "without fighting, pushing, and yelling and screaming. Or you can stay at your desks."

14   The boys comply, but it is clearly hard for them to stay still. They are squirmier, chattier and more easily distracted than the fourth-grade girls. These behaviors draw increasingly forceful reprimands until Le's discipline seems to pay off. Eventually the young scientists, raising their hands and waiting their turn, begin to explain what happened to the balloon.

15   "A lot of boys learn kinesthetically," explains principal Wright, "and it doesn't mean they're bad kids when the teacher says, 'Sit down,' and they're still moving in their seats. And it also doesn't mean they have attention deficit disorder."

16   Noted child psychiatrist Alvin Poussaint of the Harvard Medical School has studied African-American children extensively. He agrees that all-male classrooms provide an opportunity to help at-risk African-American boys.

17   "Nowadays, schools take a lot of black boys they can't work with, and they put them in special education," Poussaint observes. "They kind of give up on them, and we know that after third grade, a lot of black boys start falling behind. So how do you structure the curriculum and activities during the day to make it more appropriate to the issues around black male children?

18   "Let's say that black male children think they need to fight more. How do you set up the classroom in terms of discipline? How many recesses

should you have to let the boys run around and burn up more energy? How can you integrate some real things that they like into the curriculum—whether [it's] their greater use of black English or video games—and use them as a stepping board in helping to educate them?"

The Fight about Title IX

19 According to the Brighter Choice Foundation, which tracks single-sex education and this year launched separate boys and girls charter schools in Albany, N.Y., 17 single-sex schools were up and running when this school year began. They ranged from elementary to high school programs and reached from California to New York.

20 That number might multiply with the decision last May by the U.S. Department of Education to review existing Title IX regulations, which for more than three decades have sought to eliminate race- and gender-based discrimination in schools. The action followed a provision in the No Child Left Behind Act of 2001. The DOE recently completed a 60-day period for public comment and should announce any changes in Title IX regulations by the end of 2003.

21 "I think what we need to look at is what it means to offer 'comparable opportunities' to members of the otherwise excluded sex," says Brian Jones, the DOE's general counsel. "What we hope to be able to do is to build more flexibility into that definition of what a comparable opportunity is. If you decide that you want to have a math academy for girls because there's some research out there that shows girls learn mathematics better in a cooperative environment, where pushy boys aren't present, you may still be able to say that boys learn math very well in co-ed settings."

22 Jones adds that the DOE is also focusing on restrictions that keep co-educational schools from offering selected single-sex classes, such as a math or science course just for girls.

23 The latest review of Title IX and most single-sex experiments in recent years have raised the concerns of groups from the American Civil Liberties Union to the National Organization of Women to the NAACP. These organizations successfully opposed an attempt in 1991 to establish three all-male academies in Detroit; and the ACLU and NOW have a longstanding complaint pending with the DOE against The Young Women's Leadership School, which opened in East Harlem, N.Y., in 1996.

24 In its published response to the current challenge to Title IX, NOW spells out its position: "Unfortunately, decades of experience in related areas, such as job training, college athletics and professional sports, indicate that

female-dominated programs consistently receive fewer resources than boys in primary and secondary educational programs. Separating girls and boys in primary and secondary educational programs therefore threatens to exacerbate, rather than ameliorate, inequities between boys and girls."

25   Harvard Education School professor emeritus Charles Willie has studied racial desegregation for decades and was the architect of Boston's school desegregation program during the 1990s. He has his reservations about single-sex schools as a remedy.

26   "We think we have to set the people at the bottom apart. We can't ignore history," Willie cautions. "The reason why the Civil Rights movement in education started was that all those black students who had been set apart were not doing that well. The only way we can reach our students to catch up is to have them run the race with other students."

27   Willie says that his studies of school systems in Boston, Charleston, S.C., and Lee County, Fla., have shown that the highest achieving students tend to be in schools most diversified in terms of race, gender and socioeconomic status.

28   "You've got to be very, very careful," admits DOE general counsel Brian Jones. "We don't want to be in a position of defending discrimination on the basis of sex that doesn't have some real sound basis in educational research."

Limited Research

29   But research is not easy to compile. A 2001 study gave a mixed review of six California districts that had tried male and female academies for middle school and high school. The report concluded that single-sex education inadvertently reinforced gender stereotypes, and today the San Francisco 49ers Academy in Palo Alto is the only single-sex school left in the group.

30   In contrast, Providence College sociology professor Cornelius Riordan, who has conducted national studies of single-sex, private Catholic schools in urban areas, sees a value in their educational approach.

31   "In a nutshell," Riordan says, "what I have found is that there does appear to be a consistent positive effect on academic outcomes, largely limited to disadvantaged students. The implications are that it is a viable alternative for the kind of schools that at-risk students should attend, particularly those in African-American and Hispanic communities."

32   Recently, The Brighter Choice Charter Schools in Albany contracted with Riordan to conduct similar research.

33   In the meantime, the founders of single-sex public school programs point to other lessons learned. "If you build it, they will come," says Ann Rubenstein Tisch, who navigated the complex New York City school system in order to create The Young Woman's Leadership School in New York. Tisch's foundation has recently built another girls' academy in Chicago. She is planning four more schools in New York, including two academies for boys.

34   Back in Seattle, Benjamin Wright has been hosting a stream of school administrators from around the United States as well as from Canada, England and Australia interested in starting single-sex schools of their own. Wright also will be partnering with five other Seattle schools to help them get started.

35   "I'm not saying that single-sex education cures all problems," Wright adds. "It's not a panacea, but it's surely an alternative that we must use."

Understanding Meaning

1. How is the Thurgood Marshall Elementary School different from other public schools in America? What was its administrators' reason for trying this fairly radical change?
2. According to the article, what has been the effect?
3. Why do Title IX regulations create problems for schools wishing to separate students by gender? Why do groups like the ACLU, NOW, and the NAACP oppose single-sex classes?
4. What does research reveal about single-sex classes?
5. *CRITICAL THINKING*. Do you feel that it would have been a good idea for your elementary school to have had at least some classes segregated by gender? Explain why or why not.

Evaluating Strategy

1. As you read the first half of the essay, what seemed to be Schachter's purpose in writing it? Did you change your mind about his purpose as you read on?
2. Does Schachter eventually give a balanced view of the two sides of the issue of single-sex schools?
3. What different types of support does Schachter offer to support his main points? Are you convinced that there are merits to single-sex education? For all students? Some?

Appreciating Language

1. Notice the individuals Schachter quotes. What do the quotes add to the essay? How does Schachter work the identification of the speaker or writer into his sentences?
2. Does Schachter make use of biased language or strongly emotional language? If he is not appealing primarily to his audience's emotions, what type of appeal is he trying to use?

Writing Suggestions

1. Write an essay explaining which you think is more important for schools to provide—teaching students in the classroom setting in which they perform best academically or protecting their right to "comparable opportunities"? Can the two goals be achieved together?
2. Write an essay stating whether you believe single-sex classrooms would have been a good idea in the schools you attended.
3. *COLLABORATIVE WRITING.* Discuss this essay with a group of students and record observations regarding single-sex classes. Record comments by the group and use comparison or division to organize responses.

26

Medical Malpractice

*The health and life of my patients will be my
first consideration.*
—The Hippocratic Oath

*The problem with medical malpractice is that
it occurs far too often. It is the eighth leading
cause of death in America, killing more people
than AIDS, breast cancer, or automobile
crashes.*
—Leo Boyle

*The villain, I believe, is our legal system,
which has become a free-for-all, lacking the
reliability and consistency that are essential to
everyone, especially doctors and patients. Most
victims of error get nothing, while others win
lottery-like jury awards even when the doctor
did nothing wrong.*
—Philip K. Howard

*I am sure I could have become a millionaire
by suing my father's doctors and the
hospital. . . . But I didn't. . . . [T]o sue
someone for failing to be the god we wanted
strikes me as wrong.*
—Alden Blodget

"COMFORT ALWAYS"

A century ago, most physicians in the United States had only a fragmentary knowledge of medicine. Few medical schools were affiliated with universities, and many were not even accredited. Some medical schools did not require applicants to have a high school diploma. In a few states it was possible to obtain a medical license in six months. Apprenticed to older doctors, medical students learned primarily by observation. There were few courses in the sciences, and little connection was made between research and practice. Equipped with dubious medicines and crude surgical techniques, doctors were frequently able to provide little more than emotional support. Unable to treat many conditions, physicians attempted only to explain the natural course of a disease and inform patients and families about what to expect. Patients lived in a time when it was common for women to die in childbirth, for infants to die from whooping cough, for accident victims to bleed to death or remain disabled following life-saving but crude operations. With few diagnostic devices and limited laboratory testing, medicine was as much an art as a science. The reality of the medical profession was expressed in the popular saying, "Cure never, diagnose sometimes, comfort always."

Miracles and Malpractice

The twentieth century saw a revolution in medical science, medical education, and the medical profession. Diseases that decades before claimed millions of lives were eliminated or made manageable. Extensive operations that once required weeks of hospital care and often left patients disabled were replaced with minimally invasive procedures performed in out-patient clinics. New generations of drugs improved the quality of life for millions of people. Doctors became heroic figures, portrayed as selfless role models of skill, wisdom, and compassion in motion pictures and television dramas. For decades, public opinion polls showed that Americans rated physicians as one of the most respected professions.

Yet each year patients die or suffer severe injuries from medical malpractice. Patients are given the wrong medication or subjected to unnecessary operations. Surgeons make mistakes. Hospitals fail to follow postoperative procedures, and patients suffer from complications such as infections and drug interactions. According to an Institute of Medicine report, 98,000 hospital patients died from preventable medical errors in 1999.

In response, patients, who now view doctors as technicians rather than supportive advisors, sue when things go wrong. Attorneys who represent the injured view themselves as patient advocates, making sure victims are compensated for lost wages, disability, and pain and suffering.

To protect themselves from lawsuits, doctors and hospitals carry malpractice insurance. The cost of this insurance has soared in recent years. Some physicians who have never been sued or accused of doing anything wrong have seen their annual premiums rise from $30,000 to over $100,000. In protest, some doctors have gone on strike, refused to treat high-risk patients, or left states with records of high jury awards. Angry doctors picketed in New Jersey, carrying signs reading, "Next Time You Get Sick, Call a Lawyer!"

The War between Doctors and Lawyers

Critics of the current malpractice system claim that lawyers, who retain a third of most settlements or jury awards, care more about money than making injured patients whole. The fear of lawsuits has led doctors to practice "defensive medicine," ordering expensive but often needless tests to cover themselves in the chance that a patient will have a complication or rare condition that might not be found in normal examinations. Doctors point out that they spend valuable time documenting their actions, not to benefit patients or improve their practices but to establish records they might need in case they are sued. They argue that "capping," or limiting, jury awards and making losers pay the legal fees of both sides would reduce frivolous lawsuits and lower malpractice premiums. Physicians have switched specialties or left the profession because they cannot afford insurance.

MEDICAL MALPRACTICE INSURANCE COSTS, 2002

SPECIALTY	AVERAGE PREMIUM	HIGHEST PREMIUM
Neurosurgeon	$71,000	Chicago, $283,000
Ob-Gyn	$56,546	Miami, $210,576
Emergency Physician	$53,500	Miami, $150,000
Orthopedic Surgeon	$38,000	Philadelphia, $135,000
General Surgeon	$36,354	Miami, $174,268

Source: *Time* Magazine

Trial lawyers, however, insist the reason for the malpractice crisis is not frivolous lawsuits but bad doctors and poor hospital care. State medical boards fail to discipline bad doctors, even those who have been found guilty of malpractice. A small handful of incompetent physicians are responsible for a majority, if not all, malpractice cases in some states. Capping awards and making injured patients pay defense costs if they lose will not make doctors better, attorneys argue, but only discourage legitimate victims from seeking compensation.

The rising cost of malpractice insurance premiums, they assert, does not result from litigation but is because insurance companies have lost money in the stock market. Doctors saw their premiums rise after the terrorist attacks of September 11th, 2001, when insurance carriers braced for massive payouts and potential lawsuits. New Jersey is often cited as a

state in which rising malpractice premiums are driving physicians to change
specialties or leave. Malpractice insurance rates may be escalating, but the
state's statistics reveal no sudden increase in cases. Lawyers point out that
doctors consistently win the majority of the cases that go to trial.

MEDICAL MALPRACTICE LITIGATION, NEW JERSEY, 2002

Number of Cases Resolved	1,700
Number of Cases Dismissed	628
Number of Cases That Went to Trial	200
Cases Resolved in Favor of Doctor	146
Cases Resolved in Favor of Patient	54
Total Jury Verdicts	$59,400,000
Average Verdict	$1,100,000
Median Verdict	$325,000
Verdicts over $5 million (at least two reduced by the courts)	4

Source: New Jersey Judiciary Civil Statistics

Physicians, however, argue that even though few lawsuits are successful, the cost of defense and the pressure to make out-of-court settlements
drives up both malpractice insurance rates and the frequency of defensive
medicine.

No Solution in Sight?

Writing in *Money* in 2002, Peter Carbonara observed that suggested reforms
fail to address the basic problem:

> Capping jury verdicts or providing insurance subsidies to doctors may provide
> some relief around the edges, but the fundamental issues are unchanged.
> HMOs and health insurance companies will still try to reimburse doctors as
> little as possible, while plaintiffs' lawyers will still try to extract the largest
> amounts they can get from malpractice carriers. In the middle will remain the
> doctors—and their patients.

The full costs of the medical malpractice crisis go far beyond doctors' insurance rates and physicians refusing to treat a few high-risk patients. Philip Howard, founder of the legal reform organization Common Good, argues that the crisis has grave consequences for the health of all Americans:

> Some economists estimate that unnecessary tests and procedures, ordered by doctors to build a record just in case there is a lawsuit, costs more than $100 billion a year—enough to provide health insurance for the 40 million Americans who have no coverage. Modern medical technology is bringing us miracle cures, yet the absence of a backup system to catch human errors is causing thousands of deaths each year. In our culture of legal fear, the candor vital to improving care is also a casualty. Because doctors don't feel safe talking about mistakes, they are unable to learn from them—or even offer an honest apology.

Before reading these entries, consider these questions.

Has the medical community created false expectations in patients? Do commercials for hospitals, doctors, and drugs give the public false impressions? Are hospitals as caring and compassionate as their commercials suggest? Do drug commercials imply that chronic diseases can be immediately and painlessly cured? In promoting medical science, have medical professionals given patients unrealistic expectations? How much of perceived malpractice stems from simple lack of patient knowledge?

Do malpractice suits really help improve the quality of medicine? Trial lawyers argue that malpractice suits help discipline bad doctors and remedy poor hospital care. But in most instances court settlements are confidential. When patients prove malpractice and receive payments for injuries, they are often barred from speaking to the press or mentioning the terms of the settlement. If the terms of the lawsuit are kept secret, how is the public informed about a potential danger?

Should legal action against doctors and hospitals focus on money or reform? Do multimillion dollar verdicts force doctors and hospitals to improve their methods and procedures? Should bad doctors be suspended, required to take courses, or forced to limit their practices to low-risk medical care?

Does malpractice litigation unfairly inflate medical costs? To avoid lawsuits, do doctors practice "defensive medicine" by ordering needless tests just to have evidence in case they are sued? Does defensive medicine waste resources, raise insurance premiums, and thus deny health care to people who cannot afford it?

Should medical associations disbar more doctors?   A small number of doctors are responsible for a large percentage of malpractice lawsuits. Often, however, insurance companies pay settlements and the physicians are allowed to continue practicing. If the American Medical Association (AMA) supported the disbarment of bad doctors, could lawsuits, high insurance premiums, and defensive medicine be reduced?

Do malpractice lawsuits discourage doctors from taking high-risk cases?   Women with high-risk pregnancies can find it difficult to find a doctor to deliver their babies because physicians are afraid of being sued. Will litigation increasingly deny health care to those who need it most?

Should attorneys be compensated differently?   In the United States, attorneys usually receive one-third of any jury award. In Britain, attorneys charge clients for their time whether they win or lose. Some reformers argue this system would reduce frivolous malpractice suits and dissuade lawyers from pressing for excessive compensation. Trial attorneys, however, argue that many patients, already suffering a loss of income and medical bills, will be unable to afford additional legal fees. Changing the way attorneys are paid may reduce the number of malpractice lawsuits, they insist, but will do little to curtail malpractice.

WRITING ABOUT MEDICAL MALPRACTICE

The issue of medical malpractice can trigger a number of responses that can be useful topics for writing assignments.

Critical Thinking and Prewriting

Medical malpractice raises controversial issues. You may have strong positions about the issue. Perhaps you know or are related to a doctor or nurse who complains about frivolous lawsuits and disgruntled patients looking for money. Or you may know someone who was injured by a physician or hospital and unable to get any compensation. Although these experiences may be a good starting point, good writing is based on more than what you "feel" about a subject. Critical thinking and prewriting can help you move beyond first impressions and emotional responses to develop meaningful observations and suggestions.

Getting Started: Exploring Ideas

1. Does the malpractice crisis reveal something larger about American society? Do we believe that whenever we suffer we deserve compensation? Do many of us feel that someone has to pay when anyone is hurt? Do we live in a society where anyone with a problem is a victim?
2. What motivates the legal profession—money or reform? Why do trial lawyers resist reform that would cap jury awards or focus on disciplining bad doctors rather than compensating victims?
3. Can juries make sound decisions about medical issues? Are juries likely to be motivated by sympathy for patients even when no errors were committed? Are juries more likely to grant awards because they know the money comes from an insurance company and not directly from an individual?
4. Should insurance companies be regulated differently? Unlike auto insurance companies that raise rates on bad drivers to keep prices low for good drivers, medical malpractice companies usually raise rates for all doctors, even those who have never been sued.

Strategies for Writing about Medical Malpractice

Define key terms.
Before you can write about this issue, you have to define what you mean by *malpractice*. When, in your opinion, does a doctor commit malpractice? Can doctors make "honest mistakes" without committing malpractice?

Consider statistics carefully.
Commentators on medical malpractice use statistics to support their arguments. Attorneys present numbers to show that there is no explosion of either lawsuits or multimillion dollar awards. Doctors cite their soaring insurance premiums. Other researchers present facts about defensive medicine. Consider the source of statistics writers use and their alternative interpretations. Lawyers, for instance, point out that most doctors win at trial. They do not mention the number of doctors who feel pressured to settle before trial.

Determine if courtrooms are the best places to resolve malpractice issues.
The legal system is based on presenting opposing arguments to a judge or jury. Medical and scientific issues, however, may not always be seen in terms of right and wrong. Are courts ill-equipped to sensibly and fairly solve the problem of medical malpractice?

Discuss the importance of patient education.
How many lawsuits could be avoided if patients truly understood the nature of their illness or injury, the limits of modern medicine, and the side effects and risks of treatment? Do doctors take enough time to talk with patients? Are patients really willing to listen?

Evaluate the role of advertising professional services.
Until recently, doctors and lawyers did not advertise. Today, however, commercials feature attorneys promising big awards for those who have been injured. Doctors, clinics, and hospitals present themselves as compassionate professionals. Do these promotions only fuel the war between doctors and lawyers?

Consider patient expectations.
Previous generations accepted suffering as a part of life. Do we expect to live into old age without infirmity, pain, or disfigurement? Is a society focused on youth and appearance able to accept the reality that medicine cannot cure every disease and ease every discomfort?

WRITING IN THE MODES

You may find that selecting a particular mode is an effective way of examining a topic, organizing ideas, and shaping an essay.

Narration
1. If you or someone you know has been involved in a malpractice case, write a brief summary of the incident and describe its significance.
2. Use narration to illustrate how the malpractice crisis affects patient care. Write a hypothetical story about a doctor who decides not to treat a high-risk patient or a patient who trusts an incompetent physician.

Description
1. Describe the way doctors and lawyers advertise in your area. Do their commercials and ads encourage people to have unrealistic expectations?
2. Describe how doctors should be trained to avoid malpractice. Do you think physicians worry more about making errors or avoiding lawsuits?

Definition
1. Develop and explain your definition of malpractice. Is a doctor who orders nine tests when most doctors order ten committing malpractice? Is it malpractice if a patient suffering from several severe ailments dies during a routine procedure?

2. Provide your definition of *disability* or *pain and suffering*. At what point does a degree of incapacity or discomfort became unbearable? Should there be different definitions? If an operation for carpal tunnel syndrome leaves a symphony violinist with paralysis, would he or she have a stronger case than a disc jockey or a history teacher?

Example

1. Illustrate your definition of malpractice with a hypothetical example. Demonstrate what act you consider a genuine medical error and explain why a patient deserves compensation.
2. Present an example of "defensive medicine," in which a physician orders needless tests to protect himself or herself from potential lawsuits.

Comparison and Contrast

1. Use a "then and now" approach to show how people's attitudes about doctors and medicine have changed. How did Hollywood depict doctors in the era of Doctor Kildare and how were they depicted in films like *The Verdict*?
2. Compare and contrast doctors and lawyers. Both professionals claim to care about their patients and clients and hope to remedy their problems. Are some true professionals and others only motivated by money?

Division and Classification

1. Use division to discuss different solutions to the medical malpractice crisis.
2. Use classification to rank degrees of malpractice, such as criminal negligence, failure to follow common standards, preventable error, and questionable practices.

Process

1. Describe step by step how doctors should inform patients about drugs, surgical procedures, or their general health. Can doctors protect themselves from lawsuits by helping patients make informed decisions?
2. Outline the process by which malpractice complaints should be handled. Should a patient have to get a lawyer, or should he or she be able to file a complaint with a medical review board?

Cause and Effect

1. Discuss the effect of the malpractice crisis on medicine itself. Does it lead to tighter standards, better care, and more precise technology? Or does it retard medical research, cause defensive medicine, and deny health care?
2. What is the main cause of soaring malpractice insurance coverage—frivolous lawsuits, poor insurance company investments, or bad doctors?

Argument and Persuasion

1. Write a persuasive essay that agrees or disagrees with statements made by one of the writers in this chapter. You may respond to the entire article or a particular passage.
2. What is the single best way to solve the medical malpractice crisis? Develop an essay arguing why this reform should be instituted.

STUDENT PAPER

Taking Responsibility

Bad doctors exist. Too many of them are practicing. Too few hospitals discipline their physicians as rigorously as they should. The state medical associations, which complain about malpractice suits and the cost of insurance, do not revoke or suspend enough licenses. Greedy lawyers also exist. Too many are coaching disgruntled patients into filing suits in hopes a sympathetic jury will award a multimillion dollar settlement.

But behind all this lies something else. Part of the malpractice crisis is caused by two factors: public misperception about who is responsible for our health and the overselling of medical science by doctors and drug companies.

When we think of health too often we think of doctors, drugs, and hospitals. But the fact is that today most diseases and many injuries are preventable. The leading killers are cancer, heart disease, and diabetes. These are diseases that can be largely prevented or delayed by a healthy lifestyle. If Americans quit smoking, avoided drinking and driving, ate sensibly, and wore seat belts, the health care costs of this country would drop dramatically. The fact that 40% of American adults are obese is proof that we are not taking responsibility for our health. We expect doctors to be able to counter twenty years of poor living with drugs or painless operations.

The medical community is to blame as well. Television bombards us with commercials for a range of prescription drugs. Surgeons appear on programs extolling the virtues of the latest procedures, often failing to educate the public about complications and side effects.

Both these factors lead many people to expect doctors to work miracles, to expect pills to lower blood pressure and adjust cholesterol levels caused by an unhealthy lifestyle. Given our unrealistic expectations, we cannot accept the idea that medicine can't save us from death, pain, or disability. And so when doctors fail us, when we have to face mortality, we want to blame someone. And too many lawyers are there to help us not only find someone to blame but offer us money to ease our pain.

Malpractice exists, and bad doctors should be sued. But a good deal of the crisis has really little to do with medicine or law but with our inability to accept painful realities.

Understanding Meaning

1. What is the student's thesis? Is it clearly stated? Can you summarize it in your own words?
2. What, in this student's opinion, is the cause of the medical malpractice crisis?
3. Why does the student believe that the malpractice crisis has been caused by something deeper than medical mistakes?
4. What does the student mean by "unrealistic expectations"? Who creates the public's attitudes about health, doctors, and medicine?
5. Who, in the student's view, should be held responsible for people's health and well-being?

Evaluating Strategy

1. Do you think the title is effective? Why or why not?
2. Underline the thesis statement. Is it clear? Could it be placed elsewhere in the essay?
3. How does the student support the thesis?
4. How effective is the conclusion?

Appreciating Language

1. How effective is the student's tone and style? Is the language suitable for a college essay? Are there any words or phrases you would replace?
2. Does the student use any words that show a bias toward or against doctors or lawyers? Are they any positive or negative connotations that shape the impact of the essay?

Writing Suggestions

1. Write a brief essay that supports or opposes the student's thesis. Are people unrealistic about medicine and their own health? Are most people you know taking responsibility for their own health care?
2. *COLLABORATIVE WRITING.* Discuss this essay with several students, and write a list of three or four key issues that must be resolved to both reduce the number of medical errors and protect good doctors from lawsuits and inflated insurance premiums.

CHECKLIST

Before submitting your paper, review these points.

1. Does your paper have a clearly stated thesis? Does it express a clear point of view?

2. Do you support your thesis with reliable evidence?

3. Do you avoid making biased or illogical statements that will distract from your authority and alienate readers?

4. Do you anticipate readers' possible objections and answer them?

5. Is the paper clearly organized? Do paragraph breaks group related ideas and signal transitions?

6. Does the tone, style, and word choice of your paper suit your purpose and audience?

 Companion Website

See **academic.cengage.com/english** for information on planning, organizing, writing, and revising essays.

 E-Reading: InfoTrac College Edition
http://www.infotrac-college.com

For Further Reading
E–Readings Online

Search for articles by author or title in InfoTrac College Edition after entering your user name and password.

Mark Lopatin, *I Knew She Was Trouble: Pressured to Settle a Malpractice Case, This Doctor Is Still Outraged by the Legal System That Allowed It to Happen*
Even though he did nothing medically wrong, a physician felt compelled to follow his lawyer's advice and settle out of court to avoid a decision made by a jury moved by emotion rather than fact.

Family Practice News, *Good People Skills May Help Deter Malpractice Suits: Fire Difficult Patients*
A physician believes that doctors can avoid lawsuits by both taking time to listen to patients and firing those who don't follow their orders.

James Gray and Eric Zicklin, *Why Bad Doctors Aren't Kicked out of Medicine*
Physician competency is monitored by 63 state medical boards that lack uniform standards and rarely revoke or even suspend licenses of impaired and incompetent doctors.

Peter Carbonara, *Diagnosis: Premium Shock Rx Strike: When New Jersey MDs Walked Off the Job We Learned Just How Sick the Health-Care System Really Is*
The proposed reforms that would cap awards and subsidize doctors' insurance costs will do little to address the fundamental causes of the malpractice crisis.

James Whalen, *Warning: The Legal System May Be Hazardous to Your Health*
The malpractice insurance crisis is affecting not only the cost but also the availability of health care.

 If you have access to *Comp21*, click on Themes, then click on Medical Malpractice.

27

JAMES DILLARD

James Dillard is a physician who specializes in rehabilitation medicine. In this narra-
tive, first published in the "My Turn" column in Newsweek, *he relates an incident that*
nearly ended his medical career.

A Doctor's Dilemma

CONTEXT: *As you read this narrative, keep in mind how most people expect physicians to*
respond in a life-threatening emergency.

1   It was a bright, clear February afternoon in Gettysburg. A strong sun and
layers of down did little to ease the biting cold. Our climb to the crest of
Little Roundtop wound past somber monuments, barren trees and polished cannon. From the top, we peered down on the wheat field where
men had fallen so close together that one could not see the ground. Rifle
balls had whined as thick as bee swarms through the trees, and cannon
shots had torn limbs from the young men fighting there. A frozen wind
whipped tears from your eyes. My friend Amy huddled close, using me as a
wind breaker. Despite the cold, it was hard to leave this place.

2   Driving east out of Gettysburg on a country blacktop, the gray Bronco
ahead of us passed through a rural crossroad just as a small pickup truck
tried to take a left turn. The Bronco swerved, but slammed into the pickup
on the passenger's side. We immediately slowed to a crawl as we passed the
scene. The Bronco's driver looked fine, but we couldn't see the driver of
the pickup. I pulled over on the shoulder and got out to investigate.

3   The right side of the truck was smashed in, and the side window was
shattered. The driver was partly out of the truck. His head hung forward
over the edge of the passenger-side window, the front of his neck crushed
on the shattered windowsill. He was unconscious and starting to turn a
dusky blue. His chest slowly heaved against a blocked windpipe.

4   A young man ran out of a house at the crossroad. "Get an ambulance out
here," I shouted against the wind. "Tell them a man is dying."

5   I looked down again at the driver hanging from the windowsill. There
were six empty beer bottles on the floor of the truck. I could smell the beer
through the window. I knew I had to move him, to open his airway. I had no

idea what neck injuries he had sustained. He could easily end up a quadriplegic. But I thought: he'll be dead by the time the ambulance gets here if I don't move him and try to do something to help him.

6   An image flashed before my mind. I could see the courtroom and the driver of the truck sitting in a wheelchair. I could see his attorney pointing at me and thundering at the jury: "This young doctor, with still a year left in his residency training, took it upon himself to play God. He took it upon himself to move this gravely injured man, condemning him forever to this wheelchair . . ." I imagined the millions of dollars in award money. And all the years of hard work lost. I'd be paying him off for the rest of my life. Amy touched my shoulder. "What are you going to do?"

7   The automatic response from long hours in the emergency room kicked in. I pulled off my overcoat and rolled up my sleeves. The trick would be to keep enough traction straight up on his head while I moved his torso, so that his probable broken neck and spinal-cord injury wouldn't be made worse. Amy came around the driver's side, climbed half in and grabbed his belt and shirt collar. Together we lifted him off the windowsill.

8   He was still out cold, limp as a rag doll. His throat was crushed and blood from the jugular vein was running down my arms. He still couldn't breathe. He was deep blue-magenta now, his pulse was rapid and thready. The stench of alcohol turned my stomach, but I positioned his jaw and tried to blow air down into his lungs. It wouldn't go.

9   Amy had brought some supplies from my car. I opened an oversize intravenous needle and groped on the man's neck. My hands were numb, covered with freezing blood and bits of broken glass. Hyoid bone—God, I can't even feel the thyroid cartilage, it's gone . . . OK, the thyroid gland is about there, cricoid rings are here . . . we'll go in right here . . .

10   It was a lucky first shot. Pink air sprayed through the IV needle. I placed a second needle next to the first. The air began whistling through it. Almost immediately, the driver's face turned bright red. After a minute, his pulse slowed down and his eyes moved slightly. I stood up, took a step back and looked down. He was going to make it. He was going to live. A siren wailed in the distance. I turned and saw Amy holding my overcoat. I was shivering and my arms were turning white with cold.

11   The ambulance captain looked around and bellowed, "What the hell . . . who did this?" as his team scurried over to the man lying in the truck.

12   "I did," I replied. He took down my name and address for his reports. I had just destroyed my career. I would never be able to finish my residency with a massive lawsuit pending. My life was over.

13   The truck driver was strapped onto a backboard, his neck in a stiff collar. The ambulance crew had controlled the bleeding and started intravenous fluid. He was slowly waking up. As they loaded him into the ambulance, I saw him move his feet. Maybe my future wasn't lost.

14   A police sergeant called me from Pennsylvania three weeks later. Six days after successful throat-reconstruction surgery, the driver had signed out, against medical advice, from the hospital because he couldn't get a drink on the ward. He was being arraigned on drunk-driving charges.

15   A few days later, I went into the office of one of my senior professors, to tell the story. He peered over his half glasses and his eyes narrowed. "Well, you did the right thing medically of course. But, James, do you know what you put at risk by doing that?" he said sternly. "What was I supposed to do?" I asked.

16   "Drive on," he replied. "There is an army of lawyers out there who would stand in line to get a case like that. If that driver had turned out to be a quadriplegic, you might never have practiced medicine again. You were a very lucky young man."

17   The day I graduated from medical school, I took an oath to serve the sick and the injured. I remember truly believing I would be able to do just that. But I have found out it isn't so simple. I understand now what a foolish thing I did that day. Despite my oath, I know what I would do on that cold roadside near Gettysburg today. I would drive on.

Understanding Meaning

1. What was Dillard's goal in publishing this narrative in a national news magazine?
2. Does this narrative serve to contrast ideals and reality? How does Dillard's oath conflict with his final decision?
3. Does the fact that the victim had been drinking alcohol have an impact on your reactions to the doctor's actions? Does it seem to affect Dillard's feeling toward the man?
4. *CRITICAL THINKING.* Do medical malpractice suits improve or diminish the quality of medicine? Are lawyers or eager-to-sue patients to blame for the author's decision to "drive on" next time?

Evaluating Strategy

1. *BLENDING THE MODES.* Does this narrative also serve as a persuasive argument? Is this story a better vehicle than a standard argumentative essay that states a thesis and presents factual support?
2. Does this first-person story help place the reader in the doctor's position? Is this a more effective strategy than writing an objective third-person essay about the impact of malpractice suits?
3. Why does Dillard mention that the patient later disobeyed his doctor's orders and left the hospital so he could get a drink?
4. How do you think Dillard wanted his readers to respond to the essay's last line?

Appreciating Language

1. What words does Dillard use to dramatize his attempts to save the driver's life? How do they reflect the tension he felt?
2. What language does Dillard use to demonstrate what he was risking by trying to save a life?
3. What kind of people read *Newsweek*? Do you find this essay's language suitable?

Writing Suggestions

1. Relate an emergency situation you have experienced or encountered. Using Dillard's essay as a model, write an account capturing what you thought and felt as you acted.
2. Write a letter to the editor of *Newsweek* in response to Dillard's essay. Do you find Dillard's position tenable? Are you angry at a doctor who vows not to help strangers in daily life? Or do you blame the legal community for putting a physician in this position?
3. *COLLABORATIVE WRITING.* Discuss Dillard's essay with a number of students and list their reactions. Write a division paper outlining their views.

28

ALDEN BLODGET

Alden Blodget received his BA from Tulane University and his MFA from Temple University before being appointed to the faculty of Lawrence Academy in Groton, Massachusetts, where he is Assistant Head of the School.

Off to See the Wizard: To Sue a Doctor for Failing to Be the God We Wanted Strikes Me as Wrong

CONTEXT: *When a loved one dies unexpectedly, one wants to find a reason. If that person dies as a result of a doctor's mistake, the tendency is to want to make that doctor pay. Since with the rare exception of capital punishment we do not seek an eye for an eye and a tooth for a tooth, the way we seek justice is through our nation's legal system. Blodget proves to be a rare exception himself—the family member of a loved one who died as a result of doctors' mistakes who chooses not to sue. He chooses rather to acknowledge the doctors for what they are—fallible but well-intentioned human beings doing the best they can in a field where lives are weighed in the balance every day.*

1   On April 24, 1990, my father was killed in a Pennsylvania hospital. He was in the third day of recovery from elective reconstructive knee surgery when an error his doctors had made erupted somewhere in his abdomen. Most of his blood vessels ruptured and he bled to death. His doctors had prescribed too large a dose of coumadin, an anticoagulant used to prevent blood clots.

2   A few weeks after his death, I flew to Pennsylvania to meet with the two surgeons at the hospital. My family and I needed to know what had happened. Too many unanswered questions lingered. One of my brothers wanted to hire a lawyer and turn him loose but had agreed to wait until he knew the results of my meeting.

3   At noon, I stood before the hospital, a solid collection of brick and concrete and glass rectangles—a massive promise of competence and power. I felt small and nervous. I tried to imagine my father, who hated hospitals and was a grumpy and ill-tempered patient, as they rushed him back again to the operating room. I had been told that one of the doctors walked at his side and held my father's hand, and I wondered if Dad had been frightened.

4   I imagined the surgeons opening his abdomen and standing transfixed and impotent before the hopelessness of all that damage. My mother had called me from the hospital to say that they'd sewn my father up and wheeled him to a room where he lay unconscious and dying. There had been too much bleeding to stop it.

5   As I stood looking at this imposing building awash in the noon sun, I couldn't shake the image of Dad's small body lying alone in the dark somewhere inside. How could they open him, recognize the problem and not fix it? This was a hospital, and he had been here, not dangling from the end of a 911 call somewhere in the wilderness. It was as absurd as a fire station burning down.

6   I reached inside my jacket and touched the folded list of questions I wanted to ask, reminding myself that this hospital was now going to answer to me. I felt no reassurance. The hospital looked just as huge, and I felt no bigger.

7   My memory of the two hours I spent with the doctors is a jumbled collection of impressions wrapped in sadness and a surreal haze. The doctors seemed young, in their late 30s. They were energetic, sincere and intelligent. I was struck by their promptness and the apparent open-endedness of our meeting. I guess we all sensed the distant thunder of litigation.

8   They led me to a comfortable room—wood paneling, polished wood table, padded chairs—where we were served lunch. My father had once told me a story about having lunch with a doctor friend in a similar room. When they entered, a few doctors were eating around the table and discussing a model of an amputated leg that stood amid the napkins and plates. While the two doctors answered my questions, I felt my father's ghost settle over our conversation. I wondered if I was moving closer to the truth that fluttered elusively through the shadows of their explanations.

9   As they spoke, I understood the reason Dad had chosen and trusted them to repair his knees. He'd always insisted on finding the best people for any job—the best lawyers, teachers, mechanics, doctors. His vast network of professional friends had led him to these surgeons. And they were clearly good. They guided me carefully through the details of my father's last few days—the blood clot that appeared in a lung, the difficulty of determining quickly the level of coumadin in the blood, the unanticipated changes in my father's chemistry since an earlier knee operation.

10   When they described the sudden jump in his coumadin count and their scramble to reduce it, I noticed one doctor swallow. It was a moment in the Emerald City. The tremor of his Adam's apple shook the curtain aside to reveal the small, frantic man behind the image of the wizard. I was in a fancy

room in a big building, but these were not gods or magicians. They were men—imperfect and fallible—frightened to appear so in a society that expects perfection and infallibility from its professionals, especially its doctors.

11   These men were just like the rest of us. They'd spend years working hard to become competent in a field they care deeply about, a field that despite two or three thousand years of development is still a mixture of marvels and mystery. They hadn't been negligent or incompetent. They'd used the complex and dangerous tools of their craft as carefully as they could, guided by knowledge and understanding based on previous use of the same tools. They had improvised as intelligently as they could when the results failed to conform to previous experience. They'd made mistakes that they could see only in hindsight, the perspective from which society makes its judgments. In hindsight everything is obvious.

12   In this era of lawsuits and other lotteries, I am sure I could have become a millionaire by suing my father's doctors and the hospital—assuming my lawyer would have shared the award with me. But I didn't. I think I understand the reason. It wasn't that I wasn't angry with the doctors, that I didn't want revenge or someone to pay for my pain. I'm not so gullible that I can't recognize the crooks and quacks that move among us. It was simply my realization that we expect too much from each other. We refuse to accept that we make mistakes, that even the best of us screw up.

13   Don't misunderstand me. I know that forgetting the lettuce in a Big Mac doesn't compare to making an error that costs a life. The stakes are higher in an operating room. Nor am I opposed to lawsuits that seek to punish those who hack off the wrong leg or knowingly sell products laced with danger. But to sue someone for failing to be the god we wanted strikes me as wrong.

14   Why is it that we know so little ourselves yet expect so much from others? We refuse to recognize the flimsy curtain that separates the intention from the result, the image from reality. Andre Agassi and the Wizard of Oz may believe that "image is everything," but most of us ought to know that we're just folks from Kansas flying by the seat of our pants and doing the best we can.

Understanding Meaning

1.   What is Blodget's purpose in visiting the hospital where his father died? What is his purpose in writing about the visit?
2.   What is Blodget's opinion of the two surgeons once he meets them?
3.   Why is a simple act like the doctor's swallowing a turning point for Blodget?

4. Why does he decide not to sue the doctors?
5. Explain what Blodget means by the references to *The Wizard of Oz* in paragraphs 10 and 14.

Evaluating Strategy

1. Blodget clearly was choosing his words carefully when he said that his father *was killed* in a Pennsylvania hospital rather than that he *died* there. Why choose that term?
2. How does Blodget relate the story of the meeting with his father's surgeons to *The Wizard of Oz*, starting with the title?
3. Where does Blodget state most directly what he learned about the two surgeons as he talked with them? Is there a single sentence that best sums up the thesis of the essay?

Appreciating Language

1. How does Blodget use his description of the hospital to make a point about his own feelings as he prepares to enter the hospital where his father died? How does he use it to contrast with what he learns while he is there?
2. Where do details describing the doctors emphasize their humanity?
3. What is significant about the fact that Blodget uses the term *turn him loose* (paragraph 2) in referring to his brother's desire to hire a lawyer?
4. What analogy does Blodget use to stress the irony of his father dying in a hospital with no one able to help him?

Writing Suggestions

1. Write an essay in which you explain Blodget's references to *The Wizard of Oz*.
2. *COLLABORATIVE WRITING.* Either write down or mark on your printed copy of the text the two or three sentences that to you most concisely summarize the main point of the essay. (They do not have to be consecutive sentences.) Then share your results with at least two classmates and see if you all picked the same sentences. Whether you did or not, what does that reveal about how clear Blodget's purpose is in the essay?
3. Write an essay in which you explain whether or not you think Blodget did the right thing in not filing a lawsuit against the surgeons.

29

CARLO FONSEKA

Carlo Fonseka obtained his PhD from the University of Edinburgh before returning to his native Sri Lanka to assume the post of senior lecturer of the Department of Physiology of the Colombo Medical School. By the mid 1980s he was chair of the department. He was forced to leave the country in the late 1980s due to political unrest. During this period Fonseka served with the United Nations University in Helsinki. In 1991, he was appointed to the Foundation Chair in Physiology and dean of the new medical school at the University of Kelaniya, Ragama. He retired in 1998 and was made an Emeritus Professor. He is currently a member of the University Grants Commission, the highest controlling body for university education. He has published on diverse subjects in many medical journals including the British Medical Journal, *in which this article appeared.*

To Err Was Fatal

CONTEXT: *Because advances in medicine have made it possible to save and enhance life in cases where in the past there was no hope, there is the temptation to look upon doctors as almost godlike in their power. Like any other mortal, however, a doctor can make mistakes. In most professions, mistakes are not deadly; in the field of medicine, they easily can be. Looking back on a long career as a doctor in this 1996 article published in the* British Medical Journal, *Fonseka recalls the few times he made a mistake that had deadly consequences.*

1   Error-free patient care is the ideal standard but in reality unattainable. I am conscious of having made five fatal errors during the past 36 years.

2   After two years in state hospitals I joined the staff of my medical school in Colombo in 1962, holding the posts of lecturer, senior lecturer, associate professor, and professor of physiology. In all that time I have practised medicine because I believe that direct contact with patients makes my teaching more relevant.

3   In recounting the stories of my fatal errors the problem of guarding patient confidentiality arises. The BMJ has changed its policy from guarding anonymity to getting consent. In the most recent three of my five fatal errors, obtaining informed consent from relatives was easy. With regard to the first error, which occurred in 1960, and the second which occurred well over a quarter of a century ago, relatives could not be tracked down. So trying to achieve anonymity by changing names and some of the details was the best I could do. The *British Medical Journal* is not only British, it is also truly international. Wouldn't it be guilty of a species of ethical imperialism—the

opposite of cultural relativism—if it refused to publish material about patients dead for nearly three decades or more, merely because written consent for publication had not been obtained from relatives who cannot be traced?

4   I find myself paralysed by doubts about how best to recount the case histories. It was Hippocrates who reputedly introduced the case history to medicine. The idea that diseases have a natural history is traceable to him. It is, of course, possible to recount the history of an illness without revealing much about the sufferer. To do so would not serve the purpose of this paper.

First Fatal Error

5   The 23-year-old labourer Gunapala looked like a prize fighter. He walked into the professorial medical ward of the Colombo Medical School around 11 o'clock one morning in 1960, accompanied by his mother. His mother, a buxom, working-class woman in her 40s, gave the history. Gunapala had been discharged from another medical ward in the hospital the previous day with the assurance that he had no disease which required treatment. The visiting physician in charge of that ward was perhaps the astutest diagnostician among my clinical teachers. The assurance might well have been given by an intern.

6   The mother said that she was sure something was seriously wrong with her son because he continued to complain of a tight feeling in his upper abdomen and had difficulty in breathing. "Look," I told her, "your son was discharged from this hospital yesterday; today you bring him walking to this already overcrowded ward. All the patients on beds in this ward are too ill even to walk. Are you asking me to transfer one of them to the floor and give his bed to your son?"

7   I examined the patient cursorily, perhaps even carelessly. The trouble was that my mind was already firmly made up. My tentative diagnosis was diaphragmatic pleurisy. I prescribed penicillin, aspirin, and an antiphlogistin plaster to the upper abdomen.

8   When I came on my night round the night nurse told me that I should review Gunapala. She had given him a hospital trolley to sleep on, she said, because he looked ill. I told her that I knew better than she did, which patients required close monitoring and which ones did not.

9   About four hours later the nurse telephoned me to say that Gunapala was having fits. By then the diagnosis was obvious: a full blown case of tetanus. At the mandatory inquest the coroner, a layman, asked me whether the patient had given a history of a penetrating wound on the sole of a foot,

caused by a rusty nail. Without batting an eyelid, I said "No," although the truth was that I never asked. The coroner then judged that without such a history no doctor could reasonably be expected to diagnose tetanus.

10   The most harrowing memory of the inquest was my encounter with Gunapala's grieving mother. She looked straight into my eyes and said: "Sir, you said you would send my son home on the next day. What you sent me instead was a thunderbolt." I managed to mumble that none of the several doctors who had seen her son realised that he was suffering from tetanus until it was too late. "Is that so?" she asked. "Must be because of his 'karma'; I thought doctors knew everything about all the diseases in the world."

11   I think that I never came to terms with Gunapala's death. I suspect that his death must have been a strong influence that subconsciously drove me out of clinical medicine into a preclinical department like physiology, where in those days you killed only frogs.

Second Fatal Error

12   Miss C, a petite, shy girl in her late teens, and her lean boyfriend were students of mine in a class of paramedics in the 1970s. One day they came to see me. She had not had her periods for two months. The boy swore that the girl was still a virgin. There were early symptoms and signs of pregnancy and a urine pregnancy test was positive. A week later it was positive again. The boy told me that they had decided to end the pregnancy or to end their lives. I asked what the problem was. After all, they loved each other and were going to marry sooner or later. The boy replied that their course would end only eight months hence and that they simply could not marry then and go through with the pregnancy. The girl said that she was certain that her stern father would throw her out if he got to know the truth.

13   With her permission I visited her home and tried to persuade her mother to take a sympathetic view of the matter. She, however, only confirmed her daughter's worst fears: "Her father would kill her," she said categorically. I invited the couple to come to our home and talk things over with my wife. I hinted that it might be possible to take the girl into our home and see her through the pregnancy. The girl never came. The boy came again and again and implored me to arrange a termination. At that time there was no obstetrician who would have done a life-saving therapeutic abortion on psychiatric grounds at my request. The boy told me that there

was a senior nurse in the abortion business who, for a price, would initiate the process and send the patient to hospital. These desperate young people entreated me to introduce them to that nurse. I had grave misgivings. In a final attempt to ward them off I told them that I would agree to consider their request if they got married. Within a couple of days they fulfilled that condition too. I then sent them to the nurse. The girl died of septic peritonitis a few days later.

14   I feel directly responsible for this girl's death. Has it ultimately to do with my ethical belief that every woman has a right to control her body and that termination of a pregnancy in the first few weeks after conception is a lesser evil than permitting the birth of an unwanted child into our already overcrowded planet? Or did I become guilty of this error because I live in a society which provides safe abortions to those who can pay for them and septic abortions to those who cannot?

Third Fatal Error

15   Mrs H, a woman in her mid-30s, was the wife of a friend of a friend of mine. Her husband, a minor official in a state corporation, used to seek medical advice from me. One day, in the mid-1970s, he brought his wife to the physiology department in the Colombo Medical School. To reach the department you have to climb two flights of stairs—a total of 64 steps. Based on hundreds of casual observations, I had calculated that if a person could climb up to the department at a normal pace and not become breathless there was nothing seriously wrong with that person's heart, lungs, or blood. On the day Mrs H walked in, complaining of becoming unduly breathless on mild exertion, I asked her whether she felt breathless after climbing the 64 steps. When she said "No" I didn't bother to examine her. I placed my fingers perfunctorily on her radial pulse and assured her that there could not be anything seriously wrong with her. I did not even bother to place my stethoscope on her heart. Had I done so I believe that she would not have died three weeks later of pulmonary oedema complicating mitral stenosis. What was my error in this case? It certainly wasn't ignorance; it wasn't that I didn't care enough. Her husband continues to seek medical advice from me. He told me that he was sure that if I had seen his wife when she got her terminal attack of pulmonary oedema I would have saved her.

Fourth Fatal Error

16 Asura was an intelligent boy of 16, president of the science society in his school, the only son of an old acquaintance. Ever since he had heard me lecture to his society on scientific firewalking he had believed that I was the greatest philosopher of science in Sri Lanka. Poor lad, he had to pay with his life for that belief. He had been admitted to the neurosurgical unit at the teaching hospital for ligature of a berry aneurysm in his circle of Willis. But he had refused to give his consent for the operation unless he was advised to do so by me. I did so, using the tricks of demagogy, not the canons of scientific rationality. At the end of my harangue on the marvels of modern science he readily gave his—there is no other word for it misinformed consent. Two days later he died of a surgical misadventure on the operating table.

Fifth Fatal Error

17 Amarasiri Jayasinghe (Podi Amare), 34, was a man from my village. He became passionately devoted to Vijaya Kumaratunga, film idol, pop star, and charismatic politician, and was one of his trusted henchmen. After Vijaya Kumaratunga was assassinated on 16 February 1988 Podi Amare became depressed and declared that life without Vijaya Kumaratunga was not worth living. On 21 February, when Vijaya Kumaratunga's body was lying in the art gallery for public obeisance, some of Podi Amare's friends brought him to me because he had been threatening to commit suicide. The time was around 8 PM. It didn't take me long to diagnose that he had acute reactive depression with a strong suicidal tendency. I told his friends that there was a high probability that Podi Amare would kill himself and that the correct emergency treatment for him was to admit him to hospital for continuous observation. I asked the friends to keep him under observation for the next two hours until I was free to take him to the teaching hospital. They agreed to do so, but I noticed that some of them were in various stages of inebriation. One of them tried to call what he mistakenly believed to be Podi Amare's bluff and challenged him to translate his suicidal threat into action. Around 10 PM Podi Amare daubed himself with petrol and set himself ablaze. Onlookers quickly put out the flames but not before Podi Amare had sustained severe burns. He was admitted to hospital and when I visited him two days later he beseeched me to save his life. But he died a few days later. I believe that Podi Amare died because I erred. For various reasons, I unpardonably delayed his admission to hospital.

Synopsis and Self-Appraisal

18   Why are humans prone to error? The science of error prevention addresses that matter. According to one model, there are three levels of human performance: skill based, rule based, and knowledge based. Corresponding to these three levels of performance, three types of error have been identified: skill based, rule based, and knowledge based. Certain physiological, psychological, and environmental factors have been identified which predispose to errors. Fatigue, sleep loss, alcohol intake, boredom, anxiety, heat, and noise are examples.

19   Although the above classification of errors is perhaps too schematic to be quite true, it can be deployed for a preliminary analysis of my five fatal errors. Were they skill based, rule based, or knowledge based? I was certainly not ignorant about tetanus, which killed the first patient. I knew full well about the risks of backstreet abortions, which killed the second patient. The auscultatory signs of mitral stenosis reverberate in my memory even now and yet I failed to diagnose mitral stenosis, which killed the third patient. I know of the limitations of science more than most doctors of my time, but I brainwashed a boy to consent to an operation which killed him. And I was absolutely aware of the emergency treatment of a patient who is a high suicide risk, but I failed to apply that knowledge in the case of the fifth patient. Therefore, my fatal errors were not knowledge-based ones.

20   Nor were they skill-based ones in the sense that they were "slips" which occurred in an unguarded moment of diverted attention. By exclusion, therefore, they have to be rule-based errors. The educational task now is to identify precisely the rule that was fatally violated in each case.

21   The thought processes required for arriving at a diagnosis and for decision making that goes with treatment are governed by rules. Indeed all rational activity is subject to rules and even the rules of formal logic are abstracted from those governing effective day to day living. Therefore, it is reasonable to analyse even medical errors by the rules which govern rational day to day life.

22   In the case of Gunapala and Mrs H, I ignored the rule which enjoins me not to jump to conclusions. In the case of Podi Amare I violated the rule which enjoins me to treat an emergency as an emergency. In the case of Miss C, I erred because I condoned an inherently high-risk procedure. In the case of Asura, I erred because I deployed dishonest techniques of persuasion in the belief that sometimes the end justifies the means.

23   Further reflection generates the thought that in the first case I jumped to the wrong conclusion because of my excessive reverence for a teacher. In the

second case I condoned the risky venture because there was a "seeming possibility" of getting away with it. In the third case I jumped to the wrong conclusion because I acted merely by "considering appearances." In the fourth case I brainwashed the boy because I had too much faith in the tradition of scientific medicine. In the final case the root cause of my error was my speculation that the emergency could survive a delay of a couple of hours.

24   In the sixth century BC there lived in north India a teacher—reverentially called the Buddha—who by sheer force of mind had apprehended precisely and comprehensively the possible sources of intellectual error. Teaching the Kalamas how to avoid error he said: "Now, look you Kalamas, do not be led by reports, or tradition or hearsay. Be not led by the authority of religious texts, nor by mere logic or inference, nor by considering appearances, nor by the delight in speculative opinions, nor by seeming possibilities, nor by the idea: 'this is our teacher.'" This analysis touches the root causes of my fatal errors more insightfully than any other scheme of error analysis that I know.

25   When all is said and done a gibe at my expense must be anticipated. Although Alexander Pope did indeed famously preach that, "To err is human, to forgive divine," it will be murmured that only a fool will err fatally five times in 36 years. So the prospect must be squarely faced: this paper may embody nothing more or less than the confessions of a fool. If, however, by confessing to the world a fool could help to promote ever so slightly the ideal of error-free patient care I believe that the fool has a scientific and ethical duty to confess.

Understanding Meaning

1. Fonseka ends his introduction with this statement: "It is, of course, possible to recount the history of an illness without revealing much about the sufferer. To do so would not serve the purpose of this paper." What is the purpose of the paper?
2. Fonseka has some concerns about patient confidentiality. How does he resolve those concerns?
3. What are the five errors that led to death for Fonseka's patients?
4. According to Fonseka, under what three categories can errors be classified? What type of errors were the ones he made?
5. What rule did he ignore in each case?
6. *CRITICAL THINKING.* Each of the five errors led to a death. Do you feel that all five are similar in the reasoning that led Fonseka to act as he did? Explain.

Evaluating Strategy

1. Fonseka has an organizational pattern that is easy to follow. How would you describe the essay's organization?
2. Does Fonseka try to make excuses for his actions in the five cases that he talks about? Would doing so have made the article more or less successful, in your opinion?
3. Consider the audience for which Fonseka was writing. What different choices might he have made in writing the article for a different audience?

Appreciating Language

1. Would you say that Fonseka's language in the piece is objective or subjective? What is the effect?
2. What can you say about the ethical appeal of Fonseka's argument? What sort of person does Fonseka appear to be from what you read?
3. Fonseka uses a number of technical medical terms. Did they interfere with your ability to understand what he was saying?

Writing Suggestions

1. Write an essay in which you explain why the cases in which Fonseka's patients died were different from each in other in the reason for the mistake. What do they reveal about different levels of guilt or about the intentions behind a choice that ends in tragedy?
2. Write an essay in which you explain why you either agree or disagree with Fonseka's statement that "it is reasonable to analyse even medical errors by the rules which govern rational day to day life." Can medical decisions be made solely on the basis of reason?
3. Apply Fonseka's three types of errors to a job you have, once had, or might someday have. For that particular job, what would be examples of skill-based, rule-based, and knowledge-based errors?
4. Explain what you understand the three types of errors to be as they relate to the medical profession. Use real or hypothetical situations as examples.
5. *COLLABORATIVE WRITING.* Exchange your essay from Writing Suggestion #3 or #4 above with a classmate to see if he or she can understand the distinctions you are drawing among the different types of errors.

30

RITA HEALY

Rita Healy has worked as a staff writer for Time *magazine and for the* Denver Post.

How the System Failed One Sufferer: A Malpractice Victim

CONTEXT: *Being in the hospital can be a frightening experience. It can turn into a nightmare when something goes tragically wrong. The tragedy is intensified when added to the failure of the medical system is the failure of the court system designed to help victims seek justice for medical malpractice. In this article from the June 9, 2003, issue of* Time *magazine, Healy uses the story of one individual sufferer to show what it can be like to sue for malpractice. In some states, caps on jury awards for economic and noneconomic damages limit the compensation a victim can receive; cases can be tied up in courts for years while the victim loses almost everything; and relief from the high cost of malpractice insurance that the caps were supposed to bring does not materialize.*

1   Jim McDonough went into the hospital in 1997 to have a calcified growth, which the doctor said could be cancerous, removed from his neck. Two days later he awoke to find himself paralyzed from the chest down. Still in the intensive-care unit, he felt strangled by a noose of pain and needed three excruciating gasps of air to cry for help. "I was crushed," says McDonough, 69, a former weapons-plant inspector from Littleton, Colo. He once loved to fish and dreamed of restoring his ideal car: a 1965 Chrysler. But he soon realized that he could do neither and came to believe that his surgery had been unnecessary. A jury agreed. It found his neurosurgeon guilty of malpractice and in 2001 awarded McDonough $5.8 million. He has yet to see a dollar.

2   McDonough is a victim again, this time of the move to cap jury awards. Colorado is one of the few states that limit jury awards of both economic damages (say, for lost income) and noneconomic ones (for pain and suffering). Judge Warren Martin, now retired, cut McDonough's award to $1.33 million, concluding that although his injuries merited an exception to the $1 million cap, the jury had gone too far. (Colorado's caps limit economic damages to $750,000 and pain-and-suffering awards to $250,000. The former can be increased if a plaintiff shows future economic loss that exceeds that level.) McDonough appealed to the Colorado Supreme Court but was

denied. He later tried to settle, but the defense argued that he had waited too long, and another judge ordered a new trial to determine damages. It will begin in August—a fresh chapter in McDonough's nightmare.

3   Proponents of damage caps say they simplify malpractice cases and weed out frivolous claims. But they can also entangle victims of heartbreaking tragedy like McDonough. No longer able to work, he spends his days doing crossword puzzles and preparing again for court. That was not the intention of the first jury, whose award was based not on mere sympathy but on calculations of McDonough's direct financial burden. According to foreman Joanne Kramer, in arriving at the $5.8 million in damages, the jury considered everything from home health-care aides to a van, a wheelchair, the loss of his home, and the loss of income for his wife, who spends hours every day caring for him. Jurors also discussed whether McDonough's award would add to rising malpractice premiums but decided he should not be penalized for that. "We still had a responsibility to Mr. McDonough, who was a victim," says Kramer. "What's the point of having a jury if the judge can basically do what he wants?"

4   McDonough isn't giving up the fight. In February he wheeled himself into a state legislative hearing on damage caps. The Colorado Supreme Court ruled that "physical impairment and disfigurement" are exempt from limits on jury awards, but this spring the state's lawmakers limited the effect of the court's decision. "The doctor who performed this unnecessary operation has left the state and is continuing with his life elsewhere," McDonough testified. That neurosurgeon, Richard Branan, 59, declined to comment about McDonough. Branan practices in Los Angeles and faces two other trials this year in Colorado. His attorney in one case, in which the patient died, says, "We have a very defensible case." His attorney in the other trial, also a spinal-surgery case, says Branan "did not cause any injuries to the patient."

5   Despite Colorado's unusually strict damage cap, the state's largest insurer raised premiums 14% this year, the biggest jump in 15 years. So far at least, the cap law is failing to deliver the relief that it promised to doctors even as it blocks relief to acknowledged victims like Jim McDonough.

Understanding Meaning

1.   Healy describes Jim McDonough as having been victimized twice. What does she mean by that? Why, two years after the trial, had he not received any monetary compensation?

2. Notice that this article was published in 2003. At that time, how long had McDonough been waiting for a settlement? What of his old life has he had to give up in the meantime as a result of the surgery that was judged to have been unnecessary?

3. Some proponents of damage caps have argued that for a few patients who win their cases, it is like winning the lottery because the settlements are so large. McDonough was awarded $5.8 million. Did the jury seem to have legitimate reasons for deciding on the dollar amount that they did?

4. How has McDonough tried to use his case to try to educate others and affect legislation?

5. There is the hint in paragraph 4 that the doctor who operated on McDonough might have a pattern of mistakes. Is there any indication that he has been or will be stopped from practicing?

6. In the last paragraph, how does Healy argue against those who favor damage caps?

7. *CRITICAL THINKING.* Do you feel that there should be caps on jury awards for economic and noneconomic damages in medical malpractice cases? Explain why or why not.

Evaluating Strategy

1. *BLENDING THE MODES.* Like many writers whose primary purpose is not narration, Healy makes use of the story of Jim McDonough to structure her piece. Why is that an effective technique for her to use in getting her point across?

2. What, specifically, does Healy tell us about McDonough that appeals to our sympathy, beyond the basic fact that he was paralyzed after the surgery?

3. How does Healy supplement the emotional appeal of the McDonough case with appeal to her readers' reason or their sense of logic?

4. Is the way that Healy ends her essay a good argumentative technique? Why or why not?

Appreciating Language

1. What is the effect of Healy's use of such description as this: "he felt strangled by a noose of pain and needed three excruciating gasps of air to cry for help"?

2. What is particularly ironic about Dr. Branan's lawyer's response to the other charges against Branan?

Writing Suggestions

1. Write the speech that McDonough might have presented before the state legislative hearing on damage caps. Include appeals to the audience's emotions and to their sense of logic.
2. *COLLABORATIVE WRITING.* Exchange within your group the speeches you wrote for Writing Suggestion #1 above. Select the one from the group that offers the most effective blend of emotional and logical appeal for reading to the class.
3. Write an essay in which you argue for or against caps on jury awards in medical malpractice cases.
4. Write an essay in which you explain whether or not you believe Americans in general have doubts about the quality and cost of medical care today.

31

PHILIP K. HOWARD

Philip K. Howard is a lawyer and the founder of Common Good, a coalition for legal reform. His books include The Death of Common Sense *(1995) and* The Collapse of the Common Good *(2001).*

Yes, It's a Mess—But Here's How to Fix It

CONTEXT: *We hear in the media how expensive it is for doctors to get malpractice insurance and how much the cost of that insurance has gone up due to the number of lawsuits brought against doctors by patients who feel they have been negligent or careless. Howard examines the negative effects that the resulting "legal fear" has had on the level of care that patients receive and the inability of the current legal system to address the problem. Juries in medical malpractice cases are intentionally chosen because they are not medical professionals. Howard argues that the time has come for that system to change.*

1   Health care in America is suffering a total nervous breakdown, but it isn't just because doctors are striking and maternity wards are closing. Health-care premiums are rising at unsustainable rates. Some economists estimate that unnecessary tests and procedures, ordered by doctors to build a record just in case there is a lawsuit, cost more than $100 billion a year—enough to provide health insurance for the 40 million Americans who have no coverage. Modern medical technology is bringing us miracle cures, yet the absence of backup systems to catch human errors is causing thousands of deaths each year. In our culture of legal fear, the candor vital to improving care is also a casualty. Because doctors don't feel safe talking about mistakes, they are unable to learn from them   or even offer an honest apology.

2   With all the talent and resources devoted to health care—almost 15% of the U.S. economy—why can't somebody just use common sense and fix things? The villain, I believe, is our legal system, which has become a free-for-all, lacking the reliability and consistency that are essential to everyone, especially doctors and patients. Most victims of error get nothing, while others win lottery-like jury awards even when the doctor did nothing wrong. Because of the resulting fear and distrust, doctors and other health-care providers no longer feel comfortable making sensible judgments.

3   Yet reform is going nowhere. Both sides in the debate, horns locked, have succeeded mainly in confusing the issues. Trial lawyers talk a lot

about the "right to sue" when something goes wrong. But what about the right of doctors to a system of justice that reliably distinguishes between right and wrong? Meanwhile, the tort reform pushed by doctors is like a bandage on a mortal wound. Placing limits on discretionary "noneconomic" damages may stem today's bleeding and is certainly one element of controlling costs—$1 million to a plaintiff is $1 million less to take care of the rest of us. But merely putting caps on pain-and-suffering damages will not restore reliability or trust.

4   Recently 70 prominent figures in the field of health care came together to call on Congress to create an entirely new system of medical justice. Because neither lay juries nor most judges have the technical knowledge to weigh complex medical evidence, some of these experts believe the most effective solution is to create special medical courts—just as we have separate courts for taxes, patents, workers' compensation and vaccine injuries. Staffed with expert judges—and probably without juries—these tribunals could effectively screen claims, make rulings and award reasonable compensation for actual economic losses, plus pain-and-suffering damages based on a standard schedule: a certain amount for paralysis, for losing a limb and so on. That way we can decide how much money we want to go to victims and how much is available for future health care.

5   Creating a special medical court is an ambitious undertaking that will be opposed by trial lawyers at every step. But proposals to launch pilot projects at the state level are being drafted in the Senate. We don't really have a choice. American health care is out of control.

Understanding Meaning

1. From the beginning, Howard assumes that his readers will accept his claim that health care is, as he calls it, "a mess." According to him, why is it in such a mess? Why, for instance, are billions of dollars spent each year on expensive but unnecessary tests and procedures?
2. According to Howard, why do thousands die each year in a nation that has witnessed miracles of modern medical technology?
3. Whom does Howard perceive to be the villain in all of this? Why?
4. One proposed solution is to put a cap on how much an individual can be awarded in a medical malpractice decision. Why does Howard feel that that will not solve the problem?

5. What solution does he offer instead?
6. *CRITICAL THINKING.* Do you feel that a jury of nonmedical specialists is qualified to decide guilt and compensation in a case of medical malpractice? Do you feel that Howard's plan would be a reasonable change from the present legal system?

Evaluating Strategy

1. What assumptions could Howard make about his audience, considering he wrote this piece for *Time* magazine? How did he address the subject in ways appropriate for that audience?
2. What is his tone? In other words, what attitudes does he seem to have toward doctors and the legal system that handles malpractice cases?
3. In what ways does Howard appeal to the emotions of his readers? In what ways does he appeal to their reason?

Appreciating Language

1. What specific word choices reveal Howard's emotional response? In other words, where does he stop being objective and let his opinion show clearly?
2. In talking about the system he proposes, Howard uses words that paint the new system in the most favorable light possible. What are some examples?
3. Where in the piece does Howard make use of appropriate metaphors drawn from the realm of medicine?

Writing Suggestions

1. Freewrite for 10 minutes on whether you think lay juries are qualified to pass judgment and to determine compensation in cases of medical malpractice.
2. *COLLABORATIVE WRITING.* Share the ideas from your freewrite with a group of your classmates. Working as a group, write down some conclusions you can draw based on your group's ideas.
3. Using your group's conclusions from Writing Suggestion #2 above as a starting point, write an essay in which you explain whether or not you feel Howard's proposal for special medical courts would be a reasonable and workable solution to some of the current problems with medical malpractice suits.

4. Freewrite for 10 minutes on whether you believe there should be limits on how much a victim of malpractice could be awarded in a settlement.

5. *COLLABORATIVE WRITING*. Share the ideas from your freewrite with a group of your classmates. Write down some conclusions the group reaches as to whether or not there should be limits on the monetary compensation awarded in a medical malpractice suit.

6. Use your group's conclusions from Writing Suggestion #5 above as the basis for an essay in which you explain whether or not you feel there should be limits on awards in malpractice suits.

32

American Identity: Melting Pot or Mosaic?

There is no room in this country for
hyphenated Americanism.
Theodore Roosevelt
We hyphenated Americans are merely celebrating
the hyphen history handed us.
Julianne Malveaux

Writing about America in 1782, the French writer Crevecoeur observed, "Here individuals of all races are melted into a new race of man." A century later, American writer Ralph Waldo Emerson believed the "energy of the Irish, Germans, Swedes, Poles, Cossacks & all the European tribes,—of the Africans, & Polynesians will construct a new race, a new religion, a new State, a new literature." This concept of America as a "melting pot" was popularized in 1908 by Israel Zangwill's Broadway play, which appeared when millions of immigrants were passing through Ellis Island to build new lives in the United States. *The Melting Pot* celebrated the blending of nationalities to forge a new identity, free of the bitter ethnic rivalries that had ravaged Europe. Zangwill proclaimed:

America is God's crucible, the great melting pot where all the races of Europe are melting and reforming. . . . Here you stand in your fifty groups, with your fifty languages, and your fifty blood hatreds. . . . A fig for your feuds and vendettas! Germans and Frenchmen, Irishmen and Englishmen, Jews and Russians—into the crucible with you all! God is making the American.

The symbolic melting pot took literal form a few years later in Detroit. Henry Ford established schools to teach immigrant workers English and help them assimilate into a new society. At their graduation ceremony, employees walked across the stage dressed in their national costumes. Passing behind a large cardboard "melting pot," they ducked backstage to quickly change and emerge on the other side wearing American-style suits and ties to receive their diplomas.

In 1915 former president Theodore Roosevelt strongly advocated assimilation to prevent immigrants from being exploited or becoming a threat to national security:

> We cannot afford to continue to use hundreds of thousands of immigrants merely as industrial assets while they remain social outcasts and menaces any more than fifty years ago we could afford to keep the black man merely as an industrial asset and not as a human being. . . . We cannot afford to run the risk of having in time of war men working on our railways or working in our munition plants who would in the name of duty to their own foreign countries bring destruction to us.

Generations of immigrants assimilated into America, learning English, changing their names, and casting off ethnic customs in the process. Often fleeing persecution or oppression in their native lands, immigrants saw assimilation as a means to achieve acceptance and opportunity.

Throughout the 1950s and early 1960s the civil rights movement fought for an end to segregation, seeing integration as the solution to African American problems. *Raisin in the Sun*, a popular play of the era, depicted the struggles of a black family seeking to leave the Chicago ghetto for a home in a white suburb. Blacks, integrationists argued, should not be seen as black Americans but as Americans.

But to many African Americans, accepting mainstream society meant assimilating into a culture that had once enslaved them and continued to denigrate them. To blend into mainstream culture implied a kind of surrender, a denial of one's heritage and values. W. E. B. DuBois and other black leaders stressed Pan-Africanism, arguing that African Americans should identify with blacks living in other countries rather than other races living in the United States. In 1963, Malcolm X derided the drive for integration, telling audiences that it would only weaken and diminish African Americans:

> It's just like when you've got some coffee that's too black, which means it's too strong. What do you do? You integrate it with cream, you make it weak. But if you pour too much cream in it, you won't even know you ever had coffee. It used to be hot, it becomes cold. It used to be strong, it becomes weak. It used to wake you up, now it puts you to sleep.

Resistance to mainstream culture has been echoed by other ethnic groups. Chicanos and Native Americans have viewed the dominant culture as one that has stolen their ancestral lands and deprived them of their culture against their will. Armando Rendón, having rediscovered his Chicano

culture, abandoned his ambitions to seek traditional American ideas of success that would lead him to surrender to "the Anglo kiss of death, the
monolingual, monocultural, and colorless Gringo society."

Critics of ethnic or "identity" politics argue that the desire to maintain or
promote ethnicity can disrupt a democratic society founded on shared civic
values. Assimilation into a multicultural society, they assert, prevents the
balkanization of America and avoids the ethnic feuds that split other nations.

Those resisting assimilation and the "melting pot" prefer to see America
as a mosaic of many separate cultures. Many draw a distinction between civic
assimilation and acculturalization. The residents of Chinatowns, Amish vil-
lages, and Hasidic communities, they point out, maintain uniquely separate
identities and cultures without threatening the unity of the broader society.

Whether America is to be viewed as a melting pot or a mosaic greatly
shapes domestic politics and foreign policy. For many individuals, it means
choosing between identities or attempting to forge a personal blend that affects their education, their families, and even their career options.

Before Reading Further, Consider These Questions.

Is Assimilation Unavoidable? Can any ethnic group remain truly separate in a
highly complex society dominated by popular culture, mass media, and multi-
national corporations? Federal, state, and local laws and regulations force everyone to cooperate and interact in order to build a school, open a restaurant, or
operate a day care center. Don't these forces help create a common society?

Are Some Americans "Hyphenated" Against Their Will? While many white
Americans can embrace or ignore being originally Irish, English, or Italian,
African Americans, Asians, and Hispanics generally have no choice, being
seen as "different" by a largely white society. What difference does race
play in ethnic identity?

Do "Hyphenated" Citizens Help or Hinder American Foreign Policy? Syrian government officials were recently receptive to meeting with American legislators when they realized that the delegation consisted of three Arab American congressional representatives. Do Americans who maintain cultural links
to other countries and speak more than a single language help the United
States function as the most powerful nation in global economy? Or do ethnic
lobbies distort American policy by advancing narrow and provincial causes?

*Do Ethnic "Identity Politics" Rely on Superficial Similarities, or Do They Reflect
Genuine Concerns?* Since every ethnic group includes the poor and middle class, the unemployed and professionals, Texans and New Yorkers,

property owners and renters, men and women, can an ethnic identity alone form a consistent set of attitudes and responses to specific issues? Do those who fear a balkanization of American society mistakenly view ethnic groups as monolithic?

WRITING ABOUT ETHNIC IDENTITY

The issue of ethnic identity can trigger a number of reactions that can be useful topics for writing assignments.

Critical Thinking and Prewriting

The topic of ethnic identity can be a controversial one. You may have strong opinions about people who dress and speak differently than most Americans, or you may feel strongly about being pressured to discard elements of your heritage or faith. Effective writing does more than simply capture what you "feel" about a topic. Critical thinking and prewriting can help you move beyond first impressions and develop meaningful observations and suggestions.

Getting Started: Exploring Ideas

1. How do you define yourself? American, Asian-American, Irish-American, black, or Jewish? Or do race and ethnicity have little to do with how you look at yourself and your life? Do you perceive yourself as a woman, a Texan, a Presbyterian, a parent, or an accountant?

   What leads you to define yourself—your values, your past, the way you see yourself, or the way others interact with you?

   Point to consider: can you easily separate ethnicity from other issues that may affect your life, such as gender, age, income, family life, or career goals?

2. Explore the advantages and disadvantages of an individual or ethnic group assimilating into a dominant culture or maintaining an ethnic identity.
3. Explore the advantages and disadvantages to America of immigrants choosing assimilation or maintaining an ethnic identity.

Strategies for Writing about Ethnic Identity

Define key terms.   When writing about ethnic identity, make sure you use clear definitions. How do you define words such as *assimilation, Hispanic, identity,* or *hyphenated*?

Draw distinctions between ideological and cultural allegiances.
Few Americans in the 1930s were troubled by German-Americans who
identified with their national culturale and enjoyed German cuisine,
music, art, and literature. Many, however, felt threatened by those Germans who belonged to Nazi organizations, promoted anti-Semitism, and
encouraged German-Americans to engage in espionage and sabotage to
prove their loyalty to the Third Reich.

***Consider the role economics plays in whether people view ethnic
identity as a threat to the wider society.*** Commentators who fear
the balkanization of America—a society made up of separate ethnic
groups warring with each other, with little loyalty to the nation at large—
rarely mention groups such as the Amish or Hasidic Jews. Both these
groups live in self-contained communities, avoid contact with the wider
society, and reject many of the values espoused by most Americans. The
Amish oppose technology and do not drive cars, use electricity, teach
children how to use computers, or serve in the military. Like the Hasidic
Jews, they have a self-contained economy and do not seek government
support.

Examine America's role in the twenty-first century. Does a global
superpower benefit from ethnic diversity? Do cultural ties to other countries help build political alliances, expand trade, and create opportunities?
Or do ethnic ties distort a rational foreign policy because various groups
lobby the government to pursue their own agendas?

Place yourself in the role of an immigrant. Imagine that after graduation you accept a job in Egypt. One promotion leads to another and you
decide to stay permanently. You buy a home. You and your spouse have
children. Would you want your daughters to adopt Muslim attire to blend
in with their friends at school? Would you want them to behave according
to Islamic tradition? Would it bother you if your children spoke only Arabic,
converted to Islam, and accepted Egyptian attitudes toward America?
Would you understand why some Arabs might resent it if you celebrated
the Fourth of July, spoke English in public, and sent your children to visit
the United States? To what degree would you be willing to assimilate?

WRITING IN THE MODES

You may find that selecting a particular mode is an effective way of examining a topic, organizing ideas, and shaping an essay.

Narration

1. Write a brief history of your family. How has ethnic background affected its members? If your ancestors were immigrants, explain their degree of assimilation.
2. Relate an incident in which your ethnic background did or did not play a role in the way you made a decision or were treated by others.
3. Relate a story of ethnic conflict or cooperation.

Description

1. Describe an ethnic community you are familiar with and examine its degree of assimilation. Are there profound differences between residents of this community and mainstream society, or are the differences obvious but only symbolic, such as names of stores and restaurants?
2. Provide a positive or negative view of America in the future when a third of the nation will be Hispanic, when twenty percent of the population will be Muslim, and a quarter will be Asian. Will America improve or decline?

Definition

1. Establish your definition of a key term in the debate over ethnic identity. For example, you might define "assimilation" by stating what it is as well as what it is not.
2. Define, in your view, the best or worst approach to assimilation by immigrants.
3. Explain your definition of a multicultural or diverse society. Is a multicultural society one in which various races, faiths, and nationalities are blended to create a new common identity, or is it one in which a number of traditional cultures coexist without changing?

Example

1. Provide details about someone who symbolizes what you consider positive values about ethnic identity.
2. Choose a person, community, or organization that you feel serves as a positive or negative model of ethnic identity.

Comparison and Contrast

1. Compare how different members of the same family, organization, or neighborhood define themselves or approach ethnic identity.

2. Compare today's emerging ethnic groups with the tide of immigrants who entered this country a century or more ago. Do Muslims in America have to navigate through the same issues that Roman Catholics and Jews faced when they began to appear in larger numbers?
3. Contrast the differences between African Americans, most of whom are descended from slaves who were brought to this country by force, and immigrants who enter America by choice.
4. Compare the degrees of assimilation you see between immigrants and their American-born children.

Division and Classification

1. Use division to explain different attitudes about identity and assimilation you observe on campus, among friends, or in your neighborhood.
2. Classify the difficulty of assimilation different immigrants face. How is an English-speaking Irishman different from a Spanish-speaking Mexican or an Indonesian Muslim?
3. Use division to explain the kinds of problems immigrants face when making a new life in the United States.
4. Classify degrees of ethnic identity. Using friends or fellow students as examples, outline the differences between those who seemed steeped in their ethnic heritage, those who have limited involvement, and those who occasionally celebrate their heritage.

Process

1. Trace the process your ancestors took in either assimilating or maintaining an ethnic identity.
2. Write a lesson plan that describes step by step how our public schools should treat recent immigrants.
3. Detail the process by which ethnic elements become part of a common culture. St. Patrick's Day is celebrated by millions of Americans who are not Irish. In fifty years will Cinco de Mayo be largely forgotten or transformed into an all-American holiday?

Cause and Effect

1. Explore negative or positive effects assimilation has on an ethnic community. Are languages, art forms, and customs that could enrich the new country lost in the process? Does assimilation free people, especially women, from limitations imposed by tradition-bound cultures?

2. Explain why some immigrants cling to their heritage and others reject it. What are the different causes?
3. Examine the effects the war on terrorism has had on the issue of ethnic identity. Are many Americans suspicious of Arabs and Muslims? Is there a greater attempt to understand other cultures?

Argument and Persuasion

1. Develop a persuasive essay that states why we should or should not encourage ethnic groups to assimilate into a common culture and civic society.
2. Write an essay that favors or opposes the idea of separate student unions or campus organizations for African Americans, Hispanics, Muslims, or Asians.
3. Write a short editorial that argues for or against requiring public school children to salute the American flag each morning. Should pupils be required to recite the Pledge of Allegiance?

STUDENT PAPER

Cinco de Mayo

It was Cinco de Mayo. Hundreds of Mexican Americans jammed into El Norte on Lincoln Avenue. Mexican flags fluttered behind a Mexican band and a buffet of real—not the Taco Bell variety—Mexican food. English was a foreign language.

Maybe some of the Polish-Americans of the old neighborhood felt invaded. Maybe some of the people who speak about "Balkanization" would be concerned.

But in a strange way this ethnic enclave presented me with a greater diversity than I find on a college campus. For here at El Norte were cops and teachers, homemakers and career women, landlords and tenants, professionals and part-time restaurant workers, IBM sales reps and social workers. I found myself rubbing shoulders with people I would never meet under normal circumstances. Maybe the Carta Blanca and tequila helped, but I found myself talking to people whose views and attitudes I generally suspect and despise.

Here is the secret about ethnic identity. In a complex industrialized society, there is hardly a danger of the kind of ethnic conflict found in other nations. Aside from being Mexican I had little in common with most of the people at the celebration. Having a common ethnic bond did make me feel closer to and be willing to listen to people whose views I usually immediately reject.

A labor union meeting will help blacks, whites, Hispanics, Jews, and Asians to recognize their common need, their common humanity, their need to work together. An ethnic meeting will help labor and management, young and old, male and female, liberal and conservative to recognize their common roots.

I left a Spanish-speaking Mexican festival feeling more connected to the rest of America than many of the "melting pot" advocates will ever understand.

Understanding Meaning

1. What is the student's main point?
2. What details does the student use to support his or her thesis?
3. How does an ethnic festival create a new kind of diversity?
4. What does the student think about those who fear ethnic identity will produce a "Balkanized" culture?

Evaluating Strategy

1. How does the student use contrast to develop the essay? What role does the opening paragraph play?
2. What attitude does the student have toward his or her readers?
3. The student contrasts an ethnic meeting with a labor union meeting. Is this an effective way to support the thesis?

Appreciating Language

1. What does the tone and style of the essay reflect about the student's attitude toward the subject and his or her readers?
2. The student uses informal words like "cops" and "sales reps." Do you find these choices effective?

Writing Suggestions

1. Write a short narrative essay that recounts an event or incident that celebrated your ethnic culture. Did you feel connected with people you had little in common with? Did you feel part of the culture or too Americanized?
2. *COLLABORATIVE WRITING.* Working with other students, ask them to respond in one or two sentences to this paper. Do they think the student proved his or her point? Do they find the essay convincing? What grade would your group give it?

CHECKLIST

Before submitting your paper, review these points.

1. Does your paper have a clearly stated thesis? Does it have a clear point of view?

2. Do you support your thesis with representative facts, reliable observations, and accurate statistics?

3. Do you avoid making prejudiced or bigoted statements that will detract from your authority and alienate readers?

4. Do you anticipate readers' possible objections and answer them?

5. Is the paper clearly organized? Do paragraph breaks group related ideas and signal transitions?

6. Does the tone, style, and word choice of your paper suit your purpose and audience?

Companion Website

See **academic.cengage.com/english** for information on planning, organizing, writing, and revising essays.

E-Reading: InfoTrac College Edition
http://www.infotrac-college.com

For Further Reading
E–Readings Online

Search for articles by author or title in InfoTrac College Edition after entering your user name and password.

Richard Rodriguez, *Americans Are Just Discovering the Americas*
According to Rodriguez, "You cannot explain what is happening in the world right now without understanding the impulse to absorb the stranger."

Linda Chavez, *Our Hispanic Predicament*
Unlike other immigrants, Mexicans resist assimilation. Less than one in five seek to become American citizens, many never learn English, and most dream of returning to Mexico.

David Brooks, *People Like Us: We All Pay Lip Service to the Melting Pot, but We Really Prefer the Congealing Pot*
People are making strenuous efforts to group themselves with people who are basically like themselves ethnically, politically, and socially.

Ron Stodghill and Amanda Bower, *Where Everyone's a Minority: Welcome to Sacramento, America's Most Integrated City*
Time reporters analyze Sacramento, where a single street includes white, African American, Mexican American, East Indian, Japanese American, and Vietnamese homeowners.

If you have access to *Comp21*, click on Themes, then click on American Identity.

33

THEODORE ROOSEVELT

Theodore Roosevelt (1858–1919) was born in New York City. After graduating from Harvard, he studied law at Columbia University. In 1898 he was elected governor of New York. In 1900 he became Vice President of the United States and became President after the assassination of President William McKinley in 1901. Roosevelt initiated consumer and corporate reform at home and pursued an aggressive foreign policy abroad. He strongly advocated that the United States play a larger role on the world stage, leading critics to call him an imperialist. After leaving office, Roosevelt wrote several books about travel, conservation, and American history.

Americanism

CONTEXT: *In this article first published in 1915, Roosevelt urges Americans to abandon ethnic identities that might imperil America's sovereignty. At the time Roosevelt was advocating the United States enter the war against Germany, which was opposed by many ethnic groups. German and Hungarian Americans did not wish to see the United States declare war on their homelands. Irish Americans, many of whom were hostile to the English, did not wish to enter the war alongside Great Britain. Jews who had immigrated to America to escape Russian anti-Semitism were reluctant to view the Tsar as an ally. Roosevelt saw these ethnic ties as a barrier to developing an independent American foreign policy.*

1   There is no room in this country for hyphenated Americanism. When I refer to hyphenated Americans, I do not refer to naturalized Americans. Some of the very best Americans I have ever known were naturalized Americans, Americans born abroad. But a hyphenated American is not an American at all. This is just as true of the man who puts "native" before the hyphen as of the man who puts German or Irish or English or French before the hyphen. Americanism is a matter of the spirit and of the soul. Our allegiance must be purely to the United States. We must unsparingly condemn any man who holds any other allegiance. But if he is heartily and singly loyal to this Republic, then no matter where he was born, he is just as good an American as any one else.

2   The one absolutely certain way of bringing this nation to ruin, of preventing all possibility of its continuing to be a nation at all, would be to permit it to become a tangle of squabbling nationalities, an intricate knot of German-Americans, Irish-Americans, English-Americans, French-Americans, Scandinavian-Americans or Italian-Americans, each preserving its separate nationality, each at heart feeling more sympathy with Europeans of that nationality, than with the other citizens of the American Republic. The men

who do not become Americans and nothing else are hyphenated Americans; and there ought to be no room for them in this country. The man who calls himself an American citizen and who yet shows by his actions that he is primarily the citizen of a foreign land, plays a thoroughly mischievous part in the life of the body politic. He has no place here; and the sooner he returns to the land to which he feels his real heart-allegiance, the better it will be for every good American. The only man who is a good American is the man who is an American and nothing else. For an American citizen to vote as a German-American, an Irish-American, or an English-American, is to be a traitor to American institutions; and those hyphenated Americans who terrorize American politicians by threats of the foreign vote are engaged in treason to the American Republic.

3   The foreign-born population of this country must be an Americanized population—no other kind can fight the battles of America either in war or peace. It must talk the language of its native-born fellow-citizens, it must possess American citizenship and American ideals. It must stand firm by its oath of allegiance in word and deed and must show that in very fact it has renounced allegiance to every prince, potentate, or foreign government. It must be maintained on an American standard of living so as to prevent labor disturbances in important plants and at critical times. None of these objects can be secured as long as we have immigrant colonies, ghettoes and immigrant sections, and above all they cannot be assured of so long as we consider the immigrant only as an industrial asset. The immigrant must not be allowed to drift or to be put at the mercy of the exploiter. Our object is not to imitate one of the older racial types, but to maintain a new American type and then to secure loyalty to this type. We cannot secure such loyalty unless we make this country where men shall feel that they have justice and also where they shall feel that they are required to perform the duties imposed upon them. The policy of "Let alone" which we have hitherto pursued is thoroughly vicious from two stand-points. By this policy we have permitted the immigrants, and too often the native-born laborers as well, to suffer injustice. Moreover by this policy we have failed to impress upon the immigrant and upon the native-born as well that they are expected to do justice as well as to receive justice, that they are expected to be heartily and actively and single-mindedly loyal to the flag no less than to benefit by living under it.

4   We cannot afford to continue to use hundreds of thousands of immigrants merely as industrial assets while they remain social outcasts and menaces any more than fifty years ago we could afford to keep the black man merely as an industrial asset and not a human being. We cannot afford to build a big industrial plant and herd men and women about it without care

for their welfare. We cannot afford to permit squalid overcrowding or the kind of living system which makes impossible the decencies and necessities of life. We cannot afford the low wage rates and the merely seasonal industries which mean the sacrifice of both individual and family life and morals to the industrial machinery. We cannot afford to leave American mines, munitions plants, and general resources in the hands of alien workmen, alien to America and even likely to be made hostile to America by machinations such as have recently been provided in the case of the two foreign embassies in Washington. We cannot afford to run the risk of having in time of war men working on our railways or working in our munitions plants who would in the name of duty to their own foreign countries bring destruction to us. Recent events have shown us that incitements to sabotage and strikes are in the view of at least two of the great foreign powers of Europe within their definition of neutral practices. What would be done to us in the name of war if these things are done to us in the name of neutrality?

One America

5   All of us, no matter from what land our parents came, no matter in what way we may severally worship our Creator, must stand shoulder to shoulder in a united America for the elimination of race and religious prejudice. We must stand for a reign of equal justice to both big and small. We must insist on the maintenance of the American standard of living. We must stand for an adequate national control which shall secure a better training of our young men in time of peace, both for the work of peace and for the work of war. We must direct every national resource, material and spiritual, to the task not of shirking difficulties, but of training our people to overcome difficulties. Our aim must be, not to make life easy and soft, not to soften soul and body, but to fit us in virile fashion to do a great work for all mankind. This great work can only be done by a mighty democracy, with these qualities of soul, guided by those qualities of mind, which will both make it refuse to do injustice to any other nation, and also enable it to hold its own against aggression by any other nation. In our relations with the outside world, we must abhor wrongdoing. Finally and most important of all, we must strive for the establishment within our own borders of that stern and lofty standard of personal and public neutrality which shall guarantee to each man his rights, and which shall insist in return upon the full performance by each man of his duties both to his neighbor and to the great nation whose flag must symbolize in the future as it has symbolized in the past the highest hopes of all mankind.

Understanding Meaning

1. What danger does Roosevelt see in immigrants maintaining a strong ethnic identity?
2. How does Roosevelt see assimilation as protecting immigrants from exploitation?
3. In Roosevelt's view, what threat could unassimilated immigrants pose in times of war?
4. What must the United States provide immigrants in order for them to feel loyalty to America?
5. Roosevelt argues that those who remain loyal to a foreign country should return to their homelands. Does this seem realistic to you? Does Roosevelt assume that nostalgic or cultural ties to a homeland equate political loyalty to a foreign power?
6. *CRITICAL THINKING.* Roosevelt wrote this essay at a time when ethnic groups were lobbying the United States government to remain neutral or enter World War I. European powers, aware that America's entry into the war could change its outcome, urged immigrants to take a stand to aid their homeland in a time of crisis. As a result, immigrants were often seen as people with divided allegiances. Is there a tendency in times of war or international crisis for Americans to question the allegiance of citizens suspected of having dual loyalties?

Evaluating Strategy

1. What audience does Roosevelt seem to address? Does he seem to address only native-born Americans or immigrants as well?
2. Many people in the early twentieth century objected to immigration out of fear that American culture would be swamped by foreigners with alien customs and values. Does Roosevelt avoid appearing prejudiced?
3. Roosevelt does not advocate limiting immigration but states that immigrants owe full allegiance to their new homeland. Does this prevent his appeal from seeming racist or xenophobic to his critics?
4. Does Roosevelt's appeal for fair treatment of foreign-born workers prevent his essay from seeming anti-immigrant?

Appreciating Language

1. How does Roosevelt distinguish between naturalized Americans (those born in other countries) and what he calls "hyphenated Americans"?
2. How does Roosevelt define an "Americanized" population?
3. Does Roosevelt use any terms contemporary readers might find bigoted?
4. What does Roosevelt mean by the term "industrial asset"?

Writing Suggestions

1. Write your own definition of "hyphenated American." When, in your opinion, does a loyalty to another country or culture endanger the sovereignty of the United States?
2. Write a short essay that states the role ethnic groups should play in shaping American foreign policy. Should a representative democracy respond to lobbying groups advancing a nationalist cause or pursue policies that benefit the whole nation?
3. Write an essay that outlines your view of America's role in the world. Describe any religious, cultural, or ethnic influences that shape your beliefs.

34

ARMSTRONG WILLIAMS

Armstrong Williams (1959–), a popular talk show host and columnist, has written on a variety of issues concerning African Americans. His recent books include Beyond Blame: How We Can Succeed by Breaking the Dependency Barrier *(1995) and* Letters to a Young Victim: Hope and Healing in America's Inner Cities *(1996). Williams is a frequent commentator on cable news programs.*

Hyphenated Americans

CONTEXT: *In this column, Williams argues against Americans retaining an ethnic identity that emphasizes separateness and erodes allegiance to a common civil society.*

1   Over the past year, small, trite hyphens have been appearing on the campaign trail: Bush courts the African-American vote; the Muslim-American vote will make the difference in Michigan; Gore simultaneously appeals to California's Asian-American population and New York's Jewish-American community; Nader attempts to tap into the Native-American segment of our voting populace. Like deadly spore, these hyphens are replicating everywhere, supplanting our identities as Americans with a tribal ID card.

2   Hopefully now, our elected president will make a renewed effort to regard the citizens of this country not as rival clans, but as humans. To understand the importance of this issue, follow me for a moment, from the political to the personal. With little cultural debate, much of the country now chooses to define themselves not as Americans, but as the proud embodiments of various tribes. We no longer share this vast country. Instead, there is a nation for blacks and a nation for Asians and a nation for gays and Hispanics, one for Jews and whites, with each tribe pledging allegiance not to a unified nation-state, but to their own subjective cultural identity.

3   So what exactly is a hyphenated-American? No one really asks. They understand only that Americans must not be called "Americans" in this day and age. To do so would be to violate the tenets of political correctness, and to invite disaster—at least at suburban dinner parties. Those who dare find strength in their authentic experiences, rather than always trying to go about things as an_____-American might, are deemed traitors to their tribe and soon find themselves joined to no one. This is the new cultural narrative in America: what matters is not your unique experience as a human-American, but rather your ability to identify with some vague tribal concept.

4   Of course, there are those who swell with pride at being hyphenated-Americans. They would argue that those small hyphens keep intact their unique struggles and heritage. Such people might even point to the important symbolic function that such a hyphen serves: it pushes the hyphenated-American experience into the mainstream, therefore reducing any cultural hangover from America's less tolerant past.

5   In reality though, the argument for rooting oneself in a tribal identity seems terribly destabilizing to the concept of multicultural unity. To insist that we are all hyphenated Americans is pretty much the same thing as asserting that no one is an American. The major implication: your America is not my America. The idea of civic unity becomes clouded as hyphenated-Americans increasingly identify with their cultural "I," rather than the civic "we." The great hope that our civil rights leaders had about getting beyond the concept of warring tribes and integrating to form a more perfect union falls by the wayside of these small hyphens.

6   I fear that we are reverting from a highly centralized country to a set of clans separated by hyphens. Herein lies the danger: when you modify your identity to distinguish it from other clans, you tend to modify your personal attitudes as well. You make the "others" what you need them to be, in order to feel good about your own little tribe. The best in the other "tribes" therefore becomes obscured, as does any unity of understanding. Instead, we distill the cultural "others" into the most easily identifiable symbols: Blacks as criminals; Asians as isolationists; Italians as gangsters; Muslims as fanatics; Jews as stingy; Latin Americans as illegal immigrants; whites as racists. We perpetuate these stereotypes when we willingly segregate ourselves into cultural tribes, even when we know that in our individual lives, we are so much more than this.

7   Our cultural prophets once dreamt of achieving a nation not of warring tribes, but of humans. Presently, we fail this vision, and we fail ourselves.

Understanding Meaning

1. What observations did Armstrong make during the 2000 presidential campaign? What troubled him the most?
2. Why does Armstrong view ethnic identities as damaging to the nation and civic society?
3. Do you observe that many people on your campus or neighborhood prefer to see themselves as African Americans, Hispanics, Jews, or Irish Americans rather than "Americans"?
4. Does a cultural identity with an ethnic heritage always imply a political point of view?

5. *CRITICAL THINKING.* Is an ethnic or "tribal" identity undercut by other associations and influences? Do the poor or unemployed of all ethnic groups have more in common with each other than middle-class people who share an ethnic tie do? Do New Yorkers have a geographical identity that distinguishes them from people of the same ethnicity living in Texas? Do entrepreneurs, doctors, police officers, teachers, and small business owners have shared allegiances that overcome ethnic differences? Is there really a danger of a complex society breaking up along ethnic divisions?

Evaluating Strategy

1. Williams opens his essay by observing politicians campaigning for votes. Is this an effective device? Does it reveal how politicians see the voting public?
2. Can you easily summarize Williams' thesis in a single sentence? Why or why not? Is his point clearly stated?

Appreciating Language

1. How does Williams define "hyphenated-Americans"? How does he define "multicultural society"?
2. Williams uses the terms "tribe" and "clans" to describe ethnic groups and ethnic loyalty. What connotations do these words have? Do some people find the words "tribe," "tribal," and "clan" demeaning or offensive?
3. Williams places the word "others" in quotation marks. Today many commentators use the term "other" to describe people who are seen as outcasts, enemies, or threats. Look up this word in a dictionary. What does the word "other" mean to you? What connotations does it have?

Writing Suggestions

1. Write a short essay defining the way you vote for political candidates. Does your ethnic identity influence the way you vote? Would you be more likely to support candidates from your ethnic group?
2. Write two or three paragraphs analyzing the role ethnicity affects the way you view yourself. Is it a major or minor factor in your values, plans, and dreams? Would you rather be seen as a member of an ethnic group, a member of an age group, a student, male or female—or do any of these divisions make sense to you?

35

GEOFFREY WHEATCROFT

Geoffrey Wheatcroft was a columnist and literary editor of The Spectator *in the late 1970s. He became the first editor of the "Londoner's Diary" in the* Evening Standard. *Currently a columnist for the* Daily Express, *Wheatcroft has contributed articles to the* Guardian, *the* Wall Street Journal, *and the* New York Times. *In 1985 he wrote a book about the mining magnates of South Africa,* The Randlords. *In 1996 he published* The Controversy of Zion, *a history of Zionism.*

Hyphenated Americans

CONTEXT: *This article, which first appeared in the British journal* Guardian Unlimited, *was published shortly after a Cuban boy in the United States named Elian Gonzalez was returned to his father in Cuba. The boy's status in America became a highly political issue. Cuban exiles opposed to Castro's government sought to keep Gonzalez in America, whereas the federal government argued he should be sent back to Cuba. Eventually federal authorities removed the boy from the home of relatives and returned him to Cuba.*

1 Although the old saying that hard cases make bad law might seem to apply to the case of Elian Gonzalez, it wasn't really so hard. The law held that he should be reunited with his father, that is what most Americans thought should be done and that is what has now happened. But the case leaves ugly scars, and it raises once again the question of what should be the rights—and responsibilities—of "hyphenated Americans." The boy would have joined his father in Cuba weeks ago if he hadn't become an emblem, or a pawn, for one of the most noisiest and most feared of such groups, the Cuban Americans.

2 The United States is a land of immigrants, with complicated feelings towards their ancestral lands. It is also a free country where interest-group politics have always flourished, which does not mean that the effects of these groups or lobbies have been benign. To the contrary, the pressure exerted by the "hyphenates" has been almost unfailingly malign, for the American republic and for American people as a whole.

3 It is made worse by the cravenness of American politicians. In *Of Thee I Sing*, the Gershwin brothers' very funny 1931 musical satire on American politics, the campaign song goes, "He's the man the people choose,/Loves the Irish, loves the Jews." Real-life American polls have all too often taken this jest as a true word.

4   The US's emergence as a great power dates from the first world war, which the country entered belatedly, and despite the wishes of many Americans. Tens of millions of German Americans obviously didn't want to fight against their fathers' fatherland. Millions of Irish Americans were scarcely keener to fight for the king of England, or millions of Jewish Americans for the tsar of all the Russias whose oppression most of them had fled. And indeed the US did not enter the war until after the 1917 February revolution and the fall of tsardom.

5   Then the fun began. Irish-American pressure led towards the creation of an Irish Free State. Whatever else may be said of this, it was by no means in the American national interest. During the second world war, the most important war the Americans ever fought, once they, again belatedly, entered it, that Irish state was sullenly neutral.

6   There has recently been much bitter criticism in America of Swiss neutrality during the war. Apart from the fact that Switzerland was surrounded by the Axis and had no choice between neutrality and annihilation, Swiss neutrality did no military harm to the Allied cause. By contrast, Irish neutrality delayed victory in the battle of the Atlantic and thus the defeat of Hitler, with all that implies.

7   After the Irish came the Czech Americans' turn. Largely thanks to them President Woodrow Wilson's 14 points included the 10th point: "The peoples of Austria-Hungary . . . should be accorded the freest opportunity of autonomous development." From this light-hearted undertaking came the destruction of the Hapsburg monarchy.

8   The rights and wrongs of that aren't simple, but it is worth noting that the allegedly national "successor state" of Czechoslovakia thereby called into being no longer exists. Nor does Yugoslavia, the other state invented after the great war.

9   No other hyphenated group has been as politically powerful as the Jewish-American lobby. Although Washington politicians may tremble at the phrase "the 40m Irish Americans," they tremble more before the numerically fewer Jewish Americans. The American-Israeli Public Affairs Committee has won a reputation as the most formidable, and often the most ruthless, of all such pressure groups. Having spent some little time looking into this subject, I would merely say that the activities of that lobby will one day come to be seen as not having served the true interests of the United States, of Jewish America, or even, in the end, of Israel.

10   The behaviour of Cuban America over Elian speaks for itself, and the lobby has anyway prevented a necessary rapprochement between the US and Cuba. What has been more shocking than the hysteria of Little Havana

in Miami has been the fawning on the Cuban Americans by politicians, including both presidential candidates.

11   Yet even that is trivial compared with what may prove to be the true "legacy" (in the president's favourite word) of the Clinton administration. The eastward expansion of NATO must rank, in a hotly contested field, as the craziest single piece of American statecraft since the invasion of Cambodia 30 years ago this week. After the end of the cold war, it has no good strategic or political justification but can only justifiably inflame Russian suspicions and means, strictly speaking, that we must go to war on behalf of Hungary in a border dispute with Slovakia.

12   Why has it happened? It was inspired partly by the president's desire to enrich what his wiser predecessor Eisenhower called the military-industrial complex, but more importantly by his ingratiating himself with ethnic lobbies. Historians will date NATO expansion to Clinton's grovelling to a Polish-American audience in Chicago.

13   Even if the politics of hyphenated-America didn't produce such sorry practical consequences, it would be an affront to the "American idea." In direct contrast to European nationalism, the concept of "the American nation" is not based on ethnicity. Unlike European nation states, the American republic is founded not on a people, but on a proposition. This ideal has often been neglected, to put it mildly, and it may not say much to many black Americans, but it is noble in inspiration. If only American politicians remembered that more often.

14   In between sucking up to Cuban Americans and claiming to have invented the internet, Vice-President Gore not long ago produced an exquisite howler. The country's motto is *E pluribus unum*, which means, he told his audience, "out of one, many." It was a true Freudian slip. He made a mistake, but in his ludicrous way he expressed a truth, about the fragmentation of America into all too many fractious and competitive components.

15   What the 18th-century creators of the American republic believed in was "out of many, one." One people would emerge from many different origins, sharing common creeds (that all men are created equal, entitled to life, liberty and the pursuit of happiness), rather than common gene pools. What the 20th century has seen is a regression to the primitive atavistic group loyalties which the new country was meant to avoid.

16   More than a hundred years ago, a federal judge told an Irish-American agitator that any American was entitled to sentimental sympathies for another country, but that every American's first political duty must be to the United States. Someone should tell that to the mayor of Miami and to Al Gore.

Understanding Meaning

1. What does the Elian Gonzalez case symbolize to Wheatcroft?
2. In Wheatcroft's view, how do immigrants shape American foreign policy?
3. Why does Wheatcroft believe that immigrant lobbying groups have a "malign" effect on the United States?
4. How, in Wheatcroft's view, is the United States different than other nations? What is it founded on?
5. How do American politicians, in Wheatcroft's view, respond to the ethnic lobbies? Is it understandable that elected officials tend to pay attention to any organized group forming a voting bloc?
6. *CRITICAL THINKING.* Should a democracy be responsive to its citizens as a whole, making decisions that benefit the entire nation? Or should it represent the ideals, needs, and aspirations of various groups? Should ethnic groups be able to shape the way America deals with problems abroad? Is it realistic to expect American Jews to ignore Israel's interests or African Americans to have been indifferent to South Africa's policies during apartheid?

Evaluating Strategy

1. What historical examples does Wheatcroft use to support his thesis? Are they effective?
2. How does Wheatcroft state his thesis? Does he present a single statement or make a series of related points?
3. Wheatcroft wrote this article for a largely British audience. Does this explain his attitude toward American politicians and his emphasis on the Irish Republic? Would Wheatcroft have to revise this article to convince an American readership to accept his views?
4. How effective is Wheatcroft's concluding example? Does it create a memorable impression and summarize his point?

Appreciating Language

1. How does Wheatcroft define "hyphenated Americans"?
2. Wheatcroft claims Washington politicians "tremble at the phrase 40 m[illion] Irish Americans" but "tremble more" before the Jewish lobby. He refers to the Cuban-Americans as being "feared." What do these words suggest about American politicians?

3. In describing Irish American advocacy of a free state after World War I, Wheatcroft uses the phrase "Then the fun began." How do you interpret this phrase? What is he saying about ethnic lobbying in the United States?
4. Wheatcroft focuses on Al Gore's mistranslation of the American motto *E pluribus unum*. What does his error illustrate to Wheatcroft?

Writing Suggestions

1. Write a letter to the editor that agrees or disagrees with Wheatcroft's observations. How would you explain the role of ethnic identity to a European audience?
2. *COLLABORATIVE WRITING.* Working with a group of students, discuss the role of ethnic lobbying and foreign policy. Should the million Iranians now living in the United States influence our policy toward Iran? Should American Jews be considered when diplomats seek peace between Israel and its Arab neighbors? Work together to create a short statement that should guide American politicians. Should they determine what is good for the country independent of ethnic lobbyists or should they reflect the attitudes of their voters? If your group cannot agree, consider drafting pro and con statements.

36

ARMANDO RENDÓN

Armando Rendón (1939–) was raised in San Antonio, Texas. He is currently vice pres-
ident at a Chicago-based counseling firm. He has published articles in the Washington
Post *and* Civil Rights Digest. *Rendón has also written a film script,* El Chicano. *In*
1971 he published Chicano Manifesto, *which outlined his views of the place of Mexi-*
cans in American society.

Kiss of Death

CONTEXT: *In this passage from Chicano Manifesto, Rendón uses a personal narrative to*
argue the importance of Hispanic resistance to assimilation into mainstream American so-
ciety. Hispanics, he argues, should maintain their language and heritage to avoid being
"sucked into the vacuum of the dominant society."

1   I nearly fell victim to the Anglo. My childhood was spent in the West Side
barrio of San Antonio. I lived in my grandmother's house on Ruiz Street just
below Zarzamora Creek. I did well in the elementary grades and learned
English quickly.

2   Spanish was off-limits in school anyway, and teachers and relatives
taught me early that my mother tongue would be of no help in making good
grades and becoming a success. Yet Spanish was the language I used in playing and arguing with friends. Spanish was the language I spoke with my
abuelita, my dear grandmother, as I ate *atole* on those cold mornings when I
used to wake at dawn to her clattering dishes in the tiny kitchen; or when I
would cringe in mock horror at old folk tales she would tell me late at night.

3   But the lesson took effect anyway. When, at the age of ten, I went with
my mother to California, to the San Francisco Bay Area where she found
work during the war years, I had my first real opportunity to strip myself
completely of my heritage. In California the schools I attended were all
Anglo except for this little mexicanito. At least, I never knew anyone who
admitted he was Mexican and I certainly never thought to ask. When my
name was accented incorrectly, Réndon instead of Rendón, that was all
right; finally I must have gotten tired of correcting people or just didn't
bother.

4   I remember a summertime visit home a few years after living on the
West Coast. At an evening gathering of almost the whole family—uncles,

aunts, nephews, nieces, my *abuelita*—we sat outdoors through the dusk until the dark had fully settled. Then the lights were turned on; someone brought out a Mexican card game, the *Lotería El Diablito,* similar to bingo. But instead of rows of numbers on a pasteboard, there were figures of persons, animals, and objects on cards corresponding to figures set in rows on a pasteboard. We used frijoles (pinto beans) to mark each figure on our card as the leader went through the deck one by one. The word for tree was called: *Arbol!* It completed a row; I had won. Then to check my card I had to name each figure again. When I said the word for tree, it didn't come at all as I wanted it to; AR-BOWL with the accent on the last syllable and sounding like an Anglo tourist. There was some all-around kidding of me and good-natured laughter over the incident, and it passed.

5   But if I had not been speaking much Spanish up until then, I spoke even less afterward. Even when my mother, who speaks both Spanish and English fluently, spoke to me in Spanish, I would respond in English. By the time I graduated from high school and prepared to enter college, the break was nearly complete. Seldom during college did I admit to being a Mexican-American. Only when Latin American students pressed me about my surname did I admit my Spanish descent, or when it proved an asset in meeting coeds from Latin American countries.

6   My ancestry had become a shadow, fainter and fainter about me. I felt no particular allegiance to it, drew no inspiration from it, and elected generally to let it fade away. I clicked with the Anglo mind-set in college, mastered it, you might say. I even became editor of the campus biweekly newspaper as a junior, and editor of the literary magazine as a senior—not bad, now that I look back, for a tortillas-and-beans Chicano upbringing to beat the Anglo at his own game.

7   The point of my "success," of course, was that I had been assimilated; I had bought the white man's world. After getting my diploma I was set to launch out into a career in newspaper reporting and writing. There was no thought in my mind of serving my people, telling their story, or making anything right for anybody but myself. Instead I had dreams of Pulitzer Prizes, syndicated columns, foreign correspondent assignments, front-page stories—that was for me. Then something happened.

8   A Catholic weekly newspaper in Sacramento offered me a position as a reporter and feature writer. I had a job on a Bay Area daily as a copyboy at the time, with the opportunity to become a reporter. But I'd just been married, and there were a number of other reasons to consider: there'd be a variety of assignments, Sacramento was the state capital, it was a good town in

which to raise a family, and the other job lacked promise for upward mobility. I decided to take the offer.

9   My wife and I moved to Sacramento in the fall of 1961, and in a few weeks the radicalization of this Chicano began. It wasn't a book I read or a great leader awakening me, for we had no Chávezes or Tijerinas or Gonzálezes at the time; and it was no revelation from above. It was my own people who rescued me. There is a large Chicano population in Sacramento, today one of the most activist in northern California, but at the time factionalized and still dependent on the social and church organizations for identity. But together we found each other.

10   My job soon brought me into contact with many Chicanos as well as with the recently immigrated Mexicans, located in the barrios that Sacramento had allocated to the "Mexicans." I found my people striving to survive in an alien environment among foreign people. One of the stories I covered concerned a phenomenon called Cursillos de Cristiandad (Little Courses in Christianity), intense, three-day group-sensitivity sessions whose chief objective is the re-Christianization of Catholics. To cover the story properly I talked my editor into letting me take a Cursillo.

11   Not only was much revealed to me about the phony gilt lining of religion which I had grown up believing was the Church, but there was an added and highly significant side effect—cultural shock! I rediscovered my own people, or perhaps they redeemed me. Within the social dimension of the Cursillo, for the first time in many years I became reimmersed in a tough, *macho ambiente* (an entirely Mexican male environment). Only Spanish was spoken. The effect was shattering. It was as if my tongue, after being struck dumb as a child, had been loosened.

12   Because we were located in cramped quarters, with limited facilities, and the cooks, lecturers, priests, and participants were men only, the old sense of *machismo* and *camarada* was revived and given new perspective. I was cast in a spiritual setting which was a perfect background for reviving my Chicano soul. Reborn but imperfectly, I still had a lot to learn about myself and my people. But my understanding deepened and renewed itself as the years went by. I visited bracero camps with teams of Chicanos; sometimes with priests taking the sacraments; sometimes only Chicanos, offering advice or assistance with badly needed food and clothing, distributed through a bingo-game technique; and on occasion, music for group singing provided by a phonograph or a guitar. Then there were barrio organization work; migrant worker programs; a rural self-help community development project; and confrontation with antipoverty agencies, with the churches, with government officials, and with cautious Chicanos, too.

13   In a little San Francisco magazine called *Way*, I wrote in a March 1966 article discussing "The Other Mexican-American":

14   The Mexican-American must answer at the same time: Who am I? and Who are we? This is to pose then, not merely a dilemma of self-identity; but of self-in-group-identity.... Perhaps the answer to developing a total Mexican-American concept must be left in the hands of the artist, the painter, the writer, and the poet, who can abstract the essence of what it is to be Mexican in America.... When that understanding comes ... the Mexican-American will not only have acculturized himself, but he will have acculturized America to him.

15   If anyone knew what he was talking about when he spoke of the dilemma of who he was and where he belonged, it was this Chicano. I very nearly dropped out, as so many other Mexican-Americans have, under the dragging pressure to be someone else, what most of society wants you to be before it hands out its chrome-plated trophies.

16   And that mystique—I didn't quite have it at the time, or the right word for it. But no one did until just the last few years when so many of us stopped trying to be someone else and decided that what we want to be and to be called is Chicano.

17   I owe my life to my Chicano people. They rescued me from the Anglo kiss of death, the monolingual, monocultural, and colorless Gringo society. I no longer face a dilemma of identity or direction. That identity and direction have been charted for me by the Chicano—but to think I came that close to being sucked into the vacuum of the dominant society.

Understanding Meaning

1. What kind of childhood did Rendón have?
2. What represented success to Rendón as a young man? What does he mean by the statement, "I had bought the white man's world"?
3. What is the "Anglo kiss of death"?
4. *CRITICAL THINKING.* Rendón describes the "Gringo society" as "monolingual, monocultural, and colorless." Does he overlook the diversity of Irish, Jewish, Italian, Greek, and Russian cultures that make up mainstream America?

Evaluating Strategy

1. What tone does the first sentence create? What effect does the word "victim" have?
2. Rendón includes a quote from one of his own articles. Is this an effective device or would it be better to restate these ideas within "Kiss of Death"?
3. *BLENDING THE MODES.* How does Rendón use narration, description, and comparison in developing his essay?

Appreciating Language

1. What does the term "kiss of death" mean to you? Do you associate it with the Bible or movie images of the Mafia?
2. Rendón uses several Spanish words without providing definitions in English. What does this suggest about his idea of America becoming "acculturized" to the Mexican American?
3. What does the author mean by the term "cautious Chicanos"?

Writing Suggestions

1. Write an essay about your own version of a "kiss of death" you avoided in your own life. Perhaps you nearly lost yourself or compromised your future by taking a job, entering a relationship, or moving to a location that was initially appealing but would have had negative consequences. Emphasize how this experience could have altered your identity.
2. *COLLABORATIVE WRITING.* Discuss Rendón's essay with a group of other students, asking each one to comment on the concept of "the Anglo kiss of death." Does joining mainstream middle-class America require people to shed or deny their ethnic identity? Record the ideas of the group and collaborate on a response, agreeing or disagreeing with Rendón. If members disagree, consider writing alternative responses.

37

SHELBY STEELE

Shelby Steele (1946–) grew up in Chicago and attended Coe College in Iowa. He teaches English at San Jose State University in California. He received national attention after the publication of his 1990 book, The Content of Our Character: A New Vision of Race in America, *which included essays previously published in* Harper's *and the* American Scholar.

The Recoloring of Campus Life

CONTEXT: *In this section from* The Content of Our Character, *Steele explores how the 1960s dream of equality and integration has been supplanted by a desire for self-segregation and racial identity.*

1   In the past few years, we have witnessed what the National Institute Against Prejudice and Violence calls a "proliferation" of racial incidents on college campuses around the country. Incidents of on-campus "intergroup conflict" have occurred at more than 160 colleges in the last two years, according to the institute. The nature of these incidents has ranged from open racial violence—most notoriously, the October 1986 beating of a black student at the University of Massachusetts at Amherst after an argument about the World Series turned into a racial bashing, with a crowd of up to three thousand whites chasing twenty blacks—to the harassment of minority students and acts of racial or ethnic insensitivity, with by far the greatest number of episodes falling in the last two categories. At Yale last year, a swastika and the words "white power" were painted on the university's Afro-American cultural center. Racist jokes were aired not long ago on a campus radio station at the University of Michigan. And at the University of Wisconsin at Madison, members of the Zeta Beta Tau fraternity held a mock slave auction in which pledges painted their faces black and wore Afro wigs. Two weeks after the president of Stanford University informed the incoming freshman class last fall that "bigotry is out, and I mean it," two freshmen defaced a poster of Beethoven—gave the image thick lips—and hung it on a black student's door.

2   In response, black students around the country have rediscovered the militant protest strategies of the sixties. At the University of Massachusetts at Amherst, Williams College, Penn State University, University of California-Berkeley, UCLA, Stanford University, and countless other campuses, black

students have sat in, marched, and rallied. But much of what they were marching and rallying about seemed less a response to specific racial incidents than a call for broader action on the part of the colleges and universities they were attending. Black students have demanded everything from more black faculty members and new courses on racism to the addition of "ethnic" foods in the cafeteria. There is the sense in these demands that racism runs deep. Is the campus becoming the battleground for a renewed war between the races? I don't think so, not really. But if it is not a war, the problem of campus racism does represent a new and surprising hardening of racial lines within the most traditionally liberal and tolerant of America's institutions—its universities.

3   As a black who has spent his entire adult life on predominantly white campuses, I found it hard to believe that the problem of campus racism was as dramatic as some of the incidents seemed to make it. The incidents I read or heard about often seemed prankish and adolescent, though not necessarily harmless. There is a meanness in them but not much menace; no one is proposing to reinstitute Jim Crow on campus. On the California campus where I now teach, there have been few signs of racial tension.

4   And, of course, universities are not where racial problems tend to arise. When I went to college in the mid-sixties, colleges were oases of calm and understanding in a racially tense society; campus life—with its traditions of tolerance and fairness, its very distance from the "real" world—imposed a degree of broad-mindedness on even the most provincial students. If I met whites who were not anxious to be friends with blacks, most were at least vaguely friendly to the cause of our freedom. In any case, there was no guerrilla activity against our presence, no "mine field of racism" (as one black student at Berkeley recently put it to me) to negotiate. I wouldn't say that the phrase "campus racism" is a contradiction in terms, but until recently it certainly seemed an incongruence.

5   But a greater incongruence is the generational timing of this new problem on the campuses. Today's undergraduates were born after the passage of the 1964 Civil Rights Act. They grew up in an age when racial equality was for the first time enforceable by law. This too was a time when blacks suddenly appeared on television, as mayors of big cities, as icons of popular culture, as teachers, and in some cases even as neighbors. Today's black and white college students, veterans of "Sesame Street" and often of integrated grammar and high schools, have had more opportunities to know each other than any previous generation in American history. Not enough opportunities, perhaps, but enough to make the notion of racial tension on campus something of a mystery, at least to me.

6   To look at this mystery, I left my own campus with its burden of famil-
iarity and talked with black and white students at California schools where
racial incidents had occurred: Stanford, UCLA, and Berkeley. I spoke with
black and white students—not with Asians and Hispanics—because, as always, blacks and whites represent the deepest lines of division, and because I hesitate to wander onto the complex territory of other minority
groups. A phrase by William H. Gass—"the hidden internality of things"—
describes, with maybe a little too much grandeur, what I hoped to find. But
it is what I wanted to find, for this is the kind of problem that makes a black
person nervous, which is not to say that it doesn't unnerve whites as well.
Once every six months or so someone yells "nigger" at me from a passing
car. I don't like to think that these solo artists might soon make up a chorus,
or worse, that this chorus might one day soon sing to me from the paths of
my own campus.

7   I have long believed that the trouble between the races is seldom what
it appears to be. It was not hard to see after my first talks with students that
racial tension on campus is a problem that misrepresents itself. It has the
same look, the archetypal pattern, of America's timeless racial conflict—
white racism and black protest. And I think part of our concern over it
comes from the fact that it has the feel of a relapse, illness gone and come
again. But if we are seeing the same symptoms, I don't believe we are dealing with the same illness. For one thing, I think racial tension on campus is
more the result of racial equality than inequality.

8   How to live with racial difference has been America's profound social
problem. For the first hundred years or so following emancipation it was
controlled by a legally sanctioned inequality that kept the races from each
other. No longer is this the case. On campuses today, as throughout society, blacks enjoy equality under the law—a profound social advancement.
No student may be kept out of a class or a dormitory or an extracurricular
activity because of his or her race. But there is a paradox here: on a campus
where members of all races are gathered, mixed together in the classroom
as well as socially, differences are more exposed than ever. And this is
where the trouble starts. For members of each race—young adults coming
into their own, often away from home for the first time—bring to this site
of freedom, exploration, and (now, today) equality, very deep fears, anxieties, inchoate feelings of racial shame, anger, and guilt. These feelings
could lie dormant in the home, in familiar neighborhoods, in simpler days
of childhood. But the college campus, with its structures of interaction and
adult-level competition—the big exam, the dorm, the mixer—is another
matter. I think campus racism is born of the rub between racial difference

and a setting, the campus itself, devoted to interaction and equality. On our campuses, such concentrated micro-societies, all that remains unresolved between blacks and whites, all the old wounds and shames that have never been addressed, present themselves for attention—and present our youth with pressures they cannot always handle.

9   I have mentioned one paradox: racial fears and anxieties among blacks and whites, bubbling up in an era of racial equality under the law, in settings that are among the freest and fairest in society. But there is another, related paradox, stemming from the notion of—and practice of—affirmative action. Under the provisions of the Equal Employment Opportunity Act of 1972, all state governments and institutions (including universities) were forced to initiate plans to increase the proportion of minority and women employees and, in the case of universities, of students too. Affirmative action plans that establish racial quotas were ruled unconstitutional more than ten years ago in *University of California* v. *Bakke*, but such plans are still thought by some to secretly exist, and lawsuits having to do with alleged quotas are still very much with us. But quotas are only the most controversial aspect of affirmative action; the principle of affirmative action is reflected in various university programs aimed at redressing and overcoming past patterns of discrimination. Of course, to be conscious of past patterns of discrimination—the fact, say, that public schools in the black inner cities are more crowded and employ fewer top-notch teachers than a white suburban public school, and that this is a factor in student performance—is only reasonable. But in doing this we also call attention quite obviously to difference: in the case of blacks and whites, racial difference. What has emerged on campus in recent years—as a result of the new equality and of affirmative action and, in a sense, as a result of progress—is a *politics of difference*, a troubling, volatile politics in which each group justifies itself, its sense of worth and its pursuit of power, through difference alone.

10   In this context, racial, ethnic, and gender differences become forms of sovereignty, campuses become balkanized, and each group fights with whatever means are available. No doubt there are many factors that have contributed to the rise of racial tension on campus: What has been the role of fraternities, which have returned to campus with their inclusions and exclusions? What role has the heightened notion of college as some first step to personal, financial success played in increasing competition, and thus tension? But mostly, what I sense is that in interactive settings, fighting the fights of "difference," old ghosts are stirred and haunt again. Black and white Americans simply have the power to make each other feel shame

and guilt. In most situations, we may be able to deny these feelings, keep them at bay. But these feelings are likely to surface on college campuses, where young people are groping for identity and power, and where difference is made to matter so greatly. In a way, racial tension on campus in the eighties might have been inevitable.

11   I would like, first, to discuss black students, their anxieties and vulnerabilities. The accusation black Americans have always lived with is that they are inferior—inferior simply because they are black. And this accusation has been too uniform, too ingrained in cultural imagery, too enforced by law, custom, and every form of power not to have left a mark. Black inferiority was a precept accepted by the founders of this nation; it was a principle of social organization that relegated blacks to the sidelines of American life. So when young black students find themselves on white campuses surrounded by those who have historically claimed superiority, they are also surrounded by the myth of their inferiority.

12   Of course, it is true that many young people come to college with some anxiety about not being good enough. But only blacks come wearing a color that is still, in the minds of some, a sign of inferiority. Poles, Jews, Hispanics, and other groups also endure degrading stereotypes. But two things make the myth of black inferiority a far heavier burden—the broadness of its scope and its incarnation in color. There are not only more stereotypes of blacks than of other groups, but these stereotypes are also more dehumanizing, more focused on the most despised human traits: stupidity, laziness, sexual immorality, dirtiness, and so on. In America's racial and ethnic hierarchy, blacks have clearly been relegated to the lowest level—have been burdened with an ambiguous, animalistic humanity. Moreover, this is made unavoidable for blacks by sheer visibility of black skin, a skin that evokes the myth of inferiority on sight. Today this myth is sadly reinforced for many black students by affirmative action programs, under which blacks may often enter college with lower test scores and high school grade point averages than whites. "They see me as an affirmative action case," one black student told me at UCLA. This reinforces the myth of inferiority by implying that blacks are not good enough to make it into college on their own.

13   So when a black student enters college, the myth of inferiority compounds the normal anxiousness over whether he or she will be good enough. This anxiety is not only personal but also racial. The families of these students will have pounded into them the fact that blacks are not inferior. And probably more than anything it is this pounding that finally leaves the mark. If I am not inferior, why the need to say so?

14   This myth of inferiority constitutes a very sharp and ongoing anxiety for young blacks, the nature of which is very precise: it is the terror that somehow, through one's actions of by virtue of some "proof" (a poor grade, a flubbed response in class), one's fear of inferiority—inculcated in ways large and small by society—will be confirmed as real. On a university campus where intelligence itself is the ultimate measure, this anxiety is bound to be triggered.

15   A black student I met at UCLA was disturbed a little when I asked him if he ever felt vulnerable—anxious about "black inferiority"—as a black student. But after a long pause, he finally said, "I think I do." The example he gave was of a large lecture class he'd taken with over three hundred students. Fifty or so black students sat in the back of the lecture hall and "acted out every stereotype in the book." They were loud, ate food, came in late—and generally got lower grades than whites in the class. "I knew I would be seen like them, and I didn't like it. I never sat by them." Seen like what, I asked, though we both knew the answer. "As lazy, ignorant, and stupid," he said sadly.

16   Had the group at the back been white fraternity brothers, they would not have been seen as dumb whites, of course. And a frat brother who worried about his grades would not worry that he [had] been seen "like them." The terror in this situation for the black student I spoke with was that his own deeply buried anxiety would be given credence, that the myth would be verified, and that he would feel shame and humiliation not because of who he was but simply because he was black. In this lecture hall his race, quite apart from his performance, might subject him to four unendurable feelings—diminishment, accountability to the preconceptions of whites, a powerlessness to change those preconceptions, and finally, shame. These are the feelings that make up his racial anxiety, and that of all blacks on any campus. On a white campus a black is never far from these feelings, and even his unconscious knowledge that he is subject to them can undermine his self-esteem. There are blacks on any campus who are not up to doing good college-level work. Certain black students may not be happy or motivated or in the appropriate field of study—*just like whites*. (Let us not forget that many white students get poor grades, fail, drop out.) Moreover, many more blacks than whites are not quite prepared for college, may have to catch up, owing to factors beyond their control: poor previous schooling, for example. But the white who has to catch up will not be anxious that his being behind is a matter of his whiteness, of his being racially inferior. The black student may well have such a fear.

17   This, I believe, is one reason why black colleges in America turn out 37 percent of all black college graduates though they enroll only 16 percent of

black college students. Without whites around on campus, the myth of inferiority is in abeyance and, along with it, a great reservoir of culturally imposed self-doubt. On black campuses, feelings of inferiority are personal; on campuses with a white majority, a black's problems have a way of becoming a "black" problem.

18   But this feeling of vulnerability a black may feel, in itself, is not as serious a problem as what he or she does with it. To admit that one is made anxious in integrated situations about the myth of racial inferiority is difficult for young blacks. It seems like admitting that one is racially inferior. And so, most often, the student will deny harboring the feelings. This is where some of the pangs of racial tension begin, because denial always involves distortion.

19   In order to deny a problem we must tell ourselves that the problem is something different from what it really is. A black student at Berkeley told me that he felt defensive every time he walked into a classroom of white faces. When I asked why, he said, "Because I know they're all racists. They think blacks are stupid." Of course it may be true that some whites feel this way, but the singular focus on white racism allows this student to obscure his own underlying racial anxiety. He can now say that his problem—facing a classroom of white faces, *fearing* that they think he is dumb—is entirely the result of certifiable white racism and has nothing to do with his own anxieties, or even that this particular academic subject may not be his best. Now all the terror of his anxiety, its powerful energy, is devoted to simply *seeing* racism. Whatever evidence of racism he finds—and looking this hard, he will no doubt find some—can be brought in to buttress his distorted view of the problem while his actual deepseated anxiety goes unseen.

20   Denial, and the distortion that results, places the problem *outside* the self and in the world. It is not that I have any inferiority anxiety because of my race; it is that I am going to school with people who don't like blacks. This is the shift in thinking that allows black students to reenact the protest pattern of the sixties. *Denied racial anxiety–distortion–reenactment* is the process by which feelings of inferiority are transformed into an exaggerated white menace—which is then protested against with the techniques of the past. Under the sway of this process, black students believe that history is repeating itself, that it's just like the sixties, or fifties. In fact, it is not-yet-healed wounds from the past, rather than the inequality that created the wounds, that is the real problem.

21   This process generated an unconscious need to exaggerate the level of racism on campus—to make it a matter of the system, not just a handful of students. Racism is the avenue away from the true inner anxiety. How many students demonstrating for black theme dorms—demonstrating in

the style of the sixties, when the battle was to win for blacks a place on campus—might be better off spending their time reading and studying? Black students have the highest dropout rate and the lowest grade point average of any group in American universities. This need not be so. And it is not the result of not having black theme dorms.

22   It was my very good fortune to go to college in 1964, when the question of black "inferiority" was openly talked about among blacks. The summer before I left for college, I heard Martin Luther King speak in Chicago, and he laid it on the line for black students everywhere: "When you are behind in a footrace, the only way to get ahead is to run faster than the man in front of you. So when your white roommate says he's tired and goes to sleep, you stay up and burn the midnight oil." His statement that we were "behind in a footrace" acknowledged that, because of history, of few opportunities, of racism, we were, in a sense, "inferior." But this had to do with what had been done to our parents and their parents, not with inherent inferiority. And because it was acknowledged, it was presented to us as a challenge rather than a mark of shame.

23   Of the eighteen black students (in a student body of one thousand) who were on campus in my freshman year, all graduated, though a number of us were not from the middle class. At the university where I currently teach, the dropout rate for black students is 72 percent, despite the presence of several academic support programs, a counseling center with black counselors, an Afro-American studies department, black faculty, administrators, and staff, a general education curriculum that emphasizes "cultural pluralism," an Educational Opportunities Program, a mentor program, a black faculty and staff association, and an administration and faculty that often announce the need to do more for black students.

24   It may be unfair to compare my generation with the current one. Parents do this compulsively and to little end but self-congratulation. But I don't congratulate my generation. I think we were advantaged. We came along at a time when racial integration was held in high esteem. And integration was a very challenging social concept for both blacks and whites. We were remaking ourselves—that's what one did at college—and making history. We had something to prove. This was a profound advantage; it gave us clarity and a challenge. Achievement in the American mainstream was the goal of integration, and the best thing about this challenge was its secondary message—that we *could* achieve.

25   There is much irony in the fact that black power would come along in the late sixties and change all this. Black power was a movement of uplift and pride, and yet it also delivered the weight of pride—a weight that

would burden black students from then on. Black power "nationalized" the black identity, made blackness itself an object of celebration, an allegiance. But if it transformed a mark of shame into a mark of pride, it also, in the name of pride, required the denial of racial anxiety. Without a frank account of one's anxieties, there is no clear direction, no concrete challenge. Black students today do not get as clear a message from their racial identity as my generation got. They are not filled with the same urgency to prove themselves because black pride has said, *You're already proven, already equal, as good as anybody.*

26   The "black identity" shaped by black power most forcefully contributes to racial tensions on campuses by basing entitlement more on race than on constitutional rights and standards of merit. With integration, black entitlement derived from constitutional principles of fairness. Black power changed this by skewing the formula from rights to color—if you were black, you were entitled. Thus the United Coalition Against Racism (UCAR) at the University of Michigan could "demand" two years ago that all black professors be given immediate tenure, that there [be] a special pay incentive for black professors, and that money be provided for an all-black student union. In this formula, black becomes the very color of entitlement, an extra right in itself, and a very dangerous grandiosity is promoted in which blackness amounts to specialness.

27   Race is, by any standard, an unprincipled source of power. And on campuses the use of racial power by one group makes racial, ethnic, or gender difference a currency of power for all groups. When I make my *difference* into power, other groups must seize upon their difference to contain my power and maintain their position relative to me. Very quickly a kind of politics of difference emerges in which racial, ethnic, and gender groups are forced to assert their entitlement and vie for power based on the single quality that makes them different from one another.

28   On many campuses today academic departments and programs are established on the basis of difference—black studies, women's studies, Asian studies, and so on—despite the fact that there is nothing in these "difference" departments that cannot be studied within traditional academic disciplines. If their rationale is truly past exclusion from the mainstream curriculum, shouldn't the goal now be complete inclusion rather than separateness? I think this logic is overlooked because those groups are too interested in the power their difference can bring, and they insist on separate departments and programs as tribute to that power.

29   This politics of difference makes everyone on campus a member of a minority group. It also makes racial tension inevitable. To highlight one's

difference as a source of advantage is also, indirectly, to inspire the enemies of that difference. When blackness (and femaleness) become power, then white maleness is also sanctioned as power. A white male student I spoke with at Stanford said, "One of my friends said the other day that we should get together and start up a white student union and come up with a list of demands."

30   It is certainly true that white maleness has long been an unfair source of power. But the sin of white male power is precisely its use of race and gender as a source of entitlement. When minorities and women use their race, ethnicity, and gender in the same way, they not only commit the same sin but also, indirectly, sanction the very form of power that oppressed them in the first place. The politics of difference is based on a tit-for-tat sort of logic in which every victory only calls one's enemies to arms.

31   This elevation of difference undermines the communal impulse by making each group foreign and inaccessible to others. When difference is celebrated rather than remarked, people must think in terms of difference, they must find meaning in difference, and this meaning comes from an endless process of contrasting one's group with other groups. Blacks use whites to define themselves as different, women use men, Hispanics use whites and blacks, and on it goes. And in the process each group mythologizes and mystifies its difference, puts it beyond the full comprehension of outsiders. Difference becomes inaccessible preciousness toward which outsiders are expected to be simply and uncomprehendingly reverential. But beware: in this world, even the insulated world of the college campus, preciousness is a balloon asking for a needle. At Smith College graffiti appears: "Niggers, spics, and chinks. Quit complaining or get out."

32   I think that those who run our colleges and universities are every bit as responsible for the politics of difference as are minority students. To correct the exclusions once caused by race and gender, universities—under the banner of affirmative action—have relied too heavily on race and gender as criteria. So rather than break the link between difference and power, they have reinforced it. On most campuses today, a well-to-do black student with two professional parents is qualified by his race for scholarship monies that are not available to a lower-middle-class white student. A white female with a private school education and every form of cultural advantage comes under the affirmative action umbrella. This kind of inequity is an invitation to backlash.

33   What universities are quite rightly trying to do is compensate people for past discrimination and the deprivations that followed from it. But race and gender alone offer only the grossest measure of this. And the failure of

universities has been their backing away from the challenge of identifying principles of fairness and merit that make finer and more equitable distinctions. The real challenge is not simply to include a certain number of blacks, but to end discrimination against all blacks and to offer special help to those with talent who have also been economically deprived.

34   With regard to black students, affirmative action has led universities to correlate color with poverty and disadvantage in so absolute a way as to encourage the politics of difference. But why have they gone along with this? My belief is that it is due to the specific form of racial anxiety to which whites are most subject.

35   Most of the white students I talked with spoke as if from under a faint cloud of accusation. There was always a ring of defensiveness in their complaints about blacks. A white student I spoke to at UCLA told me: "Most white students on this campus think the black student leadership here is made up of oversensitive crybabies who spend all their time looking for things to kick up a ruckus about." A white student at Stanford said, "Blacks do nothing but complain and ask for sympathy when everyone really knows that they don't do well because they don't try. If they worked harder, they could do as well as everyone else."

36   That these students felt accused was most obvious in their compulsion to assure me that they were not racist. Oblique versions of some-of-my-best-friends-are stories came ritualistically before or after critiques of black students. Some said flatly, "I am not a racist, but . . ." Of course, we all deny being racist, but we only do this compulsively, I think, when we are working against an accusation of bias. I think it was the color of my skin itself that accused them.

37   This was the meta-message that surrounded these conversations like an aura, and it is, I believe, the core of white American racial anxiety. My skin not only accused them; it judged them. And this judgment was a sad gift of history that brought them to account whether they deserved such accountability or not. It said that wherever and whenever blacks were concerned, they had reason to feel guilt. And whether it was earned or unearned, I think it was guilt that set off the compulsion in these students to disclaim. I believe it is true that, in America, black people make white people feel guilty.

38   Guilt is the essence of white anxiety just as inferiority is the essence of black anxiety. And the terror that it carries for whites is the terror of discovering that one has reason to feel guilt where blacks are concerned—not so much because of what blacks might think but because of what guilt can say about oneself. If the darkest fear of blacks is inferiority, the darkest fear of whites is that their better lot in life is at least partially the result of their

capacity for evil—their capacity to dehumanize an entire people for their own benefit and then to be indifferent to the devastation their dehumanization has wrought on successive generations of their victims. This is the terror that whites are vulnerable to regarding blacks. And the mere fact of being white is sufficient to feel it, since even whites with hearts clean of racism benefit from being white—benefit at the expense of blacks. This is a conditional guilt having nothing to do with individual intentions or actions. And it makes for a very powerful anxiety because it threatens whites with a view of themselves as inhuman, just as inferiority threatens blacks with a similar view of themselves. At the dark core of both anxieties is a suspicion of incomplete humanity.

39   So, the white students I met were not just meeting me; they were also meeting the possibility of their own inhumanity. And this, I think, is what explains how some young white college students in the late eighties could so frankly take part in racially insensitive and outright racist acts. They were expected to be cleaner of racism than any previous generation—they were born into the Great Society. But this expectation overlooks the fact that, for them, color is still an accusation and judgment. In black faces there is a discomforting reflection of white collective shame. Blacks remind them that their racial innocence is questionable, that they are the beneficiaries of past and present racism, and the sins of the father may well have been visited on the children.

40   And yet young whites tell themselves that they had nothing to do with the oppression of black people. They have a stronger belief in their racial innocence than any previous generation of whites and a natural hostility toward anyone who would challenge that innocence. So (with a great deal of individual variation) they can end up in the paradoxical position of being hostile to blacks as a way of defending their own racial innocence.

41   I think this is what the young white editors of the *Dartmouth Review* were doing when they harassed black music professor William Cole. Weren't they saying, in effect, I am so free of racial guilt that I can afford to attack blacks ruthlessly and still be racially innocent? The ruthlessness of these attacks was a form of denial, a badge of innocence. The more they were charged with racism, the more ugly and confrontational their harassment became (an escalation unexplained even by the serious charges against Professor Cole). Racism became a means of rejecting racial guilt, a way of showing that they were not, ultimately, racists.

42   The politics of difference sets up a struggle for innocence among all groups. When difference is the currency of power, each group must fight for the innocence that entitles it to power. To gain this innocence, blacks sting

whites with guilt, remind them of their racial past, accuse them of new and more subtle forms of racism. One way whites retrieve their innocence is to discredit blacks and deny their difficulties, for in this denial is the denial of their own guilt. To blacks this denial looks like racism, a racism that feeds black innocence and encourages them to throw more guilt at whites. And so the cycle continues. The politics of difference leads each group to pick at the vulnerabilities of the other.

43   Men and women who run universities—whites, mostly—participate in the politics of difference because they handle their guilt differently than do many of their students. They don't deny it, but still they don't want to *feel* it. And to avoid this feeling of guilt they have tended to go along with whatever blacks put on the table rather than work with them to assess their real needs. University administrators have too often been afraid of guilt and have relied on negotiation and capitulation more to appease their own guilt than to help blacks and other minorities. Administrators would never give white students a racial theme dorm where they could be "more comfortable with people of their own kind," yet more and more universities are doing this for black students, thus fostering a kind of voluntary segregation. To avoid the anxieties of integrated situations blacks ask for theme dorms; to avoid guilt, white administrators give theme dorms.

44   When everyone is on the run from their anxieties about race, race relations on campus can be reduced to the negotiation of avoidances. A pattern of demand and concession develops in which both sides use the other to escape themselves. Black studies departments, black deans of student affairs, black counseling programs, Afro houses, black theme dorms, black homecoming dances and graduation ceremonies—black students and white administrators have slowly engineered a machinery of separatism that, in the name of sacred difference, redraws the ugly lines of segregation.

45   Black students have not sufficiently helped themselves, and universities, despite all their concessions, have not really done much for blacks. If both faced their anxieties, I think they would see the same thing: academic parity with all other groups should be the overriding mission of black students, and it should also be the first goal that universities have for their black students. Blacks can only *know* they are as good as others when they are, in fact, as good—when their grades are higher and their dropout rate lower. Nothing under the sun will substitute for this, and no amount of concessions will bring it about.

46   Universities can never be free of guilt until they truly help black students, which means leading and challenging them rather than negotiating and capitulating. It means inspiring them to achieve academic parity,

47   nothing less, and helping them to see their own weaknesses as their greatest challenge. It also means dismantling the machinery of separatism,
breaking the link between difference and power, and skewing the formula
for entitlement away from race and gender and back to constitutional rights.

47   As for the young white students who have rediscovered swastikas and
the word "nigger," I think that they suffer from an exaggerated sense of their
own innocence, as if they were incapable of evil and beyond the reach of
guilt. But it is also true that the politics of difference creates an environment
that threatens their innocence and makes them defensive. White students
are not invited to the negotiating table from which they see blacks and others walk away with concessions. The presumption is that they do not deserve to be there because they are white. So they can only be defensive, and
the less mature among them will be aggressive. Guerrilla activity will ensue.
Of course this is wrong, but it is also a reflection of an environment where
difference carries power and where whites have the wrong "difference."

48   I think universities should emphasize commonality as a higher value than
"diversity" and "pluralism"—buzzwords for the politics of difference. Difference that does not rest on a clearly delineated foundation of commonality is
not only inaccessible to those who are not part of the ethnic or racial group, but
also antagonistic to them. Difference can enrich only the common ground.

49   Integration has become an abstract term today, having to do with little
more than numbers and racial balances. But it once stood for a high and ad-
mirable set of values. It made difference second to commonality, and it
asked members of all races to face whatever fears they inspired in each
other. I doubt the word will have a new vogue, but the values, under whatever name, are worth working for.

Understanding Meaning

1.   In Steele's view, how serious are the incidents of campus racism? What
     causes them?
2.   How, in Steele's view, are today's black college students different than
     those who attended college in the 1960s?
3.   What anxiety do African American students bring to college?
4.   What does Steele think of "black-themed dorms" and other evidence of a
     desire to demand separation? What happens when "difference is cele-
     brated rather than remarked"?
5.   What responsibility do college officials bear in the reshaping of color on
     campuses? How does Steele think college administrations should treat
     African American students?

6. What guilt do white students reveal, in Steele's view?
7. *CRITICAL THINKING.* How should courses be arranged? Should students study disciplines such as history, art, music, literature? Or should students study history, art, music, and literature in separate programs, such as women's, African American, Hispanic, or Asian studies?

Evaluating Strategy

1. What is Steele's thesis? Can you restate it in your own words?
2. How does Steele use a comparison between the 1960s and the present to demonstrate his point?
3. What examples does Steele use to support his point of view?
4. How does Steele use interviews with students to sample campus attitudes?
5. Does Steele seem to address his concerns to white or blacks?

Appreciating Language

1. What does Steele mean by the "politics of difference"? Can you define it in your own words?
2. What role do the terms "diversity" and "pluralism" play in the politics of difference?
3. Steele states that racial tensions are more the result of "racial equality than inequality." How does he define these terms? How does "equality" cause problems?

Writing Suggestions

1. Write a short essay that describes or analyzes the ethnic composition of your campus. Are there separate areas of black, Hispanic, and Asian studies? Is there a black student union? Are students evenly distributed throughout the college or do some ethnic groups seem to cluster in certain programs or departments?
2. *COLLABORATIVE WRITING.* Discuss Steele's essay with a group of students. Do they sense that a "politics of difference" is at work in their lives? Is separateness a source of power or weakness? If people define themselves by race, does it limit their options or provide them leverage to secure opportunities? Write a brief statement that summarizes your group's observations. If there is a difference of opinion, consider creating two brief pro and con statements.

38

Welfare to Work

The lessons of history, confirmed by the evidence immediately before me, show conclusively that continued dependence upon relief induces a spiritual and moral disintegration fundamentally destructive to the national fibre. To dole out relief in this way is to administer a narcotic, a subtle destroyer of the human spirit. It is inimical to the dictates of sound policy. It is in violation of the traditions of America. Work must be found for able-bodied but destitute workers.
—Franklin Roosevelt, *State of the Union Address, 1935*

Later this year, we will offer a plan to end welfare as we know it. . . . And I know from personal conversations with many people that no one—no one wants to change the welfare system as badly as those who are trapped in it. I want to offer the people on welfare the education, the training, the child care, the health care they need to get back on their feet, but say, after two years they must get back to work, too, in private business if possible, in public service if necessary. We have to end welfare as a way of life and make it a path to independence and dignity.
—Bill Clinton, *State of the Union Address, 1993*

One-Third of a Nation

In the depths of the Great Depression, President Franklin Roosevelt declared, "I see one-third of a nation ill-housed, ill-clad, ill-nourished" and launched the New Deal, a series of federal programs to alleviate poverty and unemployment. In 1935, Congress passed the Social Security

Act, which included Aid to Dependent Children (ADC) designed to support the children of poor widows. Initial federal reimbursements to state governments were limited to six dollars a month for the first child and four dollars for each additional child.

Welfare expanded following World War II. In 1950, ADC was renamed Aid to Families with Dependent Children (AFDC). The program was revised to include unemployed parents and became a primary source of aid to poor families throughout the United States.

The Poverty Wars

> *This administration today, here and now,*
> *declares unconditional war on poverty*
> *in America.*
> –Lyndon Johnson, *State of the Union*
> *Address, 1964*

An ardent admirer of Roosevelt and the New Deal, President Lyndon Johnson increased federal assistance to the poor as part of his Great Society program. "Our aim," he stated, "is not only to relieve the symptom of poverty, but to cure it and, above all, to prevent it." In this "war on poverty," Johnson asserted the "chief weapons . . . will be better schools, and better health, and better homes, and better training, and better job opportunities to help more Americans, especially young Americans, escape from squalor and misery and unemployment rolls. . . ." Johnson signed bills for food stamps, public housing, Medicaid, Head Start, and job training.

Although payments to poor families reduced the number of households living below the poverty line, by the late 1960s welfare came under attack. Conservatives and some liberals questioned not only the cost of anti-poverty programs but also their results. The 1960s saw an increase in urban decay, riots, street gangs, drug addiction, and out-of-wedlock births. AFDC rolls swelled as single, separated, and divorced mothers became eligible for benefits once envisioned for widows.

Daniel Patrick Moynihan, an advisor in the Johnson administration, observed a troubling and ironic shift in the ratio of employment and welfare. Traditionally, welfare rolls shrank during times of high employment. But in the booming economy of the 1960s, welfare rolls in many states grew even though unemployment rates remained stable or decreased. Instead of alleviating poverty, social programs appeared to enhance it. Public housing isolated people on welfare, distancing them from the broader society and making it harder for them to enter the workforce. In 1965, Moynihan published a study on poverty and welfare, noting that families in many urban centers were "approaching complete breakdown."

Conservatives blamed the increase in crime, drugs, school dropouts, and teenage pregnancy on welfare. Dependency on government funds, they argued, eroded self-reliance and responsibility. Welfare was assailed for discouraging work and encouraging a range of social pathologies from drug use to out-of-wedlock births that created a "culture of poverty." Throughout the 1970s and 1980s, welfare was attacked as wasteful and self-defeating. Welfare, in the view of critics like William Niskanen, failed to resolve the problem of poverty:

> The national poverty rate is now about the same when the War on Poverty was instituted 30 years ago, despite the expenditure of over $5 trillion (at 1993 prices) for means tested public assistance programs in the intervening years and a 75 percent increase in average real income. More means-tested benefits may or may not have contributed to the incidence of poverty but they have clearly not reduced it.

Advocates for the poor countered that, save for some severely depressed neighborhoods, no true "culture of poverty" existed. Katherine McFate, author of *Making Welfare Work*, pointed out that 75 percent of recipients stayed on welfare for two years or less and that nearly 80 percent of children who grew up in AFDC-supported families did not become welfare recipients after leaving home. The birthrate for welfare mothers was in fact no higher than the national average, so that the average family on AFDC consisted of a mother and two children. The overall cost of welfare, blamed by many for mounting deficits, was much lower than commonly believed. In 1993, the entire AFDC program consumed barely more than 1 percent of the federal budget and 2 percent of most state budgets.

Welfare mothers formed organizations, seeking to inform politicians and the public about the realities of welfare. Benefits were barely enough to sustain a family, and regulations made it difficult for parents to move from welfare to work. Recipients attacked AFDC regulations, which penalized them if they saved too much money and threatened them with the loss of health insurance if they "cheated" by taking part-time or seasonal jobs.

By the 1990s, both Democrats and Republicans in Congress agreed there was a need to revise the Depression-era program.

Welfare Reform

In 1996 President Clinton ended the sixty-year-old AFDC program, replacing it with Temporary Aid to Needy Families (TANF), which required welfare recipients to spend thirty hours a week in "work-related activities" in order to receive benefits and limited families to a maximum of five years of support. The main goals of TANF are to move recipients into the workforce as quickly as possible, to prevent out-of-wedlock pregnancies, and encourage the formation and maintenance of two-parent families.

POVERTY AND WELFARE REFORM

Official poverty rate of U.S. households, 1959	22.4%
Official poverty rate of U.S. households, 2003	12.5%
Federal poverty line for family of four, 2004	$18,850 (slightly higher in Alaska and Hawaii)
Number of children in low-income families, 2004	26 million * 84% have at least one working parent
Number of AFDC recipients, 1993	14.1 million
Number of TANF recipients, 2000	5.7 million

TANF GUIDELINES

Under TANF the federal government provides $16.5 billion dollars annually in block grants to states to operate their own programs. States can use TANF funds for any of four purposes:

1. assisting families with needy children
2. reducing dependence of needy parents by promoting job preparation, work, and marriage
3. preventing out-of-wedlock pregnancies
4. encouraging formation of two-parent families

States can use TANF funds in a variety of ways, including cash payments and wage supplements to families, child care, education, job training, transportation, and other services assisting transition to work.

Continued

TANF REQUIREMENTS

Work Requirement
Federal law requires that 50% of families receiving basic TANF assistance (cash and other assistance) must be engaged in a work-related activity (jobs, job-training, basic education, community service, or English language classes) 30 hours a week. Failure to participate in work requirements can result in reduction or termination of benefits.

Time Limits
Federal law states that families can only receive federally funded assistance for no longer than five years. States can use TANF dollars to extend benefits for up to 20% of cases.

* Some states have received waivers and do not follow current federal guidelines.

Selected state names for TANF programs:

Arkansas	TEA	(Transitional Employment Assistance)
California	CALWORKS	(California Work Opportunity and Responsibility to Kids)
Michigan	FIP	(Family Independence Program)
Minnesota	MFIP	(Minnesota Family Investment Program)
Wisconsin	W-2	(Wisconsin Works)

Sources: Center on Budget and Policy Priorities; Joint Center for Political and Economic Studies; National Center for Children in Poverty; U.S. Census Bureau; U.S. Department of Health and Human Services

Welfare reform, in Niskanen's view, sought to undo the damage of traditional welfare by reducing recipient dependency and taxpayer resentment:

For the most part, the political support for welfare reflects a generous motive to help those who are poor, single, and with children. Welfare would provoke little controversy and benefits would probably be higher if these conditions were substantially accidental or temporary—the result, for example, of the death, disability, or temporary unemployment of the major contributor to a family's income. That is why welfare was first promoted as a widow's allowance. That is why President Clinton supports welfare as a safety net but not as a way of life. The moral dilemma, of course, is that welfare, like most forms of social insurance, increases the number of people with the insured condition.

Supporters of welfare reform measure its success in the reduction of welfare rolls. Some states saw an 80 percent decline in welfare caseloads, and nationwide the number of families on welfare dropped from four million to two million. These figures, proponents claimed, showed that welfare reform was breaking the cycle of dependency and moving families from welfare to work. "Once welfare benefits must be earned," Robert Rector argued, "the attractiveness . . . of welfare shrivels up."

Critics of welfare reform argue that those celebrating the drop in welfare rolls fail to measure what is most important—the number of families living in poverty. Welfare reform was launched during the prosperous 1990s. After 2000, outsourcing and downsizing eliminated millions of better-paying jobs. Most families who leave welfare have to support themselves on seven or eight dollars an hour. Homeless shelters and food pantries in high-rent cities like New York and San Francisco that once served single adult males with drug and alcohol problems now see more working families seeking assistance.

Tony Platt asserts that welfare reform does little to break the cycle of poverty or even provide the safety net of social services available in other developed nations:

> The United States has the most regressive system of welfare for poor people among developed nations in the twenty-first century, and in recent years it has become even more punitive. The world's self-professed leading democracy lacks a national health care policy, a universal right to health care, and a comprehensive family policy. Welfare applicants are subjected to personal intrusions, arcane regulations, and constant surveillance, all designed to humiliate recipients and deter potential applicants.

Welfare reform fails to address the steady gap between rich and poor and the erosion of jobs paying a family-supporting income. Dropping families from welfare rolls, poverty advocates insist, simply transformed the "war on poverty" to a "war on the poor."

The Work of a Nation

*In the quiet of American conscience, we know
that deep, persistent poverty is unworthy of our
nation's promise.*
–George W. Bush, *Inaugural Address, 2001*

President George W. Bush promised to continue welfare reform, noting that while poverty was unacceptable in America, its solution was not limited to government action:

> Where there is suffering, there is duty. Americans in need are not strangers, they are citizens—not problems, but priorities. And all of us are diminished when any are hopeless. Government has great responsibilities for public safety and public health, for civil rights and common schools. Yet compassion is the work of a nation, not just a government.

By recognizing both the needs of the poor and the limitations of government to resolve them, President Bush echoed the complex and often contradictory attitudes of the American people. Writing in the *Brookings Review* in 2001, Gordon Berlin observed that Americans have strong but conflicting opinions on welfare:

> Whenever Americans are polled about social welfare policies, two consistent themes emerge. Two-thirds or more of those surveyed say they support policies that help "the poor" who cannot help themselves—especially children, the elderly, and the disabled. And about two-thirds say that they do not support "welfare." Americans consistently want government to lend a hand to those who cannot provide adequately for themselves—but only if it can do so without discouraging work and promoting independence.

Before reading these entries, consider these questions.

What is the role of government in dealing with poverty? Should the government of the richest country in the world guarantee all citizens basic health care and financial support, offer temporary assistance and training to get people into the workforce, or provide assistance only to the elderly and disabled?

Do government programs eliminate poverty or just subsidize it? Do poverty programs help the poor get skills, build determination, and obtain opportunities to get jobs and become independent? Or do government programs lead to dependency and a sense of entitlement? Do some people assume it is the government's responsibility to care for their needs?

Do people make judgments about welfare based on facts or myths?   Many people who complain about welfare exaggerate both the total cost of poverty programs and the amount of money recipients get. Do people need accurate facts and statistics in order to make sensible evaluations of welfare programs?

Are there enough jobs for recipients?   With current workers facing the loss of employment because of trends like outsourcing, will there be enough private-sector jobs to employ welfare recipients who are required to work?

If meaningful jobs are unavailable, should people be required to take "make work" jobs?   Proponents of work insist that jobs, even those consisting of sweeping floors or raking leaves, teach people valuable work habits. Critics often consider these "make work" assignments wasteful, demeaning, and expensive. If recipients cannot find "real jobs," should they receive assistance until meaningful work is available, or should they be required to do "menial" tasks?

Should the poor and unemployed have a greater voice in shaping welfare policies? Are programs created by government officials and academics who have never personally lived in poverty, collected welfare, or sought entry-level jobs? Should welfare recipients and former recipients who moved from welfare to work have greater input in programs?

To be successful, do welfare-to-work programs have to be linked with programs or policies to create jobs in depressed areas?   Many poor people live in depressed rural areas and inner cities with few available jobs. Should tax breaks and other incentives be used to influence businesses to locate in areas with high unemployment?

Should the minimum wage be increased to make entry-level work more attractive? Since most welfare-to-work applicants will likely have to start out earning minimum wage, should it be increased to encourage recipients to find work and increase the income of the working poor?

WRITING ABOUT WELFARE TO WORK

The issue of welfare to work can trigger a number of responses that can be useful topics for writing assignments.

Critical Thinking and Prewriting

People often have strong opinions about poverty and welfare programs. It is important to think carefully and conduct research before advancing any point of view.

Getting Started: Exploring Ideas

1. Conduct research to determine how much federal, state, and local governments spend on welfare. Do some lawmakers exaggerate how much is spent on the poor? Do others minimize the amount?
2. Does welfare to work assume most recipients are able to work? What if more than half the people in a state needing aid are disabled?
3. Do the TANF guidelines seem like a genuine improvement over traditional AFDC payments, which had no time limits, or do they seem mean-spirited?
4. Does welfare to work seek to keep poor people from becoming a permanent underclass? Did traditional welfare become a way of life for many people?
5. Why does welfare to work emphasize reducing out-of-wedlock pregnancies and encouraging marriage? Does this address the root causes of poverty? Do you find it intrusive and unfair?

Strategies for Writing about Welfare to Work

Define key terms.
You may have to establish clear meanings of words you use, such as *recipient* or *poor* by using your own definitions or government guidelines. Some terms like *work-related activities* require specific definitions to prevent confusion.

Determine the causes of poverty.
Opponents of welfare often cite facts that indicate that welfare itself produces dependency, crime, family disintegration, and school dropouts. Advocates for the poor argue that more, not less, assistance is needed to overcome these behaviors. State your point of view and support it with facts.

Determine how much money local, state, and federal programs budget for poverty programs and how much money and assistance recipients receive.
How much money is consumed by bureaucracy, by regulations, by administration? How much goes to direct aid? Could government programs be more efficient?

Consider if welfare is more successful than most people realize.
Because of the stigma attached to being a welfare recipient, few middle-class people with good jobs are likely to tell people that at one point in their lives they or their families received support. Conduct research or poll people you know to see if you can find any welfare success stories.

Focus on the experiences of a single recipient or family.
To give readers insight into the realities of life on welfare, tell the story of one family. How hard was it for them to meet requirements? How were they treated by welfare officials? Did they abuse their benefits? Did government regulations make it harder for them to make progress?

Investigate one or more myths about welfare.
Many people make assumptions about the size and race of welfare families, the length of time families receive benefits, and the incidence of drug abuse, alcoholism, and teenage pregnancy. Select one or more assumptions you have heard and compare it with the facts.

WRITING IN THE MODES

You may find that selecting a particular mode is an effective way of examining a topic, organizing ideas, and shaping an essay.

Narration
1. Relate a personal experience with welfare, either as a recipient, someone who knows recipients, or discussions with people with strong opinions about welfare.
2. Write a narrative about a person overcoming or failing to overcome a problem or challenge because of government support. Did federal funds allow you or a friend to go to college? Did anyone you know get a free or subsidized school lunch? Did anyone you know find regulations and restrictions so cumbersome that it hindered rather than helped?
3. Relate a job-hunting experience of your own or someone you know. What challenges do job seekers face? Would being on welfare make the search more difficult? Do you think many disadvantaged people have the job search and interviewing skills needed to secure meaningful employment?

Description
1. Describe one or more of the welfare-to-work regulations. Do you think it is fair and well intentioned? Do you think it is mean-spirited and unrealistic? Should extensions on time limits be granted during times of recession?

2. Describe attitudes about welfare expressed by friends, neighbors, and coworkers. You might conduct an informal poll to measure how people feel about welfare reform.
3. Describe the way you think welfare officials should treat recipients. Do people collecting welfare need support, care, and compassion, or do they need order, discipline, and accountability?

Definition

1. Provide your definition of the government's role in assisting the poor. What should the policy or goal be? Who would you define as *poor*?
2. Look up your state's welfare-to-work policies. How do they define *work-related activities*? Do these requirements seem fair and effective? Can you detect potential abuses?
3. State your definition of *poverty* for an individual or for a family of four.
4. TANF stands for Temporary Aid to Needy Families. Federal guidelines encourage states to spend tax dollars to encourage marriage and reduce out-of-wedlock births. Does this suggest the government has a clear definition of what constitutes a family? How do you define a *family*?

Example

1. Use one or more examples to illustrate successes or problems with welfare reform.
2. Develop an essay, using the experiences of a person or people you know who struggled to overcome poverty. Use examples that illustrate a prevailing situation or condition.

Comparison

1. Contrast one or more aspects of AFDC and TANF. Which system seems more fair or more likely to help people get out of poverty?
2. Compare the current welfare system in the United States with that of another country.
3. Contrast the experiences of two people you know who received welfare benefits.

Division and Classification

1. Use division to discuss different types of welfare support—day care, cash grants, food stamps, and job training. Describe advantages and disadvantages of each type.
2. Classify welfare programs from the best to worst types. Which ones lead to dependency? Which ones help people learn skills and find jobs?

Cause and Effect

1. What are the causes of poverty? Describe one or more causes and discuss the best way to alleviate it.

374 Welfare To Work: Introduction

2. What effect does welfare have on children? Do teachers, neighbors, relatives, and government officials view them differently? Do they view themselves differently?

3. What effect do welfare-to-work programs have on other workers? Will
some people resent recipients getting benefits that they do not have? Will
some workers fear that an influx of welfare recipients will depress their
wages?

4. What are the positive and negative effects of a work requirement? Can
working teach skills and discipline and expose recipients to the world of
work? Can fellow employees or employers become valuable mentors? Can
dead-end jobs discourage recipients from making progress?

Argument and Persuasion

1. Develop a persuasive essay that agrees or disagrees with one or more
points made by an author in this chapter.

2. Write an essay that argues for what you consider an ideal welfare program.
What is the best way government can help poor people? How can the cycle
of poverty be broken? Does even a prosperous society have to accept that
there will always be those who for many reasons will be unable to function
without support?

STUDENT PAPER

Being Broke vs. Being Poor

My grandfather was born during the Depression. His father had been
a steamfitter. In fact he worked on the Empire State Building before
being laid off. For three years he had no job. My grandfather told me
they lived on relief and got handouts from a Catholic charity. He
remembers his mother arranging dimes on the kitchen table, setting
so many aside for her kids' lunch and so many for second-hand
clothes. My grandfather had one pair of shoes. When they had to be
repaired, he had to stay home from school.

When WWII started, my great-grandfather got work in the Brooklyn
Navy Yard. He worked overtime and saved his money. When the
war ended he had enough to buy a new Ford and a ranch house in
Levittown. My grandfather went to college and sent all his kids to
college. Poverty and welfare was just a piece of history for our family,
like ration coupons during the war.

"Welfare worked for us," my grandfather told me, "because we were broke but never poor."

I asked him what he meant by that. He explained that everyone knows what it means to be broke. "Being broke means you need cash," he said. "You're out of a job or have bills you can't pay. If someone gives you money, you are going to pay your rent and send your kids to school until you can make it on your own." Broke people have goals, values, and good work habits; they just need cash in hard times.

Poor people in his view would blow their money on quick thrills, booze, clothes, lottery tickets, and partying. He had one pair of shoes and grew up in a house with no radio. It is hard for him to have sympathy for people who call themselves poor today but have closets full of clothes, TVs, cell phones, and DVD players.

Government programs are geared to helping the broke. Give broke people assistance, and they will use the money responsibly. Poor people, however, have never developed the habits of work and savings. They are focused on immediate gratification and don't connect hard work today with success later. They resent work and middle-class society and somehow getting a job to them means surrendering their dignity or their identity.

Helping people who have grown up in dysfunctional families and chaotic environments find the discipline to learn and work is a major challenge. Immigrant families are often broke but not poor. Their families are intact. Their religion and traditional culture give them values. But many Americans are born into families that have been poor for two or three generations.

Some people like President Bush believe faith-based organizations can help fill the missing link. Maybe they can, but teaching people values takes a lot of compassionate conservativism and a lot of resources. To end welfare as we know it we may have to spend a lot more to really help people get their lives in order. Poor people need a lot more than money. They may need health care, counseling, education, language skills, and mentoring. It will cost a lot more, but I think spending, say, $50,000 on a person for two years to get on track is better than spending $250,000 for twenty years of handouts.

Understanding Meaning

1. What is the student's thesis? Can you state it in your own words?
2. The student draws a comparison between being "broke" and being "poor." Can low-income people be that neatly divided into two groups?
3. Do you think the experiences of the student's grandfather and great-grandfather during the 1930s are relevant today? Are the comparisons valid?
4. Have standards for what we consider "poor" changed? The student's grandfather had only one pair of shoes and no radio. Do you know people who consider themselves poor although they own appliances, TVs, computers, and lots of clothes? Just who is poor?
5. *CRITICAL THINKING.* Can government programs help teach people not only job skills but also habits about work, discipline, priorities, and saving? Is poverty as much a lifestyle, culture, and set of behaviors as it is an economic status? Are religious people, like monks, who forsake material goods and live simply "poor"?

Evaluating Strategy

1. The student bases the essay on the experiences of family members. Is this enough support? Would the essay benefit from case studies, statistics, or quotes from experts?
2. Do you think the student fully defined the terms *broke* and *poor*? Were enough details or examples presented? Can you summarize the student's definitions of these terms in your own words?
3. Poverty is a complex subject. Is it realistic to divide low-income people into two categories? Should the student have acknowledged the possibility of exceptions?

Appreciating Language

1. How would you characterize the tone and style of the essay?
2. Do you find the student's use of the terms *poor* and *broke* compelling, or is it too simplistic?

Writing Suggestions

1. Write a short essay in which you agree or disagree with the student's assessment that low-income people can be separated into the "broke" and the "poor."

2.   *COLLABORATIVE WRITING.* Review this essay with a group of other
     students. Do they accept the student's distinction between the broke and
     the poor, or do they think this division is too simplistic? Record comments
     by the group, and write one or two paragraphs stating the views of your
     group. If students have differing opinions, use comparison or division to
     organize responses.

CHECKLIST

Before submitting your paper, review these points.

1.   Does your paper have a clearly stated thesis? Does it have a clear point
     of view?

2.   Do you support your thesis with representative facts, reliable observa-
     tions, and accurate statistics?

3.   Do you avoid making prejudiced or biased statements that will detract
     from your authority and alienate readers?

4.   Do you anticipate readers' possible objections and answer them?

5.   Is the paper clearly organized? Do paragraph breaks group related ideas
     and signal transitions?

6.   Does the tone, style, and word choice of your paper suit your purpose
     and audience?

 Companion Website

See **academic.cengage.com/english** for information on planning, organizing,
writing, and revising essays.

 E-Reading: InfoTrac College Edition
http://www.infotrac-college.com

For Further Reading
E–Readings Online

Search for articles by author or title in InfoTrac College Edition
after entering your user name and password.

Erin Heath, *Welfare's 20th Century Journey*
Once dwarfed by support from private charities, public welfare spending reached $391 billion in 1998.

Gordon Berlin, *The 30 Year Tug-of-War*
Polls reveal two-thirds of the American people support policies to help "the poor" but that two-thirds also say they do not support "welfare."

Scott Winship and Christopher Jencks, *Welfare Reform Worked— Don't Fix it*
Research reveals that welfare reform lessened poverty and made it easier for low-income families to afford food and shelter.

Katherine Boo, *The Black Gender Gap*
Welfare-to-work programs that have targeted heads of households have helped many African American single mothers receive training and jobs but have failed to benefit African American males.

Isabel V. Sawhill, *The Behavioral Aspects of Poverty*
The gap between rich and poor is growing because "the rich are working and marrying as much or as more than ever while the poor are doing just the reverse."

Richard Sennett, *On Welfare and the Psychology of Dependence*
A professor of social and cultural theory criticizes the philosophy guiding welfare reform programs, arguing that "adult dependency is a condition to be managed, not avoided."

 If you have access to *Comp21*, click on Themes, then click on Welfare to Work.

39

DEEPAK BHARGAVA

Deepak Bhargava (1968–) was born in Mysore, India, grew up in New York City, and received a BA from Harvard University. He joined the Center for Community Change in 1994 and became the organization's first Director of Public Policy. Currently its executive director, he also serves on the boards of the Center on Law and Social Policy, the Applied Research Center, and the Center for Policy Alternatives.

Why Not a New War on Poverty?

CONTEXT: *Bhargava argues that the success of welfare reform has been measured not by the extent to which the incomes of the poor have increased but by the degree to which welfare rolls have been slashed. In reality, many welfare recipients have been forced into dead-end jobs, which fail to provide a living wage and often disappear altogether during times of recession.*

1 The debate in Washington over welfare policy has taken an unfortunate turn: Republicans and many Democrats seem to be in a battle over who can be tougher on poor people rather than who can be tougher on poverty. It's too bad, because in the early days of the Bush administration there seemed to be a glimmer of hope that the president might follow up on the lofty words in his inaugural address. "In the quiet of American conscience, we know that deep, persistent poverty is unworthy of our nation's promise," Bush said then. And in fact, to the surprise of those who expected little from a Republican administration and a Republican Congress, some significant steps were taken in the fight against poverty.

2 As a silver lining in the otherwise indefensible tax bill passed by Congress last year, there was the enactment of a new refundable tax credit for low-income parents, who will receive $8 billion in income support each year. This is the largest antipoverty program created in nearly a decade, and it promises to lift half a million children out of poverty. As well, the farm bill passed by Congress and signed by the president in May, which is mostly devoted to welfare for agribusiness, also includes the largest expansion of the Food Stamp Program in years. It raises benefits and allows legal immigrants once again to be eligible for the program.

3 There have been victories, too, on a range of issues at the state level, thanks to energetic grass-roots organizing in poor communities and new

sophistication in methods. Activists have pressed for wider access to Medicaid and food stamps, for living wages, for expanded education and training for low-income parents, and for new ways to give paid leave to low-wage workers. Locally and nationally, the very terms of debate have shifted: There is less discussion in the media of the supposedly lazy and shiftless poor and more focus on how hard it can be to raise a family and earn a decent living in today's economy.

4   And yet, as the president and Congress turned their attention to rewriting the 1996 welfare law, the emphasis suddenly was on how to toughen work requirements for welfare recipients. While the president has used his bully pulpit to emphasize conservatism more than compassion, most mainstream Democrats have acted as if the party has nothing to say about the problem of poverty. Given massive caseload declines and increases in work participation among poor mothers, this is a bizarre turn of events.

5   By acting as if the politics of poverty haven't changed since the Reagan era, Republicans—and many Democrats—are terribly out of touch. A recent poll by Peter Hart and Associates finds that public hostility toward the welfare system has declined substantially, and that Americans overwhelmingly reject stricter work requirements in favor of policies to support work and protect vulnerable families who are making an effort. Broader trends suggest a potential new resonant politics of economic security that connects the breakdown of the safety net for poor families with anxieties about health care, pensions, and the economy, and with the struggles most parents have in balancing their jobs and family obligations. Even the nation's governors, a conservative bunch who were the driving force behind the 1996 reform, have outlined a series of proposals to expand access to education and training, stop the clock on time limits for welfare parents who are employed, and restore benefits for immigrants.

6   And perhaps most important, the realities at ground level have changed dramatically. Welfare rolls have declined by about half (though in the current downturn they are predictably creeping back up), and millions of poor women did what the country asked (as many would have done anyway in the strong economy) and got a job. Some fundamentals of economic life for these families are what they have always been—poverty wages, no paid sick days or vacation benefits or parental leave, no health insurance, no unemployment insurance to fall back on, and uncertain child-care arrangements. Consequently, the right way to describe what's happened since 1996 is not "welfare to work" but "welfare-to-work-to-welfare-to-work."

7   The new work requirements and time limits, as well as shabby treatment at the welfare office (and, everyone should remember, the miserly

benefits averaging $300 a month), do move people to seek jobs. A sick child, a transportation breakdown, inability to pay the rent, job loss, or inadequate child care move people back to welfare. The big change since 1996 is that it is harder for families who lose low-wage jobs to get assistance when they fall on hard times. The line between the "working poor" and the "dependent poor" has become a fiction—most low-income parents are cycling in and out of low-wage jobs and on and off welfare.

8   The proposals shaping the debate in Congress don't propose to lift a finger to help these families—the vast "working poor" that everyone claims to care about. Indeed, the worst thing about these welfare plans is not what they contain—though the plans to institute unpaid workfare on a massive scale are appalling—but rather the way in which they have pushed aside all discussion about the things that really matter.

9   If leaders in Washington were serious about improving the economic lives of poor people, they would have more to offer than "Get a job." Most of the discussion about reauthorization of the 1996 welfare law has focused on the nature of work requirements imposed on states and welfare parents. But a crucial question that has gotten less attention is how best to support and reward work for parents who leave welfare for low-wage jobs and for those low-wage parents who haven't been receiving welfare. This question is important because we know that increasing incomes—rather than simply increasing labor-market participation—is the key to the economic well-being of children.

10   State studies of those who leave welfare have consistently found that families are ending up with annual earnings that leave them below the poverty line. Wages range between the minimum of $5.15 per hour and $8 per hour. And, of course, increases in income due to employment are often offset by decreases in welfare and food stamps. The poverty rate for working single mothers has actually increased slightly in real terms since the 1996 law was passed, a remarkable result in a booming economy.

11   The next step in welfare reform should therefore be to increase family incomes. Such an approach will require a combination of policies, including minimum-wage and living-wage policies to "raise the floor" in the low-wage labor market. We need to expand real education and training opportunities to increase mobility for low-income parents. And a broad range of income and related supports—including such supplements as food stamps, health insurance, and child care—need to be made more easily and broadly available.

12   One important thing Congress can do this year is to make it easier for low-wage parents to get income supplements. States have found ways to do

that, through "earnings disregards" or other means. These supplements, though frequently small, often provide the cushion necessary to get a car fixed or to meet work expenses. However, under federal law, any family that receives even one dollar of federally funded income support loses time off the 60-month lifetime limit for welfare—even if that family is working. This policy sends mixed messages to families. On the one hand, we reward work by providing additional income to supplement low wages. On the other hand, we run time limits on working families so that assistance may be unavailable to them later if they need help because of job loss or personal crisis.

13   There are other means by which to support work: by increasing funding for child care and transportation, by extending health insurance coverage to working poor parents, by creating wage-paying transitional jobs with real education and training for the hardest to employ, by increasing access to education and training so that welfare parents can move up in the job market, by expanding unemployment insurance, and by stopping time limits for those who are "playing by the rules."

14   There are also ways to show that "family values" are important: by creating paid-leave programs and good-cause exceptions to welfare rules so that poor mothers never have to choose between their jobs and their kids; by ensuring fair treatment and state accountability to guarantee that no family in crisis is ever told, as one tip sheet in a required class for welfare clients put it, that dumpster-diving is an option for those having trouble buying food; and by supporting inclusion so that immigrants who work hard and pay taxes have equal access to benefits.

15   The emerging grass-roots antipoverty movement in communities around the country has no shortage of humane and workable ideas. It also is gaining power, with impressive victories at the local, state, and national level. The public is ready for a serious effort to tackle poverty in this country. Whatever the outcome of the welfare wars this year, we are surely witnessing the death throes of an old order of politics. What we need above all is leadership in the political class to catalyze a new, progressive approach to poverty reduction. At the Democratic Convention in Chicago in 1948, Hubert Humphrey jolted the party out of its malign slumber on civil rights by challenging it to "get out of the shadow of states' rights and walk forthrightly into the bright sunshine of human rights." Who today will take on the challenge at hand: to fashion a winning politics against poverty and for economic security that will once again inspire the country?

Understanding Meaning

1. Bhargava states at the beginning that he disagrees with welfare reform, but acknowledges some progress. What victories on the welfare front does Bhargava report?
2. Where, in Bhargava's opinion, did President Bush go wrong?
3. According to Bhargava, how does the American public feel about welfare? Why has the public's attitude shifted?
4. Why does he feel that it is more accurate to describe what is supposed to be welfare-to-work as welfare-to-work-to-welfare-to-work? What problems are the poor who have found jobs still facing?
5. In a key sentence from paragraph 9, Bhargava asks "how best to support and reward work for parents who leave welfare for low-wage jobs and for those low-wage parents who haven't been receiving welfare"? He goes on, "This question is important because we know that increasing incomes—rather than simply increasing labor-market participation—is the key to the economic well-being of children." What does he mean?
6. What does he suggest be done?
7. Why does he bring up the issue of states' rights at the end of the essay?

Evaluating Strategy

1. What does Bhargava do in the second and third paragraphs to try to be fair to President Bush? What advantage is it to him as a writer to acknowledge his opponent's strengths? How does he slip in language, though, to point out Bush's flaws as well?
2. Once he points out the good things that Bush has done, what does he focus on in paragraphs 5–8? What is the final focus in paragraphs 9–15?
3. What effect do you think Bhargava hopes to achieve with his conclusion?

Appreciating Language

1. What are some specific words or phrases that show Bhargava's attitude about Republicans?
2. Where does Bhargava use language that is most directly designed to elicit an emotional response from his readers?
3. How does he use word choices to link the first and last paragraphs?

Writing Suggestions

1. *COLLABORATIVE WRITING.* Work with a group of students to create an outline of Bhargava's essay. Does anyone in your group have suggestions about how to improve Bhargava's argument?
2. Write an essay evaluating Bhargava's proposed suggestions for welfare reform.
3. *CRITICAL THINKING.* Bhargava tells us that in his inaugural speech President Bush said, "In the quiet of American conscience, we know that deep, persistent poverty is unworthy of our nation's promise." Why then do we as a nation continue to allow poverty to exist at the level it still does? State your views in a short essay.

40

BARBARA EHRENREICH AND FRANCES FOX PIVEN

Barbara Ehrenreich (1941–) has contributed social and political commentary to such leading publications as the Atlantic Monthly, Harper's, Esquire, The Nation, Mother Jones, *the* New York Times, *the* Wall Street Journal, *the* New Republic, Vogue, *and the* Washington Post. *Her books include* The Hearts of Men *(1983),* Fear of Falling *(1989),* The Worst Years of Our Lives *(1990),* The Snarling Citizen *(1995), and* Nickel and Dimed: On (Not) Getting By in America *(2001). She is a regular columnist for* Time *magazine. Frances Fox Piven (1932–) is a professor of political studies and sociology at the City University of New York. She has coauthored several books with Richard Cloward, including* Regulating the Poor *(1971),* Politics of Turmoil *(1974), and* The Breaking of the American Social Compact *(1998).*

Without a Safety Net

CONTEXT: *In the following article, published in* Mother Jones *in 2002, Ehrenreich and Piven argue that the historic welfare reform law of 1996 was based on two dubious assumptions. The first was that a job could lift a family out of poverty, and the second held that "there would always be enough jobs for anyone plucky enough to go out and land one."*

1 Just four years ago, Kimberly Hill was a poster child for welfare reform.

2 A tall, strikingly attractive mother of two, she had been on welfare off and on for several years until, in 1995, a caseworker urged her to get computer training. Her first job—for which she rated a mention in a 1998 *San Francisco Chronicle* story titled "Firms Find Talent Among Disabled, Welfare Recipients"—was no prize. "People knew I was off welfare," she told us, "and they treated me like I had the plague." Hired as an administrative assistant, she found herself being asked to clean the rest room. She got luckier with her next job, at a staffing agency, where, after a series of promotions, she was earning $65,000 a year. Then, on December 20, 2001, just as the recession became official, she was laid off.

3 Hill meets us at Starbucks because she doesn't think the neighborhood where she lives is a good place for us to be wandering around. She is confident and direct, but admits to feeling the stress of being out of work. She has found one part-time office job and is about to add another, but neither offers health insurance. We ask if she would go back on welfare if things got

bad enough. "No," she says, thrusting her chin out for emphasis. "It's too horrible, a horrible experience—demeaning."

4   Beverly Ransom was another welfare-to-work success story. We met her in Miami's Liberty City—site of the 1980 riot—at the storefront office of Low Income Families Fighting Together, a community organization that works for welfare rights and affordable housing. A bright-eyed, straight-backed woman of 50, with gray hair pulled back into a small ponytail, she speaks with pride about the catering job she found after years on welfare. But lately the work has fallen off; the catering companies that used to give her more work than she could handle just haven't been calling anymore. "Catering is based on tourism," she says. "Last year at this time I had so much work I had to beg for days off. Now I need food stamps." She gets $118 a week from unemployment insurance, but rent for herself and her children, who are 12 and 14, is $500 a month. Her biggest fear is that she'll end up in a shelter: "What do I do? My kids are at an age where they would be traumatized."

5   In 1996, when welfare reform was enacted, a recession seemed about as likely as the destruction of the World Trade Center by a handful of men armed with box cutters. The assumptions behind welfare reform were, one, that a job could lift a family out of poverty and, two, that there would always be enough jobs for anyone plucky enough to go out and land one. The first assumption was shaky from the start; women leaving welfare ended up earning an average of less than $8 an hour, hardly enough to support a family. Now the second assumption has crumbled as well: More than 2 million people lost their jobs last year, and single mothers have been especially hard hit. According to the Federal Bureau of Labor Statistics, the employment rate of women who head families fell far more sharply last fall than overall employment, by three percentage points in just three months.

6   There is, of course, a venerable New Deal program to protect laid-off workers—unemployment insurance—but it is, perversely enough, designed to offer the least help to those who need it the most. People in temporary, part-time, or very low-wage jobs—the kind most often available to someone leaving welfare—often don't qualify for benefits. According to the Economic Policy Institute, about 70 percent of former welfare recipients who have lost their jobs during the current recession are not eligible for unemployment.

7   In the past, poor single mothers had their own form of unemployment insurance—welfare. Contrary to the stereotype, most welfare recipients worked, at least intermittently, falling back on public assistance when a child got sick or a car broke down. But in their zeal to save the poor from

their supposed sins of laziness, irresponsibility, and promiscuity, the reformers entirely overlooked the role of welfare as a safety net for working
mothers. Temporary Aid to Needy Families (TANF), which is what the new
version of welfare is called, has just one aim: to push the poor into the job
market to become "self-sufficient." Whatever sense this made in the boom
years when welfare reform was devised, it makes none now. As a poster at
an East Harlem community organization put it, the acronym has come to
stand for "Torture and Abuse of Needy Families."

8   Of course, pre-reform welfare was never adequate: Grants were low (an
average of $550 a month nationwide), and recipients were routinely hassled
and humiliated by the bureaucracy. Still, under the old system, if you were
demonstrably poor and had children to support, you were entitled to cash
assistance. The new system, legislated in 1996 with the passage of the Personal Responsibility and Work Opportunity Reconciliation Act, ended that
entitlement. The law set strict time limits on assistance (no more than five
years in a lifetime for most people), encouraged private companies to bid
on contracts to administer welfare, and gave states wide discretion to cut
people from the rolls.

9   Under the current system, someone who applies for welfare is lucky to
get any benefits. More likely, the family will be "diverted"—sent to a food
bank, told to apply for child support from an absentee parent, or assigned to
a training program designed to keep them searching for a job. Those who
make it through this process may see their benefits cut for any of a multi-
tude of infractions (including, in some cases, having a child who regularly
skips school).

10   These practices, often characterized as part of an effort to endow the
poor with "self-esteem," have been extremely effective—at least at cutting
the welfare rolls. A report by the National Campaign for Jobs and Income
Support shows that welfare caseloads rose as unemployment went up in the
recession of 1990–1991, but that this time, caseloads actually fell in 14 of
the 47 states where unemployment rose between March and December
2001. In Wisconsin, the state that pioneered a particularly draconian version
of welfare reform under the leadership of former governor and current
Health and Human Services Secretary Tommy Thompson, unemployment
rose by 0.6 percentage points during the same period, but the welfare rolls
just kept on dropping—by 29 percentage points. And changes now being
debated could make the program even less accessible to poor families: With
TANF up for reauthorization in Congress by September 30, the Bush
administration is pushing measures that would make benefits more difficult
to get, and even harder to keep.

11   So what do you do when there are few jobs available and the safety net lies in tatters? We talked to former welfare recipients who recently lost their jobs in five states—New York, Oregon, California, Florida, and Illinois. Some had already exhausted their five-year lifetime benefit limit; others remained potentially eligible for welfare. None of them were having much luck. While the media tends to focus on displaced dot-commers and laid-off Enron executives, these women represent the hidden underside of the recession. In the scary new world of post-welfare America, their experience has been like that of someone who looks out an airplane window on a bright, clear day and sees nothing at all below.

12   Janet Cook is one of the many who have gone from welfare to work to nothing in a few short years. We talked to her by phone at a residential motel in Portland, Oregon, where she was paying more than $300 a week for the single room she shared with her husband and their four children. Cook, who is in her late 30s, held a job with a truck manufacturer for six years until she was laid off last April. Her husband is a construction worker, and they used to live in the houses that his company was working on, moving on as each was completed. Then, last fall, the company relocated to another city, and the couple decided to stay rather than yank their kids out of school. With no jobs in sight and their savings soon eaten up by the motel bills, there was nothing to do but apply for welfare.

13   It's "murder to get through the process," Cook says. "You have to be flat broke so you can't function. They want you to land a job, so they make you wait. They don't give you cash for the first two weeks. The first week they make you attend a job workshop. The second week is job search. If you miss one hour, you start over for the whole two weeks." On the day we spoke to her, the family was leaving the motel and moving to a shelter. (Cook ultimately did get benefits, but not until a Legal Aid attorney intervened on her behalf.)

14   All of the former welfare recipients we interviewed described the maze of obstacles that now lies between a needy family and even a paltry amount of cash assistance—a set of hurdles far more daunting than the pre-reform bureaucracy. There are long lines in welfare centers with waits, one New York woman told us, of up to nine hours. In a Latino neighborhood, there may be no Spanish-speaking caseworker on duty. In the 1960s, a federal regulation required that welfare offices accept oral applications. Now, you may have to fill out the same form three times, just to save the agency photocopying expenses.

15   "They close your case for any small thing now," reports Dulce Severino, a mother of two who lives in Brooklyn. "You can't speak to a social worker—you

have to wait a whole day to see them. And they speak badly to people when they finally see them. There are ugly words, almost fights with the social workers." Another Brooklyn woman reports that "some days there are almost riots"—and there really would be, she believes, if it weren't for the heavy police presence inside the welfare centers.

16   Applicants who aren't turned away at the welfare office often face another obstacle—the private companies that increasingly contract with states and municipalities to administer welfare programs. The 1996 law allows governments to contract with churches and community groups, but most contracts have gone to such distinctly non–faith-based entities as Maximus, Unisys, and Lockheed Martin. Some companies specialize in "job readiness" services; others do everything from conducting interviews to determining recipients' eligibility, often under contracts that reward them for any funds they do not spend.

17   Sharon Bush, a mother of four who lives in the East New York section of Brooklyn, applied for welfare in November after medical problems forced her to quit her job. After she filled out the paperwork, two caseworkers paid her a visit to investigate her claim; next, she was sent to Curtis and Associates, a private, for-profit job placement firm. There she was given a lengthy test, shown to a desk with a phone, and told to start cold-calling companies in search of a job. "They don't help, they don't provide contacts," she says. "Meanwhile there are all these people sitting there, waiting, who need back rent." She would have to report to Curtis, she was told, from 9:30 to 4:30 daily for four weeks. In the meantime she'd receive some emergency assistance—a total of $156.60.

18   The sheer hassle of "reformed" welfare is enough to discourage many people from even applying. But the best-known and most clear-cut way that TANF keeps the rolls down is through the five-year lifetime limit on benefits. The clock started ticking with the passage of the welfare reform law in 1996, with the consequence that 120,000 families exhausted their benefits just as the recession hit in 2001. Dulce Severino's family is one of them, although she has worked most of the time since 1992, packing clothes in the sweatshop factories that have sprung up in her Brooklyn neighborhood of Bushwick. Because her earnings were so low—her best wage was $5.15 an hour—Severino received a welfare wage supplement, so the clock on her lifetime limit was running even as she worked. If she had been paid better, she would still be eligible for welfare today.

19   For women without work or welfare, "luxuries" like nonemergency medical care are the first things to go. Nicey Jenkins of Liberty City took computer training to get off welfare, but ended up working at McDonald's

instead. She has given up on paying her credit card bills: "I can't give them anything. I can't make the minimum payment." Another woman we met in Liberty City has declared bankruptcy. Each woman we talked to mentioned family as a major source of support—the grown son who picks up the phone bill, the sisters who offer to babysit, the boyfriend who pitches in for the rent. Without her family, Jenkins says, "I would have killed myself."

20   Mostly, though, people talked about the daily challenge of putting food on the table. Beverly Ransom reports that "sometimes we have breakfast for dinner. . . . A lot of the times I skip the meal because I can go without. My first priority is my kids. I say, 'I'm not hungry right now.'" Nicey Jenkins buys boiling meats—like neck bones—and serves them over rice. Sometimes, to please her kids, she makes fake fast food: "We have 'KFC night,' 'Taco Bell night.' It works when they're young."

21   All across the country, the dangerous combination of recession and a damaged safety net is driving families to soup kitchens, food pantries, and shelters. A U.S. Conference of Mayors survey on hunger and homelessness in major cities showed that last year requests for emergency food assistance rose by an average of 23 percent, while requests for shelter increased by 13 percent. Another national survey of food-pantry and soup-kitchen users found that almost 40 percent had been cut off from welfare benefits within the past two years. Data gathered by Food for Survival, one of New York City's largest food-pantry groups, indicate that 1 in 5 New Yorkers—a total of 1.5 million people—use emergency food assistance at least once a year; a majority of those receiving such help for the first time are single mothers who say that what they most need is a job.

22   Even before the recession struck, welfare reform was hardly the "resounding success" President Bush called it this spring. To be sure, it was easy, at least in the boom years, to earn more in a job than the meager cash allowances welfare offered. But as critics of reform have repeatedly pointed out, the $7 and $8 an hour averaged by former welfare recipients was about $6 short of what the Economic Policy Institute calculates a family of three needs for a minimally adequate, bare-bones budget. It was in the boom year of 2000 that the nation's largest network of food banks, America's Second Harvest, reported "a torrent of need that we cannot meet," with many local charities blaming the rising demand for their services on welfare reform and insufficient wages. Milwaukee, a city whose widely publicized "W-2" program makes it the veritable capital of welfare reform, saw dramatic increases in the use of food pantries and emergency shelters through the late '90s.

23   No small part of the pre-recession misery of the poor was due to the states' Scrooge-like administration of TANF. In a number of states recipients

are not told that they might be eligible for food stamps and Medicaid—a key benefit, since many low-wage jobs don't offer health insurance—even after they leave welfare. Nor have the states reliably provided the promised support, especially child care subsidies, for women making the transition from welfare to work. You might start leaving your children with a child care provider only to find out that your subsidy had never made its way through the bureaucratic maze. One woman, whose story we learned from Eastern Michigan University researcher Valerie Polakow, took her four-year-old to work with her because the promised child care subsidy had not materialized. Her employer fired her for showing up with the child; then, in a neat Catch-22, TANF threatened her with reduced benefits for losing her job.

24   And there seems to be little inclination among politicians to fix such problems in this year's overhaul of TANF. State and local governments, knowing that they'll be left with providing emergency services as women who can't find a job are cut from the rolls, want more flexibility in extending benefits. Some Democrats in Congress are arguing for more spending on child care. But no one expects fundamental changes to the 1996 reform and its premise—that the job market holds all the answers, in good times and bad.

25   With six years' hindsight, it's hard to fathom why no one, back in 1996, seems to have thought ahead to a time when jobs would be in short supply and millions of Americans might sorely need cash assistance. We talked to Mary Jo Bane, a Harvard professor who left her post as the Clinton administration's assistant secretary for children and families in 1996 to protest the direction of reform. "People mumbled about it," she says, "but the economy was so good then. . . ." David Ellwood, who along with Bane co-chaired Clinton's welfare reform task force and who also teaches at Harvard, told us, "Many people thought about the possibility of a downturn. The real question is why the people who drafted the bill, and signed it, willfully didn't."

26   Part of the answer may lie in the peculiar economic euphoria of the mid- and late '90s, when bearishness began to seem unpatriotic and prosperity looked like a permanent entitlement. The emphasis, even among liberals, was on "making work pay" and expanding benefits such as child care and the Earned Income Tax Credit, which provides low-income working families with up to $4,000 a year in cash. Hardly anyone, welfare recipients included, wanted to see welfare-as-we-knew-it restored.

27   But the main problem, says Ellwood, was sheer irresponsibility—the very flaw the reformers aimed to eliminate among welfare recipients. "There was just enormous pressure to reduce welfare, and the attitude toward a possible economic downturn was basically, 'We'll cross that bridge when we

come to it.'" According to Ellwood, Clinton believed the money that states saved as a result of welfare reform could be used to help people in case of a recession; he did not foresee that a downturn would find states strapped for funds and eagerly slashing programs like Medicaid and child care.

28   The result has been that America entered its most recent recession as defenseless as if we had to face a terrorist attack without firefighters or emergency rescue workers. The safety net that sustained millions of the poor through previous downturns, however inadequately, has been torn to shreds.

29   We could see the current crisis, whose effects on unemployment will persist long after the recession technically ends, as an opportunity for genuine reform—including meaningful assistance for those who cannot find work, and reliable help, such as child care, for those who can. But instead, the Bush administration and Congress, like the welfare reformers who preceded them, seem poised to look the other way.

Understanding Meaning

1. How does this essay support the notion that the problems of poverty cannot be solved simply by getting someone a job?
2. In 1996, when the welfare reform legislation was passed, what were the two assumptions behind the reform, according to this essay?
3. Why do the authors argue that unemployment insurance does not help all those in need of its help? What has happened to unemployment insurance in recent years?
4. According to the authors' interviews, how are people treated when they apply for welfare?
5. What do Ehrenreich and Piven say about Wisconsin governor Tommy Thompson's welfare reforms?
6. In what way, according to the authors, were those who drafted the welfare reform act short-sighted?
7. *CRITICAL THINKING.* Why do you think our government seems to fall short of meeting the needs of the poor? Are politicians uncaring? Do they think the poor are simply lazy? Do the poor expect the government to fix everything?

Evaluating Strategy

1. How do the authors use examples to support their argument? Which ones do you find to be the most effective?

2. How effective are the statistics for making the authors' case? Why are they needed to balance the use of examples?
3. Is the article more negative at the beginning or at the end? What effect could this have on readers?

Appreciating Language

1. Explain the irony the authors use in the first sentence of the fourth paragraph.
2. How do word choices demonstrate the authors' attitudes toward politicians?
3. What could you assume about the audience for this article? Does the language seem appropriate for that audience? Why or why not?

Writing Suggestions

1. *COLLABORATIVE WRITING.* Work with a group to outline the article, using one phrase per paragraph.
2. *PREWRITING.* Summarize the article in one to two paragraphs.
3. Write a paragraph in which you discuss the image of welfare mothers that is presented in television shows and movies.
4. Write a paragraph in which you discuss the image of welfare mothers that is presented in this article.
5. Use the paragraphs you wrote for Writing Suggestions #3 and #4 above as the basis for an essay comparing the reality of welfare with the media image.

41

THOMAS W. HAZLETT

Thomas W. Hazlett received his PhD in economics from the University of California-Los Angeles in 1984. From 1984 until 2000 he taught economics at the University of California-Davis. He is currently a Senior Research Associate at the Columbia Institute for Tele-Information and a Fellow of the AEI-Brookings Joint Center for Regulatory Studies. He served as a contributing editor to Harper's *and has been a columnist for* Forbes ASAP *and* Reason. *His articles have appeared in* Barron's, *the* Wall Street Journal, *the* Economist, *the* Chicago Tribune, *and the* New York Times.

Roll Reversal: The Quiet Success of Welfare Reform

CONTEXT: *This article, published in* Reason *in 1999, argues that the welfare reform law of 1996 has been remarkably effective in trimming the welfare rolls in states across the nation. (Florida, for example, has cut its rolls by 64 percent, while Wisconsin has done so by 90 percent.) Not only are welfare recipients finding work, but, according to a study in Maryland, 93 percent of them also leave the rolls voluntarily before their time limit is up. Hazlett argues that the only states to show modest reductions in the number of welfare recipients (California is down only 16 percent) are those in which the welfare bureaucrats are resisting change to save their own jobs.*

1   NOW President Patricia Ireland, a Clinton supporter, said her organization "would not lift a finger or raise a penny to help a president who would plunge 1 million more women and children into poverty."

2   So reported the *San Diego Union-Tribune* on August 23, 1996—the day after the president signed a law ending welfare as we knew it (and as NOW preferred it). In the intervening months we have witnessed the depths of NOW's sincere commitment to the women and children who suffer at the hands (and other body parts) of Bill Clinton. But much more interesting is the great commitment to the job market made by poor people forced to move off the welfare rolls.

3   That we do not hear more about the overwhelming success of welfare reform is evidence that a fine mist of public policy peyote has been sprayed at the cumulonimbus level. Our political discourse drifts daffily at ground zero. The Urban Institute's projection that 2.6 million poor souls would be delivered into poverty; the outpouring of Democratic Party support during

the '96 election for President Clinton as the one man who could fix what he had wrought; the "where are the jobs going to come from?" taunts by welfare advocates—all are now stashed in some forgotten bin with those New Year's predictions by *National Enquirer* psychics.

4   Charles Murray set us up for all of this. When pressed to come up with a helpful solution in his 1984 book documenting the failed legacy of welfare, *Losing Ground*, Murray shrank from the challenge: Simply abolish welfare, he said, cold turkey.

5   It was irresponsible, cowardly, unthinkable—and exactly right.

6   Indeed, within a decade, states began playing with the notion in a politically thinkable way. The problem of long-term welfare dependency was seriously addressed when new and improved programs were ditched in favor of time limits, which made work "requirements" credible. The effort quietly starting taking off in the states about 1993, and federal legislation bolstered the trend in 1996. In the past five years, some 1.92 million welfare cases, 41 percent of the total, have been eliminated nationally. Three million remain.

7   Maryland's system was the subject of a 1998 study analyzing more than 2,000 welfare recipients who had gone off the dole. According to the *Baltimore Sun*, the study "found that many fears about welfare reform have not come to pass. Foster care has not been overrun with children whose parents left the welfare rolls . . . and recipients were not thrown out of programs, as many feared." Indeed, 93 percent of ex-recipients left prior to being kicked off.

8   But the horror story remains a popular genre. As the *Los Angeles Times* reports, "In states where welfare rolls have been driven to near unprecedented lows, officials are discovering that it is no longer enough to issue a 'get a job' edict and offer some firm prodding to help them make the transition." As heartening as it is that the *L.A. Times* is discovering such venerable economic concepts as diminishing returns, the bad news for horror fans is this: Florida has successfully pared its rolls by 64 percent, while Wisconsin is down 90 percent, suggesting that states like California—which has cut its rolls only 16 percent since 1993—have a ways to go before the "low-hanging fruit" get scarce.

9   Still, warns the *Times*, any further reduction in the Golden State's rolls is likely to stall because various problems—from "substance abuse to low literacy levels to clinical depression—are posing stubborn obstacles to employment." If nothing else, such analysis concedes that pre-reformers ignored such obstacles, bestowing a blanket welfare entitlement on all. You think that might have led to incentive problems? Can you spell *enabler*, boys and girls?

10   Now, much as the welfare recipient is given a deadline, policy makers are being forced to deal with choices. Having demonstrated that an open-ended, no-obligation welfare check is about the worst we can do to our fellow man, and having seen the speed with which "work-first" mandates moved people up from relief to jobs, a tougher question arises: What to do with the social service bureaucrats who work in the welfare agencies?

11   Indeed, the debilitating effects of dependency have surely gone furthest within this cohort. Thus far under the new rules, they have performed professionally, meaning that they have adroitly protected their turf. Amazingly, the old flow of dollars continues, even as there are fewer and fewer "clients" to service.

12   These vestigial civil servants will continue to scare up rationales for why diminishing welfare rolls will reverse and why "new programs" are more necessary than ever. They pray every night for an economic crash and ponder sophisticated political strategies to stem their loss of market share. After all, they need the work—and good jobs at high wages is what welfare reform is all about.

Understanding Meaning

1. When President Clinton signed a law "ending welfare as we know it," representatives of the National Organization for Women (NOW) opposed what they called "plung[ing] 1 million more women and children into poverty." Has that turned out to be the case, according to Hazlett?
2. Why does Hazlett conclude that Charles Murray was exactly right in his book *Losing Ground* when he suggested getting rid of welfare, cold turkey? Was that really done?
3. What do the statistics reveal about how the welfare-to-work program was working in 1999?
4. What does Hazlett suggest about why California is lagging far behind other states in moving its citizens off welfare?
5. What does he suggest about "social service bureaucrats"?
6. *CRITICAL THINKING.* Is there a difference between lowering welfare rolls and reducing poverty?

Evaluating Strategy

1. How would you describe Hazlett's strategy in stating his point of view?
2. How does the short paragraph 5 provide an unexpected twist?
3. Do you find Hazlett's use of statistics convincing?

Appreciating Language

1. What are some examples of Hazlett's use of humor?
2. In paragraph 3, what is Hazlett comparing to "those New Year's predictions by *National Enquirer* psychics"?
3. In paragraph 8, what is he referring to by means of the metaphor of the "low-hanging fruit"? (Why are Californians seeing welfare reform as a horror story?)
4. In paragraph 9, when he says, "Can you spell *enabler*, boys and girls?" who is he addressing? Why is he using that sarcastic tone?

Writing Suggestions

1. *COLLABORATIVE WRITING.* Bring to class photocopies or screen shots of ads that make use of the sort of sarcasm that Hazlett uses. Put all of the ads in a place where class members can look at them. Choose one of the ads as a group, and analyze it in a paragraph.
2. Use Hazlett's essay as a model to write an ironic piece about a change that has been or should be made at your college, university, or high school.
3. Using the statistics Hazlett provides, write an essay that explains whether welfare-to-work should be changed.

42

TONY PLATT

Tony Platt, who is on the editorial board of Social Justice, *is Professor of Social Work Emeritus at California State University in Sacramento. He has published several books and articles on American history, race relations, crime, and social policy.*

The State of Welfare: United States 2003

CONTEXT: *Platt argues that the historic welfare reform of 1996 was driven more by cultural politics than by a sincere desire to assist the poor. Welfare rolls have been cut and work requirements increased at a time when it has become increasingly difficult for the disadvantaged to find employment that will lift them out of poverty.*

1 The United States has the most regressive system of welfare for poor people among developed nations in the twenty-first century, and in recent years it has become even more punitive. The world's self-professed leading democracy lacks a national health care policy, a universal right to health care, and a comprehensive family policy. Welfare applicants are subjected to personal intrusions, arcane regulations, and constant surveillance, all designed to humiliate recipients and deter potential applicants. In recent years there has been a significant decrease in cash grants to the unemployed and underemployed who do not qualify for unemployment insurance. The reorganization of the welfare state began under the Clinton administration with the devolution of federal policies to the states and massive cutting of welfare rolls. The Bush administration, while distracted by September 11 and Imperial ambitions, has deepened the cuts and introduced important new policies facilitating access of private organizations to federal grants. The quickly changing economic and geopolitical climate has also generated a profound crisis in the ability of state and local agencies to provide adequate human services to the unemployed and growing ranks of impoverished citizens and immigrants.

2 Meanwhile, the middle and upper classes enjoy one of the most privileged systems of welfare in the West: a regressive system of taxation; generous government subsidies to business; and employer- and state-subsidized pension and health plans. About two-thirds of the population—some 170 million Americans—are covered by employment-based health plans and over

one-third benefit from occupational pensions. "In no other nation," observes
political scientist Jacob Hacker, "do citizens rely so heavily on private benefits
for protection against the fundamental risks of modern life." This massive system of private welfare depends extensively on government interventions in
the form of tax breaks, credit subsidies, and legislative regulations.[1] [. . .]

Legacies of 1996 – 2000

3   In August 1996, President Clinton signed into law the Personal Opportunity and Work Responsibility Act, which replaced Aid to Families with
Dependent Children (AFDC) with Temporary Assistance for Needy Families (TANF). This legislation limited aid to sixty months in a lifetime;
required work activities; prohibited legal immigrants from receiving Food
Stamps and Social Security Insurance (SSI); required teen parents to live at
home or with adult supervision; and limited food stamps for "able bodied,"
single, unemployed adults to three months every thirty-six months.[2]

4   The passage of TANF in 1996 demonstrated a bipartisan commitment to
attacking the meager gains achieved by poor and working families by the
1970s. Between 1994 and 2001, the nation's welfare caseload was reduced
from 5 million to 2.1 million families.[3] In addition to cutting welfare rolls, expanding work requirements, and imposing time limits, the legislation provides
block grants to the states, which can determine how the funds are to be used
and who is eligible for various benefits and services. Moreover, TANF provides economic incentives for state welfare systems to promote marriage and
heterosexual two-parent families, and reduce pregnancies in single women.

Long-Term Trends

5   These changes in the regulation of working-class welfare, which repeal significant aspects of the New Deal, represent a codification and consolidation
of trends, which have been under way for a long time. In 1965, the United
States ranked twenty-first out of twenty-two Western nations in per capita
welfare expenditures. Even in the 1970s, after the expansion of welfare via
President Johnson's War on Poverty, the United States still lagged far behind
most of the West. In the late 1970s, the United States spent about 14 percent
of the total federal budget on welfare, compared to 24 percent for comparable
nations in the West. By 1995, U.S. public social expenditures represented
about 17.1 percent of the gross national product, the lowest of ten comparable
nations and a little more than half the other nations' average level.[4]

6   During the Reagan and Bush senior administrations, major cuts were made by Congress and state legislatures in programs that primarily serve the unemployed poor, the working poor, single parents, and children: SSI, Medicaid, Food Stamps, school food programs, nutrition programs for women, AFDC, energy assistance grants, public service jobs and training, community development grants, and low-income housing subsidies. At the same time, profit-making human service corporations (especially nursing homes, hospitals, and childcare facilities) dramatically increased their share of public funds through the use of "contracting out" by local and state governments.

7   Even before new federal rules limiting welfare were passed in October 1996, all states had decreased their maximum grants to welfare recipients and cut their welfare rolls. Between 1970 and 1996, welfare benefits were drastically reduced throughout the country: for example, by 18 percent in California, by 48 percent in New York City, by 58 percent in Tennessee, and by 68 percent in Texas. Between March 1994 and October 1996, the number of recipients of AFDC dropped 18 percent, from 14.3 to 11.8 millions. From 1993 to 1997, welfare caseloads nationwide had dropped by 25 percent. This trend accelerated throughout the 1990s. In the three years from 1995 to 1998, New York City's welfare rolls dropped by 30 percent, from 1.16 million to 797,000. And in California, from July 1997 through April 1998, the number of families on public assistance was reduced by more than 100,000 or 12.2 percent, the largest decrease in the state's history. Los Angeles County accounted for one-third of this decrease.[5]

8   These statistics mask more profound developments that have been taking place in the organization, ideology, and programs of the welfare system.

Workfare

9   Requiring welfare participants to work in return for cash grants—a central feature of TANF—is not a new policy. Welfare grants were linked with work requirements in the federal Work Incentive Program (WIN) in 1967. "Workfare" was also promoted in the Family Support Act of 1988 under which, according to Eileen Boris, "motivational and job-search sessions constituted the extent of training, childcare funding never matched need, and the wages of welfare lagged behind rises in the cost of living."[6]

10   TANF increased work requirements without providing more funds to implement them. From 1995 to 1998, in New York City, which has the country's largest urban welfare program, some 200,000 people were processed through the city's workfare program. Less than one-third have been able to find full-time or part-time work since leaving the program. Much of the work

in the program is "so menial," notes the *New York Times*, "that it offers few, if any, skills that employers demand." Many programs that previously allowed welfare clients to undergo training and education while on welfare have been either eliminated or drastically cut.[7]

11   Contemporary welfare policies largely ignore the needs of unemployed men for education and job training. Workfare today serves primarily as a labor market regulator for hundreds of thousands of poor women, who are pushed into an already saturated low-wage labor market, thus decreasing the earning power of this whole sector of the labor force. The 1962 Community Work and Training Program (associated with the War on Poverty) was one of few welfare programs aimed at the needs of unemployed fathers. In the last three decades, policymakers have abandoned this kind of program. Ironically, one of the few places that poor men can now find work—albeit exploitative and grossly underpaid—and mental health counseling is in prison. With a daily count of over fifteen hundred people suffering from severe psychological illnesses, Los Angeles County Jail may be the country's largest mental institution.[8]

12   Imprisonment and welfare are not so much polarized opposites as they are constitutive elements of an interrelated policy. Similar to the poor houses of the past, which combined work with imprisonment, today's welfare and criminal justice policies represent a division of labor between different managerial agencies, with jails and prisons primarily containing unemployed men, and welfare agencies primarily regulating unemployed women and their children. Both sets of institutions disproportionately target the most exploited sectors of African-American, Latino, American Indian, immigrant and poor Anglo communities. Some 12 percent of African-American men ages twenty to thirty-four are currently in jail or prison, while African-American women are disproportionately on welfare. During the last twenty years, poor women have suffered the double indignity of declining welfare services and increased imprisonment rates. The number of incarcerated women in the United States tripled between 1985 and 1997, representing ten times the number of women imprisoned in Spain, England, France, Scotland, Germany, and Italy combined.[9]

Dividing the Workforce

13 The new welfare policies have aggravated divisions between workers and aspiring workers who have much to gain by joining forces to struggle for decent jobs, wages, and benefits for all that need work. These tensions will continue as long as welfare workers are denied the right to a minimum wage,

excluded from unemployment insurance, and unprotected by federal occupational health and safety standards. The new workfare requirements have created a new stratum of indentured workers who have lost previously held welfare rights without gaining any of the basic rights of "free" workers.[10]

14   Many workfare participants are taking jobs typically done by public employees. In 1998, for example, some thirty-four thousand welfare recipients did community service in New York's Work Experience Program, while the city's workforce was reduced by about twenty thousand employees, or 10 percent. Patricia Williams eloquently captures the dynamics of this process: "In New York City, the poor—many of whom are the descendants of hard-working slaves, or the grandchildren of hard-working sharecroppers, or the children of coal miners, dirt farmers and sweatshop laborers—are to be uplifted from their purportedly lazy ways through the rehabilitative effort of cleaning the subways. Subways in which some of them are living. Their instructors will be unionized workers who have spent decades organizing to improve their own lot, yet whose livelihoods are threatened by workfare's non-unionized, below-minimum-wage pools of labor."[11]

Double Standard of Morality

15   Current welfare policies limit women's ability to get financial grants and force most recipients to work outside the home under strict morality regulations. Whereas middle-class women can choose to mix work and family responsibilities, to practice their own sexual orientation, and to seek an abortion, poor women on welfare have no control over these decisions. "Dependency" has come to be associated, in the words of Rickie Solinger, with the "dangerous, pathological behavior" of poor women who make wrong choices.[12]

16   The political intent of the new welfare legislation is to force more and more poor women into low-paid drudgery with few or no benefits. Most states will use their new discretion to force or cajole women off welfare and into work irrespective of their personal wishes or family needs. "Substituting work outside the home for family labor," observes Eileen Boris, "workfare denies the value to the labor that poor single mothers already perform for their families and demands that they leave their children as a condition of welfare."[13]

17   Under the 1996 legislation, states that reduce "illegitimate" births without increasing abortion will receive a monetary bonus; teenagers on welfare have to live with their families or relatives. "This social engineering from the political Right," notes Boris, "intervenes in the lives of the poor to a degree equal to the therapeutic regimes of the Charity Organization

Societies and welfare caseworkers of the past."[14] The tax benefits received by the middle class for owning property are not dependent on their sexual behavior meeting the standards of monogamous, heterosexual marriage. Similarly, employer-subsidized health care does not require its beneficiaries to sign pledges that they do not use illegal drugs. We subject poor people to morality tests that are not required of any other class-based entitlement programs.

The Racial Divide

18   Communities of color bear the brunt of poverty and economic devastation in this country. American Indians, Southeast Asians, urban African Americans, and rural Latinos have the highest poverty rates. In South Dakota, for example, Indians made up 7.4 percent of the population, but 53 percent of welfare recipients in 1997. Prior to the 1960s, the limited beneficiaries of social insurance, public assistance and other entitlement programs were typically a small sector of Anglo, working- and lower-middle-class men. It was this group that primarily benefited from pension programs after the Civil War, New Deal public works' projects in the 1930s, and the GI Bill's educational subsidies after the Second World War.[15]

19   Until the 1960s, racism denied most poor women and men of color access to entitlement programs. For example, "mothers' aid" programs, established by states between 1910 and 1920 for single mothers with children, gave Anglos more money than African Americans and excluded Mexican Americans. In the 1930s, thousands of Chicanos were forcibly "repatriated" to Mexico in order to save welfare costs and many African Americans were kicked off welfare to meet local demands for agricultural and domestic labor. When Congress authorized grants for single women in 1949, many states used racialized criteria, such as excluding "employable" women, demanding "suitable homes," and searching for "men in the house."[16]

20   In the 1960s, as a result of the civil rights movement and liberal federal programs, for the first time poor women and men of color began to gain access to entitlement programs that gave people some chance of getting out of poverty and into work. The expansion of welfare rolls in the 1960s was in large part due to the effectiveness of the civil rights movement in demanding that welfare be made a right irrespective of race or morality tests.[17] At about the same time, there was also a momentary increase in community-based programs for first-time offenders and ex-prisoners. But by the late 1970s,

liberal social policies had been defeated: welfare programs contracted, and jails and prisons expanded at an unprecedented rate.

21   As welfare and criminal justice policies have become more punitive and vindictive, the incarcerated and welfare populations increasingly resemble a system of apartheid. Following recent changes in welfare policies, African Americans and Latino welfare recipients now outnumber Anglos by about two to one. In New York, for example, by 1998 the city's welfare rolls were 5 percent white, 33 percent black, and 59 percent Latino. As Eileen Boris puts it, "we need to understand reform in the 1990s as the triumph of a 30-year reaction against the gains of the 1960s, after African American women finally shared in AFDC and welfare finally became a right or entitlement."[18] [. . .]

Crisis in Welfare

22   While the Clinton administration changed the federal government's relationship to welfare, a changing world and new Bush policy initiatives have fundamentally altered the landscape of welfare. An expanding economy in the mid-1990s absorbed many former welfare clients—as many as 60 percent by some accounts—into low-paying jobs. Moreover, most states were able to use their growing tax revenues to maintain a pre-1996 level of services and programs. But in the last three years, economic and political changes in the United States have generated an unprecedented crisis in the welfare system.

23   First, according to Princeton economist Paul Krugman, "We are now living in a new Gilded Age. . . . Income inequality has now returned to the levels of the 1920s." The United States has more poverty and economic inequality, and lower life expectancy than most developed capitalist nations (it rates just above Portugal in life expectancy). By 1998, the thirteen thousand richest families had almost as much income as earned by the twenty million poorest households. The number of Americans with million-dollar incomes doubled from 1995 to 1999, while the percentage of their income that went to federal taxes dropped by 11 percent. Cuts in capital gains, income, and estate taxes enabled the wealthiest Americans to increase their after-tax income. According to New York University economist Edward N. Wolff, wealth is more concentrated in fewer hands today than at any time since 1929.[19]

24   Secondly, the recession and growth of unemployment and underemployment have both increased the ranks of people seeking social services and put additional pressure on the states, not the federal government, to

respond to increased demand for services. With time limits running out on the 1996 TANF legislation and the completion of prison sentences handed out to drug offenders in the 1980s, we can anticipate hundreds of thousands of former welfare recipients and state prisoners flooding the job market and service agencies.

25   Millions of unemployed men and single women with children are now living on or below the poverty line. According to the Children's Defense Fund, the number of black American children who live in extreme poverty— defined as a family of three living on $7,060 or less annually—has increased to one million, the highest level since the government began collecting data in 1980. In California, one in five children in California is growing up poor, with the child poverty rate higher today than it was twenty years ago. The number of working poor families in California reached a new high of two million in 2001, with Latinos carrying the heaviest burden.[20]

26   Moreover, declining tax revenues have plunged state governments into the worst fiscal crisis since the Second World War, according to the National Governors Association. Faced with a $35 billion budget deficit in California in 2003, Governor Gray Davis has proposed $8.3 billion in tax increases and more than $20 billion in spending reduction. Cuts are expected in Medi-Cal benefits, cash grants to recipients of SSI, and local mental health programs.[21]

27   Thirdly, the Bush response to a faltering economy has been tax cuts for the wealthy, plus increased spending on military and military-related industries. To combat the growing deficit, the Bush plan is to cut back non-military spending, including bailouts to state governments and welfare programs. Key elements of the Bush tax plan include reductions in the rate of taxation on incomes in the highest bracket, abolition of tax on dividends, and repealing the estate tax. The assumption presumably is that the wealthiest investors will take their tax refunds and reinvest in the stock market. "Almost unbelievably," says historian Robert Brenner, "the way being charted to revive the economy is to reinflate the bubble."[22]

28   Meanwhile, the "war on terrorism" and war on Iraq have required an extraordinary increase in military and security-related spending; in 2001 and 2002, the military budget increased 6 and 10 percent respectively. The U.S.-Iraq war and the subsequent occupation are projected to have cost $100 billion through next year.[23] The Bush administration justifies this budgetary increase in terms of the need to combat terrorism and defend the United States, despite the fact that the U.S. military budget is larger than the next twenty-five countries combined.

29   It is this conjuncture of geopolitical and national developments, as well as deepening crisis in the economy and state budgets, that means not only

the further lowering of the American safety net, but also consolidation of the neo-liberal model of welfare reform.

Conclusion

30   There have been rare moments in this country's history when working-class welfare policies offered poor and working people an opportunity to improve their lives without social stigma or personal humiliation. The 1944 GI Bill is perhaps the best example of welfare with dignity. Under this legislation, millions of mostly white, mostly male veterans were encouraged to seek technical and higher education with the help of free tuition and supplies, a living subsidy (including additional payments for children), and low-interest loans for housing. Typically, however, welfare has meant regulated indignity, especially in recent years as the line between imprisonment and welfare has become blurred.

Notes

1. Jacob S. Hacker, *The Divided Welfare State* (Cambridge University Press, 2002), 6, 9–10.
2. Under California's version of TANF—known as California Work Opportunity and Responsibility to Kids (CalWORKS)—all able-bodied welfare recipients are required to earn their grants through job training, job searching, or community service. Recipients, with a few exemptions, are limited to twenty-four consecutive months of welfare of a lifetime total of five years. New applicants are limited to eighteen months. CalWORKS requires twenty hours of work per week for single-parent families, thirty-five hours for two-parent families.
3. The analysis of TANF is based on Martha Coven, "An Introduction to TANF," Center on Budget and Policy Priorities, February 14, 2002; Janice Peterson, "Feminist Perspectives on TANF Reauthorization," Institute for Women's Policy Research, February 2002; Mark Greenberg and Hedieh Rahmanou, "Imposing a 40-Hour Requirement Would Hurt State Welfare Reform Efforts," Center for Law and Social Policy, February 12, 2003; and Martha Fineman, Gwendolyn Mink, and Anna Marie Smith, "No Promotion of Marriage in TANF!," unpublished position paper, 2003.
4. Hacker, 13–15.
5. "The Tough-Love Index," *New York Times*, December 8, 1996. "A Closer Look at the Decline," *New York Times*, February 2, 1997 Piven, 70. Vivian Toy, "Tough Welfare Rules Used as Way to Cut Welfare Rolls," *New York Times*, April 15, 1998. "Drop in State Welfare Load Sets Record," *San Francisco Chronicle*, July 27, 1998.

6. Eileen Boris, "When Work Is Slavery," *Social Justice* 25, no. 1, (1998): 30.
7. Alan Finder, "Evidence is Scant that Workfare Leads to Full-Time Jobs," *New York Times*, April 12, 1998. Piven, 72.
8. Men are eligible for and receive General Assistance cash grants from local governments, but they are usually small and temporary. Piven, 71. Boris, 30. Fox Butterfield, "Prisons Replace Hospitals for the Nation's Mentally Ill," *New York Times*, March 5, 1998.
9. Fox Butterfield, "Prison Rates Among Blacks Reach a Peak, Report Finds," *New York Times*, April 7, 2003. Joy James, ed., *States of Confinement* (New York: Palgrave, 2002), xi.
10. Piven, 72.
11. Steven Greenhouse, "Many Participants in Workfare Take the Place of City Workers," *New York Times*, April 13, 1998. Patricia Williams, "The Saints of Servitude," *New York Times*, October 13, 1996.
12. Rickie Solinger, "Dependency and Choice," *Social Justice* 25, no. 1, (1998): 2.
13. Boris, 41.
14. Boris, 31.
15. Pam Belluck, "A Window to Run Welfare is a Tight Squeeze for Many Tribes," *New York Times*, September 9, 1997. Anthony M. Platt, "End Game," *Social Justice* 24, no. 2, (1997): 104–106.
16. Linda Gordon, *Pitied But Not Entitled* (Cambridge: Harvard University Press, 1994), 37–64. Gordon, 192–199. Boris, 29.
17. Boris, 30.
18. Tony Platt, "Social Insecurity," *Social Justice* 28, no. 1, (2001). Jason DeParle, "Shrinking Welfare Rolls Leave Record High Share of Minorities," *New York Times*, July 27, 1998. Boris, 29.
19. Paul Krugman, "For Richer," *New York Times Magazine*, October 20, 2002. David Cay Johnston, "More Get Rich and Pay Less in Taxes," *New York Times*, February 7, 2002.
20. Jodi Wilgoren, "After Welfare, Working Poor Still Struggle, Report Finds," *New York Times*, April 25, 2002. Tyche Hendricks, "Increase in Child Poverty Found," *San Francisco Chronicle*, November 5, 2002. Information provided by California Budget Project, Sacramento, California, www.cbp.org.
21. Robert Pear, "States Are Facing Big Fiscal Crises, Governors Report," *New York Times*, January 26, 2002. Davis' budget, however, includes a $40 million increase in the state's $5.3 billion prison budget and $220 million to build a new death row at San Quentin. John Broder, "Californians Hear Grim Budget News," *New York Times*, January 11, 2003; John Broder, "No Hard Time for Prison Budgets," *New York Times*, January 19, 2003. California Budget Project, www.cbp.org.
22. Robert Brenner, "Towards the Precipice," *London Review of Books*, February 6, 2003, 23.
23. *Washington Post*, July 13, 2003.

Understanding Meaning

1. What connection does Platt make between welfare and prison?
2. What are some of the main points that Platt makes about what has happened to welfare during the 1990s? He says that the statistics mask other developments that have been taking place in the welfare system. What are those developments?
3. According to Platt, how have the changes to welfare presented a threat to other workers?
4. What does Platt mean when he says that there is a "double standard of morality" when it comes to welfare?
5. How has the history of welfare, in Platt's view, created a racial divide?
6. *CRITICAL THINKING.* In what ways is welfare more complicated than you previously thought?

Evaluating Strategy

1. *BLENDING THE MODES.* What mode is Platt using in the first two paragraphs?
2. What is Platt's purpose in paragraphs 3 and 4?
3. In paragraph 7, Platt provides statistical evidence of the number of Americans who have been dropped from the welfare rolls. What is his purpose in the paragraphs that follow?

Appreciating Language

1. Based on the language Platt uses, what audience would you assume he is trying to reach?
2. Is the language highly emotional or largely objective?
3. Describe Platt's tone. What word choices reflect his attitude?

Writing Suggestions

1. *COLLABORATIVE WRITING.* Discuss Platt's essay in a small group. Do you think the comparison between prison and welfare is accurate or misleading? Record observations of the group, using comparison or classification to organize the responses.
2. Write an essay that describes the way most people you know view the poor, especially those who receive assistance.
3. Develop an essay that discusses the responsibility, if any, you think the rich owe the poor in a democracy. Do they owe them basic resources or only the opportunity to provide for themselves?

43

ROBERT RECTOR

Robert Rector received a BA from the College of William and Mary and an MA in polit-ical science from Johns Hopkins University. He has published articles in the National Review, The World and I, Human Events, *the* Wall Street Journal, *and the* Los Angeles Times. *His book* America's Failed $5.4 Trillion War on Poverty *is a critical study of the welfare system. Rector is currently a Research Fellow in Domestic Policy Studies at the Heritage Foundation.*

Breaking the Welfare Cycle

CONTEXT: *The following article appeared in the* National Review *in 1997. Although mas-sive welfare reform on a federal level was less than a year old at this point, a similar ap-proach had been practiced in the state of Wisconsin for more than a decade. Rector praises the welfare to work program instituted by Governor Tommy Thompson. The overall wel-fare rolls were trimmed as recipients were encouraged to look for work or perform commu-nity service for their benefits.*

1   The first historic battle in the war against the welfare state has been fought and won. The field of battle was Wisconsin, where Gov. Tommy Thompson's reforms have shattered a fifty-year legacy of dependency, and have left welfare apologists fleeing in disarray. Still, a single victory does not mean the war is won—and back in Washington, DC, and in state capitals around the nation, the hosts of high liberalism are girding for their counterattack.

2   Since taking office a decade ago, Gov. Thompson has waged an un-remitting campaign against dependency and welfare bloat. The result: a 55 percent drop in Wisconsin's Aid to Families with Dependent Children caseload. In inner-city Milwaukee, the welfare caseload has dropped by a third. Throughout much of the state, AFDC has been all but eliminated: in 28 of Wisconsin's 77 counties, the welfare caseload has shrunk by 80 per-cent or more.

3   The story gets even better. Generally, as welfare rolls shrink, the most employable people exit first, leaving behind a core of more heavily depend-ent recipients. Thus, conventional wisdom would expect the decline of Wisconsin's caseload to slow and then halt. Exactly the opposite has hap-pened. As Thompson implemented more rigorous reforms over the last

two years, the pace of dependency reduction accelerated dramatically. Currently the AFDC rolls are plummeting downward by 2 percent per month in Milwaukee and 4 percent in the rest of the state. Overall, the caseload has dropped by almost one-third in the last year alone.

4   Meanwhile, . . . during much of the relevant period national caseloads were soaring. Although in the last two years the national AFDC caseload has fallen by 17 percent, this represents only a peeling back of the explosive growth of dependency which occurred in the early nineties, when AFDC nationwide rocketed up 35 percent. In the majority of states, AFDC dependency remains higher today than when Ronald Reagan left the White House.

5   The lessons to be learned from Wisconsin are of enormous importance. Thompson's reforms are based on three policy principles: (1) reducing unnecessary new entries into AFDC; (2) establishing real work requirements; and (3) erecting incentives to ensure faithful implementation of reform by the bureaucracy.

6   In developing his first principle, Thompson has rediscovered one of the key ideas of traditional charity: a rational system for offering assistance must have a gate-keeping mechanism that separates those who truly need aid from the much larger number of those who do not. Recognizing that the surest way to break the habit of dependency was to prevent it from being formed in the first place, Wisconsin's reform team established a new program, Self-Sufficiency First, with the goal of dissuading unnecessary new entries into AFDC. Self-Sufficiency First provides counseling to new welfare applicants on the negative effects of dependency. It offers short-term aid (such as money for auto repairs) which may help to eliminate the person's need to receive AFDC, and it requires applicants to complete several weeks of supervised job search before their first welfare check is issued. Finally, applicants are warned that they will be required to work in exchange for benefits within a few weeks after entry into the AFDC program. The results are clear: since the implementation of SSF, the number of new AFDC enrollments has been cut nearly in half.

7   The second reform principle is to require recipients to work. The initial step was a realization that government-run job training has a long unsuccessful history, neither reducing dependency nor raising the earning capacity of trainees. For example, a recent Labor Department study of the government's largest training program, the Job Training Partnership Act, finds that JTPA increased the hourly wage rates of female trainees by 3.4 percent and of males not at all.

8   Thus Thompson's staff de-emphasized classroom training and stressed activities leading to immediate employment. Furthermore, if applicants have not obtained a private-sector job after some six weeks of continuous

supervised job search, they are then required to perform community-service work in exchange for ongoing AFDC benefits.

9   Here, as always, the key is in the details. In a typical state, AFDC recipients may theoretically be required to perform community-service work but will receive only a financial slap on the wrist if the work is not done. In Wisconsin, all AFDC recipients are subject to a Pay for Performance rule. If they fail to perform the specified number of hours of work or other activity, their AFDC and Food Stamps benefits are reduced pro rata. Thus, if the recipient is required to perform 30 hours of work but completes only 15, welfare benefits are cut in half. Pay for Performance has eliminated the option of a free income from welfare, making Wisconsin the first state that seriously requires AFDC recipients to earn their welfare checks.

10   Once welfare benefits must be earned, the attractiveness, or economic "utility," of welfare shrivels up and the number entering or remaining on AFDC shrinks dramatically. This lesson is critical. Until now, much of the political debate about reform has envisioned creating millions of make-work jobs for welfare recipients. But the Wisconsin example shows that while mandatory community-service work drives down the caseload, relatively few recipients will actually end up in community-service positions. Instead, the prospect of being forced to do community-service work reduces new welfare enrollments and propels current recipients quickly into private-sector employment.

11   Finally, Thompson realized that the best-designed reforms could be rendered impotent by a hostile or indifferent welfare bureaucracy. Thus he created powerful incentives to guide and motivate the state's welfare establishment. County welfare offices have been forced to earn day-care and training funds by increasing the number of recipients placed in community service or private-sector employment. Moreover, welfare offices that fail to reduce caseloads dramatically face an unprecedented penalty: they can be replaced by outside contractors. Wisconsin's bureaucracy has responded well, implementing reform with unusual efficiency and zeal.

12   In radically reducing Wisconsin's welfare caseload, Gov. Thompson has demolished most of the myths buttressing the liberal welfare state. These include: welfare recipients want to work but no jobs are available; shortages of day care and transportation make work impossible; education and training are the key to cutting dependency; and sharp reductions in welfare caseload will lead to severe economic deprivation.

13   Desperate to find some pretext for dismissing Wisconsin's victory over dependency, liberals claim the drop in caseload is due to a "hot" economy. This is ridiculous; the most robust state economy has never had a fraction of this impact on AFDC dependency. Moreover, if Wisconsin is compared to

various states with lower levels of unemployment, one finds that none of the others have had a large drop in dependency. Another liberal ploy is to claim that Thompson's reforms have raised total welfare costs. This is simply untrue. During Thompson's tenure, aggregate welfare spending on AFDC benefits, administration, day care, and training has fallen some 15 percent in nominal dollars, even as this figure was nearly doubling in the rest of the nation. Adjusted for inflation, Wisconsin's total costs have fallen by more than a third.

14   The most interesting feature of the Wisconsin story is the extraordinary impact of relatively mundane policies. Pay for Performance and Self-Sufficiency First are just common sense, rigorously applied. Any state could implement these policies tomorrow. They are easy to defend politically, as well. Only 2 of Wisconsin's 77 counties currently have time limits; recipients are not booted into the street when their time runs out. True, a significant number of recipients have had all welfare benefits terminated when they failed to work in a community-service position provided by the state. However, when liberals begin to whine about these people, the response is that their checks will be resumed whenever they bother to show up at their job site and begin working. Even the most nimble-tongued apologist has a hard time depicting this as unreasonable and mean.

15   After Thompson's success story, other states must be stampeding to adopt the Wisconsin model, right? Guess again. The main problem at the state level is lack of conservative welfare expertise. The details of reform in most states are left to professional welfare bureaucrats, who are unsympathetic to genuine conservative initiatives and adept at sprucing up variants of the status quo with conservative rhetoric.

16   While sluggishness in state capitals will certainly slow the spread of Wisconsin-style welfare reform, a far more dramatic threat has now emerged from the "End Welfare as We Know It" Clinton White House. Last week the Administration suddenly "discovered" that the Fair Labor Standards Act should apply to AFDC workfare, a rule never intended by Congress and never imposed in the past. Under this ruling, AFDC recipients performing community-service work must be compensated at least at the minimum-wage rate. Of course, guaranteeing all welfare recipients a minimum-wage salary is a bad idea in the first place. Worse, following the normal rules of Clinton-speak, "minimum wage" does not actually mean "minimum wage." The way the Administration's proposed regulations are phrased, the number of hours an AFDC recipient may be required to perform community service cannot exceed his welfare benefits divided by the minimum-wage rate ($4.75 per hour). However, for the Administration, welfare benefits mean only AFDC—other assistance, such as Food Stamps, Medicaid, and public housing, will not be counted.

17 Since the AFDC cash grant is only a small portion of the welfare given to AFDC families, the net effect of Clinton's scheme is to restrict greatly the number of hours a recipient may be required to work. In a few states with very high AFDC benefits the effect would not be too severe. But in the average state, recipients could be forced to work no more than 15 to 20 hours per week. In half the states the number of hours of required work would be lower than that, falling to as little as 5 hours per week. And the effective wage rate (benefits received from all welfare programs divided by hours worked) would be nowhere near $4.75. It would average about $13 per hour and in many cases would exceed $25. The deliberate intent of this policy is to cripple mandatory community-service work, which, as we have seen, is the motor that drives dependency reduction. It is a blatant effort to preserve the status quo by banning successful reform.

18 President Clinton's hypocritical maneuver should surprise no one. For decades liberals have fought relentlessly to prohibit all effective work programs. Indeed, twenty years ago another welfare "reformer," Jimmy Carter, expelled Utah from the AFDC program for, you guessed it, making recipients work for benefits. Despite elaborate obfuscation, not much has changed since.

19 If Mr. Clinton has his way, serious workfare will be emasculated, and Wisconsin's example, like Utah's before it, will be largely forgotten. Within a few years the liberal establishment will return to its mantra: broad economic factors make vast welfare caseloads inevitable; it may be possible to cut dependency at the margin, but only if we are willing to make bold investments in new programs, and so on.

20 The good news is that Congress can easily overturn Mr. Clinton's proposed regulations through new legislation, preferably attached to the overall budget act. But whether the current timid Congress will have the will to do this remains in doubt.

21 Meanwhile, back in Wisconsin, the AFDC caseload continues to drop by 3 percent per month. If Wisconsin's polices are ever adopted by the rest of the nation, taxpayers and recipients will both be huge winners—for dependency is good for neither.

Understanding Meaning

1. What was done in Wisconsin that makes Rector declare that state's handling of welfare reform a win in the first battle against the welfare state?
2. Exactly how dramatic has been the change in the welfare system under the leadership of Governor Tommy Thompson?

3. What three lessons, according to Rector, are to be learned from Wisconsin's welfare reform?
4. What does Rector mean when he calls for "real work requirements"? What happens if an individual can't find a job?
5. What threat does Rector state Wisconsin faces because of the decision that the Fair Labor Standards Act should apply to AFDC workfare?
6. *CRITICAL THINKING.* Is there good reason for welfare recipients to work, even if only five hours per week?

Evaluating Strategy

1. What support does Rector use to convince his readers? Do you find it convincing? What objections, if any, could you raise to what he says?
2. How would you describe the essay's organizational plan? How does Rector signal shifts in focus as he moves from one paragraph to another?
3. How effective is the conclusion?

Appreciating Language

1. Would you consider Rector's language subjective or objective? Is the author trying to appeal to his audience's emotions or to their reason? Does that change in the course of the essay? Explain.
2. How effective is the battle imagery of the opening paragraph?
3. Is the author's word choice appropriate for an audience of general readers who are not experts in the field of welfare and welfare reform?

Writing Suggestions

1. Rector boasts that huge numbers of people have been dropped from the welfare rolls in Wisconsin. Does that necessarily mean that they no longer need governmental support, or does it mean they are no longer getting it? Write a short essay explaining how the success of welfare reform should be measured.
2. *COLLABORATIVE WRITING.* Discuss Rector's essay with a group of other students. Ask each member to respond to the following question. What should the goal of public support be: to provide services and assistance the poor need to survive or to provide the means for people to get jobs? Record statements of the group, organizing responses using comparison or classification.

44

Capital Punishment

*Whoever sheds the blood of a human, by a
human shall that person's blood be shed; for in
his own image God made humankind.*
–Genesis 9:6

*. . . the dignity of human life must never be
taken away, even in the case of someone who
has done great evil. Modern society has the
means of protecting itself, without definitively
denying criminals the chance to reform. I
renew the appeal . . . to end the death penalty,
which is both cruel and unnecessary.*
–Pope John Paul II

*The core of the matter is this: Murderers
volunteer for the risk of capital punishment,
and the punishment they volunteered to risk
should be imposed if, in the view of the courts,
they are guilty and deserve it.*
–Ernest van den Haag

*"Thou shalt not kill" cannot be taught by the
state sponsored execution of criminals. To tell
others not to kill by killing someone makes a
mockery of the message.*
–Sunil Dutta

*When opponents of capital punishment say to
the state: "I will not let you kill in my name,"
they are also saying to the murderers: "You
can kill in your own name as long as I have
an excuse for not getting involved."*
–Ed Koch

The Legacy of Leopold and Loeb

On May 21, 1924, two Chicago teenagers, Nathan Leopold and Richard Loeb, kidnapped and murdered a fourteen-year-old neighbor named Bobby Franks. The pair were unlikely criminals. Both had graduated college at eighteen. Leopold, a law student, spoke five languages and was a noted ornithologist. Neither needed the ransom they had demanded. Both were sons of millionaires. Under arrest, Leopold and Loeb confessed. There was no doubt about their guilt. They showed police where they had disposed of the victim's clothing and the typewriter used to write a ransom letter. They explained the murder had been an experiment, an attempt to commit the perfect crime. Previously they had contemplated kidnapping one of their fathers, raping a girl, or killing Richard Loeb's younger brother. Neither expressed any remorse. Leopold told reporters that killing his victim meant nothing more to him than "impaling a beetle on a pin."

The teenage "thrill killers" shocked the nation. Editors, commentators, legislators, and clergymen claimed they represented everything that was wrong with youth in the 1920s and deserved to be executed. The boys' parents hired Clarence Darrow, the nation's most famous attorney, to defend their sons. A strong opponent of the death penalty, Darrow begged the judge only to spare their lives. Society, he argued, could be protected without hanging them. Leopold and Loeb were sentenced to life plus ninety-nine years, outraging many who believed that less wealthy defendants would not have escaped the gallows. Loeb was killed by a fellow inmate in 1936. Paroled in 1958, Leopold published his autobiography, traveled the world, and sued a novelist who wrote a best-seller based on his case, but never expressed regret for his acts.

Opponents of capital punishment cite the case of Leopold and Loeb to prove the fundamental unfairness of the death penalty. No matter how heinous their crimes, rich defendants with skilled lawyers are rarely executed, they claim. Supporters of the death penalty use the case to prove that unrepentant killers, no matter how long their prison sentences, can be pardoned and walk free.

The United States and the Death Penalty

In 1846 the state of Michigan abolished capital punishment, making it the first English-speaking government in the world to ban the death penalty. Wisconsin followed in 1853. The majority of other states, along with the federal government, however, continue to execute criminals, long after Mexico, Canada, and most European nations have abolished or suspended capital punishment.

CAPITAL PUNISHMENT IN THE UNITED STATES

States with death penalties	38	
States with the most executions 1976–2004	Texas	321
	Virginia	91
	Oklahoma	73
	Missouri	61
	Florida	58
States without a death penalty	Alaska, Hawaii, Iowa, Maine, Massachusetts, Michigan, Minnesota, North Dakota, Rhode Island, Vermont, West Virginia, Wisconsin (also District of Columbia, Puerto Rico)	
First state to abolish capital punishment	Michigan, 1846 (last execution, 1837) *first English-speaking government in the world to ban the death penalty	
Federal executions 1927–2003	37 *includes 6 German saboteurs tried by military commission, 1942	
U.S. military executions 1942–1961	169	
Nations that have abolished the death penalty	108 countries, including the United Kingdom, France, Germany, Italy, Spain, Canada, Mexico, Brazil, Argentina, Australia, South Africa, Turkey, Haiti, Cambodia, and Israel	
Nations with the most executions	China, Iran, Saudi Arabia, the United States	

Sources: Amnesty International and Death Penalty Information Center

Capital punishment is widely supported by the American public. A 2002 Gallup poll revealed that 72 percent of respondents approved of the death penalty, with nearly half stating that it is not imposed enough. A 2003 Harris poll of 993 adults found that 69 percent supported capital punishment. Proponents of the death penalty argue that it deters other criminals, prevents murderers from killing again in or out of prison, and values life by placing the possibility of a supreme sanction against those who take life. Ed Koch, former mayor of New York City, argues that capital punishment affirms the value of life:

> Some critics of capital punishment, such as columnist Jimmy Breslin, have suggested that a life sentence is actually a harsher penalty for murder than death. This is sophistic nonsense. A few killers may decide not to appeal a death sentence, but the overwhelming majority make every effort to stay alive. It is by exacting the highest penalty for the taking of human life that we affirm the highest value of human life.

Capital punishment, however, has been strongly opposed by a variety of groups and individuals in the United States. State legislatures in the Midwest abolished the death penalty a century before European parliaments. Religious groups argue that the executions constitute state-sanctioned murder. The *National Catholic Reporter* stated that even the snipers accused of eleven cold-blooded murders in the Washington, DC, area in 2002 did not deserve to be executed because "all human life is made in the image of God. All human life is sacred. No human life is beyond redemption."

Sunnil Dutta, a police officer who opposes capital punishment, argues that the death penalty does not enhance the value of the lives of victims. Instead, it diminishes their memory and inflicts more pain on their families:

> Candlelight vigils, media coverage, and an endless judicial process turns the criminal into a celebrity while the victim's family seethes with resentment, sometimes for decades! Not only does the criminal become glorified, the taxpayer-subsidized court costs are horrendous. Victims are re-victimized repeatedly as the loss of their dear ones is downplayed and they are portrayed as despicable people because some of them want the execution to proceed.

Opponents of capital punishment argue that whatever its merits domestically, the death penalty damages the American image in the world community. At a time when the United States is attempting to influence the Middle East to accept democracy, it stands as the only major democracy that uses the death penalty. Robert Badinter, France's former Justice Minister, notes that "capital punishment brings with it all the evils of Western society: racism, social injustice, economic and cultural inequality. These traits are not unique to America, but they take on a particular intensity when viewed in the light of the death penalty." In his view the United States' continued use of capital punishment "has profoundly degraded the country's image in the eyes of other democratic nations."

In the 1990s DNA testing proved that several inmates on death row had been wrongly convicted. The prospects of innocent people being executed, coupled with more states adopting sentences of life without parole, have led to a dramatic drop in death sentences. Governor Ryan of Illinois declared a moratorium on executions in 2000. Commenting on the status of the death penalty in the United States, the *Economist* predicted that "if America ever abandons the death penalty, it is likelier to be with a whimper than a bang."

Before reading these entries, consider these questions.

Which criminals, if any, deserve a death sentence?   Should someone who kills a clerk during a robbery deserve the death penalty? Should a terrorist who followed a premeditated plan to kill a large number of civilians be executed? Should anyone under eighteen face the death penalty?

Does life without parole serve the same purpose as capital punishment?   If it can be guaranteed that a criminal will be imprisoned for life without any possibility of being released, is there reason to maintain capital punishment? Are some crimes so heinous that death seems the only appropriate punishment? In its fifty-year history, for example, Israel has executed only one person, the war criminal Adolf Eichmann.

What explains the different status of the death penalty among the fifty states?   Do Texas and Florida, which execute the most criminals, have more violent crime than New York and California, which have executed far fewer criminals? Why do you think Minnesota, Wisconsin, and Michigan have abolished the death penalty? What historical forces have shaped these regional differences?

Does the death penalty affirm or undermine the value of life?   Opponents of the death penalty believe that society should never take a life, even that of a convicted killer. Because life is sacred, it should be protected. Killing a criminal puts the state in the same category as the murderer. Supporters of the capital punishment argue that because life is sacred, people convicted of taking life should forfeit their own.

WRITING ABOUT CAPITAL PUNISHMENT

The issue of capital punishment can prompt a number of responses that can be useful topics for writing assignments.

Critical Thinking and Prewriting

People often have very strong feelings about the death penalty. You may find it racist, barbaric, and outmoded. Or you may believe that execution is the only just punishment for premeditated murder, assassination, or terrorism. To write effectively, however, you should do more than simply express what you already feel. Good writing requires careful thought.

Getting Started: Exploring Ideas

1. Why does the United States persist in executing the condemned? Mexico and South Africa have higher homicide rates than the United States but no longer use the death penalty. Does this suggest they believe it does not deter crime?
2. How does the death penalty affect America's image in the world? Can a country trying to spread democracy in the world retain the death penalty when nearly all other democracies have abolished it?
3. Consider how DNA affects capital punishment. On one hand, DNA testing has proven the innocence of several prisoners on death row, revealing flaws in the justice system. On the other hand, now that DNA testing can scientifically prove the guilt of some criminals and remove doubt about their possible innocence, does it make it easier for judges and juries to sentence defendants to death?
4. Do you think politicians are reluctant to discuss the death penalty? Does supporting the death penalty strike some voters as being harsh or racist? Would a politician advocating a national ban on capital punishment be viewed as being "soft on crime"?

Strategies for Writing about Capital Punishment

Define key terms.
Before advancing any point of view, you must create clear definitions. For instance, how do you define terms and concepts like *cruel and unusual punishment* or *deterrence* that appear in debates about capital punishment?

Poll friends, coworkers, and fellow students.
To determine current attitudes about the death penalty, ask people whether they support or oppose capital punishment. Do they support or oppose it in all cases? Do they question how it is applied? Ask them to give reasons for their views.

Evaluate use of the death penalty in your state.
Do you live in a state without the death penalty, a state that has a death penalty but rarely imposes it, or a state that uses the death penalty? Analyze the history of capital punishment in your state. Is there any current discussion to change the law?

Distinguish between death penalty opponents who condemn capital punishment in principle and those who criticize its application.
Some people believe capital punishment is wrong in all circumstances. Others argue that it is unfairly applied, so that poor or minority defendants are more likely to be sentenced to death than wealthy whites. When examining arguments by opponents, determine what their objections are.

Examine the financial costs of the death penalty.
Some jurisdictions do not pursue the death penalty because they cannot afford the state-required appeal process. Various studies show that it costs less to imprison someone for life than to execute them.

Comment on the timing of executions.
Because of lengthy appeal processes, many people condemned to death are not executed for years. The average prisoner spends nine years on death row before being executed. John Wayne Gacy, a mass murderer convicted of killing thirty-three boys and young men, spent fourteen years on death row before being executed. Some convicts have been on death row for over twenty years. Does executing someone ten or twenty years after conviction serve any social purpose? Does it become only a footnote?

WRITING IN THE MODES

You may find that selecting a particular mode is an effective way of examining a topic, organizing ideas, and shaping an essay.

Narration
1. Write an essay about a particular murder that fueled debates about the status of the death penalty in your state.
2. Develop a narrative essay to explain your views about the death penalty. When did you form your opinions? Did a particular event shape your views? If your opinions have evolved or changed, explain what happened.

Description
1. Describe how capital punishment affects America's image in the world. Do you think critics of the United States connect its use of the death penalty at home with what they consider an imperialist foreign policy abroad?
2. If you oppose the death penalty, describe what you consider to be an appropriate punishment. If you support capital punishment, describe what you consider to be an appropriate method of execution.

Definition
1. Write an essay that clearly defines in your view which crimes, if any, deserve the death penalty.
2. Define *deterrence*, then explain the role punishment might play in deterring crime. Does a swift arrest have more deterrent power than an execution ten years after the crime is committed?

Example
1. Use a hypothetical example or examples to support or reject the death penalty. You might describe a crime you feel is so heinous that death is the only appropriate punishment. Or, you might create an example of how public prejudice and incompetent defense attorneys could lead to an innocent person being executed.
2. Conduct online research and use several actual legal cases to support your position on capital punishment.

Comparison and Contrast
1. Select one argument regarding the death penalty, such as the danger of executing an innocent person or racial inequity, and contrast arguments made by supporters and opponents.
2. Compare and contrast capital punishment and life without parole. Do they provide equal protection to society? Does executing an offender have any additional impact?

Division and Classification
1. Use division to organize and discuss major arguments in support of or in opposition to capital punishment.

2. If you support capital punishment, use classification to create a scale listing crimes you definitely believe deserve the death sentence, crimes that might deserve a death sentence, and crimes that should never be punished with death.
3. If you oppose the death penalty, use classification to create a scale that describes in order of importance reasons it should be abolished or suspended.

Process
1. If your state has a death penalty, describe the appeals process. Are those sentenced to death automatically given the right to appeal? Does the process seem fair?
2. If you oppose the death penalty, describe the best process to end it. Should opponents seek to influence Congress or state legislatures to change the laws? Should they work to change public opinion?
3. If you support the death penalty, use process to describe how capital punishment should be used to eliminate racial discrimination and reduce the chances of executing an innocent person.

Cause and Effect
1. Discuss the effect the death penalty has on society. In your opinion, do executions make society coarser, less civilized, more violent? Or does capital punishment deter crime and enhance the value of life by demanding that murderers forfeit their lives?
2. Discuss causes for support for the death penalty in the United States. Why are so many Americans in favor of it when most Canadians, Mexicans, and Europeans have abandoned it?

Argument and Persuasion
1. Write an essay that addresses one issue about the death penalty. Express your opinion on the state's right to take a life, racial inequity, or the quality of legal counsel provided to poor defendants.
2. Write a persuasive essay stating how the United States should punish those convicted of an especially heinous crime such as terrorism or mass murder.

STUDENT PAPER

No Deterrence

Does the death penalty deter anyone? One of the main arguments people use to support capital punishment is deterrence—the idea that seeing someone executed will make others think before committing a similar crime. In theory it might have that effect. If a gang member murdered a police officer or shot up a liquor store and killed six people, maybe executing him within a year of conviction might influence other gang members and younger people who admired him.

But today people spend years, sometimes decades, on death row before being executed. Stays and appeals delay executions to the point that any deterrent factor is lost. When a 38-year-old man is executed for a crime he committed when he was 25, who will be deterred? No doubt his gang no longer exists. The current generation of young criminals can't relate to him and don't see his fate connected to theirs. In addition, whatever shock and horror people felt by an outrageous crime has long worn off. Executing someone years after the crime becomes only an afterthought, a minor news item. Any deterrent power is long gone.

Quicker executions, of course, are not likely to happen. In order to maintain the death penalty, state legislatures have appeased critics by building in more and more appeals. In order to allay the fear of mistakenly executing innocent people, death penalty supporters need a complex appeal process. This creates a Catch-22. People argue the death penalty deters crime. But to convince opponents the innocent will be spared, years of appeals precede executions, limiting the deterrent effect.

So we still have executions. They take place many years after the crime occurs. The only people to be affected are probably family members of the victim and the condemned. No one else is likely to be influenced. Young people, who commit most of the crime in our country, have short attention spans and generally relate only to their own generation. But do we want to become a society that executes its young people?

There may be many reasons to justify capital punishment. But the political and legal realities dictate that deterring crime is not one of them. And when the greatest threat to our nation is suicidal terrorism, the argument is even weaker. People willing to fly planes into buildings or blow themselves up are not likely to be deterred by the thought of a lethal injection.

Understanding Meaning

1. What is the student's thesis? Is it clearly stated? Can you summarize it in your own words?
2. What reasons does the student give to support his or her conclusions? Do they seem valid?
3. In the student's view, what would have to happen for executions to deter others?
4. What compromise have supporters of the death penalty made to their opponents? In the student's view, how has this affected deterrence?
5. Why does the student believe that capital punishment will not deter terrorists?

Evaluating Strategy

1. What evidence does the student present to support the thesis?
2. Can you detect any errors in critical thinking, such as hasty generalization or false analogy?

Appreciating Language

1. Is the student's tone and style suited to a college essay? Are there any words or phrases you would revise or replace?
2. The student uses the term *Catch-22*. Do you know what it means? Should a term like this be defined? Why or why not?

Writing Suggestions

1. Write a brief essay that supports or opposes the student's thesis. Is deterrence really an issue at all?
2. *COLLABORATIVE WRITING*. Discuss this paper with other students and write a statement on the deterrence factor of capital punishment. If students have differing viewpoints, consider writing opposing statements.

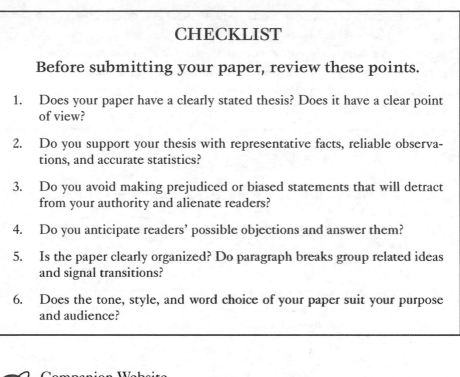

CHECKLIST

Before submitting your paper, review these points.

1. Does your paper have a clearly stated thesis? Does it have a clear point of view?

2. Do you support your thesis with representative facts, reliable observations, and accurate statistics?

3. Do you avoid making prejudiced or biased statements that will detract from your authority and alienate readers?

4. Do you anticipate readers' possible objections and answer them?

5. Is the paper clearly organized? Do paragraph breaks group related ideas and signal transitions?

6. Does the tone, style, and word choice of your paper suit your purpose and audience?

Companion Website

See **academic.cengage.com/english** for information on planning, organizing, writing, and revising essays.

E-Reading: InfoTrac College Edition
http://www.infotrac.college.com

For Further Reading
E–Readings Online

Search for articles by author or title in InfoTrac College Edition after entering your user name and password.

PR Newswire, *More Than Two-Thirds of Americans Continue to Support the Death Penalty, According to New Harris Poll Results*
Harris polls reveal that, although belief that capital punishment deters crime dropped from 59 percent in 1963 to 41 percent in 2003, support for the death penalty rose from 38 percent to 69 percent in the same period.

Robert Badinter, *Death Be Not Proud: Capital Punishment Is a Blight on America's Image in the World*
Noting that 108 countries have abolished capital punishment, the former French Justice Minister argues that the United States' "use of the death penalty has profoundly degraded the country's image in the eyes of other democratic nations."

David C. Slade, *Decades on Death Row: An "American Constitutional Tradition"?*
In the United States, prisoners spend an average of nine years on death row before being executed, creating in the minds of many legal scholars "a cruel and unusual punishment."

Joseph Rosenbloom, *The Unique Brutality of Texas: Why the Lone Star State Leads the Nation in Executions*
Although Texas represents 7.6 percent of the nation's population, it has carried out 35 percent of the executions in the United States between 1976 and 2004.

Harper's Magazine, *It's Not Like Falling Asleep*
The attempt to make execution less painful by use of lethal injection fails because "the terror of being taken to the death house" is no different than being "tossed out of an airplane."

John Steele Gordon, *Thomas Edison's Deadly Game*
To demonstrate the danger of alternating current developed by his rival George Westinghouse, Thomas Edison campaigned for its use to electrocute criminals.

 If you have access to *Comp21*, click on Themes, then click on Capital Punishment.

45

ERNEST VAN DEN HAAG

Ernest van den Haag (1914–2002) was John M. Olin Professor of Jurisprudence and Public Policy at Fordham University. A Sephardic Jew, he fled Nazi persecution in his native Holland during World War II. During the nearly six decades that he lived in the United States, van den Haag wrote and spoke frequently on behalf of conservative causes. In particular, he was a longtime contributor to National Review.

The Ultimate Penalty . . . and a Just One: The Basics of Capital Punishment

CONTEXT: *Unlike many supporters of the death penalty, van den Haag does not necessarily believe that the arguments against capital punishment are wrong. He simply thinks that they are irrelevant. Even if the death penalty has no more deterrent effect than life imprisonment and even if society could protect itself without executions, "many people would feel that the survival of murderers is morally unjustified," he writes in this June 2001 article for the* National Review. *As long as a majority of people believe this to be the case, society should have the right to impose capital punishment.*

1   The case of Timothy McVeigh reminds us that the endless dispute about the death penalty is mainly religious in origin, even if many of the arguments employed are secular. The religious belief is that only God can legitimately end a human life; no crime can justify the death penalty for anyone, regardless of how great and certain his guilt is, or how powerful a deterrent his execution would be. Theologians disagree on the death penalty—it is warranted by Biblical passages and was traditionally favored by churches—but it is currently opposed by a majority of religious leaders.

2   The secular objections to the death penalty hold that its rational purposes, such as deterrence, should be achieved by alternative means, since we can never be entirely certain that all those convicted of capital crimes are actually guilty. The possibility—in the long run, the likelihood—that some convicts are not guilty is currently the most persuasive objection to capital punishment.

3   Why execute anyone? Why not avoid the risk of miscarriages of justice by abolishing capital punishment altogether? Simply because there are no fully satisfactory alternatives. Life imprisonment is not necessarily lifelong;

life imprisonment without parole still allows governors to pardon prisoners. The finality of death is both the weakness and the strength of capital punishment. We are not ready to do without it, yet hesitate to use it: There are many convicts on death row, but only a few are actually executed. Between 1973 and 1995, 5,760 death sentences were imposed; as of 1995, only 313 had been executed, and only some 400 have been executed since. Gary Graham, executed in June 2000, spent 19 years on death row exhausting his appeals, which were reviewed by more than 30 different judges. His case is far from exceptional.

4   Abolitionists often argue as though no one would die were it not for capital punishment. Yet we are not spared death in any case; a death sentence may shorten the life span, but—unlike imprisonment—it does not introduce an avoidable event, but merely hastens an unavoidable one.

5   Even if—without executions—society would be fully and permanently protected from murder, many people would feel that the survival of murderers is morally unjust, that the death penalty for murder is deserved, that it is a categorical imperative as Immanuel Kant thought. There is no way of proving or disproving such a moral idea, but there is little question that it is widely shared.

6   The issue of deterrence is raised by the abolitionists, who often point out that the number of homicides does not decrease as the frequency of executions increases; from this they conclude that executions do not deter crime. But deterrence depends on the credibility of the threat of execution, and this credibility does not depend on the number of executions. To be sure, a threat never carried out will become incredible; to deter, it must be carried out often enough to remain credible. This does not mean it has to be carried out in all cases; but the threat of execution is currently so minuscule, compared with the homicide rate, as to be altogether ineffective.

7   It is often argued that criminals do not calculate, and that threats are therefore ineffective. Undoubtedly that is the case for some of them, but it is unlikely that all criminals are so different from the rest of the population that they do not respond to threats at all. If there are no executions over a long period, the deterrent effect of capital punishment may well be reduced to zero; but as long as the threat of execution is not entirely empty, there will be some deterrent effect. How great a deterrent it is will depend on such factors as the certainty of the punishment and the time that elapses between death sentences and executions; currently the deterrent effect is undermined by the uncertainty, infrequency, and delays involved in execution. (Indeed, a calculating criminal might look at the extreme rarity of the death penalty and thereby be encouraged in his murderous course.)

8   The existence of capital punishment is a disincentive, as threats of punishment always are. But the evidence is insufficient to prove that capital punishment deters murder more than do other punishments. Even if it did, however, capital punishment would be shown to be useful, but not morally justified. Deterring the crimes, not yet committed, of others does not morally justify execution of any convict (except to utilitarians, who think usefulness is a moral justification). If deserved, capital punishment should be imposed. If not, it should not be. Deterrence, however useful, cannot morally justify any punishment.

9   Some of the most popular objections to capital punishment do not actually deal with the punishment itself, but with its distribution. The issues that are raised are not unimportant, but they do not belong in a discussion of the legitimacy of capital punishment itself. Racial discrimination, for example, would disappear as an issue if the population were racially homogenous. Analogously, the argument that wealthy defendants can avail themselves of legal defenses not available to the poor depends on an unequal distribution of wealth; this argument is relevant to a discussion of social inequality, but is extraneous to an attempt to determine the rightness of the death penalty.

10   Although we have made great progress, we cannot ignore the remaining inequalities in the criminal-justice system. But there is no good reason to confuse such inequalities with an inherent inequity in the administration of justice. There is nothing in the nature of capital punishment that demands an unfair administration.

11   Issues of deterrence are peripheral to the moral argument at stake here, and the race and wealth issues are more peripheral still. The core of the matter is this: Murderers volunteer for the risk of capital punishment, and the punishment they volunteered to risk should be imposed if, in the view of the courts, they are guilty and deserve it.

Understanding Meaning

1. What is van den Haag's purpose in the essay?
2. What does van den Haag call the currently most persuasive objection to capital punishment?
3. Why, according to the article, is the current situation not a fair test of the deterrent effect of the death penalty?
4. What sorts of issues does van den Haag term peripheral to the moral argument about the death penalty? What, then, is the central issue?

Evaluating Strategy

1. If you have read other essays on the death penalty, how does this one compare in its effectiveness? Why?
2. How would you describe the organizational plan of the essay?
3. At what point in the essay do you know which side of the death penalty debate van den Haag is on?
4. What sort of evidence does van den Haag offer in support of his general statements?

Appreciating Language

1. Does van den Haag use emotionally loaded language? If you have read other essays on the death penalty, compare them in terms of language. How does the language affect the writers' points?
2. How would you rate the language of the piece on a scale of informal to formal? What effect does that have?

Writing Suggestions

1. *PREWRITING.* Write a paragraph explaining your personal opinion about the death penalty.
2. *COLLABORATIVE WRITING.* Meet with your group to see how the various members of the group feel about the death penalty. After sharing your opinions, write your own individual one-paragraph summary of what the group's attitudes are toward the death penalty.
3. Write an essay in which you explain whether or not you agree with van den Haag that there are "no fully satisfactory alternatives" to the death penalty.

46

SUNIL DUTTA

Sunil Dutta holds a doctorate in biology from the University of California at Davis and is a well-published research scientist. He is also a sergeant in the Los Angeles Police Department and the author of Hard Wall of Reality: Journey of a Liberal Scientist in the LAPD.

Humans Playing God: Capital Punishment and Its Follies

CONTEXT: *The British division of the Indian subcontinent into Hindu India and Muslim Pakistan resulted in rampaging violence. Sunil Dutta's great-great-grandmother and great-grandaunts were among those killed. As a result, his great-granduncle joined other Hindu vigilantes to exact retributive justice against Muslim refugees. The randomness of this violence turned Dutta away from the very notion of retributive justice. Among other things, this has led Dutta to oppose the death penalty. Better to sentence a mass murderer to life imprisonment, where he can contemplate the horror of his crime, than to have him turned into a martyr by the media. This article was published in the July-August 2002 issue of the liberal Jewish magazine* Tikkun.

1 A few months before the birth of Israel, my family lost our ancestral home in the village of Kanjrur-Duttan, a village where Duttas had lived since the time of Emperor Babar. Kanjrur-Duttan happened to be on the wrong side of the line when India was divided in two (Hindu India and Muslim Pakistan) by British colonialists. The entire Hindu village fled in the dark of the night to escape being massacred by a rampaging mob of Muslim goons who were looting, raping, and murdering. Some did not make it, and were caught and slaughtered.

2 My great-granduncle became a dispenser of retributive justice. He joined a roving gang of Hindu vigilantes in the border town of Dera Baba Nanak, where he extracted revenge for the murder of his mother and sisters. He killed many Muslim refugees who were trekking defenselessly in the opposite direction from my family—towards the newly created Pakistan from the Hindu-majority India. During my visit to India last winter, I sat across from him and asked if he felt remorse for what he had done during the time when the entire Indian subcontinent had been submerged into a bloodbath in which almost one million people died. He avoided my gaze

"Humans Playing God: Capital Punishment and Its Follies" by Sunil Dutta from TIKKUN 17(4) (July/August 2002), pp. 17–20. Reprinted from Tikkun: A Bimonthly Jewish Critique of Politics, Culture & Society. www.tikkun.org.

and kept puffing at his cigarette. I persisted, "Do you ever think that people you killed were also innocent refugees, just like you and the family members we lost?" The old man looked down and defiantly said, "I may have killed some innocent people, but there must have been some sinners in there too!"

3   When people play God and dispense the Ultimate Justice, they create Himalayan blunders. Whether they are avenging the blood of their family members by slitting their enemies' throats, blowing them up with bombs, or passing orders to execute criminals while sitting on their judge's throne, human beings cannot morally justify taking another human's life.

4   As a police officer, I often see the results of human depravity. I see incidents of such brutal behavior that my compassion dissolves like a candle flame swept by a tornado. I vividly remember responding to a double homicide scene a few weeks ago. The bodies on the grass were covered with white sheets. As soon as the news helicopters hovering above us left, detectives pulled the sheets off to look at the victims. An elderly woman with a ghostly expression stared at me through hollow eyes. Her neck was almost severed. Her skin was burnt and peeling; her body was giving off smoke. A blood-soaked, semi-burnt shirt was sticking to the torso of her husband. Though his body was badly burnt, the watch on his left wrist was still working.

5   The murderer had viciously executed his frail victims by slitting their throats, then started a fire to cover up the crime. The gentle couple, loved by their neighbors, had been married for the last fifty years. Now they were dead. I stood silently, shaken by human savagery that no other animal could match.

6   The crime-scene photographer walked slowly to me and whispered, "I hope they find the guy and hang him!" She sees a lot in her job, but the brutality of the crime and the elderly age of the victims had visibly shaken her. I didn't have the courage to tell her that executing the depraved killers would not turn back the clock and erase this blot on the sheer fabric of humanity. As I looked at the young photographer, I thought, would I have the courage to look into the eyes of the victims' daughter and self-righteously proclaim that the death penalty is immoral? Could I emphatically say that the cold-blooded monster who planned this robbery and viciously murdered these defenseless people could or should be rehabilitated? No. It would be presumptuous of me to tell the victims' families that I feel their pain. It would be even more preposterous to ask them to forgive the murderer and not root for capital punishment.

7   Nevertheless, although I am deeply aware of the suffering that murder causes, I don't believe the death penalty can be justified. When I find myself

faced with murder, I think about my great-uncle, who used senseless murder to justify senseless murder. The practice of capital punishment, particularly by our "justice system," reveals a serious failure in our humanity. We no longer burn witches or keep slaves or have monarchs dictate our lives. Capital punishment is similarly anachronistic.

8 I am not some soft-hearted ignoramus arguing for going easy on murderers. As a police officer, I am sometimes confronted by vicious people who have so lost their humanity that they don't belong in any neighborhood. Some are such cold-blooded killers and others bring such misery to the world around them that they should be locked up forever. I want the people who calculatingly and brutally murder others to pay severely for their heinous crimes. Wanting to keep dangerous people out of society is different, however, from wanting to respond to violence with violence. No society can reach a peaceful existence if its people resolve their problems with violence.

9 I have heard many arguments in favor of capital punishment. For example, some people argue that if I kill someone, I give up my right to live. That principle would qualify as a moral argument only if it were applied evenly. However, we do not sentence every murderer to death. Why isn't a reckless drunk driver who kills an entire family not sentenced to death? Because murders are different from each other, is the response—some are more cruel than others. But how do we quantitatively measure the heinousness of a murder? When mistake prone humans send some criminals to the death chamber and others to prison are we not appropriating God's authority? What could be more immoral?

10 Not only do we play the role of God by judging who will die and who will live, by supporting the death penalty we send out the dangerous message to impressionable minds that violence is a way to resolve problems. "Thou shalt not kill" cannot be taught by the state-sponsored execution of criminals. To tell others not to kill by killing someone makes a mockery of the message. We need only to look around the world to remember that subservience to violence as a way to resolve problems has brought us perpetual misery and suffering: just look at Israel, Kashmir, East Timor, Rwanda, Serbia . . .

11 Death penalty support in law-enforcement comes from a deeply-held conviction by police officers that it is a deterrent. Demagogues exploit the fear of crime in the community and use their support for capital punishment as a badge of honor. As a police officer myself, I can emphatically state that many of my colleagues are wrong: the death penalty has no deterrent effect on crime. Capital punishment fails to deter those who commit crimes

of passion. Capital punishment also has no dissuading power over criminals who are opportunistic, calculating, or overcome by drugs. A person taking a chance that he will not be caught for the crime he is planning to commit does not discriminate between the death penalty and life in prison without parole. Killing a criminal will prevent him from committing another crime—but so will putting him behind bars forever.

12   The only practical justification for the death penalty is revenge and punishment. I am not one to defend the actions of murderers. After seeing the pain and loss faced by the victims' families and the cruelty of remorseless killers, I do not find merit in the argument that criminal behavior can be explained away by childhood abuse or a lack of opportunities and therefore excused. I know countless people who grew up in miserably wretched conditions and turned out to be caring adults. I also cannot fault a victim's family's demand for revenge. Only those who have lost their family members at the hands of vicious reprobates have the right to make such judgements. However, even as a means of revenge, the death penalty is an absolute failure. Candlelight vigils, media coverage, and an endless judicial process turns the criminal into a celebrity while the victim's family seethes with resentment, sometimes for decades! Not only does the criminal become glorified, the taxpayer-subsidized court costs are horrendous. Victims are re-victimized repeatedly as the loss of their dear ones is downplayed and they are portrayed as despicable people because some of them want the execution to proceed. This sort of revenge is not sweet. Despite the hopes of most pro-death penalty victims, executing criminals does not necessarily bring resolution and healing to the victim's family. In a calculated act so depraved that even sick people would deplore it, Reynaldo Rodriguez walked into the wealthy suburban home of his ex-girlfriend Maria Calderon in Simi Valley and systematically killed three of her family members and wounded two others. After his heinous crime, he drove to a campground in Los Padres National Forest and killed himself. Maria Calderon's feelings reveal the profound flaw in capital punishment. She said to the *Los Angeles Times*, "I would have much rather he stayed alive. That way he could face the justice system and live with the fact that he murdered three people, and suffer what we're suffering. Now he took his own life—and he's not suffering anymore."

13   Even if we were to accept the arguments in favor of capital punishment, the clearest reason to forego killing criminals comes from the inevitable miscarriage of the punishment itself. I shudder at the fact that ninety-four innocent individuals in the last decade were released from death row. They had been wrongfully condemned to death for crimes they did not commit.

Some were minutes from execution. For each person exonerated, how many innocent people have we executed? This utter disgrace should make members of the criminal justice system hang their heads in shame. I cannot even imagine the anguish of a wasted life, the years away from friends and family, the disrepute and shame suffered by these poor souls who spent precious moments of their lives locked away in a maximum security prison for crimes they did not commit. What does the sword hanging over one's head do to the psyche of a wronged person who awaits the hand of the executioner while the appeals process is being exhausted? Frank Lee Smith was convicted of a 1985 rape and murder and condemned to death row. Smith died in prison after spending fifteen years there. His innocence was proven by DNA tests after his death! This is only one of many poignant examples that cries out loud against capital punishment.

14   In many of these cases, nothing in the legal appeals process helped uncover the innocence of these wrongly convicted individuals. Instead, it was investigations conducted by journalists or college students, or the confessions of the true perpetrators of these crimes that helped to exonerate the innocent. In fact, the justice system has at times worked to wrongly criminalize the innocent. Reckless prosecutors and police lab chemist teams like Robert Macy and Joyce Gilchrist of Oklahoma have been criticized for playing with the rules to convict people in murder trials. This makes a mockery of the system when professional enforcers of the law mangle the spirit of the law to get convictions, forcing outsiders to rescue the hapless victims of the criminal justice system.

15   People also make mistakes; research shows that even eyewitnesses are unable to recall events accurately. Yet we brazenly act as if we were God and condemn people to death, calmly ignoring that we are mistake-prone humans. Furthermore, our history is replete with stories of governments framing people they did not like. Individuals such as Geronimo Pratt can attest to the effectiveness with which innocent people can be framed by a determined government. Criminal cops such as Rafael Perez ride roughshod over prosecutors and juries and railroad people into prison or worse. Corruption in FBI crime labs, lying forensic analysts, biased juries, and prosecutors bending to local politics make a dangerous mixture, making the legal process highly unsafe for those on the lower socio-economic stratum of the society. I am not saying that a majority of people on death row are innocent; most are brutal killers who deserve to be there. However, even if a minute fraction of individuals on death row are innocent, it is immoral to support capital punishment. When our government executes an innocent person in our name, all of society is responsible for the death of that innocent person.

16   At least the members of death row in the United States had the opportunity to go to trial. To see the logical extension of this willingness to kill in
the name of the state we need only look to Israel, which in the last year has
begun an even more brazen and barbaric application of capital punishment:
the selective assassination by the Israeli government of those suspected of
being involved in terrorist activities. It is a disgrace that a government can
indulge in such a sinister practice. Even in the United States, an argument
to execute hard-core gang members in the inner city because that would
prevent them from killing others would jolt the conscience of the most callused hard-on-crime person. The pre-emptive executions of "suspected"
terrorists by the Israeli government are based on similarly fallacious reasoning. What about proving someone's guilt before meting out the ultimate
punishment? Not only do such executions backfire and lead to more violence against the Israeli people, they result in a complete loss of moral authority for the state; we should take heed from this example of the inherent
immorality of the state playing God.

17   People have asked me whether I would support capital punishment if
the criminal is absolutely identified beyond a shadow of a doubt. What if the
wickedness of the crime shocks the conscience of everyone? The dastardly
bombing in Oklahoma by Timothy McVeigh and the evil mass murder this
September of people in the World Trade Center come to mind. Is it moral
and practical to execute a terrorist whose sole reason for existence is causing pain and suffering? Well, I don't think that capital punishment would
make such terrorists rethink the shallowness of their reasoning and understand the insanity of their behavior. Instead, we would make them martyrs.
Capital punishment is not a deterrent to these terrorists, but a goad. It is
more important to look to social and political circumstances to prevent such
monumental catastrophes from happening.

18   Instead of using the death penalty to express society's rage at wanton
murder, we would be better off forcing remorseless and callous criminals to
confront their depravity and make them realize how much pain they cause
to others. It would be even more useful to turn our energies away from
revenge on the perpetrators of crime and concentrate them instead on community support for the victims, who are often neglected as the criminal justice
system focuses on retribution. Those of us who oppose the death penalty
should never concentrate our efforts solely on the manifold problems of the
death penalty or, as some do, on the humanity of the killer. We must pay
equal attention to compassionate support for the families and other loved
ones of the victims. We must feel the loss, agony, and anger of the survivors,
and build social and institutional support for them. It is as immoral to
ignore the pain of the victims as it is to support capital punishment.

19   An effective alternative to the death penalty exists. Life in prison without parole is moral, practical, and far less expensive than the complicated process that leads to the death chamber. With life imprisonment, the cold-blooded murderer is removed from society and immediately forgotten, so that attention can be turned to the victims and their needs.

20   Revenge may bring momentary satisfaction, but only the potential to reach into someone's callused heart can bring healing. We cannot be a civilized society while we indulge in hatred and consign forgiveness to the sidelines. Anyone can be a knee-jerk reactionary and demand blood; it takes enormous courage to forgive the depraved who have caused us such enormous pain and sorrow.

Understanding Meaning

1.   How does Dutta relate the story of his family back in India to capital punishment in the United States?
2.   What is Dutta's reaction when, in performing his duties as a police officer, he sees the two elderly murder victims? How does it affect his view of the death penalty? Why?
3.   What does Dutta see as wrong with the death penalty?
4.   What is his view of the deterrent effect of the death penalty? Why is that a complex situation in the case of terrorists in particular?
5.   Does he feel that the death penalty is effective as an act of revenge? Does he feel it provides the victims' families with what they need?
6.   *CRITICAL THINKING.* In paragraph 7, Dutta declares capital punishment as *anachronistic*, like burning witches, keeping slaves, or having monarchs dictate our lives. Do you agree with him? Explain.

Evaluating Strategy

1.   Why might Dutta have chosen to start his essay with a narrative about his family's past? Is it an effective opening?
2.   *BLENDING THE MODES.* Where else in the essay does Dutta make use of examples, and how effective are they?
3.   Which sentence sums up the thesis statement of this essay?

Appreciating Language

1. Analyze Dutta's title. Where in the essay does he link his ideas to the language of the title?
2. Notice the words that Dutta uses to describe criminals. Is such language surprising from someone who opposes the death penalty?
3. Do the references to God in the piece weaken or strengthen his argument? Consider the audience he is addressing.

Writing Suggestions

1. Write an essay in which you explain whether or not you agree with Dutta that capital punishment is never moral.
2. *COLLABORATIVE WRITING.* Work with a group of students and discuss Dutta's essay. Then write a paragraph that expresses your group's view on the morality of the death penalty. If you agree that it is moral, describe the circumstances where you think capital punishment is acceptable. If your group has conflicting opinions, consider creating opposing statements.

47

THE ECONOMIST

The Economist is a British weekly publication written expressly for business and government leaders, offering readers in-depth articles about international issues, science, the arts, finance, politics, and economics.

The Needle Paused: Executions

CONTEXT: *DNA evidence has exonerated several death row inmates, leading many states to delay or suspend executions, even as they leave capital punishment statutes on the books. If this trend continues, the death penalty may well be abolished incrementally—more "with a whimper than a bang," according to this 2003 article.*

1   Minutes before the needle was due to go into the arm of Delma Banks last week, inserting into his system the cocktail of drugs that would kill him, the Supreme Court halted his execution in Texas to consider his latest appeal. Mr. Banks was convicted of murder and robbery 23 years ago. But his trial seems to have been such a shambles that a team of former federal judges and prosecutors, led by William Sessions, an ex-director of the FBI, filed a brief with the Supreme Court maintaining that the prosecution suppressed evidence that would have exonerated Mr. Banks, paid one hostile witness, and allegedly pressed another into committing perjury. They also claim that the defence lawyer was incompetent.

2   Mr. Banks's case is not an isolated one. Next week the Supreme Court hears oral arguments in the case of Kevin Wiggins, who has been on death row since 1989. The case against Mr. Wiggins, convicted of murdering and robbing a 77-year-old woman in Maryland, was so flimsy that at one stage a federal judge not only overturned his death sentence but threw out his murder conviction as well, concluding that "no rational finder of fact could have found Wiggins guilty of murder beyond a reasonable doubt." Despite this, the prosecutors appealed and the Fourth Circuit court of appeals reinstated his conviction and death sentence, although the court's chief judge admitted that he could not "say with certainty" that Mr. Wiggins had committed the murder.

3   The issue before the Supreme Court in both cases is not the guilt or innocence of these men—although there is clearly doubt that either is

guilty—but whether the lawyers defending them were competent by the standards which the court set down in a 1984 ruling. In that ruling and subsequent ones, the Supreme Court has struggled to improve the nation's legal system to ensure that innocent people are not executed, as well as to stem the endless flow of death-row appeals that have weighed so heavily on the courts. The cases of Mr. Banks and Mr. Wiggins seem to indicate that those efforts have failed.

4   But that may be the wrong conclusion. Alarmed by the prospect of innocent people being executed, politicians have joined America's judges to try to improve the "machinery of death," as one Supreme Court justice once called it. Their efforts may yet produce results.

5   The best-known example of this was the decision in January of the departing Republican governor of Illinois, George Ryan, to commute the death sentences of 167 death-row inmates to life imprisonment. This followed a three-year moratorium on executions in the state after 13 people awaiting execution had been exonerated. Mr. Ryan's successor is keeping the moratorium in place until the state's death-penalty system can be overhauled. Maryland has imposed a moratorium on executions for the past two years. And this month Houston's mayor asked Texas's governor to declare a moratorium on 16 death-penalty cases after the local police department's crime lab was found to be so shoddy that it had to suspend DNA testing.

6   The understandable concern about miscarriages—107 death-row inmates have had to be released since 1973—masks the fact that, over the past few years, there has been a gradual improvement in the system. Many states now pay more for specialised public defenders in death-penalty cases. Many prosecutors have become more discriminating, calling for death only in the worst cases.

7   More states now have life sentences without parole as an alternative to the death penalty in murder cases, as well as a requirement that juries be told clearly that this is an option. When offered this choice, reports Richard Dieter of the Death Penalty Information Centre, more juries now seem to be choosing life sentences. The number of death sentences dropped by 50% between 1998 and 2001 and may have fallen still further in the past two years. And reform is continuing. New ideas have been floated, such as imposing the death penalty only in cases where guilt can be determined to a higher standard than normal—beyond any, rather than just a reasonable, doubt.

8   Because most Americans still support the death penalty in principle, abolitionists have had little choice but to welcome reform, even if it means improving a system they oppose. But can reform alone avoid future cases

like those of Mr. Banks and Mr. Wiggins? Mr. Dieter does not think so. "As the death penalty becomes rarer, it will come to seem more arbitrary," he says, "and mistakes will continue to be made." By then, abolition may also appear more plausible to the public, and less controversial. In other words, if America ever abandons the death penalty, it is likelier to be with a whimper than a bang.

Understanding Meaning

1. What does the author's purpose seem to have been in writing this article? What does the author ultimately decide about the death penalty?
2. Why are these two particular cases being discussed before the Supreme Court? If you have read any other essays on capital punishment, have you read about any similar cases?
3. What evidence does the author offer that the "machinery of death" has improved?
4. What does the author mean at the end when he says that America's abandonment of the death penalty is "likelier to be with a whimper than a bang"?
5. *CRITICAL THINKING.* Would you consider being kept on death row for twenty-three years "cruel and unusual punishment"? What about having your execution stopped only minutes before it was to take place?

Evaluating Strategy

1. *BLENDING THE MODES.* Why is the essay stronger with the examples than it would have been without them? Why do you think the author might have chosen these particular examples?
2. How does the author reverse the reader's expectations between paragraphs 2 and 3?
3. Is there a single sentence that sums up the main idea of the essay? If so, which sentence? If not, how would you sum up in a single sentence the main idea?

Appreciating Language

1. Analyze the effectiveness of the title.
2. Where in the first two paragraphs does the author reveal through word choice that the cases against Banks and Wiggins were not handled well?

3. Why do you think the author might have chosen to refer to the two con-
    victs as *Mr.* Banks and *Mr.* Wiggins? Is that the usual way of referring to in-
    dividuals in journalistic writing?
4. Do you know the source of the allusion at the end that America's abandon-
    ment of the death penalty is "likelier to be with a whimper than a bang"?

Writing Suggestions

1. Evaluate the changes that some states are putting into place to try to im-
    prove the death-penalty system.
2. *COLLABORATIVE WRITING.* Exchange the essay you wrote for Writing
    Suggestion #1 with a classmate. Write a response to your classmate point-
    ing out any sentences in his or her piece that you feel are not accurate. Also
    point out any sentences that may be accurate, but where the author has not
    provided enough evidence to convince you. Return to the student his or
    her essay and your response.

48

EDWARD I. KOCH

Edward Irving Koch (1924–) was born in the Bronx, New York. After attending City College of New York from 1941–1943, he was drafted into the army and subsequently received two battle stars. In 1948, he received his degree from New York University School of Law. After serving for two years in the New York City Council and nine years in Congress, he was elected the 105th mayor of New York City in 1977 and served three terms. He is the author of twelve books, including four novels.

Death and Justice: How Capital Punishment Affirms Life

CONTEXT: *In this article, first published in the* New Republic *in 1985, Koch systematically examines and rebuts various arguments against the death penalty. His primary reason for supporting capital punishment is the belief that any lesser penalty trivializes society's response to murder.*

1   Last December a man named Robert Lee Willie, who had been convicted of raping and murdering an 18-year-old woman, was executed in the Louisiana state prison. In a statement issued several minutes before his death, Mr. Willie said: "Killing people is wrong. . . . It makes no difference whether it's citizens, countries, or governments. Killing is wrong." Two weeks later in South Carolina, an admitted killer named Joseph Carl Shaw was put to death for murdering two teenagers. In an appeal to the governor for clemency, Mr. Shaw wrote: "Killing is wrong when I did it. Killing is wrong when you do it. I hope you have the courage and moral strength to stop the killing."

2   It is a curiosity of modern life that we find ourselves being lectured on morality by cold-blooded killers. Mr. Willie previously had been convicted of aggravated rape, aggravated kidnapping, and the murders of a Louisiana deputy and a man from Missouri. Mr. Shaw committed another murder a week before the two for which he was executed, and admitted mutilating the body of the 14-year-old girl he killed. I can't help wondering what prompted these murderers to speak out against killing as they entered the death-house door. Did their newfound reverence for life stem from the realization that they were about to lose their own?

"Death and Justice: How Capital Punishment Affirms Life" by Edward Koch from THE NEW REPUBLIC, April 15, 1985. Reprinted by permission of The New Republic.

3   Life is indeed precious, and I believe the death penalty helps to affirm this fact. Had the death penalty been a real possibility in the minds of these murderers, they might well have stayed their hand. They might have shown moral awareness before their victims died, and not after. Consider the tragic death of Rosa Velez, who happened to be home when a man named Luis Vera burglarized her apartment in Brooklyn. "Yeah, I shot her," Vera admitted. "She knew me, and I knew I wouldn't go to the chair."

4   During my 22 years in public service, I have heard the pros and cons of capital punishment expressed with special intensity. As a district leader, councilman, congressman, and mayor, I have represented constituencies generally thought of as liberal. Because I support the death penalty for heinous crimes of murder, I have sometimes been the subject of emotional and outraged attacks by voters who find my position reprehensible or worse. I have listened to their ideas. I have weighed their objections carefully. I still support the death penalty. The reasons I maintain my position can be best understood by examining the arguments most frequently heard in opposition.

5   (1) The death penalty is "barbaric." Sometimes opponents of capital punishment horrify with tales of lingering death on the gallows, of faulty electric chairs, or of agony in the gas chamber. Partly in response to such protests, several states such as North Carolina and Texas switched to execution by lethal injection. The condemned person is put to death painlessly, without ropes, voltage, bullets, or gas. Did this answer the objections of death penalty opponents? Of course not. On June 22, 1984, the *New York Times* published an editorial that sarcastically attacked the new "hygienic" method of death by injection, and stated that "execution can never be made humane through science." So it's not the method that really troubles opponents. It's the death itself they consider barbaric.

6   Admittedly, capital punishment is not a pleasant topic. However, one does not have to like the death penalty in order to support it any more than one must like radical surgery, radiation, or chemotherapy in order to find necessary these attempts at curing cancer. Ultimately we may learn how to cure cancer with a simple pill. Unfortunately, that day has not yet arrived. Today we are faced with the choice of letting the cancer spread or trying to cure it with the methods available, methods that one day will almost certainly be considered barbaric. But to give up and do nothing would be far more barbaric and would certainly delay the discovery of an eventual cure. The analogy between cancer and murder is imperfect, because murder is not the "disease" we are trying to cure. The disease is injustice. We may not like the death penalty, but it must be available to punish crimes of

cold-blooded murder, cases in which any other form of punishment would be inadequate and, therefore, unjust. If we create a society in which injustice is not tolerated, incidents of murder—the most flagrant form of injustice—will diminish.

7   (2) No other major democracy uses the death penalty. No other major democracy—in fact, few other countries of any description—are plagued by a murder rate such as that in the United States. Fewer and fewer Americans can remember the days when unlocked doors were the norm and murder was a rare and terrible offense. In America the murder rate climbed 122 percent between 1963 and 1980. During that same period, the murder rate in New York City increased by almost 400 percent, and the statistics are even worse in many other cities A study at M.I.T. showed that based on 1970 homicide rates a person who lived in a large American city ran a greater risk of being murdered than an American soldier in World War II ran of being killed in combat. It is not surprising that the laws of each country differ according to differing conditions and traditions. If other countries had our murder problem, the cry for capital punishment would be just as loud as it is here. And I daresay that any other major democracy where 75 percent of the people supported the death penalty would soon enact it into law.

8   (3) An innocent person might be executed by mistake. Consider the work of Adam Bedau, one of the most implacable foes of capital punishment in this country. According to Mr. Bedau, it is "false sentimentality to argue that the death penalty should be abolished because of the abstract possibility that an innocent person might be executed." He cites a study of the 7,000 executions in this country from 1893 to 1971, and concludes that the record fails to show that such cases occur. The main point, however, is this. If government functioned only when the possibility of error didn't exist, government wouldn't function at all. Human life deserves special protection, and one of the best ways to guarantee that protection is to assure that convicted murderers do not kill again. Only the death penalty can accomplish this end. In a recent case in New Jersey, a man named Richard Biegenwald was freed from prison after serving 18 years for murder; since his release he has been convicted of committing four murders. A prisoner named Lemuel Smith, who, while serving four life sentences for murder (plus two life sentences for kidnaping and robbery) in New York's Green Haven Prison, lured a woman corrections officer into the chaplain's office and strangled her. He then mutilated and dismembered her body. An additional life sentence for Smith is meaningless. Because New York has no death penalty statute, Smith has effectively been given a license to kill.

9   But the problem of multiple murder is not confined to the nation's penitentiaries. In 1981, 91 police officers were killed in the line of duty in this country. Seven percent of those arrested in the cases that have been solved had a previous arrest for murder. In New York City in 1976 and 1977, 85 persons arrested for homicide had a previous arrest for murder. Six of these individuals had two previous arrests for murder, and one had four previous murder arrests. During those two years the New York police were arresting for murder persons with a previous arrest for murder on the average of one every 8.5 days. This is not surprising when we learn that in 1975, for example, the median time served in Massachusetts for homicide was less than two-and-a-half years. In 1976 a study sponsored by the Twentieth Century Fund found that the average time served in the United States for first-degree murder is ten years. The median time served may be considerably lower.

10   (4) Capital punishment cheapens the value of human life. On the contrary, it can be easily demonstrated that the death penalty strengthens the value of human life. If the penalty for rape were lowered, clearly it would signal a lessened regard for the victims' suffering, humiliation, and personal integrity. It would cheapen their horrible experience, and expose them to an increased danger of recurrence. When we lower the penalty for murder, it signals a lessened regard for the value of the victim's life. Some critics of capital punishment, such as columnist Jimmy Breslin, have suggested that a life sentence is actually a harsher penalty for murder than death. This is sophistic nonsense. A few killers may decide not to appeal a death sentence, but the overwhelming majority make every effort to stay alive. It is by exacting the highest penalty for the taking of human life that we affirm the highest value of human life.

11   (5) The death penalty is applied in a discriminatory manner. This factor no longer seems to be the problem it once was. The appeals process for a condemned prisoner is lengthy and painstaking. Every effort is made to see that the verdict and sentence were fairly arrived at. However, assertions of discrimination are not an argument for ending the death penalty but for extending it. It is not justice to exclude everyone from the penalty of the law if a few are found to be so favored. Justice requires that the law be applied equally to all.

12   (6) Thou Shalt Not Kill. The Bible is our greatest source of moral inspiration. Opponents of the death penalty frequently cite the sixth of the Ten Commandments in an attempt to prove that capital punishment is divinely proscribed. In the original Hebrew, however, the Sixth Commandment reads, "Thou Shalt Not Commit Murder," and the Torah specifies capital

punishment for a variety of offenses. The biblical viewpoint has been upheld by philosophers throughout history. The greatest thinkers of the 19th century—Kant, Locke, Hobbes, Rousseau, Montesquieu, and Mill—agreed that natural law properly authorizes the sovereign to take life in order to vindicate justice. Only Jeremy Bentham was ambivalent. Washington, Jefferson, and Franklin endorsed it. Abraham Lincoln authorized executions for deserters in wartime. Alexis de Tocqueville, who expressed profound respect for American institutions, believed that the death penalty was indispensable to the support of social order. The United States Constitution, widely admired as one of the seminal achievements in the history of humanity, condemns cruel and inhuman punishment, but does not condemn capital punishment.

13   (7) The death penalty is state-sanctioned murder. This is the defense with which Messrs. Willie and Shaw hoped to soften the resolve of those who sentenced them to death. By saying in effect, "You're no better than I am," the murderer seeks to bring his accusers down to his own level. It is also a popular argument among opponents of capital punishment, but a transparently false one. Simply put, the state has rights that the private individual does not. In a democracy, those rights are given to the state by the electorate. The execution of a lawfully condemned killer is no more an act of murder than is legal imprisonment an act of kidnaping. If an individual forces a neighbor to pay him money under threat of punishment, it's called extortion. If the state does it, it's called taxation. Rights and responsibilities surrendered by the individual are what give the state its power to govern. This contract is the foundation of civilization itself.

14   Everyone wants his or her rights, and will defend them jealously. Not everyone, however, wants responsibilities, especially the painful responsibilities that come with law enforcement. Twenty-one years ago a woman named Kitty Genovese was assaulted and murdered on a street in New York. Dozens of neighbors heard her cries for help but did nothing to assist her. They didn't even call the police. In such a climate the criminal understandably grows bolder. In the presence of moral cowardice, he lectures us on our supposed failings and tries to equate his crimes with our quest for justice.

15   The death of anyone—even a convicted killer—diminishes us all. But we are diminished even more by a justice system that fails to function. It is an illusion to let ourselves believe that doing away with capital punishment removes the murderer's deed from our conscience. The rights of society are paramount. When we protect guilty lives, we give up innocent lives in exchange. When opponents of capital punishment say to the state: "I will not

16   let you kill in my name," they are also saying to murderers: "You can kill in your own name as long as I have an excuse for not getting involved."

It is hard to imagine anything worse than being murdered while neighbors do nothing. But something worse exists. When those same neighbors shrink back from justly punishing the murderer, the victim dies twice.

Understanding Meaning

1. Some people oppose the death penalty because of the value they place on human life. How does Koch argue that he favors the death penalty for the same reason?
2. Explain how Koch can dislike the death penalty yet still feel it necessary.
3. According to Koch, why is the death penalty perhaps more necessary in this country than elsewhere?
4. How do statistics strengthen Koch's second and third arguments?
5. How does Koch respond to the very common argument that the death penalty goes against the Ten Commandments?
6. Why, in Koch's view, is execution by the state not the same as execution by an individual?
7. *CRITICAL THINKING.* You may have read and heard a number of different points of view on the death penalty. Did Koch tell you anything you did not know before or present a more effective case for an idea you had heard before? How did that affect your views on capital punishment?

Evaluating Strategy

1. Koch tells us very directly at the end of paragraph 4 his plan for organizing his essay. What is that plan?
2. What analogy does Koch use to explain why we must continue using what seems to be the "barbaric" practice of the death penalty? Why does he say that the analogy is not perfect?
3. Koch uses a variety of different types of support for his argument. Which are the most effective?

Appreciating Language

1. How would you describe Koch's writing style? Did you find his writing easy to read? Why or why not?
2. Do you find in this essay much language that is emotionally loaded? How does his language affect the power of the essay to help readers understand Koch's position?

Writing Suggestions

1. *PREWRITING.* Koch lists seven arguments against capital punishment. List each one and then in one sentence sum up his response to that argument.
2. Choose the three of Koch's arguments that you find most convincing and use them as a starting point for an essay that supports or rejects use of the death penalty.

49

LANCE MORROW

Born in Lewisburg, Pennsylvania, Lance Morrow (1935–) was a reporter for the Washington Star *until that paper folded in the mid-1960s. Since 1965, he has been a regular contributor to* Time *magazine. His books include* The Chief *(1984),* America: A Rediscovery *(1987), and* Fishing in the Tiber *(1988).*

Why I Changed My Mind on the Death Penalty

CONTEXT: *One of the arguments frequently made on behalf of capital punishment is that it makes an important social statement and teaches an important moral lesson. Although Morrow once subscribed to this view, he now believes that our society has become so violent and decadent that even something as momentous as the ultimate punishment has simply become part of "the Jerry Springer show of American life."*

1   Christina Marie Riggs, a nurse in Arkansas and a single mother, killed her two children—Justin, 5, and Shelby Alexis, 2—by giving them injections of potassium chloride and then smothering them with a pillow. She wrote a suicide note, and apparently tried to kill herself with an overdose of 28 antidepressant tablets. She survived.

2   Or she did until last night, when the state of Arkansas put Riggs to death by lethal injection at the state prison in Varner. She was the first woman to be executed in Arkansas since 1845.

3   The state of Arkansas played the part of Jack Kevorkian in a case of assisted suicide. Christina Riggs said she wanted to die. She had dropped all legal appeals. She wanted to be with her children in heaven. Just before Riggs died, she said, "I love you, my babies." Some people said she had killed them because she was severely depressed. The prosecutor, on the other hand, called her "a self-centered, selfish, premeditated killer who did the unspeakable act of taking her own children's lives."

4   So where do we stand on capital punishment now? (And, incidentally, isn't it grand that we seem to be overcoming, at the speed of light, our reluctance to execute women? Bless you, Gloria Steinem.)

5　　Review the state of play:

- Deterrence is an unreliable argument for the death penalty, I think, because deterrence is unprovable.
- The fear of executing the wrong man (a more popular line of demurral these days) is an unreliable argument against all capital punishment. What if there are many witnesses to a murder? What if it's Hitler? Is capital punishment OK in cases of unmistakable guilt? George W. Bush says that he reviews each case to make sure he is absolutely certain a person did it before he allows a Texas execution to go ahead.

6　　I have argued in the past that the death penalty was justified, in certain brutal cases, on the basis of the social contract. That is: Some hideous crimes demand the ultimate punishment in order to satisfy the essentially civilizing deal that we make with one another as citizens. We forgo individual revenge, deferring to the law, but depend upon a certainty that the law will give us a justice that must include appropriate harshness. I favored the Texas folk wisdom: "He needs killing." If the law fails in that task, I said, and people see that evil is fecklessly tolerated, then the social contract disintegrates. Society needs a measure of homeopathic revenge.

7　　But I have changed my mind about capital punishment.

8　　I think the American atmosphere, the American imagination (news, movies, books, music, fact, fiction, entertainment, culture, life in the streets, zeitgeist) is now so filled with murder and violence (gang wars, random shootings not just in housing projects but in offices and malls and schools) that violence of any kind—including solemn execution—has become merely a part of our cultural routine and joins, in our minds, the passing parade of stupidity/psychosis/chaos/entertainment that Americans seem to like, or have come to deserve. In Freudian terms, the once forceful (and patriarchal) American Superego (arguably including the authority of law, of the presidency, of the military, etc.) has collapsed into a great dismal swamp of Id.

9　　And in the Swamp, I have come to think, capital punishment has lost whatever cautionary social force it had—its exemplary meaning, its power to proclaim, as it once arguably did, that some deeds are, in our fine and virtuous company, intolerable.

10　　I think those arguing in favor of capital punishment now are indulging in a form of nostalgia. Capital punishment no longer works as a morality play. Each execution (divorced from its moral meaning, including its capacity to shock and to warn the young) simply becomes part of the great messy pageant, the vast and voracious stupidity, the Jerry Springer show of American life.

11   Maybe most of our moral opinions are formed by emotions and aesthetic reactions. My opinion is this: Capital punishment has lost its moral meaning. Having lost its moral meaning, it has become as immoral as any other expression of violence. And therefore we should stop doing it.

Understanding Meaning

1. What does Morrow mean when he says that in the case of Christina Marie Riggs, "the state of Arkansas played the part of Jack Kevorkian"? What does he mean a few lines later when he says, "Bless you, Gloria Steinem"?
2. Why was Riggs's execution historic? Why was it important to Morrow?
3. What is Morrow's point in the two bulleted items?
4. What does Morrow mean when he says he used to believe that the social contract required the death penalty in some cases? Why does he no longer believe that?
5. According to Sigmund Freud, the superego is that part of the psyche that is bound by rules. The id is the pleasure principle. What, then, does Morrow mean when he applies these terms to the United States?
6. In paragraph 10, Morrow writes: "I think those arguing in favor of capital punishment are now indulging in a form of nostalgia." According to Morrow, what are those in favor of capital punishment nostalgic for?
7. *CRITICAL THINKING.* What is your personal response to Morrow's last three sentences?

Evaluating Strategy

1. *BLENDING THE MODES.* Why might Morrow have chosen to start this particular essay with an example? Why choose the example that he did?
2. Is Morrow making use of logical, emotional, or ethical appeal—or a combination of types?
3. An effective argument often summarizes the opponent's point of view in order to show its weaknesses. Where does Morrow do that?
4. What point is Morrow trying to make in his allusion to capital punishment as part of "the Jerry Springer show of American life"?

Appreciating Language

1. Why is the term *assisted suicide* appropriate in referring to Riggs's execution?
2. What are some specific words that reveal Morrow's emotional reaction to capital punishment and the crimes that deserve it?
3. What does Morrow mean by saying that America has "collapsed into a great dismal swamp of Id"?

Writing Suggestions

1. Write a paragraph in which you explain whether or not you believe the death penalty is ever justified.
2. *COLLABORATIVE WRITING.* Discuss with other students if they believe assisted suicide is acceptable. Record comments by the group, organizing them using contrast or classification.
3. Write an essay in which you explain whether or not you believe that assisted suicide is ever acceptable.
4. Do you agree with Morrow that America is a "great dismal swamp of Id"? Explain in an essay.
5. Write an essay in which you explain why you agree or disagree with Morrow's argument that he can no longer support the death penalty in the context of a culture already too saturated with violence.